# The China Legal Development Yearbook, Volume 2

# The Chinese Academy of Social Sciences Yearbooks: Legal Development



BEIJING
2009

# The China Legal Development Yearbook, Volume 2

*Edited by*

LI Lin

BRILL

LEIDEN • BOSTON
2009

This yearbook is the result of a co-publication agreement between Social Sciences Academic Press and Koninklijke Brill NV. These articles were translated into English from the original《中国法制发展报告 No. 5 (2007)》(*Zhongguo fa zhi fa zhan bao gao No. 5 (2007)*) with financial support from China Book International, supported by the General Administration of Press and Publication and the Information Office of the State Council of China.

This book is printed on acid-free paper.

**Library of Congress Cataloging-in-Publication Data**

ISSN 1872-7190
ISBN 978 90 04 17303 3



PRINTED IN THE NETHERLANDS

CONTENTS



GENERAL REPORT



INDIVIDUAL REPORTS

# LIST OF FIGURES AND TABLES

*Figures*

*Tables*

# PREFACE

*The China Legal Development Yearbook, Volume 2* is the English version of《法制蓝皮书：中国法制发展报告 No. 5 (2007)》(*Rule of Law Yearbook: China Legal Development Report No. 5 (2007)*), edited by the Institute of Law, Chinese Academy of Social Sciences (CASS). Professor Li Lin, constitutional law scholar and director of the CASS Institute of Law served as chief editor.

2006 marked the beginning of "the 11th Five-Year-Plan" in China. During the past year, significant progress has been made in the field of socialist democracy and the "rule of law." The Communist Party of China (CPC) advocates are working to establish a harmonious socialist society in China, which has become the guideline for China's legal reform. With Hu Jintao as the general secretary, the CPC Central Committee has put forward the "scientific concept of development" and the strategy of "building a harmonious socialist society."

In 2006, China adhered to a "people-oriented" ideology and further advanced the process of the "rule of law:" citizens' orderly participation in politics, understanding of the ideas of democracy and "rule of law" among the people, and implementation and development of a basic "rule of law" strategy. Additionally, more emphasis has been placed on respecting human rights, new achievements have been made in the protection of human rights, and impartiality and justice have also been emphasized. Despite these achievements, it is important to remember that "rule of law" in China is still at a preliminary stage. Awareness of democracy and "rule of law" needs to be heightened and the democratic supervision mechanism needs to be perfected. A mechanism for balancing and supervising power needs to be constructed, the situation of social legislation lagging behind needs to be changed, legislation relating to the livelihood of the people needs to be promoted and the protection of human rights needs to be strengthened.

In 2007, according to the scientific concept of development and the plan for building a harmonious society, and with the aim of promoting democracy, science and equality, China will make efforts in promoting lawmaking. China will work to implement the law by reducing interference from departmental interests and local protectionism and promoting the application of a platform for administration according to law. It will strive to establish a government under the "rule of law" and launch new judiciary reform, with the leadership and under the supervision of the CPC, in order to increase the effective performance of the law and its important role in the settlement of disputes.

This volume includes a general report, special reports, field work, "rule of law" in provinces and other issues. The annual general report, written by a research team at the CASS Institute of Law, describes "rule of law" in 2006–07 as China worked towards becoming a harmonious society. There are eight special reports. The first, *Report on the Development of the National People's Congress in 2006*, was written by Li Xia from the Institute of Law, CASS. The second, *Predictions on the Development and Direction of Legislation*, was written by Wang Shucheng from the constitutional and administrative law research center at Renmin University of China. The third, *Combining Punishment with Leniency, Implementing Temporary Measures and Radical Measures: An Exploration of the Criminal "Rule of Law,"* was written by Liu Renwen and Zhou Zhenjie from the Institute of Law, CASS. The fourth, *Analysis of the Response to Administrative Review and Administrative Lawsuits*, is written by Fang Jun from the Department of Administrative Redress at the State Council Legislative Affairs Office. The sixth, *The Development of Administrative Action and State Compensation*, was written by Cheng Hu from the Beijing Higher People's Court. The seventh article, *Judicial Reform and Development in 2006*, was written by Peng Haiqing from the Institute of Law, CASS. And the eighth individual report, *Protection of Human Rights and the Establishment of "Rule of Law" in China* was written by Liu Huawen from the Institute of Law, CASS.

Each year, there are certain pivotal occurrences which influence the social consciousness. In 2006, a major focus was the mechanism of resolving disputes, and due process and legal services in developing areas. On these topics, The Development of Mechanisms for Settling Disputes through Legal Channels is written by Li Lin, Mo Jihong, et al. from the Institute of Law, CASS; and a *Research Report on the Resolution of Rural Disputes* is written by Ran Jingfu, Institute of Law, CASS.

The *Rule of Law Blue Book* series is an annual report publication edited by CASS. It aims to show the development of "rule of law" in China annually, to record the progress of "rule of law," and to forecast the prospects of the coming year. These annual reports are published in Chinese every year by Social Sciences Academic Press and in English by Brill. This book is the fifth volume in Chinese, and second volume in English. Since its first publication, the Chinese version has had great social influence and has been highly praised by a wide range of civil society and governmental organizations.

We sincerely hope that this cooperation between Brill and CASS will allow more people to learn about China, particularly democracy and "rule of law" in China and will contribute to the bright future of "rule of law" in China.

Li Lin
CASS Institute of Law
April, 2007

# ACKNOWLEDGMENTS

Publication of *The China Legal Development Yearbook, Volume 2* would not have been possible without generous contributions from several parties. Chief Editor Li Lin wrote the general report and assisted with the compilation of articles throughout the publication process. Zou Hailin greatly contributed to material and data organization, and served as a liaison between Social Sciences Academic Press and the article contributors. Qi Jianjian fine-tuned the details of the yearbook. Researcher Tian He and China Academy of Social Sciences associate professor Jiang Xihui devoted themselves to oversight of the translation of this English edition from the original Chinese language version, the《法制蓝皮书: 中国法制发展报告 No. 5 (2007)》(*Rule of Law Blue Book: China Legal Development Report No. 5 (2007)*).

Social Sciences Academic Press editor Liu Xiaojun compiled the final draft of the Chinese version. The publication of the English edition would not have been possible without the hard work and dedication of translators Liu Maomin and Lin Feng. Special thanks and commendation is reserved for Chloe Garcia-Roberts for revising and editing the initial translation to meet international standards of academic level English. Her retranslation of the yearbook is one of the principal reasons these articles are now internationally accessible to readers who cannot read the original Chinese version.

Social Sciences Academic Press President Xie Shouguang oversaw the general publication process, while Guo Rongrong of the International Co-publication Center assisted throughout the course of publication, including facilitating communication between Brill, editors, and translators.

The translation of this volume, a co-publication of Brill and Social Sciences Academic Press, was made possible through financial support from China Book International, supported by the General Administration of Press and Publication and the Information Office of the State Council of China.

Social Sciences Academic Press, Beijing
Brill, Leiden

# LIST OF CONTRIBUTORS

Throughout this volume, Chinese names are always ordered according to standard practice in China, with surnames preceding given names. To clarify this ordering, surnames are in all capital letters in the following list of contributors.

CHENG Hu is a Doctor of Law. He is also a judge of the Beijing Municipal Higher People's Court.

FANG Jun is a Doctor of Law and he is also deputy director-general of the Administrative Redress Department, at the Legal System Office of the State Council.

LI Lin was born in 1955, and graduated from the Law School of the Southwest University of Political Science and Law in 1984. He received a master's degree in jurisprudence from the Postgraduate Research Institute of the Chinese Academy of Social Sciences in 1987 and in the same year, worked in the Jurisprudence Research Sector of the Law Research Institute, at the Chinese Academy of Social Sciences, where he received his doctor's degree in August 1990. From August, 1993 to March, 1995, he was a visiting scholar at the Law School of Columbia University, and completed postdoctoral studies at the East Asia Institute of the School of International Relations, at Columbia University. From 2000 on, he was a doctoral student advisor in the Research Department of Constitutional Law and Administrative Law. In February 2001, he was made a vice editor-in-chief of the Magazine Press of "Social Sciences in China." In 2005, he was appointed Head of the Law Research Institute of the Chinese Academy of Social Sciences.

LI Xia is an assistant research fellow at the Chinese Academy of Social Sciences Law Research Institute, where she is also a doctoral student.

LIU Huawen is a Doctor of Law, an associate research fellow of the Law Research Institute at the Chinese Academy of Social Sciences, and chief of the Scientific Research Section. Primary areas of research include international human rights law and the settlement of international disputes. He was a chief editor of the *Peking University International and Comparative Law Review* and was a member of the editorial board for Volume II of *Journal of International Law* (Beijing). He was a visiting scholar at the Oslo University of Norway, Lund University of Sweden and the Amsterdam University of the Netherlands.

LIU Renwen is from Longhui, Hunan Province. He holds a Bachelor of Law from the Chinese People's Public Security University, an LLM and doctorate from China's University of Political Science and Law, and completed a Post-doctorate of economics at the Chinese Academy of Social Sciences. In 1993, he worked in the Criminal Law Research Department of the Law Research Institute, at the Chinese Academy of Social Sciences. He has been a visiting scholar the Law School of Columbia University, a guest researcher at the Criminology Research Center of Oxford University, a senior visiting scholar at the Law School of Yale University, and a legal researcher at the office of the attorney general for the International Criminal Court. He has completed advanced studies at the National University of Singapore and the Nottingham University of Great Britain, and has lectured at the Max Planck Institute of Germany, and Harvard University and the Brookings Institution in the U.S. Currently he is a professor at the Law Research Institute, and assistant director of the Criminal Law Department, at the Chinese Academy of Social Sciences, and he holds a concurrent post as director of the China Society of Criminology, and the Society of Reeducation through Labor.

MO Jihong is a Doctor of Law, and a researcher at the Law Research Institute of the Chinese Academy of Social Sciences. His primary works include: *Outline on Constitutional Judicatory, Scope of Law for the Expression of Liberty, Logical Foundation of Modern Constitution* and *New Theory on Constitutionalism.*

PENG Haiqing is an associate professor of Xiangtan University. She is completing post-doctoral work at the Law Research Institute of the Chinese Academy of Social Sciences.

Pitman POTTER is a Professor of Law at UBC Law Faculty and Director of UBC's Institute of Asian Research. Dr. Potter's teaching and research are focused on PRC and Taiwan law and policy in the areas of foreign trade and investment, dispute resolution, intellectual property, contracts, business regulation, and human rights. Dr. Potter serves on the Editorial Boards of *The China Quarterly*, *The Hong Kong Law Journal*, *China: An International Journal*, and *Pacific Affairs* (chair).

RAN Jingfu is an associate research fellow at the Law Research Institute of the Chinese Academy of Social Sciences. He received a Doctor of Laws degree from Renmin University of China. Primary areas of research are: Jurisprudence, the sociology of law, comparative jurisprudence and the science of procedural law.

WANG Shucheng is a doctoral student at China's Renmin University. He specializes in Constitutional Law.

ZHOU Zhenjie is a doctoral student at the Law Research Institute at the Chinese Academy of Social Sciences.

# INTRODUCTION

This year's *China Legal Development Yearbook* (*Rule of Law Blue Book: China Legal Development Report No. 5 (2007)* in Chinese) contains a range of essays from legal scholars in the People's Republic of China, ranging from scholars at government institutions such as the Chinese Academy of Social Sciences and the State Council, to selected university scholars. The topics under discussion range from institutional reforms in areas such as the National People's Congress (Li Xia) and the judiciary (Peng Haiqing) to broad conceptual questions about the rule of law (Liu Huawen). The collection also includes treatment of specific topical areas such as criminal law (Liu Renwen and Zhou Zhenjie) and human rights (Liu Huawen). While their subject matter varies considerably, all of the essays may broadly be grouped under a generalized rubric of "rule of law studies," offering local academic and policy perspectives on the emergence and implications of a rule of law discourse in China. Just as China's process of legal institution building continues to draw on the dynamism and energy of a committed group of scholars and policymakers, so too do these collected essays offer insights to the range and depth of scholarly work in the Chinese policy and academic environments. International observers of China's law reform effort will no doubt benefit from this collection of essays, gaining greater appreciation not only for the increasingly wide range of contemporary legal discourses that is emerging in China but also for particular individual and institutional approaches to the socialist rule of law. This introduction is intended both to acknowledge the achievements of the authors and also to suggest perspectives that might sharpen discussion and further debate.

Criminal law has been the focus of significant reform efforts in the Chinese legal system dating back to the first criminal law and criminal procedure law enacted in 1979. The very interesting paper by Liu Renwen and Zhou Zhenjie offers in-depth statistical reports on a wide variety of recent criminal prosecutions in order to illustrate patterns of combining punishment with leniency. The paper combines recitations of text from the criminal code with discussion of application and practice, and provides very useful insights into the policy foundations for criminal law revisions aimed at combining punishment with leniency in order to combat bribery and other contemporary ills. The practice of adjusting punishment regimes to curtail contemporary ills such as bribery and money laundering raise important implications for China's rule of law effort. The papers suggest that changes in punishment regimes have contributed to the reduction of various criminal offences, although specific empirical linkages remain elusive.

Peng Haiqing's paper on criminal litigation system offers extensive treatment of the decline of serious criminal offences and discussion of the extent to which this is due to criminal law reform efforts. Various criminal law reforms—particularly in the area of death penalty—are addressed explicitly as efforts to strengthen the authority of law and the effectiveness of the rule of law. Reforms of particular criminal law procedures aimed at building system strength or institutional strength tell us much about the motivations underlying much of the law reform effort in China. Professor Peng's paper contains much valuable information on the operations and debates around various aspects of criminal law reform, while also addressing civil litigation to a lesser extent. The combination of criminal and civil litigation within one paper is ambitious and might well provide a foundation for separate papers in the future.

The activities of the National People's Congress in legislative developments are widely known among observers of China's legal reform efforts. The important and detailed papers by Wang Shucheng and Li Xia provide valuable information on the activities of the National People's Congress. Li Xia provides a useful overview of the National People's Congress system using a number of important examples including the property law and the process of coordinating regional legislation as examples of important institutional developments within the NPC. Li also examines important issues about the relationship between NPC deputies and civil society, as an indication of the increased dynamism of NPC policy and legislative debates, as well as interesting discussion on the supervisory functions of the legislative organs. The issue of supervision is also taken up on Wang Shucheng's paper on the development and direction of legislation. In each of these papers significant attention is given to the formal texts of legislative efforts, which reveal policy priorities of the government and the effort to bring these into operation through the legislative mechanism. In both of these papers, considerable attention to detailed regulations and debates over legislative initiatives is combined with attention to local regulatory efforts.

Administrative law has been a prominent feature of law reform over the past fifteen years. Drawing on increased access to statistical data on administrative litigation and efforts to achieve redress, the papers by Fang Jun and Cheng Hu examine patterns of administrative litigation. The statistical information on patterns of litigation, including information on respondent departments, changing patterns of case filings, and reviews of judicial outcomes, are combined with insightful analysis of implications for rule of law and Chinese society. Administrative litigation is one element of dispute settlement within the Chinese legal system, but there are many others. The useful paper on mechanisms for dispute settlement by Li Lin and Mo Jihong provides an overview of relevant regulations, patterns of case filings in both criminal and civil cases, arbitration activities and other mechanisms for resolving disputes in society. The paper would serve as a useful general introduction to dispute settlement institutions in China and also contains a number of suggestions for further development—especially in the area of labor disputes and disputes over the constitutionality of legislation. Disputes in rural areas are addressed by the China Legal and Social Development Research Group, whose paper provides an invaluable overview of the kinds of disputes that are becoming most prevalent in rural areas, including land requisition issues, "curtilage" (*zhaijidi*—land around houses), and migration labor. The paper reveals the extent to which social dislocation and disenchantment are widely reported and well known in scholarly and policy circles, inviting further critical inquiry as to appropriate and effective responses.

The papers in this volume on the NPC system and legislation, administrative law, criminal law, and dispute resolution are important efforts to illuminate institutional features of China's law reform project. Rule of law issues are addressed more specifically in papers by Liu Huawen and by the "Blue Book Task Force" of the CASS Law Institute. Linking the rule of law with policy goals of building a harmonious society, these papers reveal a range of perspectives on a wide array of socio-legal issues that have been arising in China over the past number of years, including gender relations, labor, and rural development. The recognition of a need to rectify imbalances and inequities between disparate social groups, the need to improve institutional performance and to attend to substantive goals of justice are implicit in linking the rule of law with the establishment of a harmonious society.

China's rule of law effort and local policy and scholarly depictions of it reveal a wide range of issues familiar to legal development specialists, including the role of formalism and instrumentalism. Many of the official reports on China's rule of law efforts reveal formalistic depictions of changes in legal behaviour and legal values derived from authoritative statements rather than from empirical data. The State Council's recent White Paper on the "rule of law" is perhaps the most recent example of efforts to enshrine political and ideological orthodoxies of state-controlled development and stability as indicators of the emergence of the rule of law behavior by the state. Dynamics of instrumentalism in China's rule of law effort are also evident in the extent to which law continues to be a vehicle for policy implementation. For example, the use of legal rules and structures to reward or inhibit behavior in furtherance of development goals suggests the prominence of policy objectives over protections of legal rights as the basis for legal system change.

While not entirely free from these general characteristics of formalism and instrumentalism, the papers in this collection reveal a marked effort to engage with empirical evidence and behavioral implications of China's rule of law effort. Many foreign observers of China's ongoing legal reform effort have commented on the ongoing challenges of matching legal texts and aspirations with institutional performance. Clearly, however, as demonstrated by the papers in this collection, increased attention from the scholarly and policy community in China is being devoted to this very question. While results are mixed—ranging from statistically rich and analytically insightful approaches to local dispute resolution for example to narrative depictions of rule of law and harmonious society efforts by the government, the collection of essays in this year's *China Legal Development Yearbook* reveal much about the challenges and responses of China's legal reform effort. These efforts are to be encouraged and applauded, with cautious and respectful suggestions for more intense behavioral analysis to augment depictions of governance and legislative efforts. International collaborative efforts will be an important way forward. At the end of the day, however, China's legal reform effort is a project for China's legal academic and policy specialists to carry out, and the international community is observing with great expectations and high hopes.

Pitman B. Potter
University of British Columbia
October, 2008

# GENERAL REPORT

# CHINA'S SYSTEM OF HARMONIOUS "RULE OF LAW"

—Review of "rule of law" in 2006 and forecast of "rule of law" for 2007

Rule of Law Blue Book Task Force, Institute of Law, Chinese Academy of Social Sciences

2006 marks the first year of China's "Tenth Five-year Plan." Introduced in the sixth session of the 16th CCP Conference, the "Resolution on Several Important Issues Regarding the Establishment of a Harmonious Society"[1] proposed new standards for the further development of the "rule of law" and exhibited an unprecedented vision and energy.

In 2006, state affairs were managed in accordance with the law, and a "Human-oriented" (以人为本) philosophy was maintained, the people's status as the nucleus of "rule of law" was afforded greater protection, and the regulated participation of citizens in the legal system was strengthened. The concept of Socialist "rule of law" was established with the public, and "rule of law" on the state's basic level had begun to make progress towards implementation. The importance of the development of "rule of law" had become increasingly apparent, respect for human rights was further manifested, and the safeguarding of human rights steadily progressed. The requirement for a harmonious socialist and democratic "rule of law" society which promotes equality & justice, honesty and fraternity, vigor, stability and order, and the harmonious coexistence of man and nature was in the process of research and implementation. It is anticipated that in 2007 the management of state affairs in accordance with the law will be still at a preliminary stage and that general comprehension, self-awareness, and initiative will still need development. In addition regulated public participation will need to be expanded, the basic system of democratic supervision will still need to be perfected, and the supervision of officials

---

[1] Focus Group for the Study of Theory at the Central Party Qinghai Provincial Committee Institute (中共青海省委党校理论学习中心组), "New Starting Point New Height New Subject-Learning 'Central CCP's Resolution on Several Great Issues of Building a Harmonious Society'," *Journal Title*, Volume (2006): pp. 1–3. http://www.ceps.com.tw/ec/ecjnlarticleView.aspx?atliid=626530&issueiid=43736&jnliid=2963

at various levels of governments will need to be strengthened. Also the lagging pace of social legislation needs to be changed, the legislation which promotes development of public livelihood and enterprise must be strengthened, and human rights protection must be expanded. The concepts of scientific development and the strategic ideologies of establishing a harmonious society should be used as guides for legislation, the comprehensive "legislation, modification and repeal" (立、改、废) of existing laws should be realized, and democratic, scientific and improved legislation should be achieved.

In order to diligently construct a "rule of law" government and comprehensively promote an outline for the implementation of legal administration, the administration must get rid of departmental benefits, it must strictly observe the law, prosecute legal infractions, and enforce the people's law. The judicial organ must impel new institutional reform under the party's leadership and supervision in order to function more effectively, fulfill its responsibilities, enable greater authority and increase its ability to resolve contradictions and disputes.

A harmonious society requires "rule of law," believes in "rule of law" and abides by "rule of law," and so is a democratic "rule of law" society. To establish a harmonious society with democratic "rule of law" requires not only maintaining existing legislation as a guide for the development of a "rule of law" ideology, but also unifying legislation and law enforcement and achieving a transfer of the principles of "rule of law" from legislation to law enforcement. Such a society must not only consider the systematic reform of individual integrity at every level of legislature including enforcement, judicial administration, legal supervision, compliance and service etc, but must also consider the problem of coordinating China's entire "rule of law" system in order to advance a comprehensive and harmonious development of "rule of law."

## *A Harmonious Outlook: A Review of "Rule of Law" in 2006*

### I. *Legislative Developments*

Legislation is the premise by which a Socialist "rule of law" is implemented and state affairs are administered. It is the important system which allots both justice and harmony. In 2006, the Standing Committee of the National People's Congress made new progress towards achieving the legislation goal of that session, by examining and approving in total, twenty-four laws and drafts concerning the decision of legal issues, of which fourteen have been approved and five have been submitted to congress to examine and approve. The legislation of 2006 exhibited the following characteristics: Firstly, the guiding legislative ideology was changed from one of economic development into one proponing the comprehensive implementation and realization of scientific development and the establishment of a socialist harmonious society. In his speech for the 50th anniversary of the National People's Congress on September 15, 2004, General Secretary Hu Jintao proposed a mandate for the legal manifestation of a Socialist harmonious society, one which "unified urban and rural development, unified regional development, unified development of economic society, unified environmental development, unified domestic development and expanded China's connection to the international community." This guiding ideology had proposed new more scientific explicit standards and requirements for the legislative process.

Secondly, the content of legislation changed, from emphasizing economic legislation to emphasizing a comprehensive coordinated development of economic, social, civil and criminal legislation etc., and the equal development of procedural legislation and legislation entities. This gradually shifted the economically centered legislative system towards the coordinated development of economic, social and other types of legislation. In particular, the contents and requirements of social legislation were given prominence, including employment promotion law and labor contract law. Before the tenth National People's Congress, social legislation typically comprised only 2–6% of the legislation, with the proportion of economic laws reaching as high as 40–60%. Currently, the proportion of social legislation has achieved a national level of 20–30% and even 50–60% in some areas, thereby realizing the requirement of establishing a harmonious Socialist society.

Thirdly, the form of legislation gave even more prominence to democratic and scientific legislation. Democratic participation in the legislative process became further institutionalized, standardized and established. For example, the Legislative Affairs Commission of the NPC Standing Committee held a legislation hearing for the personal income tax law, as well as a draft of the property law, a draft of the labor contract law and the draft of the employment promotion/stimulus law etc. in order to solicit opinions from experts and all circles of society. On August 27, 2006, in the 23rd session of the Tenth NPC Standing Committee,

"The Law of the People's Republic of China Regarding the Supervision by Standing Committees of People's Congresses at Various Levels" (各级人民代表大会常务委员会监督法)[2] was approved by a majority of votes. This law took twenty years since its inception in 1986 until finally being formulated and promulgated, a rarity in the legislation history of new China. During these twenty years, there were NPC deputies in all of the previous sessions of the National People's Congress to propose bills regarding the formulation of supervision law, in total two hundred and twenty-two bills, with participating signatory deputies working in total four thousand and forty-four man-hours. The drafting of the labor contract law received feedback from more than 190,000 sources from all circles of society, of which 65% were from lower-level workers. It also received feedback from various provinces, autonomous regions and municipalities and 49 larger municipal Standing Committees of the People's Congress, 45 departments connected with the Central Committee, and 45 large-scale corporations, universities, colleges and social groups. After the draft of property law was promulgated, altogether more than eleven thousand revision opinions were received. The draft of property law submitted to the fourth session of the tenth National People's Congress was deliberated on seven times by the NPC Standing Committee. In the deliberation process of that session, more than sixty sections of the property law were revised. These examples give ample explanation of the increasing role democratic legislation plays in China's legislative process.

Fourthly, the quality of legislation was further enhanced, making solid progress towards forming a Socialist legal system with Chinese characteristics in 2010. This was manifested as follows. First, in the legal draft process the opinions of experts, legal practitioners and those persons concerned, etc. were heard in order to create legal provisions and standards that better expressed public desires, and that conformed to the reality of the national condition. Second, the legislation manifested a practical and realistic approach, in that it did not indiscriminately copy western legislation codes and systems, but rather beginning from a realistic, practical, scientific and rational standpoint adopted democratic and scientific legal methods to make laws which

[2] Standing Committee of the National People's Congress, "Law of the People's Republic of China on the Supervision by Standing Committees of the People's Congress at Various Levels," August 27th, 2006, http://www.lawinfochina.com/Law/Display.asp?Id=5421

were practically applicable. Third, legislative quality and technicality was improved. In comparison with the previous decade, legislation made great advancements, from its quality of legal framing and language, to its logical positioning and awareness. Fourth, the process of formulating new laws was integrated with the process of revising existing laws. Moreover, simultaneous to the new increasing demands raised in the establishment of a harmonious society, the proportion of revised and amended existing laws grew. Not only were new laws formulated to regulate and normalize social relations, old laws were also revised in order to establish a current and relevant legal system. Presently, the quantity of laws revised has accounted for approximately 50% of total legislation.

## II. *Administrative System Reform*

The reform of the Chinese government administration in 2006 can be summarized in two words: One is "popular" and the other is "steady." "Popular" because 2006 was the year when "The 11th Five-year' Program," or the "11th Five-Year Program for National Economy and Social Development" (国民经济和社会发展第十一个五年规划纲要)," hereafter referred to as the "Program," was approved by the National People's Congress, as well as being the first year of the Program's implementation. Administrative reform figured prominently in the Program and was named as a key task in expanding of China's system of reform, which caused heated discussion in society. "Steady" is in reference to the overall steadiness and stabilization of the past year, even though major systematic reform was not accomplished. A questionnaire from China (Hainan) Institute for Reform Development showed that participants who believed administrative system reform had made a major breakthrough in the past year accounted for 2.59% of the total interviewees, 36.49% thought some progress had been made, 52.30% thought no progress had been made, 5.46% thought the system was backward and 3.16% thought it was difficult to ascertain. Those interviewees who thought no progress had been made unexpectedly accounted for more than a half of the interviews, and if we add those 36.49% of interviewees who believed some progress had been made, both sides reach as high as 88.79%, accounting for the overwhelming majority of interviewees. The results of this questionnaire reflected and supported a comparative relaxation of administrative conditions in China in 2006. In 2006, the progress of administrative system reform was prominently manifested, in that the systems and the mechanisms which, safeguarded the publicity and the transparency of administration process, were further strengthened and consummated.

In 2006, the gateway website for the central government officially opened, symbolizing new advancements in the publicity of government information and the project of E-government affairs. By 2006, 80% of above county-level governments and government departments had established a gateway website, and seventy-four State Council ministries and units and thirty-one provinces, autonomous regions and municipalities had established a news release and spokesperson system. Fifty-five ministries and units of the State Council had established small groups of public communications representatives of government affairs and its administrative body, and thirty-six ministries and units had established a public communication system for public government affairs. Twelve provinces (including autonomous regions and municipalities) and sixteen bigger cities formulated specific local laws and regulations regarding public government affairs, and the drafting of public legislation was also nearing completion that year. Villages and towns countrywide had carried out the public government affairs initiative, more than 85% of county-level governmental agencies and 83% of regional municipal-level governmental agencies implemented the public government affairs initiative, and provincial-level governmental agencies public government affairs also made distinct progress in 2006.

In addition, the use of consultants, deliberation, public hearings and public announcements etc. were utilized more widely in the process of administrative legislation and of administrative decision-making. Also a draft of the legislation regarding administrative policy decision was promulgated through the media in order to directly solicit public opinion. In 2006, China also introduced leading cadres of the party and the government to the procedure of public-opinion polls for the first time in assessing and selecting appointments. These actions thereby promoted democratic selection, review and recommendation, and further strengthened democracy and the publicizing of the personnel and employment system.

In 2006, the State Council also strengthened legislation concerning social management and public service, further accelerating the transformation of the function of China's government. New reform measures were also taken to strengthen responsibility in law enforcement administration, to expand the strength of administrative impeachment and supervision of administrative actions, especially abstract administrative actions and so on. For example, some central ministries established a supervision system or set up their own subordinate organizations on the local level to strengthen inspection and monitor and control local administrative institutions. In another example, the method of administrative impeachment changed from "a higher authority investigating responsibility" (上级问责) into "a system impeachment" (制度问责); where the object of impeachment was expanded from the investigation of offending officials to all officials committing malfeasance. The scope of impeachment was also expanded from the domain of safety in production to other domains.

## III. *Judicial Reform*

The sixth Plenary Session of the 16th Central Committee of the CCP reinforced protective standards for the administration of justice within a Socialist harmonious society, proposing the maintenance of an impartial judiciary for the people, the continued reform of the judicial system and its application, and the establishment of an impartial, efficient authoritative system whose function would be to protect and provide impartial justice. In 2006, the Central Party released the "Decision Regarding Strengthening the Supreme People's Court and the Supreme People's Procuratorate." (Zhong Fa [2006] p. 11) In accordance with the reform of the judiciary and the employment system by the central authorizes, and in accordance with "The People's Court Second Five Year Reform Program" (2004–2008) and the spirit of the "Three Year Implementation of Ideas Regarding the Development of Prosecution Reform" (2005–2008), in 2006 the Supreme People's Court and the Supreme People's Procuratorate undertook massive work on the trial and prosecution system by adopting "impartiality and efficiency" as a system-wide theme, achieving tangible results.

In 2006, the progress of judicial reform in normalizing external relations between the judicial powers and other powers (mainly legislative power and executive power), manifested as follows. First, a people's jury system was implemented, and the pilot program of the people's supervisor system was expanded. In 2006, 48,211 jurors participated in 339,965 trial cases, which greatly changed the "existence in name only" situation of the jury system. 86% of the Procuratorates carried out the pilot people's supervision program, and stipulated a detailed monitoring program for "five types of situations," including illegal search and detention etc. Second, through systems of reporting, enforcement, and inspection etc. the supervision of the National People's Congress and of its standing committee to judicial authorities was realized. For example, the Supreme People's Court reported to the NPC Standing Committee regarding progress made in developing and reforming standards of behavior in the judiciary, and cooperated with the NPC Standing Committee in the inspection of judgments, enforcement and inspection of the people's jury system implementation.

Third, public accessibility was expanded and the scope of social supervision was broadened. The court system improved the press-release system, and on its own initiative heard the testimony of various democratic parties, the Association of Industry and Commerce as well as the non-party personage's opinions and suggestions. The Supreme People's Procuratorate also formulated "Opinions on Further Expanding Public Access to the Prosecutorial Affairs of the People's Procuratorate" (关于进一步深化人民检察院检务公开的意见), increased twelve sections concerning the working system and case handling rules with public access for society and the litigant participants etc., and set up a news spokesperson in the above provincial-level People's Procuratorates. Fourth, the joining of the criminal judicature and administrative law enforcement was completed. The Supreme People's Procuratorate, with other concerned departments, jointly issued "Opinions concerning the Timely Transfer of Suspected Criminal Cases in Administrative Law Enforcement," which determined a detailed procedure for the supervision of the procuratorial organization towards administrative law-enforcement entities regarding the transfer of suspected criminal cases, and enlarged the severity of punishment for criminal offenses, especially in regards to economic crimes.

In 2006, reforms were also carried out within the judiciary's internal relations and organizational management. Primary measures included were as follows. First, the Supreme People's Court took back the right to examine and authorize death sentence cases. The NPC Standing Committee approved the decision on October 31, 2006 as a revision of the Organic Law of People's Courts, which determined the Supreme People's Court reclaimed the right to examine and authorize all death sentence cases as of January 1, 2007. At that point, the twenty-year authorization for local Higher People's Courts to examine and authorize certain death sentence cases was effectively ended. This transformation will promote unification, stricter enforcement and impartiality towards criminal trials as outlined in China's constitution which stresses the "value and protection of human rights" which itself is in accordance with the international proposition on capital punishment, the "fewer deaths" and "carefully considered death-sentencing" criminal policy.

Beginning in January 1, 2007, the Supreme People's Court will exercise this jurisdiction thereby ending a twenty-six year history of transferring such cases to the lower courts. In 2006 the Supreme People's Court made extensive preparation in the areas of ideology, systematic organization and material equipment for the repatriation of the right to examine and authorize death penalty cases. For the second primary measure, reform of the working protocol of the People's Court was completed. Provisions for organizing the management of case registration, the handling of cases within the circuit, litigation mediation and applicable summary procedure etc. of the people's court were already taking shape. Third, the judicial committee system was completed. Certain systems pertaining to the judicial committee were revised, including its method of operation, voting protocol, and its system for determining employment qualifications for committee member positions etc. Fourth, reform of the functioning judiciary system and its implementation was completed. The various government departments involved took the initiative to individually resolve problems of execution by establishing protocol for leadership coordination, systems for sharing information and precedents, and systems for examining objectives.

The court system completed development and research on the information management system of case execution and on January 1, 2007 officially implemented this system in all national courts, establishing a strong foundation for a nationwide system of unified legal practice. Fourth, the system of managing judicial personnel was completed. The Supreme People's Court revised the "Regulations on Judge Training" and formulated the "Program on Education & Training for National Courts in 2006–2010." The Supreme People's Court chose and recruited more than one hundred outstanding accomplished candidates from the lower courts, the universities & colleges, scientific research units and attorney organizations for the adjudicative work, while simultaneously, selecting many judges to concurrently serve in and bolster the local court system. Additionally, the Supreme People's Procuratorate established and completed a system for reporting the personal concerns of the leading cadres, a system for reporting work progress, and implemented an inter-regional exchange system for 662 local chief prosecutors.

In 2006, progress in judicial process reform was manifested as follows: First, the procedure of second-instance for death sentence cases and the procedure for examination and authorization of death sentence cases were completed. The Supreme People's Court and the Supreme People's Procuratorate formulated "Provisions on Certain Issues concerning the Court Trial Procedures of Death Penalty Cases of Second Instance." (关于死刑第二审案件开庭审理程序若干问题的规定).[3] And in the beginning of 2006, a session was held for all death penalty cases of second instance in which appeals who had lodged regarding material facts and evidence or protests had been lodged against the People's Procuratorate. In the second half of 2006, a session was held to hear all death penalty cases of second instance. Second, judicial proceedings for multi-party lawsuits were simplified and made more convenient. The court system carried out a direct case registration system by the in order to ease the inconvenience of filing registration applications from remote areas for litigants cases; 328 intermediate courts and 2,307 basic-level courts established a place for "one-stop" case registration, and provided a free lawsuit guide for the litigants. The court system also completed a circuit tour judicial system and went directly to the location of the litigant or crime scene to hold court hearings for convenience of mass lawsuit participation. The court system also expanded the applicable scope of summary procedure and provided judicial aid to those litigants without economical means.

Third, judicial mediation work was strengthened. The civil law principle of imposing large limitations was implemented to realize dispute settlement goals as well as dissolve societal inconsistencies. Fourth, the trial supervision system for civil and administrative cases was reformed. A coordinated mechanism was established to handle petitions and written-complaints concerning litigation and lessen the difficulty of appeals and applications for retrial in the national courts. Fifth, the working mechanism for judicial interpretation was completed. The Supreme People's Court specially formulated the working standards for judicial interpretation and before introducing its provision of judicial interpretation stipulated that the opinions of concerned departments, experts and all levels of society be solicited through the media and internet. Additionally it was stipulated that the formulation of judicial interpretation be filed with the NPC Standing Committee and put on

---

[3] Supreme People's Court, "Provisions on Some Issues concerning the Court Trial Procedures for the Second Instance of the Cases Involving Death Penalty (for Trial Implementation)," September 21st, 2006, www.lawinfochina.com/law/displayModeTwo.asp?id=5573&keyword=

record according to the provisions of "Working Procedures on the Filing and Review of Judicial Interpretations" (司法解释备案审查工作程序).[4] Sixth, supervision of investigation and evidence collection was improved. The Supreme People's Procuratorate formulated "Certain Opinions on Strengthening Evidence Examination in Investigation & Arrest and Review & Prosecution" (关于在审查逮捕和审查起诉工作中加强证据审查的若干意见) to further establish supervision of the detection of illegal actions. Seventh, whole-course synchronization video recording system for the interrogation of criminal suspects was established. After this system was established in 2005, the Supreme People's Procuratorate formulated two technical specifications in 2006 in order to perfect the details of the operational procedure.

Judicial reform in 2006 was run under the ideology of "a judiciary for the people" (司法为民). That year, the public jury system was reinforced, a system of supervision was developed, public access and judicial openness was expanded, a system of reporting protocol and a law-enforcement inspection system were established, and judicial proceedings were simplified. All advancements made also reflected a democratic reform of the judicial system. "A just judiciary" (公正司法) was another key phrase in the ideology of judicial reform for 2006. The Supreme People's Court and the Supreme People's Procuratorate strengthened the establishment of a judicial personnel core, and established a system of judicial personnel management. The Supreme People's Court developed a judicial committee system, reclaimed jurisdiction over the examination and authorization of death sentence cases, and developed a procedure of second instance protocol and examination & approval for death sentence cases. The Supreme People's Procuratorate also improved supervision of investigation and evidence collection, and implemented a whole-course synchronization video recording system for interrogating criminal suspects etc. All of which were accomplishments supporting the pursuit of impartiality in judicial reform.

Overall, the judicial reform already included the suitable location of judicial power within the state power system, and also included the equitable structuring of internal judicial affairs. Judicial reform in 2006 strengthened supervision of the National People's Congress to

---

[4] Mei Ying Gechlik, "Judicial Reform in China: Lessons from Shanghai," *Columbia Journal of Asia Law*, Vol. 19 (2005): pp. 98–137.

the judiciary, and strengthened social supervision of judicial activities, while also respecting judicial independence. The reforms in 2006 fundamentally addressed the relationship between judicial power and executive power and between the ruling party and the judiciary. It was also observed, that judicial independence as a cornerstone of a modern judiciary was not strengthened through the judicial reform. The judicial reform stressed an adjustment of judicial internal relations, and this tendency was manifested in the work protocol reform of the People's Court, the establishment of the judicial committee system, and the reclaiming of jurisdiction over the examination and authorization of death sentence cases etc.

### IV. *Eradicating Corruption and Advocating Honesty* (反腐倡廉) *According to "Rule of Law"*

In 2006, the Central Authority greatly prioritized the eradication of corruption and the promotion of honesty. On October 22, 2006, the First Annual Conference and General Meeting of the International Association of Anti-Corruption Authorities, was held in the Great Hall of the People in Beijing. General Secretary Hu Jintao attended the opening ceremony and met with high-ranking officials from various countries & regions and leaders of related international organizations. That year, the rule of law for eradicating corruption and establishing an incorruptible government made new progress, launching investigation of commercial bribes and investigating serious cases including the Chen Liangyu case. The government also continuously instituted important actions towards fighting corruption, and the Central Authority also prioritized research into the construction of an anti-corruption system.

In 2006, altogether 10,883 commercial bribes cases were investigated and prosecuted, and the total sum involved reached 3.766 billion Yuan. More than 2.6 million businesses, state-run institutions and related competent (supervision) departments practiced self-examination and self-correction for irregular trade conducts. It was disclosed by the Administration of Anti-corruption and Anti-Bribery of the Supreme People's Procuratorate that, from January to October, 2006, the national procuratorial organizations altogether registered, investigated and dealt with 8,010 cases of commercial bribery crimes, arrests for 5,117 suspects of commercial bribery were authorized, and 4,212 suspects were prosecuted, with the total sum involved at 880 million Yuan. In all levels of procuratorial (supervisory) organizations, altogether 97,260 persons were given party disciplinary punishment; 3,530 persons were transferred to the judiciary to be tried; and 37,775 persons were given administrative disciplinary punishment.

In 2006, seven ministerial or provincial-level cadres were transferred to the judiciary as suspects of embezzlement and bribery. In 2006, typical corruption cases included: (A) the social security fund case discovered by Shanghai Labor and Social Security Bureau director general Zhu Junyi, Fuxi Investment Holding Co. Chairman of the board Zhang Rongkun, Shanghai Electric (Group) Corporation Chairman of the board Wang Chengming and vice-President Han Guozhang. A case against former Shanghai Municipal Party Committee Secretary Chen Liangyu was filed and investigated by the Central Committee. (B) Former Beijing Deputy Mayor Liu Zhihua was expelled from the party and given administrative dismissal punishment because of a serious violation of regulations, and his suspected crime was then transferred to the judiciary to decide. (C) National Bureau of Statistics original Director General Qiu Xiaohua received illegal business owner's funds, lived a criminal lifestyle, and was suspected of bigamy. He was discharged from public employment and expelled from the party, and his suspected crime was transferred to the judiciary to decide. (D) On December 28, 2006, the State Food and Drug Administration original Director General Zheng Xiaoyu, who had left his post for one year and six months, was suspected of bribery and ordered to explain his illegal actions by a certain time and in a decided place by the Central Discipline Inspection Committee of the CPC (E) On August 27, 2006, the NPC Standing Committee authorized to relieve Li Jinbao's post of Tianjin People's Procuratorate Chief Prosecutor; and under authorization of the Central Committee of the CCP, Li Baojin was expelled from the Party, and his case was transferred to the judiciary to decide. (F) Chenzhou City original municipal party committee Secretary Li Dalun was suspected of, jointly with his family, using his post to acquire money and material objects of unexplained origin valued at 14.34 million Renminbi, including properties valued at 17.65 million Yuan. Cases of unreported monetary transactions included the acceptance of bribes by the original Chenzhou municipal party committee assistant secretary, Commission for Disciplinary Inspection Secretary Zeng Jinchun, and Chenzhou municipal party committee original standing committee member and minister of propaganda of municipal council, Fan Jiasheng.

In 2006, the Central Discipline Inspection Committee of the CPC investigated and prosecuted 424 persons who had breached the protocol of organizational personnel matters for applying to official positions. Nationwide, 1,269 leading cadres were investigated and prosecuted for breaching regulations by accepting and giving money, negotiable securities and payment vouchers. In 2006, 46.2% of cases investigated and prosecuted by the national disciplinary inspection and supervision institutions originated from reporting by letters and visits. For instance, the Fujian Provincial Party Committee original standing committee member and minister of propaganda of municipal council Jing Fusheng case, and the Anhui Province original Deputy Governor He Minxu case were both uncovered according to the reports of letters and visits.

In 2006, China made steady progress in eradicating corruption and establishing an incorruptible government:

(1) On February 8, the General Office of the CPC Central Committee and of the State Council jointly issued "Opinions Regarding the Launch of Special Initiatives to Eradicate Commercial Bribery" (Zhong Ban Fa [2006] Document 9). The central committee and the State Council also decided to restructure the members of the Central Committee's leading organization for eradicating commercial bribery.

(2) On February 12, China officially became a treaty power of the United Nations Convention against Corruption. The Chinese government officially submitted an instrument of ratification and a government statement to the Secretary-General of the United Nations on January 13, 2006. On February 12, 2006, the "United Nations Convention against Corruption" was officially put into effect in China. On June 13, the Central Discipline Inspection Committee of the CPC, jointly with the departments concerned, held a stage-II working conference for the implementation of the Convention in order to carry out twenty items required for the joining of the Chinese law system.

(3) The system of inspections under the guidance of the Central Discipline Inspection Committee of the CPC was strengthened. Since 2003, the Central Discipline Inspection Committee of the CPC and the Organization Department of the CPC Central Committee jointly established a special inspection organization. This inspection group can station itself at an area or within a unit for an extended period of time in order to hear the opinions of cadres and the public, and to thoroughly understand the conditions and discover existing problems. The Central Discipline Inspection Committee of the CPC promptly verified, supervised and urged related departments to investigate evi-

dence of suspected illegal activity discovered in the inspection process, and in this way discovered and investigated several important cases. For example, the cases of the Tianjin People's Procuratorate original Chief Prosecutor Li Baojin, Shandong provincial party committee original assistant secretary and Qingdao municipal party committee Secretary Du Shicheng were discovered through this inspection process.

(4) Great attention was paid to the establishment of international cooperation for anti-corruption. On April 12, in the anti-corruption seminar of Asia-Pacific Economic Cooperation (APEC), China and America issued a joint statement to appeal to APEC's various economic bodies to further strengthen exchange and cooperation, and to jointly make efforts towards the containment of corruption.

(5) On October 22, the First Annual Conference and the General Meeting of the International Association of Anti-Corruption was held in Beijing. Chairman Hu Jintao attended the annual meeting and indicated that Chinese government would continue to uncompromisingly carry out the anti-corruption struggle.

(6) In September, the primary group for the Central Committee working for the eradication of commercial bribery invited a group of famous experts to serve as consultants, as well as several expert professors from the Chinese Academy of Social Sciences.

In 2006, the rules and regulations for "eradicating corruption and establishing a corruption-free government" that were revised and implemented included, (A) "The Law of the People's Republic of China on Administrative Supervision;"[5] (B) "Regulations of the CCP Discipline Inspection Organization on Case Inspection Work;" (C) Amendment Six of the "Criminal Law of the People's Republic of China," which enlarged the scope of the definition of bribery for business personnel from the original law, and determined bribery and embezzlement as one of upstream crimes for the money laundering crime; (D) The Central Discipline Inspection Committee of the CPC issued "Provision on Party Member Leading Cadres Reporting Individual Matters of Concern" and so on.

[5] China State Department, "Implementing Regulation for the Law of the People's Republic of China on Administrative Supervision," September 17th, 2004, http://law.chinalawinfo.com/newlaw2002/SLC/slc.asp?db=chl&gid=55462

In 2006, theoretical research regarding the construction of a system for eradicating corruption made substantial progress. The Ministry of Supervision of the Central Discipline Inspection Committee of the CPC focused on theoretical research towards constructing a system of laws and regulations, and completed the international cooperation project "Building an Honest and Clean Government in China" (中国廉政建设) with the United Nations Development Program (NUDP), and did related work for the "Study on Legal System for Building a Legal and Honest Government in China" of the National Social Science Fund, all important theoretical achievements. These achievements touched on many areas of the construction of regulations on eradicating corruption and established a solid theoretical basis for the formulation of even more effective regulations and measures for preventing and controlling corruption. The leaders of the commission for disciplinary inspection of the Chinese Academy of Social Sciences along with many outstanding scholars of the Academy published the volume, *Review on Anti-corruption System of Various Countries* after publishing *Thoughts and Countermeasures on Anti-corruption* the year before last which has had a positive effect on the public.

## V. *The Development of Public Interest Law and Practice*[6]

In 2006, the movement for the practice of public interest law made great strides. Major public interest lawsuit cases included: The one-card access lawsuit, the NGO registration case, the case of discriminatory hiring practices in the Human Resource Department, the National Dental Prevention & Treatment Group lawsuit and the case in which China's University of Politics, Science and Law Master of Law Hao Jinsong sued the Ministry of Railways for the rise in transportation prices during the spring festival. As far as submitting written proposals regarding the public interest, some scholars submitted "written proposals" to the NPC Standing Committee concerning different retiring ages

[6] "Public Interest Law and its practice refers mainly to judicial actions initiated by citizens or organizations for the purposes of the protection and realization of public interests. This includes both public interest lawsuits and written statement motions for public interests submitted by citizens to the NPC Standing Committee and the State Council for legitimate inspection suggestions."—Huang Jinrong, "A Flourishing Legal Movement—Observation and Review on Public Interest Law and Practice in Contemporary China," Public Interest Lawsuit" first edition, (Beijing: China Procuratorial Press, ed. Beijing Oriental Public Interest Legal Aid Law Office, 2006).

for men and women, and price differences between "same life different costs" of the city and countryside. The response of the NPC Standing Committee for the first time to relative written statements was the single largest advancement made in public interest law last year. In 2006, the reciprocal coordination of public interest law and practice was strengthened. 2006 was an effective year for public interest law and practice. Representative public interest law and practice cases included:

(A) The public interest lawsuit against the "National Dental Prevention & Treatment Group." At least, three public interest lawsuits were initiated aiming at the false authentication of "National Dental Prevention & Treatment Group" nationwide. (1) In September, 2005, Beijing Attorney Li Gang in the Chaoyang Court sued the Ministry of Health, the Lotte Foods Co., Ltd. and the Wumart (物美商业有限公司) Stores, Inc. for committing fraud against consumers by authenticating Lotte chewing gum with the "National Dental Prevention & Treatment Group." In June, 2006, the Chaoyang District Court dismissed the case for the reason that the dispute between the Ministry of Health and the plaintiff was not related to civil rights violations (2) On February 7, 2006, Shanghai Attorney Chen Jiang sued four parties including "National Dental Prevention & Treatment Group" for the same reason in Shanghai Minhang District Court. (3) On March 15, 2006, Zhengzhou Attorney Liu Ming sued Guangzhou P&G Company, Liuzhou Liangmianzhen Co., Ltd. and the "National Dental Prevention & Treatment Group" in Jinshui District People's Court of Zhengzhou.

(B) The public interest lawsuits against the railway departments. There is a long history of the railway department being targeted by public interest lawsuits, a history which was continued in 2006. Representative cases included: (1) A case in which Hao Jinsong sued the Ministry of Railways for the rise in prices during the spring festival. The case was tried in April 2006, in Beijing's First Intermediate Court, and was afterwards dismissed. Hao Jinsong filed an appeal in Beijing High Court. In September, 2006, the Beijing Higher Court ordered the First Intermediate Court to accept and hear this case. In December, 2006, Hao Jinsong's prosecution was rejected in both the first and second instances. (2) In February, 2006, Beijing Attorney Li Subin sued the Beijing Railroad Bureau on the grounds it was illegal for the Bureau to charge passengers 2 Yuan handling charges for the railway ticket return, but the Court ultimately rejected the plaintiff's prosecution. (3) On February 17, 2006, Jiangxi passenger Ding Changxiang filed a lawsuit on the grounds that a "ticket without an assigned seat has same price as a ticket with an assigned seat, but passengers who bought the ticket without seat did not enjoy the same services as the passengers who bought the ticket with seat." He claimed this was unfair and therefore asked for a refund in the Beijing Railway Transportation Court, but lost the lawsuit in the first and second instances.

(C) Public interest lawsuits and written statements against the highway maintenance fee. The issues surrounding the highway maintenance fee were a hot topic in 2006. The legal practitioners had already begun proceedings for a public interest lawsuit, and had also started a public interest written campaign. Representative cases included: (1) on September 1, 2006, Jiangsu Province Changzhou Attorney Zhang Xiangbing prosecuted an action in Changzhou Tianning District People's Court on the grounds that it was illegal for the Changzhou Highway Maintenance Management Institution to charge the highway maintenance fee. He lost the lawsuit in the first and second instances. (2) On September, 2006, Beijing Jingyuan Law Office Attorney Song Chengjun sued the Beijing Roadway Administration Bureau in Xuanwu District Court, and requested the Court to declare it illegal for the defendant to collect the highway maintenance fee from him. (3) On October 17, Song Chengjun submitted his "Proposal to Examine 'Regulations Governing Management of Highways in the PRC'" to the NPC Standing Committee. (4) On October 30, China's Youth College for Political Sciences Associate Professor, Zhou Ze, submitted his "Proposal for Inspecting Illegal issues in Laws and Regulations on Highway Maintenance Fee Levy and Canceling Laws and Regulations on Illegal Highway Maintenance Fee Levy" to the Legislative Affairs Commission of the NPC Standing Committee.

(D) Public interest written statements against "Same life, different prices." The judicial interpretation of the Supreme People's Court on "Same life, different prices" was also the target of public criticism in 2006, and several cases had already begun to appear nationwide with sensational effect. The legal practitioners' representative public interest written statements included: (1) In March, 2006, Zhou Wei and Li Cheng of the Center for Human Rights Studies of the Sichuan University submitted "Proposal Requesting Permission to Inspect Whether Article 29 the 'Interpretation of the Supreme People's Court n Certain Issues concerning the Application of Law for the Trial of Cases on Compensation for Personal Injury'[7] Violates the Constitution" to the

[7] Supreme People's Court, "Interpretation of the Supreme People's Court of Some

NPC Standing Committee. (2) In July, 2006, Beijing Oriental Public Interest Legal Aid Law Firm submitted the NPC Standing Committee "Proposal Requesting Permission to Inspect Whether 'Interpretation of the Supreme People's Court of Some Issues concerning the Application of Law for the Trial of Cases on Compensation for Personal Injury' is Constitutional."

(E) Cases challenging irrational phenomena. There were more than two public interest lawsuits against the deposit of "One-card Access" and "corkage fees" at restaurants.

Public interest law and practice not only need to work in agreement, they must also regularly put forward new legal propositions. In 2006, new public interest lawsuits and written statements frequently appeared. Some examples of public interest law and practice included:

(1) Public interest lawsuits initiated by the Civil Affairs Bureau. In March, 2006, the Civil Affairs Bureau of Gaochun County sued the accused instigators of two accidents and the insurance company on behalf of the family of two homeless persons in Gaochun County People's Court. Compensation for funeral expenses as well as 300,000 Yuan was requested, however ultimately the Court overruled the case by reason that the plaintiff was disqualified.

(2) Public interest lawsuits initiated by the taxpayers. On April 3, 2006, Jiang Shilin, a village Director of Changning, Hunan Province sued Changning Municipal Financial Bureau in the capacity of an ordinary taxpayer, and asked the court to determine that it was illegal for the Municipal Financial Bureau to exceed the year fiscal budget in order to purchase two cars, and to order the two cars bought illegally to be recovered and turned over to the State Treasury.

(3) Cases for the protection of worker's rights in the reform of the state-owned business system. This kind of case was not common. On July 25, 2006, Jiangsu Tongyu Textile Group Co., Ltd. employees Yin Zihong, Xu Zhiming and Cui Xiaohua instituted administrative proceedings against Yangzhou city government which made the decision to reform the business system in Yangzhou Intermediate Court. Beijing Oriental Public Interest Legal Aid Law Firm and Beijing King & Capital Lawyers provided joint legal aid for this case.

---

Issues concerning the Application of Law for the Trial of Cases on Compensation for Personal Injury," December 26th, 2003 http://law.chinalawinfo.com/newlaw2002/SLC/slc.asp?db=chl&gid=51002

(4) Cases concerning the citizen's rights of association. Cases concerning rights of association were not common as of yet, and cases where the national ministries and commissions were defendants were even rarer. In February 2005, Dong Jian sued the Ministry of Health because his eight applications within four years to the Ministry of Health for the establishment of the "Love-eye Association" (爱眼协会) were not replied to. In March 2006, Beijing First Intermediate Court officially accepted this case. Beijing Impact Law Firm provided the legal aid for this case.

(5) Public interest written statements concerning discrimination in the retirement ages of men and women. On March 7, 2006, the Center for Women's Law & Legal Service of Peking University proposed to the NPC Standing Committee "Proposal on Inspecting Constitution Violation for the Provision of Retirement Age in Guo Fa (1978) Document 104."

(6) Public interest written statements concerning a student's right to an equal educational during the compulsory education stage at rural private schools. In September, 2006, Oriental Public Interest Legal Aid Law Firm proposed to the State Council "Proposal on Asking the State Council for Inspecting Related Provisions of 'Notice of Ningxia Hui Autonomous Region People's Government on Deepening the Reform of Fund Security Mechanism for Compulsory Education in Rural Areas' and 'Opinions of Fujian Province People's Government on the Implementation of Notice of the State Council on Deepening the Reform of Fund Security Mechanism for Compulsory Education in Rural Areas.'"[8]

(7) The people challenged the cross-banking enquiry fee for the first time. In June, 2006, Shanghai resident Deng Weijie sued the Bank of Communications, the Industrial & Commercial Bank of China and the Construction Bank in Shaihai Xuhui District Court for the reason that charging a cross-banking fee was illegal.

[8] "Deepening the reform of funds guarantee mechanism for rural compulsory education; raising the level of the development of rural compulsory education in an all-round way—Interviewing Tian Zuyin, the Vice Director of Finance Department of the Ministry of Education," Developing Small Cities and Towns, (Journal title) Third Quarter, 2006, http://scholar.ilib.cn/A-xczjs200603007.html

Overall, public interest law and practice made remarkable achievements in 2006: First, the NPC Standing Committee responded to written statements regarding public interest for the first time. With reference to Zhou Ze's and Song Chengjun's written statements questioning the legitimacy of the highway maintenance fee, on November 23, 2006, the persons in charge from the NPC Legislative Affairs Commission and the Legal System Office of the State Council responded with a tactful interview about progress made in tax reform, the cost of communication and the collection of highway maintenance fees etc. Although the interview confirmed the validity of highway maintenance fee, it was however the first time a public response was made to a written statement regarding public interests. Second, the Ministry of Railways announced the spring festival transportation would no longer rise in prices. On January 10, 2006, news spokesperson of the Ministry of Railways disclosed that all kinds of train ticket prices in the spring festival transportation would not be raised, and expressed the railway transportation would also no longer use the variable system of ticket pricing during the spring festival in the future. Third, the China National Regulatory Commission for Certification and Accreditation and the Ministry of Health stopped the authentication for oral health products produced by the "National Dental Prevention & Treatment Group." Beijing Chaoyang District People's Court had sent out judicial suggestions to the China National Regulatory Commission for Certification and Accreditation criticizing the evaluation of oral health products discovered in the case of "National Dental Prevention & Treatment Group," and the suggestions made were carefully considered by the Commission. The Commission then replied that in accordance with the Ministry of Health, they had made the decision to require "National Dental Prevention & Treatment Group" to cease authenticating oral health products. Fourth, the Supreme People's Court pledged to revise the judicial interpretation of "Same life, different price." On March 14, 2007, when accepting the interview, the Supreme People's Court chief justice indicated that the Supreme People's Court had conducted extensive research regarding the judicial interpretation of "Same life, different price," and had already formed a preliminary opinion, which would be released shortly.

## VI. *Refinement of the System for Dispute Settlement*

Along with the continuous reform of the economic structure, the GDP per person has surpassed 1,000 US dollars, discrepancies between city and rural areas, between incomes, and between eastern areas and mid-western areas have grown, and community disputes have become an outstanding problem in current social disputes.

### (A.) *Review of the Status Quo of Current Disputes*

According to the report of the Supreme People's Court in the fifth session of the Tenth National People's Congress, in 2006, social disputes settled by all levels of people's courts have greatly increased, and the daily functioning of the people's court has improved in settling various kinds of social disputes. The Supreme People's Court dealt with and closed 3,668 cases altogether, and the number of cases closed increased by 14.77% over last year. All levels of local people's courts altogether dealt with and closed 8,105,007 cases, and the number of cases closed increased by 2.07% over last year. Altogether 245,254 cases were adjudicated including cases of explosion, voluntary manslaughter, robbery, rape and kidnapping and so on, and 340,715 criminals were condemned, including 825 above county-level staff, 92 regional department-level officials and 9 provincial department-level officials. In all 153,724 criminals were condemned with imprisonment for 5 years or more, life imprisonment and the death penalty. Altogether 1,159,437 cases concerning marriage & family, heritage and dispute were adjudicated; 986,082 cases concerning the disputes of property and right infringement were adjudicated; 179,637 cases of labor dispute were adjudicated, and the funds involved in these litigations reached 3.189 billion Yuan. 4,755 cases concerning disputes over annexation, bankruptcy and transfer of property rights of the state-owned businesses etc. on were adjudicated. 717,526 cases of finance dispute were adjudicated. 2,236,888 cases of contract dispute were adjudicated, and the funds involved in these litigations reached 475.7 billion Yuan. 14,056 first-instance civil cases concerning the intellectual property were adjudicated, and the object of litigation reached 2.71 billion Yuan. 7,375 cases concerning maritime affairs and marine trade were adjudicated, and the funds involved in these litigations reached 4.445 billion Yuan.

According to a symposium for the national arbitration work held in Beijing on January 23–25, 2007, 185 arbitration committees nationwide accepted a total of 60,844 cases in 2006, more 12,505 cases than in 2005, and the rate of increase was 21%; Total funds involved in litigation reached 72.5 billion Yuan, an increase of 7.1 billion Yuan over 2005, with a 10% rate of increase. The people's courts ruled against 124 arbitration awards in the whole year, or 0.2% of cases accepted. The people's courts ruled against 71 arbitration awards, or 0.12% of cases accepted. Overall, national arbitration work continued to develop but the number of cases accepted and undertaken for arbitration as well as regional cases fell short of the target quota, a phenomenon which must be watched. According to the sixth national letter-or-visit working conference which ended on March 28, 2007, there were "four decreases" in Chinese litigation in 2006: in the total numbers of letters and visits, the quantity of collective appeals, the quantity of unusual appeals and the quantity of community events. In particular, formal complaints dropped in 2005 for the first time in twelve years and then in 2006 dropped once more a total of 15.5%.

Generally speaking, China's current social disputes have three characteristics: (1) they can still be classified as typical social contradictions and conflicts, which are inevitable in the process of social transformation and development. The overwhelming majority of these are social conflicts among the public, which can be solved through legal channels and other system measures. (2) There is an increase in the number of disputes, which is in accordance with the phase of social development. The income per capita of our country is 1,000 US dollars to 3,000 US dollars, and while this period could be called a "golden age of expansion," it also could be called a "period of magnified contradictions (矛盾)" one in which the various profit entities struggling for power has had chaotic effects in society. (3) The reasons for legal disputes are multifaceted, and this could possibly intensify. Judging from the present social disputes, the reasoning for these actions is diverse. If those disputes cannot be settled properly and reasonably, it is possible they could cause societal turbulence, in particular large-scale incidents in response to compulsory relocation of residents, corruption cases and compensation for land requisition could all possibly bring about chaos within the social order.

(B.) *Analysis of the System for Dispute Settlement*

In China, social disputes have many types and extremely complex manifestations; however, the majority of social disputes can be divided into four classes. Class I is disputes between the state entities and the public regarding matters of authority; Class II is disputes between state entities in regarding matters of authority; Class III is internal disputes occurring within state entities, businesses and institutions and social groups; Class IV is disputes among the public. Among them, Class I & IV are currently the primarily social disputes. Community disputes have the greatest negative influence towards a well-functioning and stable society. In recent years, community disputes have increased in scope, a phenomenon which all departments and levels of government would do well to monitor. Tradition, the economy, society, the culture, the current system and ideologies etc. can all become possible reasons for social disputes. However, from a "rule of law" standpoint, an incomplete legal system, low-quality legislation, disrespect and disregard for the law, slack law enforcement, leniency for law-breakers, an corrupt administration, an impartial judiciary, an obstructed legislative system, and an unsound system are all reasons for most social disputes as well the inefficiency of their resolution. Stemming from these causes community disputes caused by land requisition and relocation, reforms of the state-owned enterprise system, unemployment settlement, the labor-capital contradictions, environmental pollution, the right to taxi management, the protection of the legitimate rights of special communities and the level serious corruption are some of the most intense problems facing Chinese society at present. Pointed measures must be taken to resolve these issues.

According to our analysis of dispute resolution in 2006, we observed that, at present, dispute resolution can be basically divided into two classes, namely dispute resolution within the legal channel and dispute resolution using other non-legal methods. The legal channel has explicit laws and regulations, concrete organization and a clear legal procedure. Also the settlement outcome has certain legal effect. The objective of the legal channel of dispute resolution is the establishment of a harmonious and stable society; it has stability, far-reaching applications and the potential for consistent and unified adoption. There are generally two kinds of legal mechanisms for resolving disputes through the legal channel. The first type is litigation, including civil action, criminal prosecution and administrative proceedings; the second type is non-legal, and includes administrative arbitration, internal affairs, civil & commercial arbitration, legal mediation, letters and visits and the investigation of constitutional violation etc. Litigation is the most effective legal channel and the final legal means for settling social disputes. The non-legal channel is however an important auxiliary channel which settles the social disputes using legal means outside of litigation. According to the newest statistics, using disputes involved in written complaints as an example, typical problems that have garnered intense public reactions are, land expropriation, urban construction and relocation, environmental protection, business system reform and bankruptcy all of which have become important issues for formal complaints.[9] The dispute resolution through legal channels is required for the rapid rise of disputes in a current "rule of law" society.

## VII. *The Improvement of Law Enforcement and Supervision*

In 2006, in regards to law enforcement and the legal supervision, the NPC Standing Committee promulgated the Supervision Law, which strengthened filing, inspection and supervision of normative documents and organized law-enforcement inspection on several occasions to inspect and supervise the implementation of the Patent Law, the "Law of the Peoples Republic of China on the Protection of the Rights and Interests of Returned Overseas Chinese and the Family Members of Overseas Chinese," the "Energy Conservation Law of the Peoples Republic of China," the Judges Law, the Prosecutors Law and a Law concerning environmental protection.

On August 27, 2006, in the 23rd session of tenth NPC Standing Committee, a draft of the Supervision Law was approved by vote and was put into effect on January 1, 2007. The Supervision Law specifically defined the constitutional supervision authority for every level of the People's Congress and its standing committee, which is evidence of the increasing standardization, institutionalization, and routine applicability of the legal supervision system. That the National People's Congress and its standing committee hold the power to investigate and inspect the standard legal documents, including administrative rules and regulations, local laws and regulations, regulations on the exercise of autonomy, specific regulations and judicial interpretations

[9] "Deepening the reform of funds guarantee mechanism for rural compulsory education; raising the level of the development of rural compulsory education in an all-round way—Interviewing Tian Zuyin, the Vice Director of Finance Department of the Ministry of Education," *Developing Small Cities and Towns*, (Journal title) Third Quarter, 2006, http://scholar.ilib.cn/A-xczjs200603007.html

is an important official right. They are then authorized to repeal those standard legal documents which are not in accordance with the constitution and the laws.

Social organizations and individual also may put forward inspection proposals to the NPC Standing Committee if they discover that these standard legal documents are at variance with the constitution and the laws. In 2006, the public was enthusiastic about submitting written statements and inspection proposals for standard legal documents. For instance, on September 8, 2006, the Oriental Public Interest Legal Aid Law Firm proposed that the NPC Legislative Affairs Commission inspect the judicial interpretation of "Same life, different prices," and suggested that the National People's Congress change judicial interpretation of the Supreme People's Court ruling on "Same life, different prices." On October 31, 2006, China's Youth College for Political Sciences, Associate Professor Zhou Ze, submitted a proposal for the inspection of laws and regulations to the Legislative Affairs Commission of the National People's Congress, and requested to inspect the laws & regulations on collection of highway maintenance fee and to repeal those existing rules and regulations.

China uses a constitutional system of democratic centralism. The National People's Congress and its standing committee not only are the legislature, but they also simultaneously supervise the implementation of the constitution and its laws. In 2006, the NPC Standing Committee organized frequent inspections of law enforcement. In May, it inspected the implementation of the Patent Law, and heard the reports of the State Intellectual Property Office, the Ministry of Science and Technology, the State Development and Reform Commission, the Ministry of Commerce, the State-owned Assets Supervision & Administration Commission and the Supreme People's Court on the implementation of the patent law. Three inspection teams were then formed to conduct inspection in 6 provinces (cities) Beijing, Shanghai, Liaoning, Jiangsu, Guangdong and Sichuan. The Standing Committee of the People's Congress of 8 provinces (cities), such as Tianjin, Chongqing, Hebei, Zhejiang, Fujian, Hubei, Hunan and Shaanxi, were also entrusted to carry out an internal-examination in regards to the implementation of the patent law in local administrative regions. From April to May, 2006, the National People's Congress (NPC) and its standing committee set up the law-enforcement inspection team to inspect the implementation of the "Law of the Peoples Republic of China on the Protection of the Rights and Interests of Returned Overseas Chinese and the Family Members of Overseas Chinese."

At the beginning of April, the NPC and its standing committee heard the reports of 10 departments of the State Council, the Supreme People's Court, the Supreme People's Procuratorate and the Chinese Overseas Residents Association on law enforcement and the maintenance of overseas Chinese benefits. From April 9 to May 22, the inspection team was divided into three groups to conduct inspections in six provinces (regions, cities) including Guangdong and Shanghai, Fujian and Shandong, Guangxi and Shaanxi. In May, 2006, the National People's Congress and its standing committee set up a law-enforcement inspection team to inspect the implementation of the "Energy Conservation Law," and heard the reports of the State Development and Reform Commission, the Ministry of Finance, the Ministry of Construction, Ministry of Communications, the General Administration of Quality Supervision, Inspection and Quarantine and the National Bureau of Statistics of China. This team was divided into five groups to go to 10 provinces (regions, cities) Tianjin, Shanxi, Xinjiang, Chongqing, Hubei, Henan, Hebei, Inner Mongolia, Zhejiang and Jilin to enquire into the situation, conduct a special investigation and research energy conservation in the industry, as well as construction, transportation and civil facilities.

In 2006, a law-enforcement inspection team was set up to inspect the implementation of the Judge Law[10] and the "Public Prosecutor Law," and conduct an investigation of the implementation of the two laws in Guangdong, Zhejiang, Yunnan and Xinjiang, and hold a forum on judicial work for internal affairs in the local People's Congress. From June to July, the team inspected the implementation of two Laws in 5 provinces (autonomous regions) Heilongjiang, Jiangsu, Hubei, Guangxi and Guizhou on site. The Standing Committees of the People's Congress of 5 provinces (autonomous regions, municipalities) Shanxi, Jilin, Henan, Shanghai and Ningxia etc. were also entrusted by the General Office of the NPC Standing Committee to inspect the local implementation of the two laws. The Supreme People's Court and the Supreme People's Procuratorate cooperated with the NPC Standing Committee to inspect the enforcement of the laws through an internal examination and delivered a special report.

---

[10] "Judges Law of the Peoples Republic of China," promulgated by the Eighth People's Congress, February 28th, 1995, http://www.the1.com.cn/infosort_the1/info/99524-1.htm

In May, 2006, a team was established to inspect the implementation of the laws concerning the environmental protection. On May 22, after hearing the reports of the State Environmental Protection Administration, the National Development and Reform Commission, the Ministry of Finance, the Ministry of Water Resources, the Ministry of Construction and the General Administration of Customs, the team was divided into five groups to investigate five provinces (cities) Sichuan, Hubei, Shanxi, Beijing and Shaanxi. During inspection, the groups separately heard the reports of local authorities of five provinces (cities) and partial respective cities and counties. On site they observed urban sewage and garbage treatment facilities, the prevention and treatment of industrial pollution, medical & dangerous waste treatment facilities, the prevention and treatment of drainage basin pollution and the protection of drinking water and water sources. At the same time, the Standing Committees of the People's Congress of 10 provinces (regions, cities) Tianjin, Liaoning, Inner Mongolia, Shanghai, Fujian, Jiangxi, Guangdong, Chongqing, Gansu and Ningxia were entrusted to inspect work in local areas. The movement of environmental protection in China cooperated with this law-enforcement inspection, carried out interviews and reported to key areas and businesses inspected by the standing committees in the past three years.

In 2006, the judicial departments made special effort to reorganize and standardize judicial acts in order to guarantee the impartiality and authority of the judiciary. According to the Commission of Politics and Law of the CPC Central Committee's unified deployment, the Supreme People's Court and the Supreme People's Procuratorate carried out reorganization to standardize the judicial actions for more than a year beginning in May, 2005. The goal of the Supreme People's Court in reorganization was mainly to standardize the filing acts and to open the channels for public to legally file claims to standardize trial action, to resolve issues of judicial unfairness especially in civil & commercial trials, to normalize protocol for the execution of laws. The SPC also aims to alleviate the problem of execution difficulties with a strong response, to normalize retrial protocol, to solve the difficulty of retrial application, to strengthen judicial management, and to establish an institutional framework for separate powers and responsibilities and mutual checks within the court system. The Supreme People's Procuratorate's special reorganization main activities included: (1) Strengthening of ideological education, in order to establish correct ideas of law-enforcement idea. (2) Thorough reorganization in order to resolve unprecedented problems in law enforcement. (3) Establishment of a comprehensive system of rules and regulations, and a standard for law enforcement. (4) Strengthening of supervision and inspection, and the efficacious execution of system criterion. (5) The establishment of supervision restriction, and the promotion of a correct exercise of the criteria for prosecutorial power.

## VIII. *"Rule of Law" in the Hong Kong, Macao and Taiwan Regions*

### (A) *Development of "Rule of Law" in the Hong Kong Region*

Since the return of Hong Kong, the central committee upholds the basic principle of "one country two systems" and has strictly handled Hong Kong affairs according to the relevant provisions of the Basic Law of the Hong Kong Special Administrative Region of the People's Republic of China (hereinafter referred to as the HK Basic Law), while fully respecting the implementation of the self-government system in the Hong Kong Special Administrative Region. In the past ten years, since the return of Hong Kong, the central government has respected completely the independence of Hong Kong judiciary which has a particular function as determined by HK Basic Law. The NPC Standing Committee has played a crucial role in the interpretation of HK Basic Law, in the settlement of legal disputes concerning Hong Kong, and in the effective implementation of HK Basic Law. In the past ten years, the NPC Standing Committee has interpreted HK Basic Law in three ways. The first was the interpretation of the Articles 22 and 24 of HK Basic Law (namely the interpretation concerning "Children's Right of Abode in Hong Kong") in 1999; second was the interpretation of the appendixes of HK Basic Law in 2004, this interpretation of the National People's Congress on the HK Basic Law was to voluntarily interpret the HK Basic Law; third was the interpretation of Article 53(2) of HK Basic Law in 2005, which clearly defined a new chief executive's tenure in office as the remainder of the original chief executive's tenure in office.

The NPC Standing Committee has always taken a cautious approach to the interpretation of Basic Law. It has carried out only necessary interpretation with unequivocal implications, thereby stabilizing Hong Kong society and enhancing public confidence at all levels. Although there is a contingency in Hong Kong of those who believe the NPC Standing Committee interpreting the Basic Law did not conform to the provisions of Basic Law, injured the autonomy of Hong Kong jurisdiction, and disobeyed the spirit of "one country, two systems," the interpretation of Basic Law was supported by the majority of the Hong Kong public at all levels. These new issues arose regarding the implementation of HK Basic Law because of misunderstanding of Basic Law, insufficient research into its implementation as well as insufficient communication between the legislative communities of the Mainland and Hong Kong. There is evidence to the fact that the interpretation of the NPC Standing Committee of the Basic Law has worked in maintaining prosperity, stability and development of Hong Kong society and the benefits of its inhabitants.

In addition, the so-called "issue concerning the general election by universal suffrage" was also an important issue in the development of the Hong Kong political system. In Hong Kong, some organizations and individuals proposed the immediate implementation of a general election for all seats in the chief executive and the legislative council. Although Articles 45 and 67 of HK Basic Law certainly do not exclude this possibility, under existing conditions, it should be understood that immediately implementing a general election would not conform to the requirements, namely that "the method for the formation of the chief executive and the legislative council of the Hong Kong Special Administrative Region should be prescribed according to the practical situation of the Hong Kong Special Administrative Region and by an ideology of gradual progression" as stated in the provisions of Basic Law. Pushing the gradual development of Hong Kong democracy has been the central government's consistent guideline and policy. First, that the development of Hong Kong democracy is in keeping with the nature of China's state system, as this nature evolves directly from the People's. And since the return of Hong Kong, the central government has guaranteed the Hong Kong inhabitants the right of autonomy and taken the lead in establishing a democratic electoral system in Hong Kong.

Second, the gradual development of a Hong Kong democracy is an integral idea in the autonomous government of "Hong Kong people governing Hong Kong," and is an important motivation behind the Basic Law. That the Hong Kong Special Administrative Region's high-level of self-government is based on the central committee's authorization through the Basic Law, and that the Hong Kong inhabitants exercise the rights as master of their own affairs according to the provisions of the Basic Law, is an important manifestation of democracy. The HK Basic Law has not only has made specific provisions for the immediate future of Hong Kong's democratic development, it has also planned long-term goals for Hong Kong's democratic development, which fully manifests the determination and confidence of the central committee in promoting the gradual development of a Hong Kong democracy. Third, in the 10 years since the return of Hong Kong, Hong Kong's democracy has continuously developed according to the process stipulated in the Basic Law under the support of the central committee.

Undoubtedly, Hong Kong's current level of democracy is the highest in Hong Kong history, and this progress could not have been possible without the central committee's support. The central committee will continue to support and promote the development of democracy in Hong Kong, according to the provisions of the Basic Law, just as it has in the past. Advancing the development of Hong Kong political system must be carried on pragmatically, and according to the track stipulated in the Basic Law. To seek the truth is to seek the truth of Hong Kong's practical situation, and to function pragmatically is to develop Hong Kong's democratic system gradually according to the reality of Hong Kong's situation. Seeking the truth, doing things pragmatically and strictly following the provisions of the Basic Law are the keys to solving differences and disputes in the process of developing Hong Kong's political system. The Basic Law and the NPC Standing Committee's related interpretations and decisions have indicated the direction for advancement and development of the Hong Kong political system, while also leaving room for discussion regarding Hong Kong's development. What is urgent now is to work together to continue advancing in the direction stipulated by these interpretations and decisions.

### (B) *"Rule of Law" in the Macao Region*

Since the return of Macao, the central committee has upheld the basic principle of "One country, two systems," administering the city according to law to handle Macao's affairs according to related provisions of the Basic Law of Macao Special Administrative Region (hereinafter referred to as Macao Basic Law), and it has fully respected the high-level of self-government in the Macao Special Administrative Region. The Macao Special Administrative Region's administrative, legislative and judicial organizations all are running according to the blueprint of Macao Basic Law, which has resulted in a smooth transition of the government framework, and has created a miracle in Macao history. Before the return of the Macao Region, the economy experienced negative growth continuously for four years, the unemployment rate steadily increased, the public security situation worsened (which caused disaster after disaster for Macao's economy which is based on tourism), the legal system was incomplete, and government efficiency was low. Public complaints were rampant and the quality of government officials was lacking quality and the high-level officials had become provincial and territorial.

As a result of this history, after the return of Macao, the entire leadership of this special administrative region was replaced with new personnel. For example, the Macao chief executive as well as nine main officials and the Legislative Council president have all held their posts only since the return, and more than two-thirds of officers in nearly 50 bureau-level departments were appointed only on the eve of or after the return. However, they all have qualifications of being permanent Macao inhabitants which conforms to the ideology of "Macao people administering Macao." The localization of leadership in the government of Macao government was an impossible goal under Portugal's rule of more than 400 years. The Macao Special Administrative Region has also newly established a court of last instance, a procuratorate, an audit administration, a customs and the police headquarters and has reorganized and adjusted several government institutions. It has established non-regime municipal organizations, basically completed the construction of the political system and the administrative framework of a high-level self-government (finalizing the shift from "Portugal administering Macao" to "Macao administering Macao").

After the return, the public security situation in Macao's showed marked improvement. Through the strengthening of the internal construction of the police departments, an adjustment in efficiency, and the joint effort of two police departments, the rate of criminal cases has been greatly reduced. Compared to before, the rate of instances of serious crime has markedly dropped, and the rate of solved criminal cases has greatly increased, especially heartening is the rate and speed at which major cases are solved. Certainly, Macao's "rule of law" construction also faces many difficulties and problems. Legal localization, the massive legislation work of linking up the Macao Basic Law, the revision and consummation to the partial original laws which are in disagreement with the return, and the enhancement of the overall social "rule of law" level and so on, all are the arduous legal missions which Macao currently faces, extremely arduous work for such a recently formed legislation team.

(C) *Impact of Taiwanese Independence Movement on Cross-Strait Relations*
In 2006, the Taiwanese independence movement was active. Chen Shui-bian attempted to accelerate this independence[11] (法力台独) and used obscure means to force its progress. Presently, the development of Cross-Strait Relations is exhibited by the fact that on one hand, economic and cultural contacts between the two sides of the Taiwan Straits are daily growing closer. More and more Taiwanese businessmen are investing in the Mainland, and investment funds are continuously growing. The bilateral volume of trade is fast increasing and in 2006, it reached 100 billion US dollars, of which the export of Taiwan Area to the Mainland Area had reached 80 billion US dollars. All levels of Taiwanese society strongly supported the "Three links" (三通) (namely, trade, travel and post between the two sides of the Taiwan Straits). In regards to the relations between the two sides of the Taiwan Straits, the Mainland authorities maintained a method of positive advancement. For example, opening a "green channel" (绿色通道) for the increased import of Taiwan agricultural products, etc. The Mainland authorities also focused on the protection of the Taiwanese compatriots' legitimate rights and interests, and positively promoted the implementation of the "three links." The Taiwanese authority could not help but face reality, and opened a limited scale category for Taiwanese investment in the Mainland, and opened limited sightseeing sites in Taiwan to the Mainland people.

Additionally on traditional holidays, such as the Spring Festival and the Tomb-sweeping Day etc., a chartered plane for Taiwanese businessmen was established one way. Conversely, the Taiwanese authority stiffly maintained a standpoint of Taiwanese independence, and repeatedly created disturbances and obstacles to the unification of the Taiwan Straits, gradually advancing the agenda of Taiwanese independence. In 2006, the Taiwan authorities disregarded their commitments, and undertook the so-called "Program on Abolishing the National Unification Council and the Guidelines for National Unification," to abolish "the National Unification Council" and "the Guidelines for National

[11] Translator's Note: Taiwanese independence is not recognized by the Chinese government and is so considered a *de jure* independence movement by the Chinese authorities.

Unification." Chen Shui-bian also put forward the so-called "four desires and one lack" (四要一没有), namely "the desire for independence, the desire for an official name, the desire for a new constitution, and the desire for development. The only difference between unification and independence, being that this new plan lacked coordination in the relations between the two sides of the Taiwan Straits, a fact which did not stop public opinion from supporting Taiwanese independence. It should be noted that, currently the Taiwanese independence forces within the Taiwanese authorities and the Democratic Progressive Party are very adept at manipulating the law as a political instrument to manipulate procedure, glossaries, proposals, the election and the drafts in order to promote Taiwanese independence. They confuse right and wrong, regression for progress, and their motivation is to dominate state political power, and to realize the goal of Taiwanese independence.

In 2006, the legal principles of the Taiwanese independence movement grew increasingly intense, as the Taiwanese authorities had incited those politicians with leanings towards Taiwan independence to draw up a so-called "Draft Constitution for a Second Republic" (第二共和宪法) in support of Chen Shui-bian's idea to "renew the constitution for Taiwan." The Taiwanese independence forces went into action without delay, and drafted various editions of a "new draft constitution" one after another; in total more than 15 editions together comprising an organic representation of the Taiwanese independence movement. It could be said the basis for evaluating the independence movement could be decided by whether "the Constitutional Reform" has even touched on "sovereignty" and other sensitive issues.

## IX. *Progress in Legal Education*

Since the country restored the college entrance examination system in 1977, the system of legal education in China has developed rapidly. However it has also contains large inconsistencies and flaws. In 2006, legal education reform was manifested in:

(A) The dispute on the preservation or abolishment of an undergraduate law education was the focus of a legal education discussion in 2006. In July, 2006, during the "Forum for Representatives from Chinese and African Universities," Chinese universities suggested that higher education in China should abolish undergraduate legal education, as they believed it very difficult for legal graduates an undergraduate education level to be engaged in relevant work. Furthermore, advanced and intermediate legal education was the direction of development and reform in the international community. At present, the opposite viewpoint still dominates. The Guidance Commission on Legal Education of Law Schools under the Ministry of Education Director Zhang Wenxian expressed concern that the Guidance Commission did not research the issue of canceling undergraduate legal education, and said nothing of considering the cancellation. Under the current social system of China, undergraduate legal education within the field of legal education has been decided as an integral part in the foundation of a functioning university.

(B) The dispute regarding the quality of education of graduate law students was also a hot topic in legal education discussion in 2006. Detractors believed that though there were many graduate law students, and though they published large numbers of papers and works, the quality of these students and their scholarship was not verified. Presently, there are no specific teaching materials for the education of graduate law students, no specific teaching method and no teaching objectives. There is a "high yield" of graduate law students but a "low rate of utilization" in other words, they can be engaged in work concerning legal affairs, but they are not actually competent enough for professional legal work, which indicates a worrying phenomenon in legal education. The solution lies in the determination of education goals for graduate law students. The main target of legal education is to cultivate capable law practitioners, possessing namely practical abilities and abilities to handle complex tasks. The task of fostering legal abilities in academia should be handled by a national team of legal experts. It should not be handled hastily on a mass scale, but rather comprehensively at all levels so that performance levels do not drop again.[12]

On September 30, 2006, assessment for the first Qian Duansheng Prize for Law Research Findings was announced. This prize was initiated by China's University of Political Science and Law, and is named after the country's first jurist. The prize is awarded to law students in the populace. The establishment of this prize commemorates Mr. Qian Duansheng's tremendous contributions in law research to China;

---

[12] Huo Xiandan, *Unbreakable bond—Testimony of Legal Education for 20 Years* (City: Law Press of China, 2003).

its purpose is to promote the prosperous development of research in Chinese law, and to promote the advancement of national rule-of-law construction. The establishment of this prize not only significantly promotes law research, but also more importantly establishes a tradition of respect for accomplished scholars in Chinese legal education and law research. The field of academic legal research needs accomplished scholars, the field of legal education severely needs accomplished scholars, and the process of constructing a "rule of law" society in China will doubtless require more accomplished scholars. In 2006, international exchange and cooperation in the field of legal education & research continued to expand. (1) From July 4~5, 2006, more than 100 deans and jurists from nearly hundred Australian and Chinese law schools attended a joint conference, and discussed the future of legal education. (2) On November 8, 2007, the first "Forum for Chinese-African Legal Education and Law Culture" was sponsored by the Legal Education Institute of China's Law Society, the Law Culture Research Center of Renmin University of China, the Zeng Xianyi Legal Education and Law Culture Foundation and the Centre for African Laws and Society of Xiangtan University in order to carry out the "China-Africa Cooperation Forum—Beijing Action Plan."[13] This was the first academic large-scale meeting of the Chinese and African law and legal science circles. (3) On December 13~14, 2006, the establishment ceremony of the China—United States Joint Commission on Legal Education was held in the Great Hall of the People. This Commission was proposed and established by the Guidance Commission on Legal Education in Law Schools under the Ministry of Education and the Association of American Law Schools. The establishment of the Commission has made a contribution to establish regular mutually beneficial exchange between China and America in the legal education field, and to promote the development and progress of legal education in China.

In 2006, in order to promote educational fairness and establish a harmonious society, the plan of recruiting students by provinces for undergraduate education at the China University of Political Science and Law was changed for the first time into one divided according to the

[13] Information Office of the State Council of the People's Republic of China, "Environmental Protection in China (1996–2005)," June 1st, 2006 http://www.lawinfochina.com/Wbk/display.asp?id=52&keyword=

population proportion. In 2006, the school planned to recruit 2,000 students for undergraduate education. After the student recruitment target was assigned according to the population proportion of various provinces, in Shandong, Henan and Sichuan three provinces with large populations, the recruitment population historically exceeded hundred students. Two core values of a socialist harmonious society is the democratic "rule of law," and impartiality and justice. The motivating force behind the "rule of law" is justice, and fairness in education is always a concern of society as a whole. As a "trailblazer" university, China's University of Political Science and Law recruited students according to the division of population proportion, which brought widespread public controversy. This attempt not only established fair opportunities for legal education, but will also serve as model in the future reform of the college entrance examination and enrollment system.

On April 26th 2006, Beijing Normal University established a Law School and an Institute of Criminal Law Science, and the University Dean, Zhao Bingzhi, was appointed dean of the Law School. The teachers for the Law School at Beijing Normal University increased from the original 16 to more than 60. On November 9th of the same year, the Chinese University of Hong Kong established its Law School while maintaining its dedication to a bilingual and "dual-culture" teaching philosophy in order to cultivate professional legal students who met the demands of globalization and the fast-growing Chinese inland economy. In 2007, the school began officially recruiting students. On November 8th 2006, under the authorization of the Ministry of Education, the Northwest Institute of Political Science and Law officially changed its name to the Northwest University of Politics and Law and held a grand unveiling and opening ceremony in the new school campus in Chang'an.

In 2006, the Guanghua Law School at Zhejiang University received a donation of a hundred million Yuan. The Guanghua Education Foundation representative Yin Yanliang and Zhejiang University Principal Yang Wei signed an agreement at Zhejiang University detailing they use the 100 million Yuan funds to construct "the Guanghua Law School at Zhejiang University." The Guanghua Law School is only the second school on the Chinese mainland after the Guanghua School of Management at Peking University which received substantial funding from the Guanghua Education Foundation. Continuing study and research produced in the economics field, this attempt opens the door for future cooperation, study and research in the field of legal science.

## X. *Harmonious World Politics and International "Rule of Law"*

The goal of international "rule of law" in China is to establish a more harmonious world. International "rule of law" in 2006 can be reviewed in three domains, public international law, private international law and international economic law.

### (A) *Public International Law* (国际公法)

2005 was the 60th anniversary of the end of WW II and the establishment of the United Nations. In 2006 international "rule of law" maintained development in international human rights law, international constitution law, collective security law, international environment law and international criminal law, playing an increasingly vital role in international relations and human life.

In the domain of international human rights law, the United Nations Commission on Human Rights was officially abolished by the United Nations Economic and Social Commission in 2006. It was replaced by the United Nations Human Rights Council established by the Resolution 60/251 approved in the United Nations General Assembly on March 14, 2006. On May 19, 2006, the United Nations General Assembly elected 47 members for the Human Rights Council. On June 19, 2006, the first conference of the Human Rights Council was held in Geneva, marking the official start date of the Human Rights Council.

At the end of 2006, Ban Ki-moon was elected as the eighth Secretary General of the United Nations. This is only the second time which an Asian was elected to hold this highest international administrative post. These United Nations reforms were widely followed by the international community. In June 2006, the United Nations Peace-building Commission[14] held its first conference, and discussed the problems of Burundi and Sierra Leone. The United Nations also started up the "Peace-building Fund" on October 11 to provide immediate support for the countries after conflicts, and to help them to solve the problem of insufficient short-term funding so that peace could be established. The

[14] On December 20, 2005, the United Nations General Assembly and the Security Council approved the resolution to establish a United Nations Peace-building Commission. This Commission will help various countries transition from war to peace, propose consultation opinions for peace building and the recovery work after conflict, and focus on the reconstruction and the system construction needed for recovery after conflict.

Peace-building Commission's establishment and its work all indicate the priority the United Nations places on peace, moreover its efforts have developed from conflict prevention and peace maintenance to establishing the development of systems advantageous to maintaining long-term peace after a conflict.

In the public security domain, on October 9, 2006, North Korea carried on the nuclear test. The United Nations Security Council unanimously approved Resolution 1718 on October 14 to condemn North Korean's nuclear test and to implement embargo sanctions against it. This resolution also established a sanction committee to supervise implementation of the resolution. The North Korean nuclear crisis and the Iranian nuclear problem are representative of the severe trials we currently face as a result of international nuclear proliferation. In 2006, attacking terrorism through international cooperation was still a key task of the United Nations, but there had been no substantive progress made in completing and approving the "Comprehensive Convention on International Terrorism." The International Law Commission of the United Nations approved "Draft Articles of Diplomatic Protection"[15] in 2006 and submitted it to the United Nations General Assembly. Simultaneously it was still carrying on research and drafting of certain subjects, which had powerfully impelled compilation and development of the international law. In addition, the world court, the international criminal court and the court of maritime international law also proposed the application and development of international rule of law in respect to their particular domains.

In the domain of international environment law, in 2006 the United Nations climate change conference was held in the Nairobi, Kenya on November 6. During the conference, it held the 12th contracting party session for the United Nations Framework Convention on Climate Change[16] and a series of international sessions on the global climate, including the 2nd session of the contracting parties for the Kyoto Protocol[17] etc. The main subject under discussion was the problem

[15] Song Ran, "The Rights, Duties and Obligations of a State and the Human Rights Protection—Comments on the Draft Articles of Diplomatic Protection," Yunnan University Journal, 6th Period of 2007, http://vip.ilib.cn/A-yndxxb-fxb200706026.html.

[16] "United Nations Framework Convention on Climate Change," Xinhuanet, June 1992, http://news.xinhuanet.com/ziliao/2003-07/10/content_966008.htm.

[17] Chinese Climate Change Network, "United Nations Framework Convention on Climate Change and the Kyoto Protocol," posted June 24th, 2005, http://www.ipcc.cma.gov.cn/Website/index.php?ChannelID=15&NewsID=101

of "after Kyoto," namely how to reduce the emission of greenhouse gasses further after 2012.

In the domain of international criminal law, on December 10, 2006, the first conference of contracting states for the "United Nations Convention against Corruption"[18] was held in Jordan. The attendee representatives discussed how to put into effect the Convention against Corruption, reinforce international cooperation against corruption, to recover losses of assets, as well as how to provide necessary technical means for prevention and punishment of corruption.

In 2006, the main achievements and the main problems faced in the domain of public international law included: (1) Chen Feng Fuzhen was elected as the director general for World Health Organization. This is the first time that someone Chinese has held the chief administrative post of major international organization. This also indicated the increasing role that China was playing in international affairs. (2) The five-year transition-period for the WTO entry had expired, and China was facing the problem of how to comprehensively fulfill the obligations prescribed in WTO, while simultaneously maintaining China's benefits under the WTO. (3) Though certain problems associated with China's national territories and ocean benefits, including the Diaoyu Island problem and the East China Sea continental shelf problem etc., are still unresolved, they continue to receive attention from the government, scholars and the public. The Shanghai Cooperative Organization, which China plays a vital role in, is also developing smoothly.

### (B.) *Private International Law* (国际私法)

Since the 1990s, along with the trends of global economic integration and global legislation, various countries have had a rise in domestic legislation regarding private international law. Dozens of countries formulated new private international laws or revised preexisting private international laws. The development of private international law

---

[18] The first legal document approved by the United Nations Convention against Corruption to instruct the international efforts to eradicate corruption, officially came into force on December 14, 2005. This document legally standardized certain problems concerning the prevention of corruption, the definition of corruption, international cooperation against corruption, and the recovery of illegal assets etc. Additionally this document was significant for various countries to strengthen their domestic anti-corruption actions, enhance their effectiveness and to promote international cooperation against corruption.

legislation in various countries presented great variety, including legislation centralization and the unification of legislative structure which exhibits a combination of stability and flexibility. Overall, in 2006, various countries' legislation for private international laws and practice was developing steadily. In the hearing of civil and commercial cases concerning foreign interests, international conventions were increasingly respected by the judiciaries of various countries, and the application and verification of foreign laws was widely discussed.

Private international law received increasing attention in China, and a draft of the civil code already created more than ninety ad hoc articles regarding private international law. According to academic statistics, 48 of the total judicial interpretations of the Supreme People's Court from 2000 to 2005 were associated with private international law. Taiwanese private international law was in the drafting process. Additionally, the development of private international law in 2006 focused on legislation and practice, the settlement of interregional legal conflict, interregional civil litigation, and the international commercial arbitration system as well as on those private international laws made after joining the WTO.

In the practice of the private international law in 2006, the abuse of litigious right increased, as shown by: (1) prosecution of parties in countries unconnected to the case; (2) agreement between both parties to sue the court; (3) prosecution of parties in the courts of several countries with concurrent jurisdiction; (4) repeated prosecution of parties in those countries associated with the case. China has signed and ratified the "Convention on the Protection of Children and Cooperation in Respect to Inter-country Adoption,"[19] and the legislation for adoption involving foreign nationals has received much attention. In the domain of private international air law, after the Montreal Convention[20] came into force in our country on July 31, 2005, the State Council ratified the "Provisions on the Limited Compensation Liabilities of Carriers in Civil

[19] Office of the Commissioner of the Ministry of Foreign Affairs of the People's Republic of China for the Hong Kong Special Administrative Region, "A Table of Various Treaties that have been Signed but not yet Approved, Granted or Accepted by China" (中国签署但尚未批准、核准或接受的多边条约一览表), Current up to December 2004, posted on July 13th, 2005 http://www.fmcoprc.gov.hk/chn/szyw/t203414.htm.

[20] Civil Aviation Administration of China, "A Brief Introduction to the Montreal Convention," (蒙特利尔公约), http://www.caac.gov.cn/L1/L5/L5_3/.

Aviation Transport"[21] on January 29, 2006, which expanded the applicable scope of limited liabilities in the civil aviation transport, enhanced the compensation quota for the carriage of passengers by air, introduced a quota adjustment mechanism, increased the carrier's liabilities, and strengthened protection for consumers of aviation transport. Thereby establishing coordination of a "double-track pricing system" (双轨制) adopted from civil aviation law and the "double gradient responsibility system" (双梯度责任制) adopted from the Convention. China is also researching legislation on private international law, the jurisdiction of civil cases concerning foreign interests, the legal system of succession concerning foreign interests, and the application of private international law for micro credit.

Academic circles have widely discussed the practice of the private international law, and have held numerous seminars on the topic. For example, the 2006 "Joint Academic Seminar for the Private International Law of Japan, China and Korea" sponsored by the Law School at Waseda University in Japan, or the second session of "Academic Seminar for the Private International Law of Chinese Mainland and Taiwan" sponsored in turn by both sides of the Taiwan Straits, the annual meeting of the Private International Law Association of China hosted by the Law School of Liaoning University in 2006, and the third academic seminar "Forum on International Law" sponsored by the Center for International Law Study and the Chinese Academy of Social Sciences. The *Chinese Yearbook on Private International Law and Comparative Law* (2005) sponsored by the Private International Law Association of China, was published by the Law Press of China, and Volume I of *International Law Research*, sponsored by the Center for International Law Study and the Chinese Academy of Social Sciences, was published by the Press at the Chinese People's Public Security University.

### (C.) *International Economic Law* (国际经济法)

The current force of economic globalization is overwhelming, and the tendency towards the melding and infiltration of separate economies is increasingly apparent. Additionally, international economic law, which aims to regulate international economic relations, simultaneously faces huge development opportunities and challenges.

---

[21] Civil Aviation Administration of China, "Provisions on the Limited Compensation Liabilities of Carriers in Civil Aviation Transport," (国内航空运输承运人赔偿责任限额规定), February 28th, 2006 http://www.lawinfochina.com/law/displayModeTwo.asp?id=4992.

In 2006, China had become the third largest trade power in the world. China also participated on a large scale in various campaigns, including the WTO, the International Monetary Fund, related economic organizations of the United Nations, regional economic organizations as well in negotiations for a bilateral free trade agreement, all of which made important contributions towards the innovation and development of international economic law. In the area of international economic law, theoretical research and practice concerning the revision and implementation of WTO legislation, legal regulations concerning a trade code of conduct, the trade & environment and the multinational corporation etc., in the action of international economic organizations including the International Monetary Fund etc. as well as in the consummation and formulation of detailed legal rules all have made the important progress. The right to contribute of emerging market countries, such as China and India etc., has increased day by day in the formulation of international trade rule, the regional trade liberalization as well as the bilateral free trade agreement kept a strong growth.

2006 marked the 5th anniversary of China's WTO entry, and at the beginning of that year, the WTO carried on a comprehensive review of China's trade policy. Famous economist, WTO secretariat and Trade Policy Review Division Director-general Mr. Clemens Boonekamp lead the compiling of "Trade Policy Review: A Report of the WTO Secretariat on the People's Republic of China"[22] (hereafter referred to as the report). This report provided detailed commentary on macroeconomic policies, the legal system of trade, specific policies & measures and trade policies for specially designated departments within China's larger economic trade policies and practices since its WTO entry. This report made a comprehensive introduction to China's economic system, the implementation of its commitments upon entering into the WTO, its trade policies and laws as well as its contributions to a multilateral trade system etc., and determined China to be "a responsible WTO member." At the same time, this report also pointed out that China's macro-economic and trade policies should "pay attention to"[23] the fact that trade and investment policies and systems have received only partial revision or annulment, the pace of exportation and exportation reform has fallen behind importation, the strength of intellectual

[22] WTO Secretariat, trans. Liu Jingdong, *Trade Policy Review—Report of WTO Secretariat on the People's Republic of China*, (China Financial & Economic Publishing House, 2006).

[23] The Shanghai WTO Affairs Consultation Center website "First Trade Policy Review of WTO to China" (April 30th, 2006), www.sccwto.net.

property protection is insufficient, and the establishment of freedoms for certain crucial departments in the service industry had fallen behind other departments.

On July 24, 2006, for the first time since its establishment, the WTO multi-round multilateral trade negotiations were compelled to announce a suspension, resulting in serious and unprecedented setbacks in global trade negotiation as well as in the legal system for WTO multilateral trade. This was the inevitable result of the new protectionist ideologies pursued by certain developed western countries. The topics of the Doha Round were extremely wide-ranging, and mainly included had the open distribution of agricultural products, market access for non-agricultural products and for the service industry, as well as intellectual property protection etc., including certain new topics, such as trade convenience, trade and the environment and electronic commerce etc. Because the United States, Europe and other countries were diametrically opposed and uncompromising regarding subsidies for agricultural products and the opening of the market opening, ultimately the Doha Round was compelled to end.

In 2006, there were unceasing trade frictions between China and America and between China and Europe concerning the export of textiles and shoes and the import of automobile parts and components. In regards to China's intellectual property protection and the reform of the RMB exchange rate, the U.S. has repeatedly exerted pressure on the Chinese government. Regarding import duties and prohibited subsidies for automobile parts and components and so on, U.S. etc. had initiated WTO procedures for conflict settlement. Trade relations between China and America and between China and Europe faced severe trials.

In 2006, in the area of foreign trade law practice, the Ministry of Commerce initiated an antidumping investigation of five types of import products, including imported potato starch originally produced in the European Union, imported electrolytic capacitor paper originally produced in Japan, imported sulfanilamide originally produced in India, imported bisphenol-A and butanone originally produced in Japan, South Korea, Singapore and the Taiwan area. The Ministry of Commerce ruled that eight different types of dumped imported products registered before 2006 had committed dumping and collected anti-dumping taxes. In the antidumping investigation, China followed related WTO rules and domestic laws and regulations throughout. According to the newest statistics from the Ministry of Commerce, from the year of 1997 when China started to take the first antidumping measure to import newsprint paper to the end of 2006, China initiated forty-seven antidumping investigations towards forty-four types of imported products from twenty-four countries and regions. Thirty-two antidumping cases were definitively ruled as such, and levied additional antidumping taxes; two were ruled harmless, and four investigations were terminated. These products involved the chemical industry, the light industry, the steel industry, the textile industry, the electron industry, the medicine industry and the agricultural industry of China. At the same time, in 2006, China was still the country which suffered the most antidumping investigations world-wide. Up until October 2006, there were a total of seventy-one antidumping investigations. Following the substantial increase of trade and China's establishment as a great trade power, China will face steadily increasing frictions regarding bilateral trade, especially after implementing the trade relief law which includes antidumping and anti-subsidy protection measures.

## XI. *Moving Towards Harmony: The "Rule of Law" Forecast for 2007*

Maintaining harmony was a key concept for "rule of law" in 2006, and is also a continued focus for "rule of law" in 2007. Chinese "rule of law" in 2007 will continue to center around fulfilling a scientific development view and building a Socialist and harmonious society. This will be achieved by strengthening legislation, expanding judicial reform, promoting administrative reform, further developing "rule of law" for the people, expanding the strength of law promulgation and administration, and promoting a socialist "rule of law" ideology, thus building a foundation for the construction of a harmonious "rule of law" society.

### A. *2007 will be a Key Year in the Formation of a Socialist Legal System with Chinese Characteristics*

2007 will be as key year for completing the task of the tenth session of the National People's Congress, namely the formation of a socialist legal system with Chinese characteristics. In 2007, the National People's Congress and its standing committee will arrange to review 20 draft laws: (1) two of which were submitted to the fifth session of tenth National People's Congress to review, the draft of the Property Law and the draft of the "Business Income Tax Law."[24] (2) Five of which were proposed for reconsideration, the draft of the "Labor Contract Law," the draft of the "Emergency Response Law," the draft of the "Administrative Coercion Law," the draft of the "Drug Prohibition Law" and the draft of the Antitrust Law; (3) thirteen of which were proposed for primary review. The 26th session of the standing committee in February reviewed the "Employment Promotion Law" (draft). The 27th session of standing committee in April reviewed the "Labor Dispute Mediation and Arbitration Law" (draft) and the "Urban and Rural Planning Law" (draft). The 28th session of standing committee in June reviewed the "Energy Saving Law" draft (revision), the law draft regarding lawyers (revision) and the law draft of civil procedure (revision). The 29th session of standing committee in August reviewed the "Recycling Economy Law" (draft), the draft of the "Law for Science and Technology Advancement" (revision), and the draft of the amendment of the Criminal Law. (7) The 30th session of the standing committee in October reviewed the "Illegal Acts Correction Law" (draft), the draft of "Criminal Procedure Law" (revision). The 31st session of the standing committee in December reviewed the draft of the Insurance Law, and the draft of the "Food Hygiene Law" (revision). (4) The legislation plan in 2007 also covered nine preparative projects, namely the formulation of a law on liabilities for torts, a law on primary health protection, a law on national defense mobilization and a telecommunication law; as well the revision of Postal Law, Insurance Law, Conscription Law, "Fire Protection Law" and "State Compensation Law." All elements concerned with these nine legislations are in the drafting process and are being revised. This process of formulation and revision was included in the legislation plan for this year, and when the opportunity arises, deliberation will be arranged. Overall, after the above draft laws were submitted for review or approval, the legislation goal of establishing a Socialist legal system with Chinese characteristics in this tenure of National People's Congress and its standing committee will be realized as scheduled. In the beginning of 2008, active effective laws will reach about 230.

Another important legislation plan of note in 2007 was the State Council and its role in the construction of a "rule of law" government. The state council will comprehensively settle 655 current administrative

[24] According to the results of two national conferences in March 2007, the "Property Law" and the "Business Income Tax Law" have been approved, and will be implemented soon.

rules and regulations, 3,031 rules and regulations of the State Council departments and 9,664 rules and regulations of the local governments. This large-scale legislation settlement was proposed for completion at the end of October, 2007 in order to guarantee a unified, harmonious and ordered socialist legal system, which would have important influence in the maintenance of socialist "rule of law" authority and the promotion of legal administration.

The mission of developing Chinese legislation includes the arduous and weighty responsibilities of comprehensively and thoroughly advancing democratic and scientific legislation, establishing a legislation quality assessment system, noticeably reducing "department protectionism" and "regional protectionism" in legislation, further improving and consummating legislation work and continuously improving the quality and level of legislation.

B. *The Establishment of Protocol for the Prevention and Aid of Emergencies*
In 2007 the dispute mechanism protocol will be completed. On one hand, the construction of a legal system for dispute settlement must be improved, and the legal channel for dispute settlement must be strengthened in order to control social disputes within the approved system. On the other hand, a protocol for the prevention and resolution of emergency disputes must be established, in particular, a protocol to develop awareness and help prevent those types of community disputes which garner widespread attention, cause intense conflict and involve complex issues. In analyzing countermeasures, China must transform the ideology of "submitting petitions on a large scale" (大信访), and encourage the use of other legal channels such as litigation etc. It must emphasize the construction of a complaint filing system, formulate a "complaint filing law," implement a centralized management source for complaint processing, and reduce the role of leadership in the administration, refinement and standardization of the procedure for complaint filing. China must also promote positive and safe judicial reform, continuously develop litigation protocol, and increase the real outcome of such litigation. It must revise administrative procedure law and administrative redress law, and establish an examination system to review administrative litigation and administrative redress behavior. It must establish a protocol for internal dispute settlement, establish a connection between personnel dispute arbitration and litigation and the unified national complaint filing system for state personnel, as well as advance the system for collective labor bargaining and dispute resolution. It must establish a mediation system, strengthen the legal effects

of non-judicial mediation, and fully encourage the role of mediation in the settlement of social disputes.

In the interest of judicial reform evaluation system regarding the constitutionality of laws, regulations and rules should be established, regional and departmental protectionism must be overcome, and a basic system to safeguard the settlement of social disputes through legal channels should be provided.

C. *The Gradual Expansion of Administrative Reform*

In 2007, China had to face the fact that pre-existing issues still existed in its current administrative system. Namely, power is overly centralized, and the mechanisms of regulating power are so ineffective they cause corruption and various abuses such as the abuse of authority, dereliction of duty, and illegal use of vested authority etc. The primary target of administrative system reform should be to establish a feasible mechanism of authority restriction and supervision, one in accordance with "rule of law" Democracy that has precedence over other approaches of administrative reform. If these ideologies are not established, the simplification of administrative structure, the adjustment of responsibilities, the formation of social public administrative structure, and the construction of a service government will all be difficult to implement.

In this age, the key to administrative reform definitely does not lie in the division of power, the reduction of scale, demotion of rank or adjustment of responsibilities. This is so even in the case of largely used systems or the basic Western new public management theory, which introduces the market competition mechanism to the public administration and establishes a so-called "corporate" government etc. Rather, the key to such reform lies in the development and expansion of an internal power restriction mechanism within the administrative system concurrent to the development of an external power restriction mechanism, thereby truly bringing the controlling power in line with the "rule of law." The "rule of law" principle and protocol need be continuously applied from the exterior of an administrative system to its interior. The system of responsibility for administrative leaders needs be explored and encouraged to change from the traditional approach of centralized state power to one which implements several patterns and modalities that unite practice and theory. Internal policy decisions in administrative systems should be promoted and in order to assure suitable separation, the three basic rights and functions should be implemented. Policy decisions in politics and in general administrative affairs should be separated. Additionally, public officers on the front lines should be endowed with the authority to unify their rights and duties and according to law independently fulfill their responsibilities and obligations etc.

The development of openness and transparency in the administration process in order to encourage the participation and supervision of public opinion, and the expansion of a judiciary investigation protocol are both indispensable to a modern administrative system in a democratic "rule of law" society. Since the current reform and opening of Chinese society, especially since 16th session of the National Congress of Communist Party of China (hereinafter referred to as 16th NCCPC), the external supervision mechanism of administrative power has quickly developed, relevant law structures and basic systems have been formed and are being continuously improved and perfected. However, the internal restriction protocol for administrative power has been constructed and reformed relatively slowly.

### D. *Judicial Reform that Emphasizes an Impartial Judiciary in Service of the People*

In 2007, judicial system reform will be carried out according to the goals determined by the Commission of Politics and Law of the CPC Central Committee. Namely that a reformed judiciary will, (1) Provide convenient access for public litigious activities and enforce laws for the people. (2) Strengthen litigious activity, and supervise, restrict and promote judicial impartiality. (3) Expand public access to the judiciary to promote impartiality. (4) Revise and perfect criminal policy and protocol for group conflict mediation in order to continue the development of the elements of a harmonious society. As well as reform supervision to further enhance judicial efficiency, and reform the litigation system in order to promote judicial democracy. (5) Reform the division of powers and the managerial system in order to further safeguard human rights. (6) Reform the personnel administration system and the protocol for the safeguard of funds in order to lessen the influence safeguarding concerns influencing political and legal work.

The core of judicial reform lies in the problem of deploying and dividing the three powers. Judicial power should be reformed and structured reasonably, and be reformed according to procedure. It is foreseeable that, in 2007, the judicial organs will further implement judiciary measures in order to facilitate public party participation at various levels of litigation including filing, trials, enforcement, and retrials etc. Additionally the applicable scope of litigation mediation will be broadened, and suitable mediation will be attempted in self-incriminating criminal cases and other minor criminal cases. A protocol for inquiring about case handling will be established, as well as a system of public record for judicial documents. The judicial demands of indigent communities will be a focus, and also the further development of a judicial reparation system. The construction of a system for petitioning information pertaining to lawsuits will be established to facilitate mass on-line petitions and inquiries. The judiciary will also gradually increase reform in various areas, including the litigation system, and judicial organization and judicial management in order to promote an impartial judiciary and a harmonious society.

For example, a ratification procedure and a judgment standard for death sentence cases will be established, protocol for the court appearances of important witnesses and expert witnesses will be established; leniency and strictness will be implemented according to criminal policy, measures for the aid of criminal victims will be established, a simpler trail system for defendants who have admitted guilt will be established, a system for the research of legal precedents will be developed and the judge's discretionary behaviors will be expanded.

E. *The Continuous Fight against Corruption and the Promotion of Honesty*

In 2007, efforts to eradicate corruption will revolve around (1) the establishment of an impartial and comprehensive social security system; (2) impartial supervision and direction over the development of a public fiscal system and the establishment of basic public services for all levels of party organization and government; (3) the establishment of a normalized ordered income distribution system. Implementing a comprehensive social security system, would realize the important agenda of protecting the life and work of the public on the most fundamental level and would advance the realization of the principle of social equality.

The effort to eradicate corruption in China will focus on the establishment of a unified employee placement policy, an education & training policy, a medical health policy, a cultural development policy and an environmental protection policy. Further work to this aim would include the establishment of an effective and incorruptible social management system to carry out the supervision and inspections, as well as research and formulation of a special "Anti-Corruption Law" to effectively eradicate official and commercial corruption.

F. *Legal Implementation and Supervision Will Yield Greater Actual Results*

In 2007, enforcement and supervision of the law was still an arduous process. According to investigation and research on the topic in 2006, non-compliance with the law and lax enforcement were both the key points and largest difficulties for municipalities in implementing the general plan for managing state affairs according to the "rule of law." Additionally the quality of implementation and execution varied according to location.

Conditions, environment, and demographic fluctuations specific to each location are all important and influential factors in the implementation and effect of laws. Take population as an example: in the Midwest inland area, there is a large population of migrant workers and a reduced population of local residents. Because the majority of the migrant workers are young adults, those left behind tend to be primarily the elderly, women and children. These elders, women and children left behind, are called the "386199 Army" by the local cadres. In east coast area, whether in urban or rural areas, massive floating populations are gathering. The high-speed development of economic society has created an unprecedented challenge for law enforcement.

From 2002 to 2006, the NPC Standing Committee successively heard and reviewed 44 special reports from the people's government, the people's court and the Supreme People's Procuratorate. The NPC Standing Committee also inspected the implementation of 21 laws, which guaranteed the correct implementation of laws according to the supervision of the National People's Congress, promoted administration by law and an impartial judiciary, and maintained the people's legitimate rights and interests. 2007 is the first year that the Supervision Law will be implemented. The NPC Standing Committee took this as a turning point to further strengthen and improve the standardization, function and effects of supervision. According to the report of the NPC Standing Committee, three aspects of law enforcement were slated for inspection in 2007. Nine special reports were slated for hearing and review: (1) the report of the State Council on advancing new socialist rural reconstruction, and on energy conservation and environmental protection. (2) The reports of the State Council on urban and rural medical healthcare reform, the development of safe supervision of foods and drugs, the continued provision of employees' legitimate rights and interests, and the inspection and implementation of the compulsory education law. (3) The report of the Supreme People's Court and the Supreme People's Procuratorate on implementing trial supervision and prosecutorial supervision, as well as tracking the implementation of suggestions made in inspection reports regarding the enforcement records of judges and prosecutors. (4) The reports of the State Council on overseas Chinese affairs and on the protection of the legitimate rights and interests of Taiwanese investment, as well as tracking the implementation of suggestions made in inspection reports regarding the enforcement of regional and national autonomy laws, and the formulation of relevant laws and regulations.

In 2007, the NPC Standing Committee will strengthen its supervision of the budget and economy. It will hear and review the reports of the State Council on the Central Committee's final accounts and audit in 2006, the report on standardizing financial transfer payments, and the report of the State Council regarding the national economy, the execution of the social development plan to strengthen filing inspection of standard documents, including administrative rules and regulations, local laws and regulations and judicial interpretations etc, and the further development of a petitioning and feedback system.

According to the report of the Supreme People's Procuratorate, in 2007, continued implementation and supervision of law will take three forms: First, it will expand the serious implementation of legal supervision responsibilities. This will result in the development of an arrest authorizations system in accordance with the law, prosecution of particular problems in the criminal underworld, and renewed attention towards official offenses and commercial bribery. Additionally, it will increase legal supervision of litigious activities, civil trials, administrative suits and sentencing. Second, the implementation and supervision of law in 2007 will function to lead existing prominent criminal policies. In order to focus on the implementation of a criminal judiciary policy with both lenient and strict penalties, the Supreme People's Procuratorate formulated "Certain Opinions on Implementing Both Strict and Lenient Criminal Judiciary Policies in Prosecutorial Work" (关于在检查工作中贯彻宽严相济刑事司法政策的若干意见). Third, it will strengthen the construction and reform of procuratorial organizations. This will be accomplished by establishing and improving supervision of malfeasance on the part of judicial personnel, establishing supervision and restriction within procuratorial organizations, and promoting the standardization and institutionalization of the people's supervisor system.

In 2007, according to the report of the Supreme People's Court, the implementation and supervision of the law of the Supreme People's Court would assume three forms: First, continued fulfillment of judicial functions in accordance with the law in order to maintain social stability;

and in particular, the expedited handling, prevention and avoidance of collective administrative disputes for the reason that, inappropriate working conditions can intensify existing problems resulting in public condemnation. Second, emphasis on key issues and development of legislative implementation measures, for example, anti-corruption efforts, regulation and careful deliberation of death penalty cases, criminal victim relief, and simplified trials in the case of confessions. Lastly the development of legislative implementation would result in an expansion of the scope and methods of legislative application and a comprehensively realized system of legislative implementation. Third, development of a comprehensive system of supervision and restriction to guarantee the correct application of judicial authority, Also, emphasis on a system of supervision and restriction within the courts, for instance, strengthened supervision of trial grades and adjudicative work, and establishment of a comprehensive retrial system.

G. *Promoting Prosperity and the Development of "One Country, Two Systems"* (一国两制)

July 1, 2007, will be the tenth anniversary of the return of Hong Kong to mainland China. It is also the tenth anniversary of the effective implementation and successful practice of HK Basic Law and the great conception of "One country, two systems." In this time, Basic Law had been gradually learned, accepted and supported by the Hong Kong people.

In the continued "rule of law" work for Hong Kong and Macao in 2007 and beyond, the following issues should be addressed: First, the legal systems of Hong Kong and Macao Regions should be thoroughly researched, and effective communication with Hong Kong and Macao law circles and jurisprudential circles should be maintained in order to eliminate differences in understanding regarding Basic Law which could result in bifurcation. Second, Hong Kong and Macao political system reforms should be closely monitored, and advance research on possible legal issues should be conducted. "To gradually develop Hong Kong's democratic system according to the practical situation of the Hong Kong Special Administrative Region" is the consistent standpoint the Central Committee advocates in its support of developing democracy in the Hong Kong Special Administrative Region. In Macao, the Central committee maintains an identical standpoint. Third, judicial cooperation between Hong Kong & Macao and the inland should be strengthened, and a space of legal cooperation should be created for resolving issues, for example, cooperation in extraditing criminal, etc. Fourth, the construction of Macao rule of law should pay ample attention to the problem of legal language, the problem of localization of legal professional and the problem of judicial costs. Other risks and issues of particular relevance include the impact of strong foreign capitals on the local market because of the gambling industry, employment, education for teenagers and the price of real estate all of which could possibly affect Macao national security.

Presently, the cause of de jure independence is the main ploy used by the independence movement to incite disturbances between the two sides of the Taiwan Straits. It is the single largest barrier to a peaceful cooperation between the two sides of the Taiwan Straits, and it is also a subject of urgency which the legislative and judiciary circles should fully research. So-called independence, in general refers to the Taiwan independence movements attempts to realize Taiwanese independence legally through legislative procedures in the Taiwan region. In particular it attempts to complete the so-called establishment of "the country of Taiwan" in legislation through revision of "the constitution" of the Taiwan Region or the formulation of a "new constitution."

At present, the Taiwanese authorities and the Taiwan independence movement have begun real preparation and implementation measures for independence, with the elimination of Chinese culture as one of its goals. For example, the term "Taiwanese self-identity" is used instead of "Taiwan independence." In order to carry out this so-called "Elimination of Chinese culture," China is substituted for the original terms of "our country," "us" and "the Mainland" in the textbooks to show Taiwanese separation; additionally the "The Republic of China's Postal Service" has been changed to the "Taiwan Postal Service," and so on.

Even if one takes the legal principle of independence as division, one can also still divide it further into a direct method of independence and an indirect method of independence. Direct independence has three basic positions. First, the title of "Republic of China" should be changed, and the "Constitution of the Republic of China" should be changed into the "New Taiwan constitution" through a revision of the "constitution." Second, the authority of "the constitution of Republic of China" should be suspended while the "new constitution" is being formulated. And finally, the direct independence method uses a more direct approach to replacing "The Constitution of the Republic of Taiwan" for "The Constitution of the Republic of China." Indirect independence also has three basic positions. First, the title of the Republic of China would not be changed, but changes would be made to the language of the laws; for example, "The sovereignty of the Republic of China extends to all nationals" would be changed to "belongs to all Taiwanese people." "The territories of the Republic of China are compliant with the rest of the domain" would be changed to "the territories of the Republic of China are only restricted in the Taiwan Islands, Pescadores, Jinmen Island and Mazu Island areas" or only "restricted in Taiwan." Second, relevant terms and conditions in "The constitution of the Republic of China" would be suspended, and new terms and conditions increased. The contents of these new terms and conditions are actually indirect formulations of Taiwanese independence; for example, in Chen Shui-bian's speech on New Year's Day in 2006 he said: "Taiwan is our country, with a total land area is 36,000 square kilometers. Taiwan's 'national sovereignty' belongs to its 20 million people, and it is not subordinate to the People's Republic of China." Third, the administrative division of "Republic of China," and its defined "sovereignty" and jurisdiction over Taiwan, Pescadores, Jinmen Island and Mazu Island areas, would be revised and changed into "four provinces and a special region" (四省一特区) and so on. Therefore, the containment of the independence movement will be an urgent matter for 2007 and the future.

The independence offensive of the Taiwan independence movement should not be underestimated nor allowed to divert the efforts of the People's Republic to use theoretical innovation to solve the problem of Chinese unity and establish a unified national legal ideology instead of responding aggressively. China should use historical fact and unified comprehensive ideology as responses to the provocations of the independence movement. Through the construction of legal system, the relationship between the people on both sides of the Taiwan Straits would become closer, creating a greater public understanding of unification, and turning unification into a legal requirement. Also in-depth research into the political trends of the Taiwan Region should be conducted.

China must also conduct institutional analysis and research on the politics and the laws of Taiwan Region, as well as new patterns, changes, theories and practices of party politics in the Taiwan Region. China must maintain multi-level multi-channel contact and communication with the various political parties and social strata of Taiwan, and eliminate barriers with those Taiwanese compatriots who are also seeking unification. We must clarify misunderstandings, promote understanding and seek common ground while respecting differences in order to promote a cooperative system as the major premise for unification.

Maintaining peace and stability in the Taiwan Straits is the key to relations between the two sides. We should firmly protest against any form of separatist activity, including Taiwan's independence etc. and closely watch the motions and secession scheme which the Taiwanese independence force is using. We must not allow Taiwan to change its long history and its accepted international legal status as an inalienable part of Chinese territory. The "Anti-Secession Law"[25] approved by National People's Congress in March, 2005 is a basic law protesting secession and promoting unification. On the one hand, we must steadfastly implement this law, firm in the standpoint against secession, earnestly conduct theoretical research regarding "Anti-Secession Law," continue to develop the theory behind the "Anti-Secession Law," and develop legislation research into the de jure independence of Taiwan in order to strengthen legislation work against an independent Taiwan. On the other hand, we must strengthen cooperation between those opposing an "Independent Taiwan," promote unity between the two sides of the Taiwan Straits and strengthen communication with all circles of Taiwanese society. All forms of the Taiwanese independence movement must be met with a unified front by strengthening communication between those supporters of developing unified relations, by increasing public contact, by strengthening economic and trade contacts, and by strengthening exchange and cooperation in law etc.

H. *Comprehensively Promoting Quality Legal Education*

Over the past several decades, the legal education of China could be basically defined as being in an "expansion" or "limited construction" stage. Presently, this historic phase has been basically completed.[26] In 2007, we should advocate comprehensive quality in legal education. Presently our pressing responsibility is to create innovation in the

[25] China's Taiwan Web (中国台湾站), "Anti-Secession Law" (反分裂国家法), March 15th, 2005, (http://2006.chinataiwan.org/web/webportal/W5266604/index.html (website loading problems).

[26] Xu Xianming, "Speech Given at the Closing Ceremony of the Seminar on 'Strengthening the Construction of Specialized Discipline and Improving the Overall Quality of Legal Education'," *Chinese Legal Education Research* Volume 3 (2006): 5. China University of Politics and Law Press.

traditional mode of legal education development, and to enhance the quality of legal education.

A comprehensive and quality legal education system includes high-level applicants, faculty, and training, as well as quality educational management and administrative conditions. The primary goal of a high quality legal education is the education of civic virtues, secondarily the education of higher-level legal professional ethics, and the final level is the education of political ethics.[27] The current legal education system only addresses education problems of civic virtues, and legal professional ethics education and political ethics education are universally absent.

At present, the legal education system still uses the traditional classroom teaching method, preventing students from utilizing practical experience. Judiciary departments have also generally reported that law graduates are lacking in the ability to practically apply their knowledge, and can only apply legal provisions in a proscribed manner. After graduating and entering judiciary departments, students generally need at least 3 years or more of professional experience in order to be able to meet the demands of handing cases and legal affairs as a prosecutor.

The Institute of Law at the Chinese Academy of Social Sciences has led the way in successfully offering legal clinic courses and training full-time Master's level law students. It is estimated that eventually this method of legal clinic education will be more and more widespread. Law teaching materials will also diversify, both according to teaching characteristics, and according to teaching objectives (such as, coursework for undergraduate education, LLM or the Master of Judicial Science). Teaching materials could also focus on law knowledge education and emphasize the cultivation of professional law skills. The form of teaching materials could also be diversified, to include the traditional system materials, reading materials, CDs based on case precedents, and film & television programming etc.[28]

Since the country implemented a unified judiciary exam in 2002, the exam has focused on memorization, instead of comprehension, articles of law, instead of not legal principles and elementary knowledge,

---

[27] Ibid.

[28] Wang Liming, "Several Opinions on Construction of Legal Teaching Materials," *Chinese Legal Education Research*, China University of Politics and Law Press, Volume 3 (2006): 17~23.

instead of the evolution of legal applications. Legal education in China has gradually lost its diversity and has moved towards the single goal of examination-oriented education, which will become increasingly apparent in future legal education.

Additionally in 2005 there occurred a series of events in graduate education which caused the public to question the rationality of the current system of examination and matriculation, they included, the resignation Chen Danqing, the bribery of Professor Ouyang by female examinees, and He Weifang's ceasing to recruit students etc. Regarding graduate matriculation in 2006, the types of self-directed test questions were reduced, and their quality was improved. Examination of the examinees professional skills was conducted through secondary examination, and the weight of this secondary examination was moderately expanded. In 2007, this reform will still be in progress.

## XII. *International "Rule of Law": Working Towards a Harmonious World*

The principal tasks facing international law in the future are to promote a connection between peace and security, development and human rights; to avoid violation of the "United Nations Charter" and the international law principles; to increase the authority of the United Nations and the actual effects of international law; and finally to promote the establishment and refinement of international rule of law in order to solve those important problems which international law faces in the immediate future. The Human Rights Council established in 2006, has hopes of becoming one of the United Nation's primary organizations, and also of establishing human rights as one of the United Nation's primary areas of focus along with peace and security. The Human Rights Council set up a universal periodic review protocol, in which all member nations of the United Nations must submit a report to the Council for deliberation on the situation of its protection and promotion of human rights. This system replaced and supplemented the existing mechanism in which only nations belonging to the International Human Rights Convention needed to submit reports. The United Nations and the international community have placed great expectations on the Human Rights Council, that it more effectively promote human rights all over the world.

The Human Rights Council will be reviewed within a year after the first conference and will afterwards then improve and reasonably adjust its missions, protocols, functions and responsibilities as necessary.

This reform will be a focus of the Council work in 2007. In 2007, Ban Ki-moon officially accepted the post of Secretary General for 5 years. The performance this new chief of the United Nations, who until this point has kept a low profile, has yet to be seen. The international community will be closely following his actions as he leads the United Nations in enhancing its efficiency, reconstructing its prestige and authority, responding to increasingly complex international situations, and in resolving increasingly intractable international issues. In 2007, the North Korean nuclear crisis will become a key issue in international rule of law. On the one hand, international society should make great efforts to properly resolve this issue within the framework of the United Nations according to the regulations of international law by preventing nuclear proliferation and banning weapons of mass destruction. On the other hand, countries should absolutely avoid resolving this problem outside of the UN framework or in a way that violates international law. In 2007, more than twenty countries with latent nuclear potential will be awaiting the decisions of the international community in regards to the resolution of the North Korean nuclear issue in the "Six-Party Talks," and the direction of developments in the Iranian nuclear issue. However the coordination and resolution protocols of the great powers and the United Nations Security Council seem to have difficulties in effectively addressing the issue of regional nuclear proliferation. The unilateral doctrine of the United States, international antiterrorism and the nuclear issue will continue to be key issues for international society in 2007.

The problem of legislating private international law in China will be the center of much attention. The 21st century is a new century of information, economic knowledge, economic globalization and the development of an unprecedented network. In order to adapt to this new century, private international law should also exhibit innovative development tendencies. The question of how to forecast and lead these development tendencies will be a major issue facing private international law in the new century. Since the beginning of China's political reforms increasing connection with the international community, foreign, civil and commercial relations have experienced unprecedented development. However at the same time China lacked an independent system of private international law, and only had established certain sporadic rules and regulations regarding private international law in the correlative laws. At that time, China was drafting and formulating a civil code, in which the ninth section was specific to private international law, comprising altogether more than 90 articles. Academic circles connected to private international law were researching the importance and feasibility of legislating Chinese private international law, including its system and protocol, the establishment of concrete laws and regulations, and the coordination of Chinese private international law and international conventions on private international law as well as the private international laws of various countries.

In 2007, China will also address issues related to private international law since its WTO entry and those issues of private international law brought on by Internet development, as well as the general unification and convergence of private international law. Under the frame of "One country, two systems," China would also strengthen the research and implementing of Chinese law in interregional conflicts.

In summary, the theory behind China's system of law on interregional conflicts was not perfect, the legislation was imperfect, and there were also many problems of practice which proved difficult to solve. Included in these problems were: the refinement of the Law on Interregional Conflicts, its status quo and characteristics, its resolution methods and channels, and the comparison between private international law and the Law on Interregional Conflicts on the four areas of the law (四法域). Other outstanding difficulties included the establishment and coordination of jurisdiction for interregional civil & commercial cases, the refinement of interregional civil litigation procedure and the coordination of laws and judicial cooperation among the four areas of Chinese law. Additionally, in 2007, the private international law of Taiwan Region of China will be drafted.

At the beginning of 2007, all of the WTO member countries unanimously agreed to hold Doha round negotiations again. It is anticipated that the U.S and the European Community will concede on the agricultural product subsidies and market admittance in order to facilitate the smoothness of the Doha round negotiations. Simultaneously, also it is also anticipated that the Doha round could promote WTO regulations, the revision and refinement of the dispute settlement protocols, and promote the establishment of a system of regulations for competition in trade, trade and environment, increasing trade convenience and electronic commerce.

In 2007, China will still be faced with the huge pressures of trade conflicts with the Western great trade powers, especially regarding import duties for auto parts and components, prohibited subsidies and the protection of intellectual property etc. Also China will possibly have to respond to the USA's appeal for WTO dispute settlement.

In the area of trade relief measures, Chinese business is still under the huge pressure of effecting antidumping litigation from other countries. To remedy this The Ministry of Commerce and related business organizations should further expand the coordination and management of the activities of enterprises sued protecting their own lawful rights and interests. Additionally the Ministry of Foreign Affairs should increase consular protection for the legitimate rights and interests of Chinese business investment abroad. Supervision and management of foreign investments and import-export goods should be advanced as well as the application of those rights endowed the WTO member countries in anti-dumping, anti-subsidy and protection measures etc. which protect the impartiality and order of China's domestic market. WTO regulations and conflict resolution protocol should also be revised and refined.

A tendency that must be closely followed is the liberalization of regional trade. Presently, the WTO multilateral trade system is widely challenged, while the practice of interregional or bilateral free trade agreements has been welcomed. This has created serious challenges for multi-lateral trade organizations that have been successful for over half a century, which raises the question, should international trade adopt the multilateral system or the free trade system?

Generally it is believed that implementation of regional trade liberalization should not negate a multilateral trade system. Those WTO member countries that have participated in regional trade liberalization should seek a suitable balance between the policy goals of regional trade liberalization and maintenance of basic order of the multilateral trade system.[29] Finally, China upholds this principle and resolutely participates in regional trade liberalization.

---

[29] WTO Secretariat, trans. Liu Jingdong, *Trade Policy Review—Report of WTO Secretariat on the People's Republic of China*, (China Financial & Economic Publishing House, 2006).

# INDIVIDUAL REPORTS

# REPORT ON THE DEVELOPMENT OF THE NATIONAL PEOPLE'S CONGRESS SYSTEM IN 2006

Li Xia[1]

The National People's Congress system made important progress towards its goal of "building a socialist harmonious society" at all levels. On the legislation front, central legislation experienced new breakthroughs and local legislation also improved. Democratic and scientific legislation also made continued advancements. The scope of ordered public participation in the legislative process was further expanded, and enthusiasm for legislative participation increased. Regional legislation cooperation also yielded new perspectives and insights and legislation assessment was gradually standardized and institutionalized while local legislation regarding petitions and complaints was active. In addition, all levels of the People's Congress and its standing committee undertook massive work towards enhancing the outcomes of supervision, expanding representative function, and strengthening the system construction etc., which made new contributions towards maintaining and refining the system of the National People's Congress, and advancing the establishment of a socialist democratic legal system, as well as promoting the comprehensive advancement of Chinese "rule of law" in order to establish a socialist harmonious society.

## I. *Speeding Up the Legislation Process*

### A. *Central Legislation: Achieving New Breakthroughs*

In March, 2003, after changing session, the tenth National People's Congress proposed that the goal of legislation work of the National People's Congress and its standing committee was "forming the foundations of a socialist legal system with Chinese characteristics," and

[1] Li Xia is an assistant researcher at the Law Institute of the Chinese Academy of Social Sciences.

that the emphasis of legislation would be "enhancing the quality of legislation." The tenth National People's Congress and its standing committee approved altogether 70 laws, legal interpretations and decisions concerning legal issues of the past four year tenure (2002~2006), including one constitutional amendment, more than 20 newly-made laws and nearly 30 law revisions, by which the legislation of China in the areas of politics, economy and society were comprehensively strengthened.

2006 was the fourth year of the five-year legislation plan, and was undoubtedly a key year in the realization of legislation goals of the National People's Congress and its standing committee. That year, based on the progress of former legislations, the National People's Congress continued to strengthen legislation work aimed at comprehensive economic & social development, and supporting a socialist market economy legal system, thereby coming closer to realizing the legislative goals.

Compared with the previous two years, the quantity of legislation further shrunk in 2006,[2] but there were new breakthroughs in the complexity and quality of legislation, both crucial to establishing a socialist "rule of law" society. The tenth National People's Congress and its standing committee approved in total 70 laws, legal interpretations and decisions concerning legal issues during the past four years of their tenure, including one constitutional amendment, more than 20 newly-made laws and nearly 30 law revisions of law. Among them, in 2003 the National People's Congress and its standing committee reviewed altogether 12 laws and draft decisions concerning legal issues, and approved 10. In 2004, the NPC reviewed altogether 33 laws, legal interpretations and draft decisions concerning the legal issues, and approved 25. In 2005, it reviewed in total 25 laws, legal interpretations and draft decisions concerning the legal issues, and approved 18. In 2006, it reviewed 24 laws and draft decisions concerning the legal issues, and approved 15 (see Figure 2.1).

[2] The Ninth National People's Congress and its standing committee reviewed altogether 124 laws, legal interpretations and draft decisions concerning the legal issues in its tenure (1998~2002). Among them, the standing committee reviewed and approved 102, and submitted 7 to the National People's Congress to consider and approve after review. Another four decisions concerning legal issues were reviewed and approved by the National People's Congress.

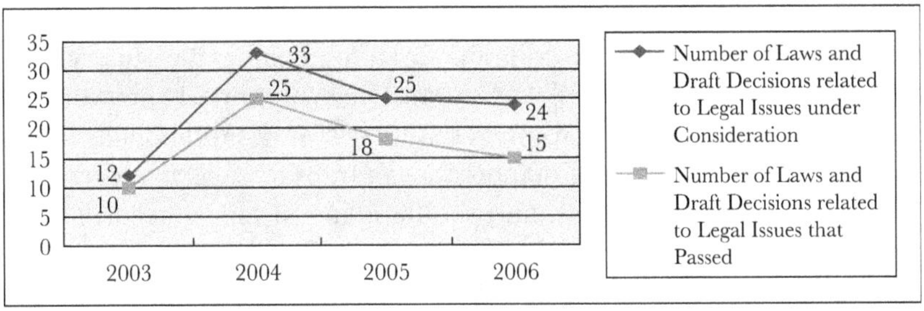


Figure 2.1: Laws and Drafting Decisions Concerning the Legal Issues Examined (in Draft Form) or Approved by the National People's Congress and its Standing Committee from 2003–2006

In 2006, the promulgation and implementation of the Supervision Law[3] and the review of the Property Law (Draft) were the most noticeable acts of legislation of the People's Congress. Both of these laws, one which involves the national political system and the state system, and the other which is basic civil law that standardizes property relations, have lasted many years and have only appeared publicly after repeated studies, argumentations, revisions and innumerable reviews.

In August, 2006, the 23rd session of tenth NPC Standing Committee approved the Supervision Law, to be implemented on January 1, 2007. The Supervision Law included the collective input of the deputies of the National People's Congress, the members of the standing committee, all levels of local People's Congress and experts. This input was significant for the Standing Committees of all levels of People's Congress to legally exercise supervision authority, refine supervision protocol, to strengthen and improve supervision work, to enhance the actual results of supervision, and to effectively promote the characteristics and the superiorities of the system of National People's Congress. This law has fully manifested the organic unity maintained by party leadership, as has also maintained the central role of the public in the management of state affairs. It has correctly handled those relations which strengthen

[3] The process of ratifying the Supervision Law from research and drafting to consideration and approval took twenty years (1996–2006). This important law underwent the longest legislation process since China's reform and international involvement. The Property Law from drafting (in 1993) to approval (in 2007) underwent deliberation eight times, with the entire legislative process and consideration lasting 14 years, a rarity in China's legislative history.

the supervision work of the National People's Congress and maintained party leadership, which in addition to strengthening the supervision work of the National People's Congress has supported the work of the "government, court and procurator" (一府两院). Additionally it has maintained the principle of democratic centralism, collective exertion, collective decision questions, and the handling of affairs according to the law and procedure, which conforms to the national situation and the practical work of the National People's Congress.

As in 2005, in 2006 the Property Law was still the legislation which received the most attention from the public. The Property Law is a basic law which standardizes property relations, supports a socialist legal system with Chinese characteristics, and emphasizes politics, as well as adherence to policy and specialization. After massive investigation and study, and extensive deliberation of opinions and suggestions, the draft Property Law underwent significant revision. It has comprehensively defined the basic principles of Property Law, including property protection, usufructruary rights, including state, collective and private property, structural zoning rights, land contracting and management rights, construction use rights, house site land use and easement rights etc., and the actual rights for security, including the right to a mortgage, the right of pledge and lien and so on. The formulation of Property Law has refined the socialist property rights system with Chinese characteristics, which it is extremely important in maintaining a basic national economic system, standardizing an ordered socialist market economy, maintaining the vital interest of the public, stimulating the creativity of society as a whole, achieving the goal of comprehensively constructing an affluent society, and building a socialist harmonious society.

In 2006, several important legislation projects related to the overall economic development situation were completed. For example, "Law of the People's Republic of China on Agricultural Product Quality Safety" (农产品质量安全法),[4] "Passport Law of the People's Republic of China" (护照法),[5] "Amendment 6 to the Criminal Law of the

[4] Standing Committee of the People's National Congress, "Law of the People's Republic of China on Agricultural Product Quality Safety," promulgated April 29th 2006, http://www.lawinfochina.com/law/display.asp?id=5142.

[5] Standing Committee of the People's Congress, "Passport Law of the People's Republic of China," promulgated April 29th, 2006, http://www.lawinfochina.com/law/display.asp?id=5143&keyword=.

People's Republic of China" (刑法修正案 [六]),[6] "Decision of the Standing Committee of the National People's Congress Regarding the Revision of the Organic Law of the People's Courts of the People's Republic of China" (关于修改人民法院组织法的决定)' and so on were reviewed and approved. Many draft laws were also reviewed, such as the "Employment Contract Law" (劳动合同法),[7] "Anti-Drug Law" (禁毒法), "Business Income Tax Law" (企业所得税法)[8] and "Emergency Response Law" (突发事件应对法)[9] and so on. Among them, the "Law of the People's Republic of China on Agricultural Product Quality Safety" established a standardized system of agricultural product quality safety, strengthened the production management of agricultural products, standardized the production process of agricultural products, and refined the system of supervision and inspection of agricultural product quality safety. This was advantageous in improving the level of agricultural product quality safety, safeguarding public health and safety, enhancing the competitive standing of agricultural products, and achieving greater income levels for farmers. The "Passport Law of the People's Republic of China" defined types, issuance targets, application and issuance procedures and the legal liability of the passport etc. in order to meet the demands of China's rapidly increasing overseas negotiations and personnel exchange as well as its rising immigration numbers, which created a demand for the further standardization and institutionalization of passport supervision work.

In order to guarantee prudent and fair death penalty sentencing, the NPC Standing Committee revised related terms and conditions of the "Organic Law of the People's Courts" (人民法院组织法), canceled the provision in which the Supreme People's Court was allowed to authorize the Higher People's Court to exercise partial competence for examination and approval of death sentence cases, and reclaimed authorization to examine and authorize death sentences for the Supreme

[6] Chinese Laws in English Online (法律英语网), "Amendment 6 to the Criminal Law of the People's Republic of China," 2008, http://www.21lawyer.cn/english/04c/8.html text

[7] The Legal Enterprise Online (企业法律网), Law on Employment Contracts, posted December 10th, 2007, http://www.hnqylawyer.com/ldqy/ShowArticle.asp?ArticleID=717.

[8] National People's Congress, "Enterprise Income Tax Law of the People's Republic of China," promulgated March 17th, 2007, http://www.lawinfochina.com/Law/display.asp?id=5910&keyword=.

[9] Standing Committee of the People's National Congress, "Emergency Response Law of the People's Republic of China," promulgated August 30th, 2007, http://www.lawinfochina.com/law/display.asp?id=6358&keyword=.

People's Court, which strictly controlled and prudently applied the death penalty, and fully manifested respect and protection for the human right of life.

The "Business Income Tax Law" is an important law which is related to the overall situation of economic and social development. The NPC Standing Committee carried on an earnest review of the Business Income Tax Law (Draft), and thought it advantageous to the reform of the current business income tax system and the unification of foreign capital business income tax to create a fair competitive market environment, and further refine the socialist market economy system. The "Business Income Tax Law (Draft)" was submitted to the fifth session of the tenth National People's Congress for review.[10] The Antitrust Law (反垄断法) is an important legal mechanism which protects market competition, maintains the order of market competition, and fully expresses the foundational function of market disposition resources. It is usually referred to as "the economic constitution." After twelve years of studies and drafts, in June 2006, the 22nd session of the tenth NPC Standing Committee reviewed the Antitrust law (Draft) for the first time. This draft contained 56 articles and 8 chapters. It mainly stipulated the prohibition of monopoly agreements and the abuse of market ascendancy and established three systems to control centralization of management. The abuse of administrative power for the removal and limitation of competition was also prohibited, an antitrust organization was established and legal liabilities were delineated. The related operating mechanisms of NPC Standing Committee will continue to be revised according to investigation and research of the law draft. In addition, according to the legislation plan, aimed at the representative issues in compulsory education and the protection of minors, the NPC Standing Committee comprehensively revised the "Law on Compulsory Education" (义务教育法)[11] and "Law on the Protection of Minors" (未成年人保护法).[12] The "Law on Compulsory Education" after revision fixed

[10] The "Business Income Tax Law" was approved in the fifth session of the tenth National People's Congress on March 16th, 2007. The approval of this law meant that in the future, foreign-owned and domestically-funded businesses could compete with the same advantages.

[11] Foreign Language Education Online (外语教育网), "Compulsory Education Law of the People's Republic of China, May 18th, 2006 http://www.for68.com/new/2006%5C5%5Cwu14212414418156002202 02-0.htm.

[12] CN-Teacher (中国教育展), "Law of the Peoples Republic of China on the Protection of Minors," May 3rd, 2007 http://www.cn-teacher.com/yyjy/flyy/flyy1/200705/209765.html.

the funding safeguard protocol for compulsory education by law, which determined that the compulsory education system would not collect tuition fee and other miscellaneous expenses. The law also determined the promotion of a balanced development of compulsory education as the leading requirement, and explicitly stipulated that all levels of government should reasonably disburse educational resources.

Additionally, the Law made implementing quality education into law to further establish the policies and objectives of compulsory education. These important revisions provided powerful legislative support to guarantee that compulsory education funds were included in the fiscal budget and were promptly appropriated in full. Countrywide development of compulsory education was also promoted, especially in rural, impoverished areas and in areas with high minority populations. Finally, the immediate integrated development of quality education, moral education, intellectual education and physical education for primary scholars and middle school students was also stipulated in order to safeguard the sound development of compulsory education. The "Law on the Protection of Minors" after revision further strengthened the protection responsibility of family, school, society and country, and gave prominence to the right to education for minors, which would play a vital role in protecting the physical and intellectual integrity of minors and safeguarding their legitimate rights and interests.

### B. *Frequent Innovation in Local Legislation*

In 2006, local legislation reform was quite active, and there were frequent innovations. Regional legislative coordination and the institutionalization and standardization of legislation assessment can aid local legislation practice in that it gradually increases the accumulation of experience and the exploration of beneficial precedents and initiatives.

#### 1. *The Appearance of Regional Legislation Coordination*

Regional legislation coordination was a highlight of Chinese local legislation work in 2006. In July, 2006, the first Chinese regional legislation coordination framework was established. With the signing of the "Agreement of Three Northeast Provincial governments (Liaoning, Jilin and Heilongjiang) on a Legislation Coordination Framework" (辽宁、吉林、黑龙江东北三省政府立法协作框架协议), an interprovincial legislation coordination mechanism which respected regional characteristics while coordinating the sharing of legal system resources between governments, was officially established. This act was the first instance of interprovincial legislation coordination in China. With regards to the establishment of a legislation coordination framework between these three northeast provincial governments, the most outstanding practical significance is the regional sharing of legislation resources and complementary legislation advantages, and ultimately the reduction of legislation costs and the improvement of legislation quality. Regional legislation cooperation is advantageous for communication between the local legislation departments, and can effectively maintain the harmony of local legislation systems and the unity of the national legal system by eliminating inconsistencies in local laws and regulations. According to differences in legislative objectives, cooperation methods between the three provinces took three forms, unified, partially unified and divergent. At the same time, the three provinces exchanged legislation information promptly, and established a regular notification system. After the "Agreement of Three Northeast Provincial governments (Liaoning, Jilin and Heilongjiang) on a Legislation Cooperation Frame" appeared, the correlative departments of these three provinces determined to immediately launch legislation coordination in the following five domains: the encouragement and safeguarding of legislation cooperation in non-public economic development, the promotion of honesty and good faith, the handling of unexpected public incidents, in the management and establishment of state institutions, and in the supervision of administrative law enforcement.

2. *Systemization of Quality Assessment for Local Laws and Regulations*

"Strengthening legislation work and improving legislation quality" was one of the overall requirements for legislation work proposed in the 16th Party Congress and the NPC Standing Committee. Over the past three years, the local government had explored many types of effective methods and approaches for improving the quality of local legislation. Establishing a system of quality assessment for local laws and regulations was one of these.[13]

[13] For example, in 2004 Chongqing launched a "review of the legislation" and established a local law assessment subject research group to research "Regulations on Administrative Punishment in Forestry," "Regulations on Administration of Job Referral Agencies," "Provisions on the Administration of Job Fairs" and "Regulations on Supervision of Product Quality." In 2004 Beijing launched research on the subject of a law quality assessment mechanism, and in 2005 chose "Measures of Beijing on Implementing the 'Law of the People's Republic of China of the Prevention and

Post-legislation assessment (立法后评估) refers to the process that happens after a law is formulated. It is when the legislation department, the law-enforcement department the public and experts and scholars etc. analyze and assess the effect of the law's implementation through social investigation, quantitative analysis and cost-benefit calculations etc. to promptly rectify and remedy any faults. In function, it is an assessment of the cost-benefit aspect of the legislation and a re-adjustment of legislation according to the actual situation.

As an independent law assessment mechanism, legislation assessment involves many levels of legislation technology, the enforcement of laws and regulations, and institutional background and social context etc. Its function is integral to provisional legislation inspection. Legislation assessment also has greater focus in that it provides assessment and inspection specific to the implementation conditions of the law. Additionally, it encourages broader participation in that those primary societal organizations associated with laws and regulations can widely participate in the inspection process. Furthermore it is more comprehensive in that a complete assessment of the laws and regulations from formulation to implementation is provided. And finally, it offers more direct feedback so that legal loopholes and remedies are promptly discovered. Therefore, the practice of legislation assessment should not be the testing and inspection of certain regulations chosen by the legislative body, but rather the integration of assessment into the legal track with legislation that specifically stipulates the scope, the body, the method and the procedure of legislation assessment as well as the influence of assessment results in the legislation, amendment and abolishment of laws etc. This approach guarantees the standardization and scientific systematization of legislation assessment and better displays its ability to guarantee the vitality of the legal system in providing a sustainable source of sound law for a "rule of law" society.

Presently, the basic methods of legislation assessment in the Beijing, Shanghai, Chongqing and Shenzhen provincial and municipal Standing Committees of the People's Congress etc. are as follows. First, the standing committee organization is responsible for implementation. Second, assessment is provided for overall or partial provisions of the

---

Control of Water Pollution"' and "Urban Planning Regulations" as the objects of this assessment. Shanghai chose "Regulations on the Protection of Historic and Cultural Landmarks" as the object of their assessment.

laws and regulations. Third, the basis for assessment is the result of practice and investigation. Fourth, the standard of assessment is focused on validity, operability and pertinence etc. This system has different names in practice, the majority of areas called it "local post-legislation assessment," some areas called it "review of the legislation," "assessment of local legislation quality," "assessment of the effects of local legislation," "tracking the effects of local legislation" and "local legislation feedback system" etc.

3. *Active Local Legislation Concerning Letters and Visits* (信访)

On January 10, 2005, the State Council promulgated the newly revised "Regulations on Letters and Visits." (信访条例)[14] In 2006, local legislative activities concerning complaint letters and petitions were very active. Jiangsu province and the Beijing municipality revised the existing regulations regarding letters and visits, and included many legislation highlights that further revealed the value and importance of a petitioning system to the local legislation. These highlights were closely followed by the media and the public. The "Regulations of Jiangsu Province on Letters and Visits" passed with a majority vote, manifested a strong emotional tone and omitted many of the terms in the original which had offended the sensibilities of the petitioners. Also the provisions in the regulations regarding the bypassing of immediate leadership in the complaint process were afforded even more attention by the media. The "Regulations of Beijing Municipality on Letters and Visits[15] approved in September, 2006 explicitly stipulated that those state organizations which handled complaint letters and petitions were not allowed to ignore any voiced complaints, as to do so would be regarded as illegal, and would warrant criminal punishment if the circumstances were serious. The media generally supported the formulation of a responsibility to respond respectfully to all complaints, and applauded legal repercussions for those who did not do so.

[14] State Bureau for Letters and Calls, "Decree of the State Council of the People's Republic of China No. 431," March 7th, 2007, http://gjxfj.gov.cn/2006–03/07/content_6399309.htm.

[15] Standing Committee of the People's Congress of Beijing Municipality, "Catalogue of the Local Regulations of Beijing Municipality Currently in Effect," July 19th, 2003, http://www.lawinfochina.com/law/displayModeTwo.asp?id=3029.

4. *Local Legislation Fulfills Various Necessities*

In 2006, the legislation work of the local People's Congresses was extremely active. Under the premise of following Legislation Law, and leading the Central authorities, the local People's Congresses addressed and filled the gaps in several areas of local legislation, advancing with the goal "there must be laws for the people to follow" (有法可依). Examples of such legislation include:

– On September 27, the "Regulations of Jiangsu Province on Protection of Non-Material Cultural Heritage" (江苏省非物质文化遗产保护条例) was approved in the 25th session of tenth Standing Committee of the Jiangsu Provincial People's Congress. This was the first local legislation for the national protection of non-material cultural heritage. Promulgation and implementation of this regulation will promptly bring the Jiangsu Provincial work for protection of intangible cultural heritage onto the track of being made into law.

– On September 29, the 24th session of tenth Standing Committee of the Inner Mongolia Autonomous Region People's Congress reviewed and approved "Regulations of the Inner Mongolia Autonomous Region on Company Employee Directors and Employee Supervisors" (内蒙古自治区公司职工董事职工监事条例). This was the first local regulation which standardized specifically the powers and responsibilities of company employee directors and employee supervisors in China. It also established that business staff representatives should join the board of directors and the board of supervisors according to legislation, and guaranteed employee status within the legal personnel management framework of the company. This was a guarantee which would establish a system and protocol for the employee to participate in democratic management and supervision, and was also important work toward establishing scientific and democratic decision making in business and management.

– On December 1, concerning the special requirements for water pollution prevention and control of the regions along the south-north water transfer project of the Shandong section, the Standing Committee of Shandong Provincial People's Congress reviewed and approved "Regulations of Shandong Province on Water Pollution Prevention and Control of the Regions along the South-north Water Transfer Project" (山东省南水北调工程沿线区域水污染防治条例). These regulations stipulated pointed measures necessary for water pollution prevention and control in the regions along the south-north water transfer project for the first time on a local level. The regulations also adopted the small basin pollution control strategy combining "governing, utilization and protection" (治、用、保) as one of its legislation principles, which has provided an advantageous legal instrument in the process of guaranteeing the water quality of the south-north water transfer project.

– On November 21, the draft of "Regulations of Chongqing City on National Education Examination" (重庆市国家教育考试条例) was reviewed for the first time in the 27th session of second Standing Committee of Chongqing People's Congress. In this review, all members of the standing committee unanimously believed that taking the lead in enacting local legislation in the national education examination system was advantageous to standardizing the protocol of the national education examination in the city, and to maintaining the authority and public credibility of the national education examination system. Until this point, China did not have a law that adjusted the legal relations of education examination, and that standardized the protocol of a national unified education examination system.

### C. *Legislative Procedure: Democratic Legislation Continues to Advance*

All levels of the People's Congress are making developments, innovations and progress towards further advancing scientific and democratic legislation based on prior legislation experience.

The National People's Congress and its standing committee carefully considered opinions from concerned departments, deputies to the National People's Congress, experts and scholars, and especially the beneficiaries of the legislation process. Based on the experiences of announcing the full text of the draft Property Law to the public in 2005, the NPC Standing Committee also released the full text of the "Employment Contract Law (Draft)" in order to hear opinions from all levels of society in March, 2006. After the announcement of the draft of the "Employment Contract Law," public response was positive. In a month, the NPC Standing Committee had received 191,849 opinions from all circles on this draft law, of which more than 180,000 were received through the internet website of the Chinese National People's Congress. These were record numbers in the legislation history of the National People's Congress. Of these opinions, 65% came from the workers of basic units. In addition, many opinions were also collected from various provinces, autonomous regions and municipalities and 49 bigger municipalities' Standing Committees of the People's Congress, 45 central departments concerned, and 45 large-scale businesses, universities and colleges, and social groups.

The NPC Standing Committee comprehensively analyzed opinions from all circles, in order to sort out 11 central issues, and held separate forums to earnestly hear the opinions of concerned central departments, deputies to the National People's Congress, employer organizations, the public and experts. In this process, the opinions and suggestions of many lower-class workers were highly regarded. Legislation suggestions which addressed the signing of labor contracts, insurance for lower-class workers and the prevention of in-arrears wages etc. were manifested in the revision of the draft of the Employment Contract Law. The revision of the "Law on the Protection of Minors" also fully integrated suggestions regarding the regulation of internet information potentially harmful to minors, the protection of the legitimate rights and interests of children left in rural areas, and a strengthened campus security management etc. as proposed by the deputies to the National People's Congress.

In the process of legislation, a special meeting was held to discuss the relatively urgent issue of professional specialization, which had become a powerful action in improving legislation quality. According to statistics, in the process of formulating the Property Law, the Law Committee of the National People's Congress and the Legislative Affairs Commission of the standing committee etc. had held more than 100 forums to hear opinions or suggestions concerning important issues. In 2006, regarding the order of priority in property rights and creditor's rights, the definition of public interests, and whether a statute of limitations was applicable to property protection and the possibility of using received funds as guarantees etc. In the draft of the Property Law, the NPC Standing Committee held special legislation argumentation meetings to carefully listen to and consider the experts' opinions. The NPC Standing Committee repeatedly studied and revised the draft laws through various kinds of scientific and democratic measures in order to connect the approved laws with objective principles, the Chinese national condition and practical situation, and to withstand the verification process of actual practice. The revision and refinement process of the draft of the Property Law was regarded as a vivid example of how the NPC Standing Committee persisted in scientific and democratic legislation.

The proposals and the suggestions from the deputies (人大代表) to the National People's Congress are an important basis for democratic legislation. In 2004, the NPC Standing Committee began inviting these deputies to attend a meeting as non-voting delegates in order to carefully consider their opinions. At present, this procedure has become a system, and an increasing number of deputies are able to express their opinions on the draft laws. In the standing committee conference in December, 2006, more than 36 nonvoting delegates attended, and equal attention was paid to both their opinions and the opinions of actual members of the standing committee.

This new approach not only facilitated the delegates' professional function, it was also an indispensable link in the process of scientific legislation. Since that session of the standing committee, it is clearly felt by the deputies to the National People's Congress that the subjects of legislation stemmed mostly from public suggestion, and that the legislation subjects determined by the NPC Standing Committee as well as the bills and proposals of delegates and commissioners, were representative of those issues most widely followed by the public. Of these issues, the majority were reflected in the work of the "Two Conferences" (两会)[16] which truly manifested a legislation directed at attentively listening to and respecting public opinion.

Also worth mentioning, in the National People's Congress system, legal practice respected the traditional method of legislation, namely "from bottom to top" while also emphatically practicing "from top to bottom" legislation. These basic levels of exploration and practice received support and approval from the Central Party. Additionally this approach was manifested in the legislation, and is prominently represented in the formulation and promulgation of the Supervision Law. For many years, each local area carried on positive exploration to strengthen and improve supervision work of the People's Congress, and some areas also formulated local laws and regulations concerning supervision of the People's Congress. Truly, it was the positive exploration on the part of the local People's Congress which provided the practical experiences necessary for the revision and refinement of the draft of the Supervision Law.

The local People's Congress had also made many contributions towards increased public participation and enhanced democratization in legislation. In 2006, Guangzhou promulgated the first regulation to standardize public participation in administrative legislation, the "Measures in Guangzhou on Public Participation in the Formulation of Rules and Regulations" (广州市规章制定公众参与办法). This action

[16] Translator's Note: *Liang Hui* means the National People's Congress and the Chinese People's Political Consultative Conference.

indicated that thereafter, the Guangzhou government would allow public participation in the formulation of all rules and regulations. And furthermore, if the department concerned did not fully consider public opinions or if they did not all the public to voice their opinions when drafting the rules and regulations, the municipal legal system office was allowed to refuse the draft and the public was allowed to make complaints directly to the legal system office. The implementation of this measure also created enforceability in the public participation procedure. This was the first local government regulation that standardized public participation in administrative legislation, which created a new forum for the open hearing of opinions or suggestions and established a timely feedback system for public opinions.

On January 11, in Yinchuan, 21 legislative representatives vehemently debated the draft of the "Regulations of Ningxia Hui Nationality Autonomous Region on Road traffic Safety Management" (宁夏回族自治区道路交通安全管理条例) in a 3 hour hearing. These representatives came from all walks of life and from across the entire region, they were legal workers, graduate students, public officers, taxi drivers, the self-employed (个体经营者), farmers and managers. This hearing was significant in the guaranteeing the rationality and feasibility of the law, and improving the quality of legislation. On July 14, in Yunnan Province, 9 citizens who submitted the legislation suggestions were given rewards by the Standing Committee of Yunnan Provincial People's Congress. The advisers of 5 legislation items and 4 draft laws and regulations were separately rewarded 300 Yuan and 3000 Yuan. On November 25, the 25th session of tenth Standing Committee of Hebei Provincial People's Congress approved "Measures of Hebei Province on Implementing the Law of the People's Republic of China on Road Traffic Safety" (河北省实施〈中华人民共和国道路交通安全法〉办法)[17] by a majority vote. This measure took two years to complete from its inception in 2005.

The entire process spanned from the initial stages of listening to public opinion in the drafting process, to undergoing three reviews of the standing committee. In these two years, the Provincial People's Congress held 8 different forums and 1 public hearing to solicit the

[17] Standing Committee of the People's National Congress, "Decision of the Standing Committee of the National People's Congress on Amending the Law of the People's Republic of China on Road Traffic Safety," December 29th, 2007, http://www.lawinfochina.com/law/display.asp?id=6570&keyword=

opinions of the deputies to the municipal Standing Committees of the People's Congress, deputies to the Provincial People's Congress, as well as concerned departments directly under the provincial party committee. The general office of the Standing Committee of Provincial People's Congress also announced the draft measure in the main news media outlets, and on the website of the Provincial People's Congress, where they opened a text-message platform for the first time to widely solicit opinions through the internet and text-message. Guangzhou's public participation method of legislation, Ningxia's legislation hearing method, Yunnan's reward for legislation suggestions method and Hebei's method of implementing several different channels to "open the door to legislation" varied in approach but were equally satisfactory in result, and all instilled praise and encouragement for legislation participation on the part of the citizens. These methods of local legislation reform also symbolized a transformation of local legislation from a bureaucratic model to a democratic model as well as a change in the legislative ideology from one of control to one of service, which was significant for institutional innovation and breaking through traditional legislative methods.

## II. *Strengthening the Actual Effects of Supervision*

The supervision of the National People's Congress over the "one government two courts" system includes professional supervision and legal supervision. It is an important authority endowed by the constitution to the National People's Congress, and it is an important mechanism of the party and the national supervision system. The supervision objective of the National People's Congress is to guarantee that the constitution and the laws are correctly implemented, to guarantee executive, judicial and prosecutorial powers are correctly exercised, and to guarantee that the legitimate rights and interests of the citizens, legal persons and other organizations are respected and maintained.

In recent years, the supervision work of the National People's Congress and its effects have increased yearly. In its tenure of five years (1998~2002), the former session of NPC Standing Committee altogether inspected the implementation of 22 laws and legal decisions, and heard and reviewed 40 special reports from the State Council, the Supreme People's Court and the Supreme People's Procuratorate. And, in the first four years of the tenure of this session of National People's Congress (2003~2006), the NPC Standing Committee inspected the implementation of 29 laws and decisions concerning the legal issues, and heard and reviewed 43 special reports from the State Council, the Supreme People's Court and the Supreme People's Procuratorate. In 2003, the NPC Standing Committee successively inspected the enforcement of 5 laws, and heard and reviewed 11 special reports from the State Council and the departments concerned. In 2004, it inspected implementation of 6 laws, heard and reviewed 11 special reports from the State Council, the Supreme People's Court and the Supreme People's Procuratorate. In 2005, it inspected implementation of 6 laws, heard and reviewed 10 special reports from the State Council, the Supreme People's Court and the Supreme People's Procuratorate. In 2006, it inspected enforcement of the implementation of 12 laws, heard and reviewed 11 special reports from the State Council, the Supreme People's Court and the Supreme People's Procuratorate (see Figure 2.2).

### A. *Central Level*

In 2006, the National People's Congress and its standing committee increased supervision of those issues widely followed by the public. After a year, this session of the NPC standing committee established the working ideology, "revolve around the center, give prominence to key points, improve actual outcomes" (围绕中心、突出重点、增强实效) in order to better resolve the widely followed "three issues concerning agriculture" (三农), the issue of environmental protection and the issue of an impartial fair judiciary etc.

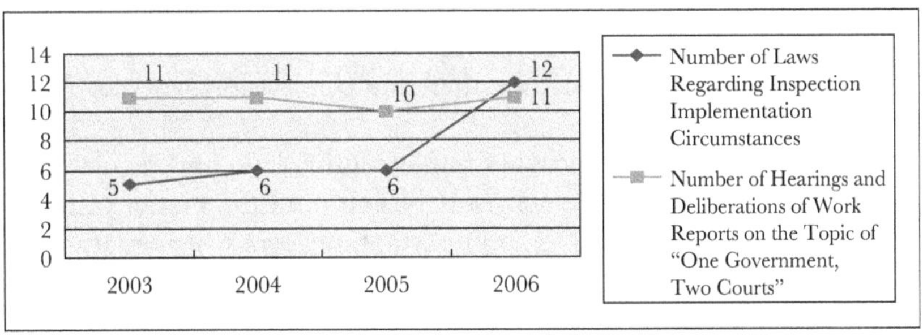


Figure 2.2: Laws and Drafting Decisions Concerning a Supervision System from 2003–2006

The Standing Committee also adopted a long-term inspection method in order to comprehensively and systematically review the implementation of laws concerning agriculture and environmental protection. Additionally, it heard the reports of the Supreme People's Court and the Supreme People's Procuratorate on launching a special reorganization of standardized judiciary and law-enforcement behavior. This played a vital role in further encouraging the "government, court and procuratorate" system to adopt more powerful measures to guarantee the effective implementation of laws, to support and supervise related state organizations to legally exercise their authority and to practically maintain the legitimate rights and interests of the people.

The State Council, the Supreme People's Court and the Supreme People's Procuratorate paid great attention to the opinions and suggestions of the NPC Standing Committee, implemented positive measures, and earnestly improved their work, which brought about unprecedented results.

1. *Increasing Supervision and Long-Term Supervision* (跟踪检查) *of the Enforcement of Laws*

Law enforcement supervision is a form of supervision that organically combines legal supervision and professional supervision. It has been practiced from the end of 1980s, and has been generally carried out in all levels of National People's Congress in the 1990's. However, the former law-enforcement inspections ended when the inspection was completed. This method only paid attention to immediate inspection, and neglected to conduct extended supervision. It paid attention only to appearances, and neglected to consider actual effects, therefore, the effects of this type of supervision were negligible. In light of this situation, this session of NPC Standing Committee proposed to carry out long-term law-enforcement inspection. This was an important institutional innovation to strengthen the supervision work of NPC Standing Committee.

Understanding the problems of implementing laws and regulations, and developing law-enforcement supervision until the matter at hand has been realistically solved, is an important measure which guarantees that law enforcement supervision does not become a formality.[18] The following work has been done in this area:

[18] The Supervision Law also defines the standards and routines of law enforcement

(1.) Supervision work regarding the construction of a new socialist countryside was implemented. From August to October, 2006, vice chairpersons Wuyun Qimuge and Jiang Zhenghua separately led a team to inspect and supervise six provinces over an extended period regarding the execution of the laws concerning agriculture. The law-enforcement inspection group went to villages and farm households to hold forums with representatives, cadres from basic units and farmers. This group researched first-hand materials extensively, and proposed suggestions about how to strengthen the "three agricultural problems." (2.) Supervision work regarding the settlement of in- arrears of lower-class workers' wages was implemented. This is one of the most frequently mentioned problems in complaint letters of recent years. In 2003, in a law-enforcement inspection of the building law, the NPC Standing Committee discovered that in-arrears wages were a serious problem, and that behind this problem was the issue of in-arrears engineering project funds. It was requested that all levels of governments and those departments concerned take practical measures to solve this problem, and carrie d out long-term supervision and inspection of engineering project funds and worker wages continuously for several years.

A joint supervision group was also established, composed of those State Council departments concerned to travel to various areas for long-term supervision. Through joint efforts, until June 2006, various local governments and enterprises pooled funds to repay 175.3 billion Yuan of in-arrears project funds, which accounted for over 94% of the total amount in arrears liquidated for those projects completed before 2003. Funds were also raised to repay 33.6 billion Yuan of lower-class worker wages before 2003, which accounted for above 99% of total lower-class worker (农民工) wages in arrears, and upheld the legitimate rights and interests of lower-class workers. (3.) Supervision regarding the encouragement of innovation and invention in China was implemented. In 2006, the NPC Standing Committee inspected the implementation of

supervision and long-term supervision. Before the promulgation of the Supervision Law, only the "Certain Provisions on Strengthening Inspection and Supervision of Law Enforcement," approved by the Standing Committee of the National People's Congress in 1993, made the stipulation of law-enforcement inspection. These "Certain Provisions" are a law document not a law. The Supervision Law is the first comprehensive systematic definition of law enforcement inspection within the law, which symbolizes that law enforcement inspection has become a method for the Standing Committee of the National People's Congress to exercise supervisory power.

the Patent Law, heard and reviewed special reports of the State Council on enhancing independent innovation (自主创新能力) capabilities and strengthening the protection of intellectual property and so on.

The State Council issued policy to encourage finance and taxation in regards to independent inventions as well as policies on government procurement of these innovations. Also several science and technology projects of wide-reaching implication were earmarked for government procurement. The Supreme People's Court also strengthened judicial protection of intellectual property. (4.) Supervision work regarding the construction of a conservationist and environmentally aware society was implemented. The standing committee strengthened its monitoring of resources and the environment based on the work of recent years. (a.) It combined inspection of the implementation of "Law on the Prevention and Control of Atmospheric Pollution" (大气污染防治法),[19] with the monitoring of the implementation of "Law on the Prevention and Control of Environmental Pollution by Solid Wastes" (固体废物污染环境防治法)[20] and "Law on the Prevention and Control of Water Pollution" (水污染防治法) etc.

Additionally, the reports of the State Council concerning the current water environment situation and the prevention and control of water pollution were heard and reviewed. Also supervision, monitoring and reporting on the reorganization of the key areas and businesses etc. were carried out through the China Century Environmental Protection Campaign. (b.) The advancement of energy conservation in the industrial sector and the building industry was a key goal of the "Energy Conservation Law" implementation inspection. And State Council reports concerning the rational utilization, protection and supervision of mineral resources were heard and reviewed. (5.) Supervision work regarding the promotion of an impartial judiciary was implemented. In 2006, the implementation of the Judge Law and the "Law of Prosecutors" (检察官法) was inspected. The reports of the Supreme People's Court and the Supreme People's Procuratorate

[19] Eduzhai, "Law of the Peoples Republic of China on the Prevention and Control of Atmospheric Pollution," November 8th, 2007, http://www.eduzhai.net/yingyu/615/763/yingyu_246450.html.

[20] Chem YQ, "Law on the Prevention and Control of Environmental Pollution by Solid Wastes of the People's Republic of China," http://www.chemyq.com/xz/xz7/65901kxlmf.htm.

concerning the implementation of a special reorganization of standardized judicial and law-enforcement behaviors were heard and reviewed. The members of the standing committee affirmed the effects of this special reorganization, and in light of the serious problems reflected by the reorganization as well as the existing achievements, the Supreme People's Court and the Supreme People's Procuratorate were requested to further strengthen the construction of a contingent base (队伍建设), to vigorously promote the implementation of a system, to maintain openness and transparency, to strengthen internal supervision, and to strictly investigate responsibility, all of which will continue to advance the special reorganization.

(6.) Law enforcement inspection of the "Law on Regional National Autonomy" (民族区域自治法)[21] and the "Law of the Peoples Republic of China on the Protection of the Rights and Interests of Returned Overseas Chinese and the Family Members of Overseas Chinese" (归侨侨眷权益保护法) was implemented. This inspection was the first since these two laws were promulgated and implemented, and was also a key goal of the supervision work of the standing committee in 2006. The law-enforcement inspection group went to 11 provinces and autonomous regions to conduct their inspection, and carried out the special investigation and study of 22 minority nationalities. The law-enforcement inspection group of the standing committee for the "Law of the Peoples Republic of China on the Protection of the Rights and Interests of Returned Overseas Chinese and the Family Members of Overseas Chinese" went to 6 provinces, autonomous regions and municipalities to conduct their inspection. A forum was held for returned overseas Chinese, the family members of overseas Chinese, overseas compatriots, overseas Chinese deputies who had returned to the National People's Congress, members of the National Committee of the CPPCC of the Returned Overseas Chinese Federation and those persons in charge of the departments concerning oversea Chinese. Also extensive research was conducted on first-hand materials gathered through travels to overseas Chinese farms, ventures and homes.

[21] Eduzhai, "Law of the Peoples Republic of China on Regional National Autonomy," November 8th, 2007, http://www.eduzhai.net/yingyu/615/763/yingyu_246009.html.

2. *Supervision of Budgetary and Economic Work*

The Supervision of budgetary and economic work is an important authority of the NPC Standing Committee. In 2006, the NPC Standing Committee heard and reviewed the central final report, the audit report and the report on plan execution. It examined and approved the central final accounting of revenue and expenditure in 2005, and heard and reviewed the report of the State Council on advancing the joint stock system reform of state-owned commercial banks and expanding the reform of the monetary system. The execution of the national economy and social development plan was satisfactory, and finance and audit work was approved. Simultaneously some suggestions were proposed for standardizing the budgetary procedure, refining the finance transfer payment system, maintaining a strict budget, strengthening audit supervision, curbing excessive growth in investment, increasing energy conservation and environmental protection, reducing energy consumption, and giving increased attention to social development and the livelihood problems of the people. In December, 2006, the State Council submitted its report on excess budgetary revenues and the reorganization plan for those problems discovered in audit to the NPC Standing Committee.

3. *Hearing Special Reports Regarding the "One Government, Two Courts" System*

In 2006, the NPC Standing Committee heard and reviewed many special reports on the major issues concerning the stability of overall reform & development and key concerns of the public. In particular, those reports proposed in recent years by the standing committee regarding the urgently needed reorganization of work supervision. This session of NPC Standing Committee continuously named problems concerning resources and the environment as key issues in supervision work. In 2006, the NPC Standing Committee also supervised and encouraged departments concerned to improve in this aspect through careful long-term supervision. (1) Long-term supervision of the execution of environmental protection laws was implemented while an inspection of the enforcement of the energy conservation law was carried out. The reports on these two law-enforcement inspections were heard and reviewed by the standing committee in August. (2) Reports of the State Council regarding the current water environment situation, the prevention and control of water pollution, and the rational utilization, protection and supervision of mineral resources were heard and reviewed.

The standing committee also heard and reviewed the reports of the State Council about developing joint stock system reform of state-owned commercial banks and about reforming the monetary system. While affirming the positive results of the joint stock system reform and the reform of non-tradable shares of state-owned commercial banks, the standing committee also requested monetary system reform, construction of a rural finance service system, that financial supervision be strengthened and developed, and that financial risks be to prevented and dissolved. In the 23rd session of tenth NPC Standing Committee held in August, 2006, the report of the State Council about the execution of this year's national economy and social development plan was also heard and reviewed.

4. *Registration and Examination of Standardized Documents*

The registration and examination of standardized documents is an important part of the supervision work of the NPC Standing Committee. In 2006, the NPC Standing Committee examined the handling of possible inspection suggestions proposed by citizens and organizations, with the intention of maintaining a unified national legal system. At the same time, the NPC Standing Committee paid great attention to the petitions and suggestions of the public. In 2006, altogether more than 150,000 letters were received, and more than 75,000 visits were made regarding this matter. In regards to the laws and litigation related to those problems reflected in public awareness such as, land expropriation (土地征收征用), reservoir caused immigration (水库移民), forced relocation and demolition (房屋拆迁), medical treatment service and education, social security and environmental protection, the NPC standing committee increased assignation, supervision and handling abilities and also urged those parties concerned to handle these issues according to law. This advancement impelled the settlement of a group of problems raised in the letter and visit system, and provided a positive example on how to dissolve social contradictions and promote a harmonious society.

## B. *The Local Level*

In 2006, all levels of People's Congresses and their standing committees took the implementation of the Supervision Law as a turning point in legislation that would increase the relevance and outcomes of supervision work when used in accordance with the practical needs of the locality.

*1. "Monitoring the People's Livelihood Project"* (民生工程), *and "Resolving Problems of Popular Sentiment"* (民心问题)

In 2006, issues concerning the "people's livelihood" and "problems of popular sentiment" will serve as legislative focal points in all levels of the People's Congress from the central level to the local level.

At the end of 2005, a serious water pollution event took place in the Songhua River. The Standing Committee of Heilongjiang Provincial People's Congress paid great attention to this event, and organized partial Deputies to the National and provincial People's Congresses to survey the prevention and control of Songhua River water pollution on January 9~13, 2006. Hereafter, the Standing Committee of Provincial People's Congress heard and reviewed the special report of the provincial government concerning the prevention and control of Songhua River water pollution, and organized and carried out the Longjiang century environmental protection campaign of "let the people drink clean water." All opinions and suggestions on effectively preventing and controlling of Songhua River water pollution were proposed separately on several occasions to the national and provincial parties concerned, efforts which greatly supported the prevention and control of Songhua River water pollution.

On January 29, the 30th session of tenth Standing Committee of the Jilin Provincial People's Congress heard the report of the inspection group of the Standing Committee on the progress of shantytown (棚戶区) reconstruction in the province. The Jilin Provincial government decided to take three years to comprehensively implement a citywide shantytown reconstruction project, and to change the shantytown inhabitants' housing conditions in the entire province. The Standing Committee of Jilin Provincial People's Congress has promoted this "issue concerning popular sentiments" since its inception. It has supervised the reconstruction work through professional inspection and government report hearings, and raised some practical and feasible proposals. According to the suggestions of the Standing Committee of Jilin Provincial People's Congress, the departments concerned further refined the policy benefits for the people for shantytown reconstruction.

In March, the Standing Committee of the Qinghai Provincial People's Congress heard the "Report of the Law Enforcement Inspection Group of the Provincial People's Congress on the Province's Practice of Implementation, Inspection and Opinions regarding the Drug Administration Law of the People's Republic of China" (关于省人大执法检查组对本省实施〈中华人民共和国药品管理法〉执法检

查意见的整改落实情况的报告) of the provincial government, and also reviewed opinions. In order to supervise and review opinions, the Standing Committee of Provincial People's Congress increased its monitoring of the supervision system and encouraged the resolution of the problem of difficulty and cost associated with seeing a doctor. Under the monitoring and supervision of the Standing Committee of Provincial People's Congress, the government constructed a respective Sub-bureau of Food and Drug Administration in those counties which had originally jointly set up a Food and Drug Administration Additionally, every effort was made to build independent management substations in those 16 counties (Area Committee on Administrative Unions) without sub-bureaus during the "11th Five-year Plan" time-frame. By doing this the government would fundamentally solve the lack of enforcement entities, keep watch on un-monitored areas and bypass the local enforcement problems.

The provincial government also further strengthened the construction of a medicine supervision network and medicine supply network for agricultural and rural areas throughout the entire province. This medicine supervision network was established in 396 villages and towns and 4071 villages and rural committees throughout the province. After these actions were implemented, the price of medicine supply and delivery had dropped on average, 10~20% in agricultural and rural areas in entire province.

In August, the Standing Committee of the Hainan Provincial People's Congress combined its special investigation and research of the deputies to National People's Congress with the "looking back" (回头看) law-enforcement inspection initiative of the "Law on the Prevention and Control of Water Pollution" in order to inspect 13 reorganization enterprises and 8 enterprises of serious pollution in 8 counties and cities, including Haikou and Qionghai and so on. Through on-the-spot investigations, selective examinations and secret inquiries and so on, a thorough understanding of the reorganization situation was gained. The Hainan Provincial People's Congress then urged those government departments connected with the issues to carry out reorganization work, and to solve the problems in these units on the most fundamental level. Carrying out these "looking back" law-enforcement inspection initiatives is an innovation and practical action of the National People's Congress law-enforcement inspection. This initiative has been widely followed and supported by the public.

During National Day Golden Week,[22] Guangxi Fangchenggang cut off the water supply for two days because of certain undisclosed reasons, but did not inform the residents about it, which affected the resident's daily life. After receiving inquiry calls and letters from the public, the Standing Committee of Municipal People's Congress immediately initiated inquiry procedures, and heard the reports of the functioning departments of the municipal government regarding the accident of cutting off the water supply. The members of the standing committee proposed 8 correlative suggestions and opinions, and assigned these suggestions to the related departments to carry out. Also, the urban construction & environmental protection committee of the People's Congress monitored and supervised the process. The supervision of the Standing Committee of Municipal People's Congress urged the Municipal Public Works Bureau, the Municipal Planning Bureau and the Municipal Commodity Pricing Bureau (市物价局) to immediately carry out reorganization, and implement "major surgery" (大手术) on the Municipal system to solve the water supply problem.

### C. *Refusal of the "Government, Court and Procuratorate" Reports* (对"一府两院"报告说"不")

Hearing and reviewing reports is an important mechanism by which the People's Congresses and their standing committees exercise their supervisory authority of the "government, court and procuratorate" system. In 2006, the supervision work of the People's Congresses ran smoothly and followed a prescribed order. However, the People's Congresses were no longer accepting (照单全收) all of the "government, court and procuratorate" reports, a move that showed an increasing "boldness" on the part of the People's Congresses.

On September 22, 2006, in the 40th session of Standing Committee of fifth Jinchang Municipal People's Congress of Gansu Province, the chief of the Jinchang municipal public security bureau submitted a report on the work of public security and traffic police in the city. The Committee for Internal and Judicial Affairs under the Standing Committee of Jinchang Municipal People's Congress simultaneously submitted an investigation report on the work of public security and traffic police in the city. This report presented certain problems regarding the vehicle management station and the Vehicle Inspection

[22] Translator's Note: A week of national holidays beginning on October 1st.

Station such as bad customer service and hidden charges (搭车收费) etc. The Standing Committee of Municipal People's Congress thought the report was inconsistent with the investigation results in the review. The report was not accepted because exaggerated results and evasion of the actual problem were suspected. Afterwards the Standing Committee of Municipal People's Congress gave their opinions, and requested the municipal government and the public security department to deliberate on the problems, reorganize, and submit the status of their reorganization within six months to the conference of standing committee for re-review.

On October 27, the 24th session of the Standing Committee of 12th Zhengzhou Municipal People's Congress of Henan Province heard and reviewed the report of the municipal government on the situation of the proposals regarding "resolving the difficulties involved for urban and rural populations to visit a doctor" (解决城乡弱势群体看病难、看病贵问题) proposed by the deputies to the People's Congress. The conference of Standing Committee did not approve this report when voted on. The conference believed that, although the government had done the massive work, much of it was done insufficiently and could be done better, and it requested that the municipal government re-submit a report after resolving this problem. The results of this vote were closely followed by the public as well as by the municipal government. The municipal government held a mayoral meeting to conduct specialized research on the subject. In this meeting the deputy mayor was assigned to manage this investigation, and the departments concerned implemented a series of measures to resolve the issue.

### D. *The Materialization of Examination and Registration*

Although many local authorities formulated locally specific laws and regulations to stimulate and standardize the registration and examination of rules and regulations,[23] as the right of registration and examination

[23] After the Legislation Law was promulgated, the registration and examination work of the local People's Congress regarding rules and regulations entered high speed. The partial provincial municipal People's Congress quickened system construction and made the registration and examination of rules and regulations part of the legislative system. For example, some provinces such as Shaanxi, Sichuan, Hainan, Changchun and Zhuhai etc. formulated specific local laws and regulations regarding registration and examination. And although some cities, such as Fuzhou, Shantou, Shijiazhuang and Jilin etc., did not formulate special laws and regulations, they included stipulations for registration in local legislation regulations.

were often described with the statement "We have the rights, but they are not often used" (备而不用). This situation was overcome in Zhejiang in 2006. From January to September 2006, the Standing Committee of Zhejiang Provincial People's Congress for the first time carried on a comprehensive examination of the provincial government's rules and regulations registered in 2005. Additionally, examination results were that certain provisions in the "Measures on Management of Breeding Livestock and Poultry" were "inconsistent with upper law or not suited to the new situation." The Zhejiang Provincial government carefully considered these results and earnestly discussed and enacted the revision of related laws and regulations and the abolishment of correlative provisions. The Standing Committee of Zhejiang Provincial People's Congress examined the provincial government' rules and regulations, and strengthened the legal supervision of government acts, which was a new and positive act on the part of the local People's Congress.

## III. *Deputies' Responsibilities Advance to a New Level*

In 2006, all levels of People's Congress and its standing committee continued to earnestly implement those ideas put forth in the Central Committee's Document 9 of 2005. Much attention was given to combining the handling of deputies' proposals in conjunction with legislation work, combining the handling of deputies' suggestions in conjunction with promotion work, combining the expansion of deputy participation in conjunction with the improvement of the standing committee's work level, and combining the organizing of deputies for special investigations and research with the enhancement of the quality of proposals and suggestions. All of which were initiatives that further expanded the deputy's function while maintaining the momentum of the People's Congress.

### A. *The Quality of Proposition and Proposal Handling by Deputies is Enhanced*

The legal proposals of the Deputies to this level of People's Congress play an important role for the responsibility and authority of the People's Congress. The Central Committee of the CCP issued Document 9 in May of 2006, and outlined explicit requirements to improve the quality of deputy proposals and the handling of propositions and proposals. The general office of the NPC Standing Committee then formulated the "Measures on Handling of the Deputies to the National People's

Congress" (全国人民代表大会代表议案处理办法) specifically to standardize the scope and condition of the proposals, and also to outline a handling procedure for the proposals. These measures strengthened the efficiency of deputy proposals.

In the four year tenure of this session of the National People's Congress (2003~2006), the deputy proposals increased yearly. In 2003, during the first session of the tenth National People's Congress, the delegation and deputies jointly proposed 338 proposals. In 2004, during the second session of the tenth National People's Congress, there were 641 proposals. In 2005, during the third session of the tenth National People's Congress, there were 991 proposals. In 2006, during the fourth session of the tenth National People's Congress, altogether 1006 proposals were received (see Figure 2.3).

Of these 1006 proposals received during the fourth session of tenth National People's Congress, 1003 proposals were from deputies and 3 were from the delegation. In that conference, the deputies initiated more proposals than ever before, and the proposal quality also improved. These proposals included a clear cause and basis for action, a specific plan, and were attached with the necessary interpretations. 541 of these 1003 legal documents provided the draft text of law, which accounted for 53.9% of total. Of all the proposals, 256 were the result of special investigation and research, and intensive inspection on the part of the deputies, accounting for 25.5% of the total. Additionally, 448 of these proposals were the result of discussions, interviews and opinion solicitation etc., accounting for 44.5% of total. Other proposals were

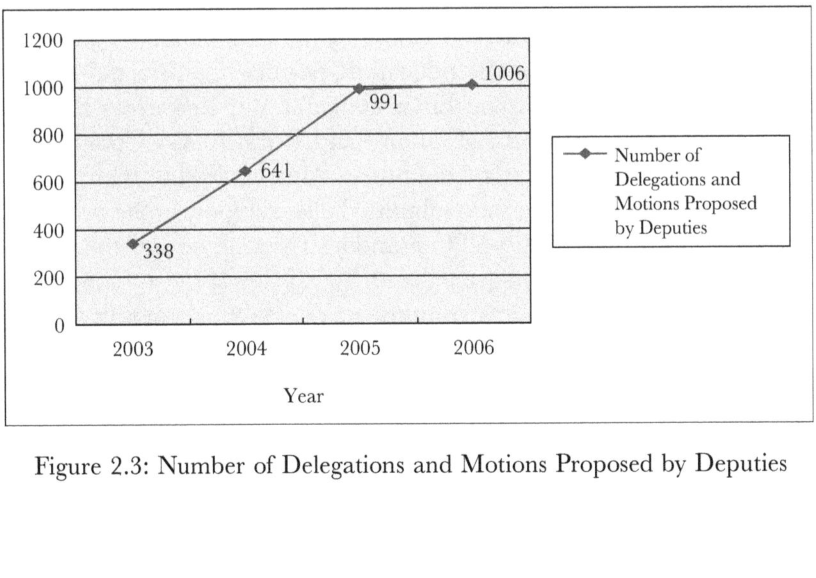


Figure 2.3: Number of Delegations and Motions Proposed by Deputies

proposed mainly on the basis of each deputy's own combined responsibilities and experiences.

The overwhelming majority of deputy proposals at this time were legal proposals that analyzed the progress and quality legislation. 436 of these proposals were already included in the Five-Year Legislation Plan of the standing committee and the legislation plan of 2006, accounting for 43.3% of total. In this division of legal documents, some are in the process of being reviewed or drafted, and some are being prepared for investigation and research in order to be drafted. The deputies have requested that the standing committee use the existing content of the draft law text proposed when drafting and reviewing these legal documents. Of the other 567 legal documents, 270 were proposed as revisions of current laws, accounting for 26.8% of total, and 297 were proposed as formulations of the law, accounting for 29.5% of total. These proposals were classified according to the seven legal departments of a Socialist legal system with Chinese characteristics, the breakdown is as follows: there were 333 proposals concerning administrative law (33.1% of the total); there were 202 concerning economic law (20.1%); there were 127 concerning social law (12.6%); there were 117 concerning constitutional law (11.6%); there were 99 concerning litigation and non-litigation procedure law (9.8%); there were 74 concerning civil law and commercial law (7.4%); and there were 51 concerning criminal law (5.1%). Additionally, 3 of these were proposals to be decided by the NPC Standing Committee (see Figure 2.4).

According to the Special Committee's division of responsibility, these proposals were reviewed separately by the related Special Committee. Among them, 296 were reviewed by the Finance and Economy Committee, 283 by the Law Committee, 160 by the Committee for Internal and Judicial Affairs, 136 by the Education, Science, Culture and Public Health Committee, 78 by the Environmental and Resources Protection Committee, 50 by the Agriculture and Rural Affairs Committee, and 3 by the Foreign Affairs Committee. After reviewing them, each related Special Committee then submitted a legal report of the proposal consideration results to the NPC Standing Committee. Of the 1,006 proposals, 100 proposals associated with 10 existing laws were reviewed and approved by the standing committee. Thirty-one proposals associated with 7 draft laws were submitted to the standing committee for review, and 353 proposals associated with 51 legislation items were included in the legislation plan or annual plan. Of the other proposals, some were submitted to the State Council to deliberate and formulate

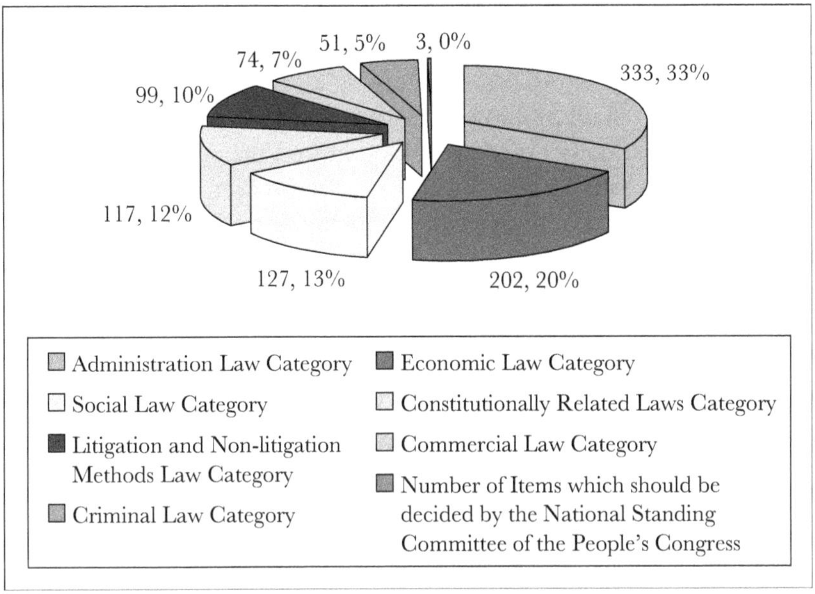


Figure 2.4: Breakdown of Laws according to Legislative Type

administrative rules and regulations, and those which still did not meet the legislation requirements at that time were separately explained by the deputies themselves. The report of the Special Committee on the results of deputy proposal consideration was reviewed and approved in a conference of the standing committee.

### B. *The Deputies Play an Important Role in Proposal Handling Work*

In 2006, during the fourth session of tenth National People's Congress, the deputies proposed 6,511 suggestions regarding the overall work of the party and state as well as those the issues widely followed by the public. These suggestions mainly focused on the following topics: 1.) 1,369 of these were related to science and technology, education, culture and sanitation, which accounted for 21.03%. 2.) 1,023 were related to society and public affairs, which accounted for 15.71%. 3.) 844 were related to the development plan and economic work, and accounted for 12.96%. 4.) 759 were related to agriculture, forestry and water conservancy, and accounted for 11.66%. 5.) 580 were related to finance, tax revenue and banking, which accounted for 8.91%. 6.) 575 were related to court work, procuratorate work and the development of the legal system, which accounted for 8.83%. Additionally, 1,361 were related to other miscellaneous aspects of legislation and accounted for 20.9% of the total number (see Figure 2.5).

The research of all proposals was undertaken by 174 units classified according to the contents of the proposal and the responsibility level of the various units. Under joint efforts, the problems of 1,810 of the deputy proposals were settled or were being settled, which accounted for 28% of the total proposals. Solutions were formulated or included in the work plan for 3,148 of the proposals, which accounted for 48%, an increase over 2005. Each research unit carefully considered the work suggested by the deputies. And the leaders of each unit personally took charge of the work, and communicated with deputies in order to improve the handling and monitoring of the problem. Twelve related departments from the State Council, such as the Supreme People's Court, the Supreme People's Procuratorate and the State Development and Reform Commission and so on, submitted written reports on the status of the deputy proposals to the standing committee.

Each research unit further strengthened communication and contact with the deputies in order to fully utilize them in the process of handling proposals. Before beginning, deputies' opinions were heard,

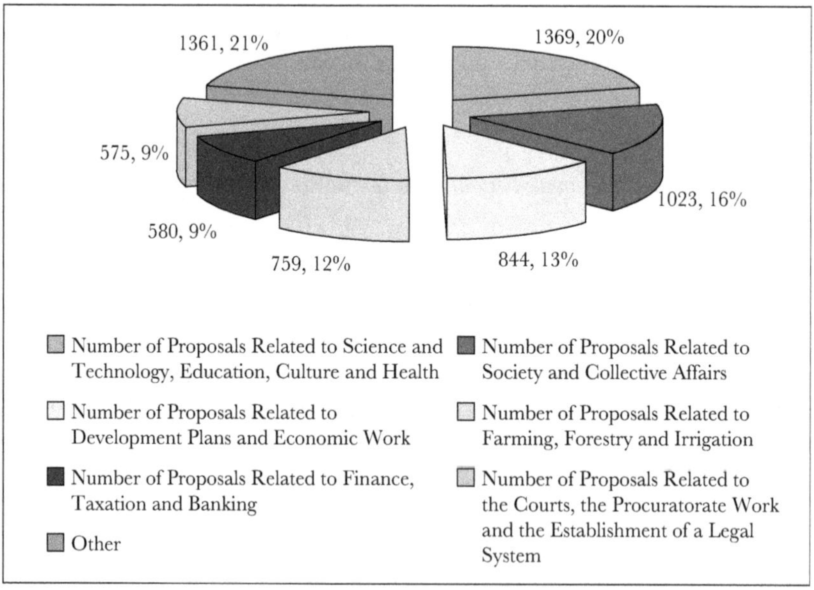


Figure 2.5: Breakdown of Laws according to Subject Matter

original intentions were clarified, and requirements for the proposals were suggested. While in process, communications were improved from "mouth to mouth" telephone conversations to "hand to hand" in-person transactions. Additionally, the deputies who initiated the proposals were invited to investigate, research, and negotiate a means of settlement. After the proposal was handled, the deputies' opinions regarding the handling process and the unit response were solicited through many channels, including sending out the "Questionnaire for Handling and Replying to Deputy' Proposals" etc. According to the processing statistics 850 suggestions were undertaken by 10 units, including the Supreme People's Court, the Supreme People's Procuratorate and the Ministry of Construction and so on. Of these, 582 were handled through direct contact with the deputies or had invited the deputies to be directly involved in the process. These 582 accounted for 68.47% of the total suggestions handled, an increase of 18 percentage points over 50.47% in 2005. The processing unit for key suggestions invited a total of 77 deputies with proposals to participate in field investigation and research in 18 provinces, autonomous regions and municipalities in order to resolve the specific issues. Shanxi Province opened "a green channel" for the suggestions of deputies to the National People's Congress. On March 23, 2006, the Shanxi Provincial people's government officially opened "the green channel," and distributed the first batch of specially marked paper and envelopes to more than 500 deputies of the tenth provincial People's Congress for suggestions. Postage for these envelopes was paid for by the general office of provincial government. At the end of November 2006, the Shanxi Provincial government had received the twenty-nine deputy letters through "the green channel," and the problems outlined in these letters were responded to successively.

### C. *The People's Congress Strengthens Communication with Its Deputies*

As a result of the fact that the responsibilities of deputies to the National People's Congress are non-specialized, the quality of the reviews conducted by the conference of the National People's Congress was criticized on several fronts. In light of this, in 2006, the NPC Standing Committee and other related state organs provided extensive information, informed deputies of related situation and posted correlative data in order to increase awareness of the case details, political affairs and ultimately to enhance the quality of the review. In 2006, the deputies received more than 20 kinds of written materials, including related state organizations' bulletins, standing committee plans for related work, data concerning the national economy and social development, and information regarding this electoral unit and so on. The deputies also obtained related information provided through modern network technology etc. These efforts greatly strengthened the deputies' understanding of certain significant matters regarding the functions and powers of the National People's Congress and its standing committee as well as regarding certain major issues of the national economy and society.

At the same time, the participation of the deputies in the activities of the NPC Standing Committee was further expanded in 2006. Altogether 185 deputies attended the conference of standing committee as non-voting delegates, and more than 500 deputies participated in the law-enforcement inspection and legislation investigation of the standing committee. According to the needs of the review agenda and, the deputies that attended the conference of standing committee as non-voting delegates increased from 24 to 36 each conference (including deputies from Hong Kong and Macao), and 38 at the most. In the entire year, non-voting delegate attendees increased from 140 in 2005 to 185, which was the highest increase in recent years. Inviting the deputies to attend the conferences of the standing committee as non-voting delegates was established as a standardized system and the resulting improvements have included to the preliminary viewing of related proposals before meetings, hearing opinions and suggestions of the deputies regarding the work of the standing committee during meetings, and notifying other deputies of the conference results after meetings etc. The deputies who participated in law-enforcement inspection, legislation investigation and research for the standing committee increased from nearly 400 in 2005 to more than 500 that year. When participating in these activities, the deputies proposed many sound opinions and suggestions, which played a vital role in improving legislation quality and enhancing supervision outcomes as well as other improvements.

Based on the deputies' special investigation and research in 2005, the projected work for 2006 was "one union, four improvements" (一个结合、四个改进), namely unify special investigations & research with high-quality deputy proposals & recommendations, and expand time-limits and the investigation scope for unified provincial-level organizations, regulations and activities. Altogether 1,874 deputies participated in special investigation and research in 2006, with the participation rate reaching 63%, which was an increase of nearly 10 percentage points over 2005. The deputies who participated in special investigation and research did so diligently, overcoming many difficulties to participate and secure substantial results. 183 special investigation reports were compiled and submitted to related ministries and commissions of the State Council and the Supreme People's Court, and the Supreme People's Procuratorate to deliberate. Many deputies wrote high-quality proposals or suggestions based on special investigation and research. In connection with this research, at the end of 2006, furthering the goal of building a socialist harmonious society, the deputies to the National People's Congress also carried out inspection work and related investigation and research in order to ascertain the status of the "Tenth Five-year Plan," the status of the annual plan for the national economy and social development as well as the status of the "one government, two courts" system of administration by law and impartial judicial administration in local areas, which was prepared for the National People's Congress in 2007. Deputies to the National People's Congress also made new progress in organization, and also documented several good experiences (经验). The deputies were also in close contact with the public through several channels in order to understand and promote their opinions and desires.

Since May, 2005, according to the ideas of related documents put forth by the central committee and correlative working documents of the general office of the NPC Standing Committee, each provincial region, autonomous region and municipal People's Congress set up liaison offices for the deputies to the National People's Congress in order to provide services for local deputies to the National People's Congress in order to carry out their duties and responsibilities. Without a doubt, this initiative is an attempt to connect the responsibilities of the delegates to "collective activities." In 2006, 31 administrative bodies of the Standing Committees of provincial-level People's Congresses set up deputy liaison offices, and more than 90 comrades provided considerate careful special service work to aid these deputies in the fulfillment of their obligations, a service which strengthened protection for the work entrusted to the deputies.

### D. *Closing the Gap between the Deputies and the Public*

At the same time that work is underway to facilitate a clear "channel" of communication between the deputies to the National People's Congress and the National People's Congress itself, many local authorities are also emphasizing the importance of establishing "a bridge" between these deputies and the public. For example, the Sichuan Provincial People's Congress made the deputies' proposals and suggestions available to the public for the first time. In January, 2006, the fourth session of tenth Sichuan provincial People's Congress made use of the internet and media platform in order to set up the column "connecting with proposals and motions." This column would post majority of the proposals and motions submitted by the deputies and make them available to the public. Public appraisals of the proposals and motions s can be submitted through text messages, a newspaper hot line and the internet (网路点评). This action has had an immediate impact on the participant deputies and all of the involved parties since its commencement.

According to incomplete statistics, during conferences the number of on-line visits to this column reached nearly 30,000. On-line visitors left more than 1,100 letters, proposals and opinions and Sichuan citizen participation in the proceedings of the People's Congress achieved unprecedented levels. This initiative also encouraged the correlative departments to improve their handling efficiency and the quality of proposals and suggestions. In Anhui Province, all circles of society participated in the assessment of the deputies' work. In April, 2006, the Standing Committee of Anhui Provincial People's Congress carried out assessment and commendation for outstanding proposals and suggestions of deputies, the most advanced deputy group and most advanced unit for handling the suggestions of the deputies etc. This initiative lasted nearly 7 months, and appraised and commended 8 outstanding proposals, 10 outstanding suggestions, 9 advanced deputy groups and 12 advanced units handling the deputies' suggestions. This initiative was a positive accomplishment that achieved new levels of influence. It was also a powerful impetus for the deputies' work; as it inspired and mobilized enthusiasm fulfilling their responsibilities, while simultaneously enhancing public awareness of the People's Congress, and strengthening the positive interaction between the Deputies to the People's Congress and the public they represent.

### E. *Training for the Deputies to the People's Congress is Gradually Launched*

Improving the quality of Congress deputies is the key to developing and refining the National People's Congress system. Since the third session of tenth National People's Congress, the NPC Standing Committee has achieved tangible results by implementing systemic learning and training for the deputies to the People's Congress based on prior experience. In 2006, the general office of the NPC Standing Committee continued to hold training courses in systemic learning for the deputies, and also held training courses specifically on the subject of the implementation of "Tenth Five-year Plan" program and the legislation and supervision work of the National People's Congress and so on. Simultaneously a special lecture for deputy learning using a long-distance video system was held to explore new methods for deputy training, which could further increase the relevance of learning and training.

In 2006, the general office of the NPC Standing Committee held a five stages training course for the deputies to the National People's Congress. Within this course, two stages were training for deputies regarding the fulfillment of their obligations, and three stages were special learning seminars. The first training course for the deputies to the National People's Congress started in Shanghai in April. More than 90 deputies to the National People's Congress from 13 provinces and cities, a Taiwanese delegation, and a People's Liberation Army delegation participated in this training course. During training, the deputies systematically studied curricula on maintaining and refining the People's Congress system, building a socialist harmonious society, protocol for reviewing reports, protocol for deputy examination of budget report, strengthening the foundation of the NPC Standing Committee system, enhancing the quality of proposals and motions, and enhancing deputy activity outcomes etc. Through this training, the deputies' ability to legally fulfill their obligations was further enhanced, thereby improving their function as deputies to the National People's Congress. In August 2006, special courses in energy conservation and environmental protection were held in Xinjiang, and several positive field investigation sites were arranged. Through field investigations of the Dabancheng wind-power Station, the Bositeng Lake, the Takelamagan Desert and the *Populus Euphratica* (胡杨) Forest and so on, the vital significance of environmental protection was emphasized on many levels. From September 7 to 11, 2006, the third stage of the training course for deputies to the National People's Congress was held in Nanchang City, this training course was also a seminar of special learning for building a new socialist countryside. 77 deputies from 28 provinces, autonomous regions and municipalities participated in this training course, of which 24 deputies were agricultural technology personnel who were there on behalf of the farming population or were directly connected to the "three agricultural issues" (三农). On November 3, 2006, the fifth training course on the following three areas was begun in Shenzhen: (1) implementing the ideas of the sixth Plenary Session of the 16th Central Committee of the CCP; (2) implementing the Supervision Law which was officially put into practice on January 1, 2007; (3) deliberating the draft of the Property Law.

## IV. *Future Prospects*

Building a socialist harmonious society was an important mission proposed in the fourth Plenary Session of the 16th Central Committee of the CCP, and significant strategic deployment was made by the party in order to build an affluent society and found a new evolution of a Chinese Socialism. Proposing this theory was of strategic significance to the party in that it sharpened ruling ability, fulfilled the ruling mission and realized a national stability and peace. It also set a higher requirement for the development and refinement of the People's Congress system.

In 2006, the People's Congress system made great progress, however some issues were also brought to the surface. For example the coordination of certain issues in the legislative process was insufficient, the relevance and outcomes of supervision work needed to be further developed, the processing of deputies' proposals and motions was lacking, and the protocol of deputy work needed to be further refined etc.

On a macroscopic level, the objective practice of building a constitutional government over the last fifty years, the way by which the People's Congress system was perfected, has included on the most basic level the following approaches:

First, there are the planning of reform measures and the advancement of system innovation in regards to the designated center of the People's Congress system. Any system is operated by a specific group of people, and the accomplishment and behavior of these specific people influences the discernable function of the system as well as its overall image. The fundamental goal and development direction of China's rural reform and business reform innovations is to encourage the enthusiasm, initiative and creativity of the employees within each specific economic organization. Therefore, in the case of deputy politics, this approach is helpful to attaining the basic reform of the People's Congress system. In the case of deputy politics, only by implementing the following measures can the People's Congress system and the construction of a constitutional government establish itself as the fundamental source of authority and vitality in China. These measures include: refining the methods of deputy election, gradually improving the structure of the deputy organization, improving the accomplishments of the deputies, implementing a solid platform for all activities, establishing an honest environment and safeguard measures for the fulfillment of deputy obligations, strengthening supervision & restrictions for deputies, enhancing the authority and function of the People's Congress, and strengthening the actual provisions offered by the People's Congress system.

Second, there is the approach of emphasizing procedure, focusing on concrete details, and adopting the reform ideology of moving from easy to difficult in order to positively, safely, methodically and comprehensively promote the People's Congress system. The People's Congress system has made its development progress the impetus for reform and refinement since its inception. However, the appeal for the establishment of a principled and eloquent system has overwhelmed the creation of a cautious and concrete system. The People's Congress system is the fundamental political system, though any macroscopic system requires the generous extended support of concrete microscopic systems, in order to be put into practice and produce effective results. Although the system of the People's Congress had been established on the macroscopic level, the concrete systems on the microscopic level are as yet imperfect, a fact already analyzed in the proceeding text. Emphasizing the refinement of the internal organization system and the working procedure of the People's Congress system will be important to the process of perfecting the People's Congress system for some time. In fact, the substance of democratic politics is inseparable from concrete procedure and operation; and without ascertaining democratic procedural safeguards, no true realization of democratic politics is possible. Presently this phenomenon has gradually been realized by the public, and they have started to support the construction of a concrete system with the belief that, only when political culture is founded on concrete connections, can an overall constitutional government be achieved.

Third, there is the approach developing on the basis of China's national condition and practical experience, while simultaneously taking advantage of the achievements of the international political culture without imitating the Western political system. Although the People's Congress system differs from the Western political system of the three separate branches of power, they are both representative systems, and share certain common traits. China cannot copy the separation of the three powers system though the tenants of this system can be used by China as guides in researching the development and accomplishments of science and of human political culture since ancient Greece. The exclusion and denial of the Western system of constitutional government and the overemphasis of differences between the Chinese political system and the western one can result in an imbalanced knowledge of the achievements of human civilization. This lack, and potential reference source, must be remedied in the process of reforming and refining the People's Congress system and building a constitutional government. On a microscopic level, necessary concrete reform measures include refinement of the electoral system, structural reform in the People's Congress and standing committee, establishment of a professional deputy system, refinement of the agenda, and the research and application of accomplishments of other countries' parliamentary systems etc. These issues still require prudent and careful argumentation and research in theory and in practice. And in order to reach a resolution, it is necessary that all levels of People's Congresses be involved in the constant exploration of practice and application.

# PREDICTIONS ON THE DEVELOPMENT AND DIRECTION OF LEGISLATION

Wang Shucheng[1]

In 2006, China experienced a legislation boom. The Standing Committee of the National People's Congress (hereafter referred to as "the NPC Standing Committee") altogether promulgated 6 laws, such as the "Supervision Law of the Standing Committee of All Levels of People's Congress of the PRC" (中华人民共和国各级人大常委会监督法) etc. Promulgation of these laws has played a vital role in standardizing Chinese society. At the same time, the NPC Standing Committee had correspondingly revised seven laws which were not meeting the demands of society. For example, the "Criminal Law of People's Republic of China" (中华人民共和国刑法) and the "Audit Law of People's Republic of China" (中华人民共和国审计法) were properly revised. In addition, the NPC Standing Committee also approved 22 decisions.[2] In 2006, the State Council altogether promulgated 23 administrative rules and regulations, for example, it promulgated the "Regulation on the Protection of the Great Wall" (长城保护条例) and so on. The quantity of State Council administrative legislation on rules and regulations associated with newly-emerged social issues surpassed that of 2005. This phenomenon is inseparable from the many new problems which emerged in society in 2006. At the same time, the State Council also properly revised some former administrative rules and regulations and altogether revised 4 administrative rules and regulations such as "Provisions on Administrative Penalty against Price-related Unlawful Practices" (价格违法行为行政处罚规定)[3] and so on. The object of this legislation

---

[1] Wang Shucheng is a Doctoral candidate, and a constitution and administrative law major, at Renmin University of China. He is also a research assistant at the Center for Constitutional Government and Administrative 'Rule of law' Research, at Renmin University of China.

[2] In 2006 the decisions approved by the NPC Standing Committee mainly related to authorization of the international conventions and agreements and so on, such as the "Decision on Acceding to the 'WPO Copyright Treaty'" and the "Decision on Acceding to 'WIPO Performances and Phonograms Treaty'" etc.

[3] CN-Teacher, "Provisions on Administrative Penalty against Price-related Unlawful

report is to discuss the formulation and legal revision of laws by the NPC Standing Committee in 2006, as well as those administrative rules and regulations promulgated by the State Council.

## I. *The Formulation of Laws*

In 2006, the NPC Standing Committee altogether promulgated 6 laws, they were respectively, the "Supervision Law of the Standing Committee of All Levels of People's Congress of the PRC," the "Law of the People's Republic of China on Agricultural Product Quality and Safety," the "Law of PRC on Farmers' Professional Co-operatives" (中华人民共和国农民专业合作社法), the "Law of the People's Republic of China on Business Bankruptcy" (中华人民共和国企业(破产法)), the "Law of the People's Republic of China on Eradicating Money-Laundering" (中华人民共和国反洗钱法) and the "Passport Law of the People's Republic of China" (中华人民共和国护照法).[4]

### A. *Supervision Law of the Standing Committee for All Levels of People's Congress of the PRC*

The National People's Congress has received deputy proposals regarding the formulation of the Supervision Law since 1987. On August 27, 2006, the Supervision Law was finally reviewed and approved by the 23rd session of tenth NPC Standing Committee. Because China uses the People's Congress system, other state organizations are generated by and are responsible to the National People's Congress. As the executive body of all levels of People's Congress, the Standing Committee exercises many authorities over all levels of People's Congress when Congress is not in session. Of these authorities, the two most important are legislative power and supervisory authority. The Legislation Law specifically defines how legislative power should be exercised. However, the implementation consistently falls short of the standards. In recent years, the Standing Committee for all levels of People's Congress has

---

Practices," May 3rd, 2007, http://www.cn-teacher.com/yyjy/flyy/flyy1/200705/209229.html.

[4] Standing Committee of the National People's Congress, "Passport Law of the People's Republic of China," promulgated April 29th, 2006 http://new2007.lawinfochina.com/law/displayModeTwo.asp?id=5143&keyword=.

enacted a positive exploration of this phenomenon, and has accumulated valuable information on the topic. The formulation of Supervision Law is necessary for the National People's Congress to legally fulfill its supervisory authority, to strengthen its supervision work, and to promote administration by law and an impartial judiciary.

1. *Main Contents*

According to the provisions of the Supervision Law, this law applies to the procedure by which the Standing Committee of all levels of People's Congress exercises the supervisory authority. Other related laws are only applicable to what is not defined by the Supervision Law. The Supervision Law has increased the provisions supporting the authorities of the Standing Committee for all levels of People's Congress, and includes the following points:

(A.) To hear and review the specialized reports (专项工作报告) of the People's Government, the People's Court and the People's Procuratorate. This law stipulates that the Standing Committee of all levels of People's Congress may choose certain major issues every year, and according to a plan arrange to hear and review the specialized reports of that level of government, court and procuratorate on these issues. Before hearing and reviewing these specialized reports, the standing committee is authorized to inspect related work or do special investigation and study. Before 20 days when the standing committee holds conference, the administrative bodies of the government, the court or the procuratorate should submit the reports to the related Special Committee of this level of People's Congress, or the related operating organization of the standing committee, in order to solicit opinions. If the standing committee decides it is necessary, they may decide the outcome of these reports. This level of government, the court or the procuratorate should report to the standing committee regarding the status of enforcing the decision within the prescribed time limit.

(B.) To examine and authorize the final accounts. Hear and review reports regarding the execution of plans, and the budget for the national economy and social development, as well as hear and review the audit reports. This law stipulates that, the State Council and all levels of local governments above county-level should submit drafts of their final accounts for the previous year to the Standing Committee within the prescribed time limit for examination and authorization. Simultaneously, they should report to the Standing Committee within the prescribed time limit regarding the previous budget for the national economy and social development as well as on the status of implementing the current budget. In regards to an authorized plan and budget for the national economy and the social development, if the implementation needs to be adjusted, the readjustment plan should be submitted to the Standing Committee of this level of People's Congress for examination and authorization. The government should submit a written report on the research and processing status of the proposals made by members of the standing committee in the review, to the standing committee. The standing committee may decide the resolution for the audit report. When the budget funds need to be readjusted and reduced, this should be submitted to the Standing Committee of this level of People's Congress for examination and authorization. Simultaneously the government should submit a midterm evaluation report on the implementation of the Standing Committee of this level of People's Congress for review.

(C.) To inspect the implementation of laws and regulations. This law stipulates that, the Standing Committee of all levels of People's Congress may inspect the implementation of all relevant laws and regulations according to plan. After the law enforcement inspection is completed, the law enforcement inspection group should promptly submit a law enforcement inspection report to the standing committee for review. Review opinions on the law-enforcement inspection report along with the law-enforcement inspection report itself, should be submitted to the government, the court or the procuratorate for consideration and processing. After the processing results of the government the court or the procuratorate are handed over the related special committee or related operating organization of the standing committee in order to solicit the opinions of the administrative body the report should be submitted to the standing committee. If necessary, the standing committee may organize a long-term inspection.

(D.) To register and examine standardized documents. This law stipulates that, the Standing Committee of all levels of local People's Congress above county level will examine the validity of the resolutions and decisions made by the lower level of People's Congress and its standing committee as well as the decisions and orders made by that level of the people's government. In those instances when the State Council, the Central Military Commission and the provincial, autonomous region and municipality People's Congress think the interpretation of a specific law's application is at variance with the provisions of the law, they may request a written examination from the NPC Standing

Committee. Other state organizations and social groups, businesses and institutional organizations as well as citizens may make written inspection proposals. In those instances when the Law Committee of the National People's Congress and related specialized committees believe think the interpretation of a specific law's application is inconsistent with the provisions of the law after examination, they may put forward a motion for the revision and abolishment of the law, or put forward a motion for legal interpretation of the law.

(E.) Inquiry and interpellation. This law stipulates that, when reviewing proposals and related reports, this level of government, court or procuratorate or the departments concerned should send a staff member with related responsibilities to attend a meeting for hearing opinions or suggestions and answering questions. If the necessary legal quantity of deputies to the People's Congress jointly signs; then they may propose a bill addressing inquiries on this level of government, the court and procuratorate and its departments in writing to the standing committee. The institution of inquiry should reply to the bill addressing all questions. If the reply is unsatisfactory, the institution of inquiry should reply again.

Concurrently, the Supervision Law also defines the investigation of specific issues as well as the issue of reviewing and resolving employee dismissal cases.

2. *Evaluation*

As mentioned above, the Supervision Law has also increased comprehensive provisions regarding the supervisory authority of the Standing Committee for all levels of People's Congress. The implementation of the Supervision Law has also functioned to safeguard and supervise the building of a socialist harmonious society. Even so, the Supervision Law is still a newly promulgated law. Consequentially in its specific implementation process, certain issues arose that could not be effectively settled solely by the Supervision Law. Therefore, when the Supervision Law is unable to effectively safeguard the supervisory authority of the Standing Committee, the supervision system should be refined by continuously adopting supplementary standards, and must expand beyond the existing Supervision Law. Considering the provisions of procedure, although the Supervision Law contains many procedural standards, they are generally macroscopic, and the included possible and exercisable procedural provisions still need to be refined through continued implementation. Indubitably, the promulgation and implementation of Supervision Law will lay a solid standardized foundation for the refinement of the supervision system of the People's Congress, and for further development of the People's Congress system.

### B. *"Law of the People's Republic of China on the Quality and Safety of Agricultural Products"* (中华人民共和国农产品质量安全法)

In order to guarantee the quality and safety of agricultural products, to preserve public health and to promote development of the agriculture and the rural economy, on April 29, 2006, the 21st session of tenth NPC Standing Committee reviewed and approved the "Law of the People's Republic of China on Agricultural Product Quality Safety." This law has implemented specific provisions regarding producing areas, production, packaging and labeling, and the supervision and inspection of agricultural products.

#### 1. *Main Contents*

(A.) Provisions regarding the producing areas (农产品产地) for agricultural products. This law stipulates that, the local government agricultural administrative department of the local or above county level local government should report to that level of government for approval to announce those areas designated as unsuitable for agricultural production on the basis of the various special characteristics of the agricultural products and the levels of poisonous or harmful substances in the atmosphere, the soil and the water of the producing area. No areas where poisonous or harmful substances can be found in excess of the prescribed standards can produce, catch or gather edible agricultural products or establish production of agricultural products. No waste water, waste gas, solid wastes or other poisonous or harmful substances can be discharged or dumped in an area producing agricultural products. Also, the water supply for agricultural production and the use of solid wastes as fertilizer should conform to state specified standards.

(B.) Provisions regarding the production of agricultural products. This law stipulates that agricultural chemicals, veterinary medicines, livestock feed and feed additives, fertilizer and veterinary instruments which could possibly affect agricultural product quality and safety must be used in accordance with a licensing system and relevant laws, administrative rules and regulations. The various responsible agricultural administrative departments should carry out regular supervision and spot-checks of agricultural chemicals, veterinary medicine, feed and feed additives, fertilizer and other substances which could possibly endanger agricultural product quality and safety. The results of these investigations should also be announced. Agricultural product manufacturing businesses and farming collectives (农民专业合作经济组织) should establish a record of agricultural product production. This record should be preserved for two years. No record of agricultural product production shall be fabricated. No agricultural additives specifically prohibited by the state may be used in agricultural product production. Any agricultural product which does not conform to the standards of agricultural quality and safety after examination cannot be sold.

(C.) Provisions on the packaging and labeling of agricultural products. This law stipulates that, agricultural products should be packaged or labeled according to legal provisions, before being sold. The name, place of origin, producer, production date, shelf life and the quality grade of products, etc. should be displayed on the wrapping or labels according to provisions. Products that use chemical additives must be labeled with the names of the chemical additives used according to provisions. Anti-staling agents, antiseptics and chemical additives etc. used in packing, preservation, storing and transportation of agricultural products should conform to the related mandatory national technological specifications. Those agricultural products which belong to the category of agricultural transgenic biology (农业转基因生物的农产品) should be labeled according to the related provisions on agricultural transgenic biology safety management. Those animals, plants and products which need to be quarantined should have the quarantine acceptance symbol and the quarantine certificate attached.

Also, this law has also made detailed provisions regarding supervision and examination. For example, agricultural products which contain agricultural chemicals, veterinary medicines or other chemical substances etc. which are prohibited from use cannot be sold.

2. *Evaluation*

The promulgation and implementation of the "Law of the People's Republic of China on the Quality and Safety of Agricultural Products" was of vital significance to safeguarding the quality of agricultural products, and public health. This law has made specific provisions on overall control of agricultural products' quality and safety. However the particular process of implementation of this law still needs to be refined through the detailed standardization of administrative regulations and local laws and regulations etc. It has also been observed that the efficacy of this law is inseparable from the concrete implementation of the lower laws. For example, Article 13 of this law stipulates that the standards of quality and safety for agricultural products must be revised according to scientific advancements and technological developments as well as according to the public demands regarding quality and safety of agricultural products.

However these safety standards must also be decided through other standards, "The compulsory technical specifications" (强制性的技术规范) in the "Law on Quality and Safety of Agricultural Products" must also pass the specific provisions of other standards. In Article 18, it states that "the water supply for agricultural production and the solid wastes used as fertilizer must conform to nationally regulated standards," showing that the standards contained in the law must also fulfill specific standards of their own. So long as the concrete system contained in the "Law on Quality and Safety in Agricultural Products" is strictly enforced, the quality and safety of Chinese agricultural products will be effectively safeguarded.

### C. *"Law of PRC on Farmers' Co-operatives"* (中华人民共和国农民专业合作社法)

This law was approved on October 31, 2006, by the 24th session of tenth NPC Standing Committee, and has made specific provisions regarding the establishment and registration, membership, and organizational framework of Farmers' Cooperatives. The law also includes provisions governing the financial management, merging and separation, dissolution and liquidation, and the support policy for these cooperatives.

#### 1. *Main Contents*

(A.) The establishment and registration of Farmers' Professional Co-operatives. This law stipulates that, an established Farmers' Cooperative should include more than five members in accordance with the provisions. It should implement regulations, establish an organizational framework and determine a name and location in accordance with the provisions of this law and the administrative rules and regulations. Member investments should also conform to the regulations. A meeting should be held when establishing a Farmer's Cooperative for all establishing members to participate in. Established Farmers' Cooperatives should apply to the industrial and commercial administrative department for incorporation. Applicants who conform to the registration requirements will be issued a business license. Processing of the registration should have no fees.

(B.) Members of Farmers' Professional Co-operatives. This law stipulates that, the citizens who possess civil capacity (民事行为能力), as well as businesses, institutions or the social groups engaged in production and operation directly related to the businesses of the Farmers' Cooperative may take advantage of the services provided by the Farmers' Professional Co-operatives. And, that those individuals who acknowledge and observe the regulations of the Farmers' Cooperative while fulfilling the stipulated membership procedure may become the members of the Farmers' Cooperative. The unit (单位) responsible for the management of public affairs is not eligible to join. In regards to the members of the cooperatives, farmers should account for the membership proportion prescribed in this law. Members enjoy the right to attend member meetings, the right to vote, and the right of suffrage and eligibility for elections. Other rights include the use of services and the production operation facilities provided by the co-operative, the right of earnings sharing, and the rights included in the regulations of the co-operative, its member scroll, the member meetings or the record of member congress, the council conference resolutions, the resolutions in the conference of board of supervisors, the financial statements and the account records etc. The members fulfill the all obligations stipulated by the regulations.

(C.) Organizational framework of the Farmers' Professional Co-operatives. The member meeting of Farmers' Professional Co-operatives is composed of all members, and is the agency of power of the cooperative. The Farmers' cooperative appoints a chairperson of the board of directors, and may appoint the council. The chairperson of the board of directors or the council of the Farmers' Professional Co-operatives may appoint a manager and a financial accountant according to the decisions of the member meeting. The chairperson or the director may hold a concurrent post of manager. According to the regulation or the council's decisions, other personnel may also be appointed as manager. The chairperson, the director and the manager cannot hold a concurrent post of chairperson, director, supervisor, and manager of other farmer's cooperatives which have the same area of business.

(D.) Financial management of the farmer's cooperatives. This law stipulates that, the treasury department of the State Council formulates the financial and accounting system for the farmer's cooperatives. The chairperson of the cooperative or the council organizes the compiling of the annual business report, plans for distributing earnings, loss handling plans as well as other financial statements according to the regulations. These documents are made available in the work place for the member's reference. Deals between the cooperative and its members, and the non-members who use the services provided by it must be separately calculated. The cooperatives should set up a member account for each member. The cooperatives' distributable earnings are the yearly earnings after covering losses and withdrawing reserved funds. Distributable earnings should be returned or distributed to the members according to the provisions, and specific measures are determined according to regulations or are resolved in a member meeting.

(E.) The merging, separation, dissolution and liquidation of farmers' cooperatives. Merging cooperatives will inform creditors within 10 days from the date of the merging resolution. Creditor's rights and the debt of all merging sides will be inherited by the surviving organization after merging or the newly established organization. In the case of cooperative separation, property should be divided accordingly. The debts before separation should be borne jointly by the organizations after separation, with the exception of agreements otherwise. In regards to the dissolution of farmers' cooperatives, a liquidation commission should be formed in order to dissolve the cooperative's assets. If the liquidation group cannot be composed within the time limit, the members and the creditors may apply to the courts for liquidation.

Simultaneously, this law also stipulates a support policy. For example, the farmers' cooperatives enjoy those correlative tax incentives as stipulated by the country for agricultural production, processing, circulation, and services as well as for other economic activity relating to agriculture.

2. *Evaluation*

The "Farmers' Cooperative Law" clearly defines the status of the cooperatives as a mainstay in the economic market. This action makes farmer cooperatives a continuance of the precedent of laws which protect market entities, after the Company Law (公司法), the Partnership Law (合伙企业法) and the "Law on Individual Proprietorship Businesses" (个人独资企业法). This law is advantageous for farmers who are establishing cooperatives according to law, and in defining the scale of production operation and promoting the development of a market economy. This law has emphasized the role of the farmer and the democratic management of cooperatives as important market entities, which is advantageous in encouraging farmers and realistically protecting their benefits.

## D. *"Law of the People's Republic of China on Business Bankruptcy"* (中华人民共和国企业破产法)

On August 27, 2006, the 23rd session of tenth NPC Standing Committee approved the "Law of the People's Republic of China on Business Bankruptcy."

### 1. *Main Contents*

The new Bankruptcy Law has surpassed the scope of the prior Bankruptcy Law on many levels. The specific contents of the new Bankruptcy Law as compared with the prior law are outlined below:

(A.) The new law has expanded the range of application, has introduced the administrator system, and has emphasized the creditor's rights. The "Law on Business Bankruptcy (Trial)"[5] was only applicable to those businesses owned by the public but not individual and privately owned businesses, therefore the creditor's benefits were frequently discounted (大打折扣). The range of application of the new Bankruptcy Law has been expanded to include all legal persons of business, including state-owned enterprises, corporate private enterprises and the three types of foreign-funded enterprises, listed companies and non-listed companies, limited liability companies and joint-stock limited companies, even financial institutions. Bankruptcy in state-owned businesses is no longer guided by the administrative system but instead is decided by the situation of the market. In addition, the government will no longer decide affairs of bankruptcy for state-owned businesses, meaning that all businesses will be governed by market rules. Because the original Bankruptcy Law emphasized the role of the government in deciding various bankruptcy matters, it lacked marketability.

The new Bankruptcy Law has introduced a bankruptcy trustee system to be operated according to the market which stipulates that the social

[5] Supreme People's Court, "Notice of the Supreme People's Court on Implementing the Rules on Some Issues concerning the Application of Law to Enterprise Bankruptcy Cases pending Trial upon the Effectiveness of the Enterprise Bankruptcy Law of the People's Republic of China," promulgated on May 26th, 2007, http://big5.chinalawinfo.com/eng.chinalawinfo.com/law/display.asp?id=6317&keyword=.

intermediary organizations mainly hold the post of trustee, including law firms, accounting firms or bankruptcy liquidation firms etc. This causes the bankruptcy procedure to conform more to the rules of a market economy. In liquidating debts due, the creditor may apply to the people's court for rectification or bankruptcy liquidation on the part of the debtor. Article 22 (2) of the new Bankruptcy Law stipulates that, "Where it is decided at the creditors' meeting that a bankruptcy administrator fails to perform or fulfill his duties and functions in a lawful and impartial manner, the creditors may apply to the people's court for changes." Article 68 (2) stipulates that "When the creditors' committee performs its functions and duties, it has the right to require the relevant bankruptcy administrator and debtor to give an explanation on any matter within the scope of his functions and duties or provide the relevant documents." These provisions prove that the creditor's rights are considered. Simultaneously, the administrator must be supervised by the creditor conference and the board of creditors when fulfilling his duties according to the provisions. Moreover, the administrator also should attend the creditor conference as a non-voting delegate and report on the execution of his duties to the creditor conference, and reply to inquiries. In the rectification (重整程序) procedure, the creditor may legally apply directly to the people's court for consolidation on the part of the debtor, and the creditor conference holds the right to vote on the consolidation draft plan, which has the decisive function of executing the consolidation procedure. From this we can see that creditor's rights are a fundamental part of the new Bankruptcy Law.

(B.) The rectification system and the bankruptcy procedure of financial institutions are regulated. Rectification refers to a system of liquidation of the insolvent debtor's properties which is not immediately carried out, instead an agreement between the debtor and the creditor under the court's intervention is reached, and a rectification plan is made which stipulates that the debtor completely or partially discharges a debt according to an agreed upon manner within a certain timeframe. The debtor may also simultaneously continue running his business. Article 73(1) of the new Bankruptcy Law stipulates that "For the duration of rectification, a debtor may, upon filing an application and obtaining an approval from the people's court, manage its assets and business operation under the supervision of the bankruptcy administrator." The provisions of the rectification system give the debtor business the opportunity to recover. The former Bankruptcy Law did not make provisions for the bankruptcy of financial institutions. The new Bankruptcy Law has stipulated that, when certain financial institutions including commercial banks, insurance companies and security companies etc. are insolvent etc., the finance supervision institution of the State Council may file an application with the people's court for rectification, compromise or bankruptcy liquidation. With respect to inability on the part of commercial banks, securities dealers and insurance companies to pay the debts due, takeover, trusteeship or bankruptcy liquidation and rectification etc. must be reported separately according to instructions requested from the related supervision departments.

(C.) To standardize misfeasance in bankruptcy and specific bankruptcy responsibilities. Compared with the former Bankruptcy Law, the new Bankruptcy Law has established more complete rescission rights and an invalid act system. Article 31st of new Bankruptcy Law stipulates that, a bankruptcy administrator has the right to request the court to revoke any act relating to the debtor's assets, including transferring assets free of charge, trading at obviously unreasonable prices, providing asset guaranties to those debts without any asset guaranty, paying off the undue debts in advance or giving up the creditor's rights within one year before the people's court accepts an application for bankruptcy. At the same time, Article 33 of the new Bankruptcy Law stipulates that, any act involving the debtor's assets which conceals or transfers the assets in order to avoid debts, fabricates any debt or acknowledges any unreal debt shall be deemed invalid. This has standardized the misfeasance of "false bankruptcy" (虚假破产) and "malicious bankruptcy" (恶意破产) to a certain degree, which it is advantageous in the protection of creditor's benefits. According to the former Bankruptcy Law, after bankruptcy, even if the businesses' large sum debts are unable to be paid off, the businesses' chief employee does not bear any legal liability. The new Bankruptcy Law has made a new provision that "mangers are subject to legal liabilities." Article 125 stipulates that, "where a director, supervisor or senior manager violates his obligations of being honest and diligent and thus leads to business bankruptcy, he shall be subject to the relevant civil liabilities according to law. In addition, no person under any circumstance as prescribed in the preceding paragraph may, within 3 years of the day when the procedures for bankruptcy are concluded, assume the post of director, supervisor or senior manager of any business."

(D.) Secured creditor's rights have precedence over staff creditor's rights, and legal stipulations regarding cross-border insolvency issues are implemented. Regarding the discharging sequence of secured creditor's rights and the staff creditor's rights, the new Bankruptcy Law stipulates that when bankruptcy occurs before the promulgation of new law, the staff creditor's rights have precedence over the secured creditor's rights. When the bankrupt entity's unsecured properties are insufficient to cover staff wages, the wages must be paid off from secured properties. After the new Bankruptcy Law was promulgated, secured creditor's rights would be paid off first, and the staff wages and other welfare costs would be paid off from uncovered properties. The new Bankruptcy Law stipulates that "The procedures for bankruptcy initiated according to the present Law shall have binding force over the assets of the concerned debtor beyond the territories of the People's Republic of China." At the same time, the Chinese court also rules to accept and execute foreign courts' rulings on bankruptcy under the conditions of reciprocal benefits, judicial aid and international covenants. Such provisions of the Bankruptcy Law foreshadow future international cooperation regarding the Bankruptcy Law.

#### 2. *Evaluation*

The new Bankruptcy Law effectively guarantees that, under the market economy, all creditors can be fairly compensated, and that failing businesses can withdraw in an orderly manner. At the same time, through the system of bankruptcy rectification, those businesses facing difficulties with future possibilities for improvement can resolve their financial problems, which can reduce unemployment and losses of public wealth caused by the depreciation of bankrupt property because of bankruptcy liquidation. Overall, the provisions of the new Bankruptcy Law are more systematic, clear and careful criteria. For example, the new law has made provisions for the declaration of creditor's rights with 15 articles in the sixth chapter, which determines the declaration methods of various types of creditor's rights and so on. The new Bankruptcy Law will play a vital role for the development of Chinese business as well as the economic prosperity of the market.

### E. *"Law of the People's Republic of China against Money Laundering"* (中华人民共和国反洗钱法)

On October 31, 2006, the 24th session of tenth NPC Standing Committee approved the "Law of the People's Republic of China against Money Laundering". The law mainly defines, prevents and monitors certain criminal activities, such as money laundering etc.

1. *Main Contents*

The "Law against Money Laundering" contains 37 articles, which define eradicating money laundering as the prevention of any money laundering activity for the purpose of concealing or disguising, by any means, the source and nature of criminal proceeds generated from any drug-related crime, organizational or gang crime, terrorist crime, smuggling, corruption or bribery, disruption of the financial management order, or financial fraud, etc. Its main contents include:

(A.) This law stipulates that the administrative department on eradicating money laundering of the State Council shall take charge of supervision and administration of this problem throughout the country, and has determined the responsibilities of this administrative department of the State Council, relevant departments and organizations under the State Council and judicial organizations regarding the eradication of laundering. Financial institutions established within the territory of the People's Republic of China or a special non-financial institutions will adopt relevant measures for the prevention and supervision of any money laundering activity according to law, by establishing and improving the a client identity identification system, a system to preserve the privacy of clients' identification materials and transactional records, and a reporting system for large sum transactions and questionable transactions, in order to perform its anti-money laundering obligations. Any client's identification materials or transactional information acquired in the performance of duties or functions regarding the eradication of money laundering will be kept confidential. Identification materials and transactional information acquired by the administrative departments or by any other department or organization in regards to money laundering investigations in the process of performing their functions and duties shall only be used in the administrative money laundering investigation.

(B.) This law determines the scope of financial institutions in fulfilling their obligations in regards to eradicating money laundering and it establishes specific obligations. Financial institutions will establish and improve an internal system to control money laundering, and the chief officer at each financial institution will be responsible for the effective implementation of the internal system, while simultaneously establishing a special organization to undertake eradicating money laundering related work. This organization must also establish a client identification system, a system for protecting clients' identification materials and transactional records, and implement a reporting system for large sum transactions and questionable transactions according to the relevant provisions.

(C.) This law stipulates the performance conditions, the principal subject, and the granting procedure and deadlines for an investigation concerning money laundering. For example, in the investigation of a questionable transaction, there shall be no fewer than 2 investigators, who will show their legal certificates as well as the investigation notice produced by the administrative department of eradicating money laundering of the State Council or by its dispatched organization at the provincial level. A transcript will be made of the inquiry and will be checked against the testimony of the person being interrogated. When further examination is required in an investigation, the investigator may, upon the approval of the principal of the administrative department of eradicating money laundering of the State Council or its dispatched organ at the provincial level, consult and photocopy any relevant account information, transactional records or other materials of the investigated institution or persons, and may seal any document or material that could be transferred, concealed, tampered or destroyed. When a client requests to transfer account capital involved in a foreign investigation, temporary freezing measures may be adopted. A temporary freeze shall not exceed 48 hours. If any notice on prolonging the freeze is not received from the investigation organization within 48 hours after temporary freezing measures are implemented, the freeze will be immediately lifted. These procedures and provisions provide a strong base of criteria for investigation concerning the eradication of money laundering.

In addition, the law also stipulates the basic principles of international cooperation to eradicate money laundering as well as the legal liabilities of violating the "Law against Money Laundering." China will also carry out international cooperation in regards to eradicating money laundering, according to the international treaties that China has implemented or acceded to, and according to the principles of equality and reciprocity. The provisions of legal liability include legal liability of any functionary of the administrative department concerning the eradication of money laundering or any other department or organ performing the functions and duties of supervision and administration of eradication efforts, and for financial institutions and directly liable chairpersons, senior managers or any other directly liable persons.

2. *Evaluation*

The "Law against Money Laundering" has played a vital role in promoting stable politics, social stability, and economic security as well increasing the security of the international political economic system. It has accomplished this by focusing on many types of current economic criminal activities, including embezzlement, bribery, smuggling, terrorism and tax evasion. It has also investigated criminal organizations illegal banks and money laundering operations etc. The formulation of the "Law against Money Laundering" encourages the prompt discovery and investigation of illegal money laundering activities, the investigation and confiscation of criminal earnings, the investigation of money laundering crimes and also of related or causal crimes (上游犯罪的蔓延). This law also helps to eliminate the risks incurred by financial institutions as a result of money laundering, it aids in the discovery and appropriation of criminal capital, and in the prevention of new criminal acts. The law also increases protection of property rights for victims of related crimes.

F. *The "Passport Law of the People's Republic of China"*

In order to regulate the application, issuance and management of passports of the People's Republic of China, guarantee the rights and interests of the citizens of the People's Republic of China exiting and entering the People's Republic of China and promote the intercourse with foreign countries, the 21st session of tenth NPC Standing Committee approved the "Passport Law of the People's Republic of China" on April 29, 2006.

1. *Main Contents*

(A.) The law stipulates the issuance authority for ordinary passports. The "Passport Law of the People's Republic of China" establishes the exit/entry administrative departments of the public security organization as the legal central entities for the issuance of ordinary passports. Article 4 of the "Passport Law of the People's Republic of China" explicitly stipulates that "ordinary passports shall be issued by the exit/entry administrative departments of the Ministry of Public Security or the exit/entry administrative departments of the public security organizations of the local people's governments at or above the county level as authorized by the Ministry of Public Security, and by the embassies or consulates of the People's Republic of China stationed abroad or other institutions stationed abroad upon the authorization of the Ministry of Foreign Affairs." Article 5 stipulates that "When a citizen goes abroad for residence, visiting relatives, study, employment, travel, business activities or other non-official service reasons, he shall file an application with the exit/entry administrative department of the public security organization of the local people's government at the county level or above in the place of his permanent residence."

(B.) The law contains provisions regarding passport application and holding. When applying for an ordinary passport, a citizen will submit his resident identity certificate, residence registration, recent full-face photos without a hat and other materials related to the reasons for the application. When a state functionary applies for an ordinary passport, he/she will additionally submit relevant certification documents according to the relevant provisions of the state. The ordinary passport will be issued within 15 days, in remote regions or areas of minimal official traffic, the time limit may be extended to 30 days. The items registered on an ordinary passport will include name, gender, birth date and birth place of the passport holder, as well as the issuance date, valid period, issuance place and issuance organization of the passport. The original provision to include the resident identification card number in the registration items of passport, has been canceled. Considering the practice of reissuing or exchanging passports is quite complex, provisions included in the law regarding reissues or exchanges are quite broad.

(C.) The law contains requirements for passport agency personnel. When any functionary of a passport issuance department commits any of the following acts during the process of handling a passport, administrative sanctions will be imposed, and if any crime is committed, it will be subject to criminal liabilities: (I.) failing to accept an application that should be accepted; (II.) failing to issue a passport within the statutory time limit without any justifiable reason; (III.) charging any fee above the criteria as prescribed by the state; (IV.) extorting or accepting bribes from any applicant; (V.) impairing the legitimate rights and interests of any citizen by leaking personal information accessed during the making or issuing of a passport; (VI.) other acts such as abuse of power, neglect of duties, seeking private benefits and so on.

At the same time, the law also makes specific provisions as to the punishment for illegal acts, the conditions for reissuance and exchange of ordinary passports etc.

2. *Evaluation*

In some legal norms such as the "Administrative License Law," (行政许可法)[6] the "Law on Administrative Penalties," (行政处罚法) "Administrative Law," (行政诉讼法)[7] and "Administrative Reconsideration Law" (行政复议法) etc., the contents have been inconsistent with the present entry and exit administration system of China. The formulation of the "Passport Law of the People's Republic of China" has completed the process of aligning legal norms. Based on many years of field experience, the Passport Law has stipulated the type, the issuance authority, the application procedure, the time limit of issuance, the objects not to be issued and the penalty provisions etc. in regards to the passport, an important part of the legal system for entry and exit administration. The Passport Law also sets new requirements for the public security organizations and so on. For example, the Passport Law has reduced the processing time limit for the ordinary passport, which requires the public security organization to further improve its services, to strictly enforce the law, and to maintain a standard process of managing passport issuance.

## II. *Law Revisions*

In 2006, the NPC Standing Committee has completed the revisions of the following seven laws, "Law of the People's Republic of China on the Protection of Minors" (中华人民共和国未成年人保护法),[8] "Banking Supervision Law of the People's Republic of China" (中华人民共和国银行业监督管理法), "Organic Law (组织法) of The People's Courts of the People's Republic of China,"[9] "Business Partnership Law of the People's Republic of China" (中华中华人民共和国合伙企业法),[10] "Amendment to the Criminal Law of the People's Republic of

[6] Chinese Law in English Online (法律英语网), "Administrative License Law of The People's Republic of China," 2008, http://www.21lawyer.cn/english/03a/6.html.

[7] Chinese Law in English Online (法律英语网), "Administrative Procedure law of the People's Republic of China," 2008, http://www.21lawyer.cn/english/03a/5.html.

[8] Standing Committee of the National People's Congress, "Law of the People's Republic of China on the Protection of Minors," promulgated September 4th, 1991, http://www.lawinfochina.com/law/display.asp?id=148.

[9] Foreign Language Education Online, "Organic Law of the People's Courts of the People's Republic of China," posted May 18th, 2006, http://www.for68.com/new/2006%5C5%5Cpa1271533518156002600-0.htm.

[10] Standing Committee of the National People's Congress, "Partnership Enterprise

China (VI),[11] "Compulsory Education Law of the People's Republic of China" (中华人民共和国义务教育法)[12] and the "Audit Law of People's Republic of China" (中华人民共和国审计法).[13]

### A. *"Law of the People's Republic of China on the Protection of Minors"*

For the purpose of protecting the physical and mental health of minors, safeguarding their lawful rights and interests, promoting their comprehensive moral, intellectual and physical development, as well as for the purpose of training minors to promote and adapt to the ideals of the socialist cause and develop sound morality, better education and a good sense of discipline, the 25th session of tenth NPC Standing Committee approved the revision of the 'Law on the Protection of Minors' on December 29, 2006.

#### 1. *The Law Explicitly Stipulates That Minors Enjoy Five Rights*

The "Law on the Protection of Minors," after revision, explicitly stipulates that minors enjoy the right to survival, development, protection, the right of participation and the right to receive education.

#### 2. *The Law Emphasizes the Protection of Identity and the Dignity of Minors by the Schools*

The teaching and administrative staff in schools, kindergartens and nurseries will respect the personality and dignity of minors, and may not commit corporal punishment either directly or in disguised forms against minors, or commit any other act that humiliates the identity and dignity of minors. The teaching and administrative staff will also safeguard the legitimate rights and interests of minors, such as personal safety etc. in all ways. For example, when a personal injury accident occurs in an activity of minor students within the school or in an activ-

---

Law of the People's Republic of China," promulgated on August 27th, 2006, http://www.lawinfochina.com/law/display.asp?id=5428&keyword=.

[11] Standing Committee of the National People's Congress, "Amendment to the Criminal Law of the People's Republic of China," promulgated on February 28th, 2005, http://www.lawinfochina.com/law/display.asp?id=3938&keyword=.

[12] Standing Committee of the National People's Congress, "Compulsory Education Law of the People's Republic of China," promulgated June 29th, 2006, http://www.lawinfochina.com/law/display.asp?id=5299&keyword=.

[13] Standing Committee of the National People's Congress, "Audit Law of the People's Republic of China," promulgated February 28th, 2006, http://www.lawinfochina.com/law/display.asp?id=4980.

ity organized by the school outside of school, the school will organize timely aid for the injured, provide appropriate treatment and promptly report the matter to the relevant competent department.

3. *The Law Strengthens the Protection of the Rights and Interests of Minors in the Area of Social Protection*

This law stipulates that, no site that is unsuitable for minors to carry out activities in, such as a commercial singing and dancing recreation site or Internet access service site, etc. will be established next to elementary or high schools, or the transgressor will be closed by the department responsible, and incur administrative punishments according to law. No site that is unsuitable for minors to carry out activities in, such as commercial singing and dancing recreation site or Internet access service business site, etc. will allow minors to enter. The business operator will prominently display a sign prohibiting the entry of minors. It is prohibited to sell tobacco and liquor to minors, and a sign that prohibits these sales must be displayed in a conspicuous position.

4. *The Law Emphasizes the Legitimate Rights and Interests of Minors in Regards to Judicial Protection*

This law stipulates that, when handling minor crime cases and the cases involved with the protection of the rights and interests of minors, the public security organization, the procuratorate and the court must consider the physical and mental development of minors, respect their identity and dignity, safeguard their legitimate rights and interests, and set up specialized institutions or specially assign personnel to handle the needs of minors.

## B. *"Banking Supervision Law of the People's Republic of China"* (中华人民共和国银行业监督管理法)[14]

On October 31, 2006, the 24th session of tenth NPC Standing Committee approved "Decision of the Standing Committee of the National People's Congress on Amending the Banking Supervision Law of the People's Republic of China."[15] The "Banking Supervision Law" after

[14] UN Lawyer Blog, "Banking Supervision Law of the People's Republic of China," posted November 24th, 2006, http://unlawyer.blog.bokee.net/bloggermodule/blog_viewblog.do?id=399028.

[15] Standing Committee of the National People's Conference, "Decision of the

revision has added an article based on the original law, stipulating that the banking regulation organization has the right to carry on extended inspections to businesses and individuals when inspecting banking organizations in accordance with the law. These extended inspection powers include: inquiring about the relevant entity or individual, and requiring him to explain the relevant matters; inspecting and copying relevant financial accounting, property registration and other documents and materials; conducting advanced registration and preservation of documents and materials that may be transferred, concealed, destroyed or falsified.

The revised "Banking Supervision Law" also adds a new provision, that in the case of someone hampering any inspection or investigation legally carried out by the functionaries of the banking regulatory organ, he shall be given a public security administrative penalty, and if any crime is committed, he shall be subject to criminal liabilities.

The third revision of the "Banking Supervision Law" emphasizes the protection of confidential business information and individual privacy. When any functionary conducting supervision or administration in the banking regulation organization embezzles public funds, accepts bribes, divulges state secrets, commercial secrets or personal privacy, or if any crime is committed, he will be subject to criminal liabilities. If no crime is committed, he will incur administrative sanctions. After revision, the "Banking Supervision Law" stipulates that, the banking regulatory organization will be compromised of no less than two functionaries when taking the above measures. These functionaries will present lawful certificates and investigation notices, otherwise the concerned entity or individual has the right to refuse the investigation.

### C. *"Organic Law of the People's Courts of the People's Republic of China"* (中华人民共和国人民法院组织法)

On October 31, 2006, the 24th session of tenth NPC Standing Committee approved "Decision of the Standing Committee of the National People's Congress on Amending the Organic Law of the People's Courts of the People's Republic of China."[16] This decision has revised

Standing Committee of the National People's Congress on Amending the Banking Supervision Law of the People's Republic of China," promulgated October 31st, 2006, http://www.lawinfochina.com/law/display.asp?id=5601&keyword=.

[16] Standing Committee of the National People's Conference, "Decision of the

Article 13 of the "Organic Law of the People's Courts" to read "cases involving death sentences, except for those cases with sentences imposed by the Supreme People's Court, shall be submitted to the Supreme People's Court for approval." From this point on, all authority for the examination and authorization of death sentence cases is returned to the Supreme People's Court, and the Supreme People's Court uniformly exercises this authority.

D. *"Business Partnership Law of the People's Republic of China"*

When the "Business Partnership Law" appeared in 1997, the legislation only made the provisions regarding ordinary partnerships, namely partnerships in which all investors bore the unlimited joint responsibility and liability for business debts. However, owing to the exceedingly narrow range of adjustment in the "Business Partnership Law," the full implementation of its function was affected to a certain degree. Several new issues have emerged in the area of economics (经济生活); in addition to the development of public investments and risk investments, the professional service organization has set new requirements as to the structure of business partnership. For example, the "Business Partnership Law" did not stipulate a limited partnership system. It is of urgent necessity to the development of related professional service organizations that a limited liability partnership structure be provided to satisfy development needs. For this reason, it is necessary to revise much of the content of the "Business Partnership Law." The 23rd session of tenth NPC Standing Committee revised and approved the "Business Partnership Law of the People's Republic of China" on August 27, 2006.

The new "Business Partnership Law" has increased its provisions concerning the limited partnership system. It stipulates that the limited partner's rights and obligations, the business execution of limited partnership, as well as the special provisions of limited partnership other than the ordinary partnership, etc. It also increases the content concerning the limited partnership system, and determines the circumstances in which the legal personage may participate in the partnership. This

---

Standing Committee of the National People's Congress on Amending the Banking Supervision Law of the People's Republic of China," promulgated October 31st, 2006, http://www.lawinfochina.com/law/display.asp?id=5601&keyword=.

law has also made the corresponding revisions to other content areas, for example, "No wholly state-funded company, state-owned company, listed company, public-welfare-oriented institution or social organization may become a common partner."

## E. *"Amendment to the Criminal Law of the People's Republic of China (VI)"*

The Standing Committee of National People's Congress approved the "Amendment to the Criminal Law of the People's Republic of China (VI)" on June 29, 2006. The "Amendment to the Criminal Law of the People's Republic of China (VI)" contains 21 articles.

Except for Article 21 which is a provision regarding the time this amendment goes into effect, the rest are the revisions to the articles of criminal law. Among them, Articles 1–4 concern crimes of serious safety accidents in production; Articles 5–9 concern crimes of upsetting the company management order; Articles 10–16 concern crimes of upsetting the financial order; and Articles 17–20 concern crimes of upsetting the social management order and the arbitration order.

### 1. *Amendment Regarding the Crimes Concerning Serious Safety Accidents in Production*

Articles 1–4 of "Amendment to the Criminal Law of the People's Republic of China (VI)" amended Articles 134 & 135 of the original criminal law in the following ways; (a.) The central subject of the serious crime of safety accidents in the production process is amended as a common subject. (b.) The act of forcing other people to conduct risky operations by violating the relevant provisions is distinguished from an act in which anyone violates the provisions concerning the safety management in production or operations, and the former is assigned a more serious statutory sentence. (c.) "Facilities for safe labor" (劳动安全设施) is amended as "facilities or conditions for safe work" (安全生产设施或者安全生产条件), and the important provision establishing the crime of "not adopting measures to fix the hidden risk of accident after the departments concerned or the staff unit had voiced concerns" (经有关部门或者单位职工提出后，对事故隐患仍不采取措施) was cancelled. (d.) Acts in violation of any of the provisions concerning safety management in the organization of large-scale public activities resulting in serious casualties or any other serious consequences are considered crimes. Additionally acts resulting in safety accidents, where the individual obliged to report it fails to do so or makes a false report so that the rescue efforts are affected are also stipulated as crimes.

2. *Amendment to the Crime that Hinders Company and Business Management Order*

Articles 5–9 of the "Amendment to the Criminal Law of the People's Republic of China (VI)" amend the original crime of hindering the company and business management order, including: (a.) an amendment for important constructive conditions. The main body and the object are expanded as "any of the employees of any company or enterprise or any other entity;" adding "fails to disclose any other important information that shall be disclosed according to law" as the modes of conduct of Article 161 of the new Criminal Law. (b.) The act of falsely declaring bankruptcy so that the interests of the creditors or any other person are severely injured, as well as the violation of fiduciary duty to the company and to the manipulation of employment status within the listed company resulting in serious losses to the listed company are stipulated as crimes.

3. *Amendment to the Crime of Destruction of the Financial Management Order*

Articles 10–16 of the "Amendment to the Criminal Law of the People's Republic of China (VI)" amends the crime of destruction of the financial management order: (A.) the act of manipulating the price of securities or futures is expanded as the act of manipulating the securities or futures market, including manipulating the trading volume of securities or futures. The tenable important condition of the crime of "obtaining illegitimate benefits or transferring the risks" has been deleted. Limitation of the fines as "equal to the illegal earnings or up to five times their value" has been cancelled. Additionally in order to handle "extremely serious circumstances" (情节特别严重), it was established that the statutory sentence to "be sentenced for a fixed-term imprisonment of no less than five years and no more than ten years and will include a fine." (B.) The crime of illegally granting loans to relatives and the crime of illegally granting loans has been unified. Additionally, the illegal granting of loans to relatives has been assigned a heavier punishment than the crime of illegally granting loans. The provision for "the conditions of granting unsecured loans or secured loans to relatives at an advantage over similar loans for other borrowers" has been deleted. Also the provision has been added that "the amount in question be large" as one of the conditions of the crime existence. The statutory sentence has also undergone corresponding changes. (C.) It deletes "seeking personal gain" and "the illegal use of funds on short-term daily interest bearing loans and in the granting of loans" as important factors proving the perpetration of a crime, punishment is also increased for those situations. (D.) In Article 188(1) the circumstances with heavier punishment for the tenable condition of this crime, those which "cause larger losses" and the crime which "results in heavy losses" are deleted. Instead, it stipulates "serious circumstances" and "extremely serious circumstances," and these consequential offenses will be reclassified as circumstantial offenses (情节犯). (E.) The related crime of money laundering is expanded as including bribery and embezzlement, the destruction of finance management order, and financial fraud. (F.) Circumstances in which financial institutions, including the commercial banks or the stock exchange, violate their fiduciary duty or unlawfully utilize funds or any other entrusted client property, are defined as crimes if the circumstances are serious. This also includes swindling of loans, bill acceptances, and letters of credit and indemnity.

4. *Amendment to the Crime of Hindering the Social Management Order and the Arbitration Order*

Articles 16–20 of "Amendment to the Criminal Law of the People's Republic of China (VI)" amend the original criminal law: (A.) The act of organizing gambling parties or engaging in gambling as the main form of business is distinguished from the act of establishing or running any casino, and the two are assigned different statutory sentences. (B.) In Article 312 of the criminal law, criminal targets (犯罪对象) have been expanded to include those who benefit from criminal gains, and criminal behaviors have been expanded to include alternative methods of covering up or concealing perpetrations. The provision "in serious circumstances, the perpetrator will be sentenced to a fixed-term imprisonment of not less than three years but not more than seven years, and will be fined." (C.) The act of arranging for any disabled person or any minor below the age of 14 by force or coercion to beg is stipulated as a crime. Additionally, the act of undertaking the duties of arbitration according to law in a manner that intentionally goes against the facts or law or affects any wrongful ruling in the process of arbitration, if the circumstances are serious, is also stipulated as a crime.

### F. *"Compulsory Education Law of the People's Republic of China"*

The 22nd session of tenth NPC Standing Committee amended and approved "Compulsory Education Law of the People's Republic of China" on June 29, 2006. The "Compulsory Education Law" has been changed from original 18 articles to 63 articles.

The new "Compulsory Education Law" further determines public welfare and the obligation for compulsory education in China. It stipulates that the state adopt a funds guarantee mechanism for compulsory education. Explicit provisions as to the management protocol of compulsory education are also made, and various measures are adopted to guarantee all school-age children receive an equal compulsory education. This law further impels the implementation of a quality-oriented education, by determining the quality requirements of compulsory education. Also the law makes new provisions regarding the status and treatment of teachers at the compulsory education stage. At the same time, the new "Compulsory Education Law" also makes certain provisions regarding the structure of running a school.

### G. *"Audit Law of People's Republic of China"*

On February 28, 2006, the 20th session of tenth NPC Standing Committee approved "Decision of the Standing Committee of the National People's Congress on Amending the Audit Law of the People's Republic of China."[17]

#### 1. *The Scope of Audit Supervision is Adjusted*

The amendment decision expands "the state-owned financial institution" in the Audit Law into "the state-owned financial institution and the financial institution in which the state asset holds stock ownership." At the same time, it has amended "the national reconstruction project" as "construction projects that are invested in by the government or a state-owned business and construction projects that are invested in or mainly invested in by the government or state-owned businesses." Also a provision was added that, "The auditing organization carry on an audit or investigation into the reality and the validity of capital projects funds obtained by the entities of building, design, construction, reconnaissance, supervision and purchase and so on that are directly associated with construction projects in preceding clause." Also, "the institutions of the state" in the Audit Law are amended as "institutions with state assets."

---

[17] Standing Committee of the National People's Congress, "Decision of the Standing Committee of the National People's Congress on Amending the Audit Law of the People's Republic of China," promulgated February 28th 2006, http://www.lawinfochina.com/law/display.asp?id=4979&keyword=.

2. *The Audit Supervision System is Further Refined*

"Electronic data on government or financial revenues and expenditures stored and processed by computers and necessary computer technical documents" and "the specific circumstances of opening an account in a financial institution," were added to "the materials which the auditing organization requests of the entity under audit to provide" as stipulated in the Audit Law. Also the provision is added that, "The auditing organization is authorized to request the person in charge of the entity under audit to make a written pledge as to the authenticity and the integrity of the financial accounting data provided by the entity." In addition, two other provisions are added, "The auditing organization is authorized to inquire into accounts held in financial institutions by the unit under audit under the authorization of the chief of the auditing organization above the county-level." Additionally, it is included that "If the auditing organization can prove that an entity under audit deposits public money in the name of individuals, it shall be entitled to look into the deposits of the entity under audit in the name of individuals at the financial institution upon the approval of the person in-charge of the auditing organization of the people's government at or above the county level."

In addition, this law emphasizes the integration of audit supervision protocol, and it stipulates that "For the appointment and dismissal of the chief employee of the local auditing organization at any level of government, it is necessary to solicit the opinions of the auditing organization at the superior level in advance of any action." The audit law also makes concrete amendments to the legal status of the auditing organization's delegated agency; for example, it amends the expression "special audit delegate" (审计特派员) to "the delegated agency." (派出机构)

## III. *The Formulation of Administrative Rules and Regulations*

In 2006, the State Council altogether promulgated 23 administrative rules and regulations, and completed the amendment to 4 administrative rules and regulations. These newly promulgated administrative rules and regulations mainly involve five subjects, and they are: the protection and the management of natural resources, the expropriation system, social management in regards to security and sanitation etc., the protection of intellectual property and rural systems and other administrative rules and regulations.

### A. *Regarding the Protection and Management of Natural Resources*

#### 1. *"Regulations on the Protection of Great Wall"* (长城保护条例)[18]

In order to increase the protection of the Great Wall, and to standardize the activities that make use of the Great Wall, it was necessary to specially formulate administrative regulations that protected it in view of the outstanding problems regarding its protection according to the provisions of "Law on the Preservation of Cultural Relics." (文物保护法) On September 20, 2006, the State Council approved "Regulation on the Protection of Great Wall." This Regulation contains 31 articles, and its contents supplement and refine related systems and measures in view of Great Wall's particular characteristics and the outstanding problems regarding its protection according to the provisions of the "Law on Preservation of Cultural Relics," a measure which increases it capacity for operation. The protection and management of the Great Wall is implemented by sections, and the liability of local people's government is determined by the location of each section of the Great Wall. The law also stipulates the responsibilities of the entities that use the Great Wall, and sets up a security system to standardize the actions that make use of the Great Wall, as well as determines whether certain principles and conditions are maintained and required etc. in order to open up these sections of the Great Wall as visiting and sight-seeing areas.

#### 2. *"Administrative Regulations Regarding the Prevention and Treatment of the Pollution and Damage to the Marine Environment by Marine Engineering Construction Projects"* (防治海洋工程建设项目污染损害海洋环境管理条例)[19]

In order to implement the "Marine Environment Protection Law of the People's Republic of China" (海洋环境保护法)[20] well, the State Council approved the "Administrative Regulations on the Prevention and Treatment of Pollution and Damage to the Marine Environment

[18] Yuanhui People's Court Online, "Regulations on the Protection of the Great Wall," October 11th, 2006, http://www.lhfy.cn/law/zyfg/xzfg/5486.html.

[19] State Council, "Administrative Regulation on the Prevention and Treatment of the Pollution and Damage to the Marine Environment by Marine Engineering Construction Projects," promulgated September 19th, 2006 http://www.lawinfochina.com/law/display.asp?db=1&id=5649.

[20] Standing Committee of the National People's Congress, "Marine Environment Protection Law of the People's Republic of China, August 23rd, 1982 http://www.lawinfochina.com/law/display.asp?id=20.

by Marine Engineering Construction Projects" on August 30, 2006. This Regulation contains 59 articles, and its specific contents include environmental impact assessment, the prevention and treatment of the pollution by marine engineering construction, the management of pollutant discharge, the prevention and processing of pollution accidents, supervision inspection and relevant legal liabilities etc.

3. *"Regulations Regarding Designated Scenic and Historical Areas"* (风景名胜区条例)

Along with social and economic development, the "Provisional Regulations on the Management of Scenic and Historical Areas" promulgated in 1985 was unable to meet the requirements of managing designated scenic and historical areas (风景名胜区). For example, plan compilation and modification work etc. regarding designated scenic and historical areas failed to keep pace. Development was a focus, though ultimately protection for these areas was lacking. The established managerial structure was in disorder, and the power and responsibility system was unclear. The designated scenic and historical areas charged for use and employed an admission ticket system that was flawed. Additionally the regulations governing these areas were too theoretical and impractical in their operability. In order to practically solve these apparent problems, the State Council approved the "Regulations Regarding Designated Scenic and Historical Areas" on September 6, 2006. This Regulation contains 52 articles and 7 chapters, and stipulates the establishment, the layout, the protection, the use and management and the legal liabilities of landscape and famous sceneries, etc.

4. *"Ordinance on Yellow River Water Volume Regulation"* (黄河水量调度条例)

At present, the amount of development and use of Yellow River water resources has been critical, and the river is constantly in danger of running dry. The Yellow River contains a disproportionate amount of sand to water, uneven spatial distribution, an erratic and fluctuating water-table and many annual changes etc. The Yellow River's particular characteristics require the establishment of a managerial system and measures specific to the Yellow River's characteristics under the basic frame of water law. On July 5, 2006, the executive meeting of the State Council approved the "Ordinance on Yellow River Water Volume Regulation." This Ordinance contains 43 articles, and main contents include water allocation, water regulation, emergency regulation, supervision & management and legal liabilities etc.

In addition, in order to protect and manage the natural resources, the State Council also promulgated "Regulations of the People's Republic of China Regarding the Administration of the Import and Export of Endangered Wild Fauna and Flora." (中华人民共和国濒危野生动植物进出口管理条例)[21] (approved on April 12, 2006)

B. *Regarding the Expropriation System*

1. *"Interim Regulation of the People's Republic of China on Tobacco Leaf Tax"* (中华人民共和国烟叶税暂行条例)[22]

In 2005, the NPC Standing Committee abolished the "Regulations Concerning Agricultural Taxes." (农业税条例)[23] The agricultural taxes of agricultural special local products were originally levied according to the "Regulations Concerning Agricultural Taxes." The cancellation of these taxes meant that the agricultural taxes of agricultural special local products also had to be canceled. Thus, the levy of agricultural taxes on agricultural special local products, including tobacco leaf, also lost all legal basis. Ending the levy of agricultural taxes on tobacco leaf products would tremendously influence the local financial revenue of those areas producing tobacco leaf. According to the current financial system, the revenue from the agricultural taxes of tobacco leaf products is completely incorporated into the finance of the county or township; moreover this part of the revenue has a greater proportion in local financial revenues. Ending the levy of agricultural taxes on tobacco leaf special products could increase local finance difficulties to a certain degree, especially for those county or townships that produce tobacco leaf products. Therefore, the State Council promulgated the "Interim Regulation of the People's Republic of China on Tobacco Leaf Tax."

[21] State Council, "Regulation of the People's Republic of China on the Administration of the Import and Export of Endangered Wild Fauna and Flora," promulgated April 29th, 2006 http://www.lawinfochina.com/law/display.asp?db=1&id=5188&keyword=china.

[22] State Council, "Interim Regulation of the People's Republic of China on Tobacco Leaf Tax," April 28th, 2006 http://www.lawinfochina.com/law/display.asp?id=5155

[23] Food and Agriculture Organization of the United Nations ed. Gerard Ciparisse, "Multilingual Thesaurus on Land Tenure," (Rome: FAO, 2003).

2. *"Provisional Regulations of the People's Republic of China Regarding Vehicle and Ship Taxes"* (中华人民共和国车船税暂行条例)[24]

The "Provisional Regulations Governing the Vehicle and Vessel License Plate Tax" (车船使用牌照税暂行条例)[25] in 1951, employed a license plate tax in order to collect taxes from vehicle and vessels. The "Provisional Regulations of the People's Republic of China on Vehicle and Vessel Usage Tax" (车船使用税暂行条例)[26] in 1986, collected taxes on vehicle and vessel usage, but was not applicable to foreign investment businesses and the foreign businesses. Along with the development of a market economy and especially after China's WTO entry, practical problems concerning the two provisional regulations listed above developed emerged. For example, the two categories of domestic and foreign taxes did not conform to the requirements for a unified tax policy and for a simplified tax system and lacked the necessary means to monitor tax sources. Along with the economic development, the standard amount of the two categories of taxes was also lower. For these reasons, the State Council promulgated the "Provisional Regulations of the People's Republic of China for Taxes on Vehicles and Ships."

3. *"Regulations on Management of Water Usage Permits and Water Resource Charges"* (取水许可和水资源费征收管理条例)[27]

According to the amended water law of 2002, the water collection needed to reinforce the unified management and unified basin regulations in order to avoid local and departmental division in water resource management. At the same time, according to the provisions of the administrative permit law, the conditions and the procedure for water use permits needed to be further delineated in order to increase transparency in the water resource allocation process. However because water resource charges were not standardized, certain practical problems emerged, including differing water resource charges, an non-standardized

[24] "Provisional Regulations of the People's Republic of China for Tax on Vehicles and Ships," *China Shipbuilding,* Volume 2, 2007, http://ilib.cn/A-zghs200702005.html.

[25] Government Affairs Council, "Provisional Regulation Governing the Vehicle and Vessel License Plate Registration Tax," September 13th, 1951, http://www.lawinfochina.com/law/display.asp?id=1221.

[26] State Council, "Provisional Regulations of the People's Republic of China On Vehicle and Vessel Usage Tax," promulgated September 15th, 1986, http://www.lawinfochina.com/law/displayModeTwo.asp?id=1268.

[27] *Chinese Water Conservation and Irrigation* (中国水利), "Regulations on Management of Water Abstraction Licenses and Water Resources Charges," Volume 7, 2006, http://scholar.ilib.cn/A-zhonggsl200607007.html.

expropriation procedure, and unreasonable usage circumstances etc. In order to solve these problems, the State Council approved the "Regulations on Management of Water Usage Permits and Water Resources Charges" on January 24, 2006. This regulation contains 58 articles, and the contents mainly cover the application & acceptance procedure, the examination & the decision process for water usage, charges and use management, and the supervision and legal liabilities regarding water resources charges etc.

In addition, the State Council also promulgated "Measures on the Payment of Litigation Costs" (诉讼费用交纳办法)[28] (approved on December 8, 2006) and "Regulations on Land Requisition Compensation and Resettlement for Construction of Large and Medium-sized Water Conservancy and Hydropower Projects" (大中型水利水电工程建设征地补偿和移民安置条例) (approved on March 29, 2006), etc.

### C. *Regarding Social Management, Including Security and Sanitation etc.*

#### 1. *"Regulations on Firework and Firecracker Security Measures"* (烟花爆竹安全管理条例)

The production and sale of fireworks and firecrackers has become the leading industry and source of economic development in certain areas of China. The production of fireworks and firecrackers is a high risk and small scale industry that employs simple equipment and low-level technology, and runs on small high-risk investments. In recent years, as a result of the neglect of certain local authorities regarding firework and firecracker safety control, several safety accidents in this industry have occurred. After the Beijing municipality implemented "limited use instead of restriction" (禁改限) in regards to the firing of fireworks and firecrackers this year, approximately more than 170 cities divided into districts also followed suit or ceased regulation altogether. As a result, the requirements of the firework and firecracker market increased, as well as safety problems. In order to strengthen safety control of fireworks and firecrackers, prevent explosion accidents and safeguard the public security, personal safety and property security, the executive meeting of State Council approved the "Regulations on Firework and Firecracker Security Measures" on January 11, 2006. These Regulations contain

[28] State Council, "Measures on the Payment of Litigation Costs," promulgated December 19th, 2006, http://www.lawinfochina.com/Law/display.asp?id=5765&keyword=.

46 articles, and include provisions and liabilities regulating production safety, operation, transportation and the firing off of fireworks and firecrackers etc.

2. *"Regulations on the Safe Administration of Explosives for Civilian Use"* (民用爆炸物品安全管理条例)[29]

In 1984, the State Council promulgated and executed the "Regulations of People's Republic of China on the Safety Administration of Explosives for Civilian Use," regulations necessary for the legal management of explosives for civilian use. However in recent years, occasional safety accidents involving explosives for civilian use occurred. These occurrences warranted the revision of the original regulations and called for a revised safety management system in accordance with the new specifications and situation. At the same time, because safety management also involved the production, sale, purchase, transportation and blasting of explosives etc., the original regulations needed to be revised in order to further determine the safety management responsibilities of the concerned departments and businesses, and their concrete legal liabilities also needed to be further developed. In order to strengthen the safety management of explosives for civilian use, to prevent explosion accidents, and to safeguard the lives and property of citizens as well as their public security, an executive meeting of the State Council approved the "Regulations on the Safe Administration of Explosives for Civilian Use" on April 26, 2006. These regulations contain 55 articles, and include provisions regarding the production, sale and purchase, transportation, blasting and storage of explosives for civilian use and the correlative legal liabilities etc.

3. *"PRC Law on HIV/AIDS Prevention and Control"* (艾滋病防治条例)

In order to prevent and control the occurrence and spread of AIDS and to safeguard human health and the public health, the executive meeting of State Council approved the "PRC Law on HIV/AIDS Prevention and Control" on January 18, 2006 in accordance with existing law on the prevention and control of infectious diseases. This Law contains 63 articles, and includes provisions concerning propaganda and education, prevention and control, treatment and rescue, safeguarding measures

[29] Yuanhui Area Court Online, "Regulation on the Safety Administration of Explosives for Civilian Use," May 10th, 2006 http://www.lhfy.cn/law/zyfg/xzfg/5429.html.

and correlative legal liabilities etc. This law stipulates the responsibilities of all levels of government regarding AIDS prevention and control, and determines the rights and obligation of AIDS infected persons and AIDS patients. For example, it stipulates that, above county-level people's governments must provide free curatives of the AIDS virus to rural AIDS patients and impoverished urban AIDS patients. Free treatment and consultation to AIDS infected pregnant women must be provided to prevent mother-to-infant transmission of the AIDS virus. Those persons infected with the AIDS virus and AIDS patients must take the necessary protective measures to prevent the spread of infection to other people, and may not intentionally transmit AIDS in any manner.

In addition, the State Council also approved "Regulations on Management of Entertainment Venues" (娱乐场所管理条例)[30] (approved on January 18, 2006) etc.

### D. *Regarding the Protection of Intellectual Property*

#### 1. *"Regulations on the Protection of the Right to Transmit Information through the Network"* (信息网络传播权保护条例)

Along with the development of network technology, the transmission of individual's works, performances, and audio & video recordings through the information network is increasing exponentially. The question of how to adjust the relationships between individuals, the network service providers and professional users has become a question imperative to Internet development. The World Intellectual Property Organization approved the "WIPO Copyright Treaty"[31] and the "WIPO Performances and Phonograms Treaty"[32] in December, 1996. The Internet treaty endows individuals with the right to provide works to the public in a wired or wireless manner, and enables the public to obtain this work at an individually designated time and place. The Chinese copyright law defines this right as the right of information network transmission,

---

[30] CN Teacher, "Regulations on Management of Entertainment Venues," May 3rd 2007, http://www.cn-teacher.com/yyjy/flyy/flyy1/200705/209251.html.

[31] "World Intellectual Property Organization Copyright Treaty," Xinhuanet, December 20th, 1996, http://news.xinhuanet.com/ziliao/2007–06/14/content_6240441.htm.

[32] "World Intellectual Property Organization Performances and Phonograms Treaty," Xinhuanet, December 20th, 1996, http://news.xinhuanet.com/ziliao/2007–06/14/content_6240453.htm.

and the State Council has been requested to formulate concrete protection measures for this right. Therefore, in order to protect the right of information network transmission of the copyright owner, the performer and the maker of audiovisual products, and to encourage the production and transmission of the works which are beneficial to the construction of socialist spiritual civilization and material civilization, according to the "Copyright Law of the People's Republic of China,"[33] the executive meeting of State Council approved the "Regulations on the Protection of Information Transmission through the Network" on May 10, 2006 and the regulation contains 27 articles.

2. *"Regulations of the People's Republic of China Concerning the Administration of Achievements in Surveying and Mapping"* (中华人民共和国测绘成果管理条例)

In 1989, the State Council promulgated the "Provisions Concerning the Administration of Achievements in Surveying and Mapping," (测绘成果管理规定) which played a vital role in strengthening the management of surveying and mapping achievements and in promoting the application of these achievements. Also in conjunction with social development, the investment in the field of surveying and mapping had multiplied on many levels. The industry achievements need to be coordinated and their preservation and use raises new demands. Simultaneously the actual form of surveying and mapping products has transformed from simply a map form to a digitized product of many different incarnations. Also the original management methods are already not suitable to present developments. In order to strengthen the management of surveying and mapping achievements, to maintain the national security, to promote the use of these, and to meet the requirements of economic development, construction and the development of national defense and society, in accordance with the "Surveying and Mapping Law of the People's Republic of China," the executive meeting of State Council approved the "Regulations of the People's Republic of China concerning the Administration of Achievements in Surveying and Mapping" on May 17, 2006. These regulations contain 32 articles, and include provisions regarding remittance, management, storage and the usage of surveying and mapping achievements, as well

[33] "Copyright Law of the People's Republic of China," Xinhuanet, December 20th, 1996, http://www.cn-teacher.com/yyjy/flyy/flyy1/200705/209841.html.

the verification and announcement of important geo information data and correlative legal liabilities.

E. *Regarding the Rural System*

1. *"Regulations on the Five Guarantees in Support of Rural Areas"* (农村五保供养工作条例)

In 1994, the State Council promulgated the "Regulations on the Five Guarantees in Support of Rural Areas." However with advancements in rural tax reform, the rural areas had canceled the village deductions and rural unified costs, though in the "Regulations on the Five Guarantees in Support of Rural Areas" promulgated in 1994, the capital related to the five guarantees was "listed as expenses from the village's deductions and rural unified costs" which was unsuitable for meeting actual demands, additionally the "Regulations on the Five Guarantees in Support of Rural Areas" faced new situations and new problems. In order to complete the work of supporting the rural five guarantees, to safeguard the typical rural lifestyle, and to promote the development of a rural social security system, the executive meeting of State Council approved the "Regulations on Five Guarantees Supporting in Rural Areas" on January 11, 2006, and the original Regulation was abolished. The new regulation contained 26 articles, and included provisions regarding the object, content and form of support, as well as supervision and correlative legal liabilities etc.

2. *"National Agricultural Census Regulations"* (全国农业普查条例)

The national agricultural census is not only a large-scale operation involving a large amount of investigation work, the participation of various government departments, and high-levels of specification; it also entails many investigation issues, and the coordination of complex social systems. In order to scientifically and effectively organize and implement the national agricultural census, to safeguard the accuracy and timeliness of the agricultural census data, according to "Statistics Law of the People's Republic of China," (中华人民共和国统计法)[34] the State Council approved the "National Agricultural Census Rule."

[34] Standing Committee of the National People's Congress, "Statistics Law of the People's Republic of China," promulgated December 8th, 1983, http://www.lawinfochina.com/law/display.asp?id=37.

This rule contains 42 articles, and includes provisions regarding the object, scope and contents of an agricultural census, the organization and implementation of an agricultural census, data processing and quality control, data announcement, materials management, development and application and citations and punishments etc.

### F. *Other Administrative Rules and Regulations*

1. *"Regulations of the People's Republic of China on the Administration of Foreign-funded Banks"* (中华人民共和国外资银行管理条例)[35]

Along with China's WTO entry, the quantity of foreign-funded bank organizations has greatly increased in China, and the types of businesses and the regions of management are constantly expanding. In accordance with international commitments, China will open the Renminbi businesses (人民币业务) of Chinese citizens within the country to foreign-funded banks before December 11, 2006. Additionally regional restrictions for business operation and other un-circumspect restrictions would be cancelled, and national treatment (国民待遇) would be granted to foreign-funded banks. In order to adapt to the needs of increased international involvement and economic development, to strengthen and refine the supervision and administration of foreign-funded banks, and to promote a stable banking operation, an executive meeting of the State Council approved the "Regulations on the Administration of Foreign-funded Banks" on November 8, 2006. The original "Regulations of the Peoples Republic of China Governing Financial Institutions with Foreign Capital" (外资金融机构管理条例)[36] was abolished at the same time. The new regulations contain 73 articles, and include provisions regarding the establishment and registration of foreign-funded banks, the business scope, the supervision and administration, the termination and liquidation, and correlative legal liabilities and so on.

---

[35] Mingxin Zhang, "Regulations of the People's Republic of China for the Administration of Foreign Banks, http://www.eastwestlaw.com/c_legis/show.asp?id=244.

[36] CN-Teacher, "Regulations of the Peoples Republic of China Governing Financial Institutions with Foreign Capital," May 3rd, 2007, http://www.cn-teacher.com/yyjy/flyy/flyy1/200705/209648.html.

2. *"The Rule of Maintaining Local Records"* (地方志工作条例)
The maintenance of local records is a fundamental cultural undertaking which serves to connect the future and the past, and which is beneficial to later generations. However, at this new historic stage, the keeping of local records has been unorganized and compiled only according to past administrative protocol. In addition, the work of compiling local records has been chaotic because of the lack of relevant nationwide laws and regulations. In order to maintain, further develop and promote the outstanding cultural traditions of the Chinese nation, to comprehensively objectively and systematically compile the local records, to scientifically and practically develop and use the local records and to emphasize the function of these records promoting the development of an economic society, the State Council promulgated the "Local Records Work Rule." This Rule contains 22 articles.

In addition, the State Council also promulgated the "Regulations on Compulsory Traffic Accident Liability Insurance for Motor Vehicles," (机动车交通事故责任强制保险条例)[37] the "Regulations on Organizational Management of Public Security Organizations," (公安机关组织管理条例) and the "Provisions on the Reporting Activities Conducted in China by Foreign Journalists during the Beijing Olympic Games and the Preparatory Period" (北京奥运会及其筹备期间外国记者在华采访规定)[38] and so on.

During the formulation of administrative rules and regulations, the State Council also amended partial contents of 4 administrative rules and regulations according to actual social actual demands. The administrative rules and regulations amended are the "Regulations of the People's Republic of China on the Control of Nuclear Exports," (中华人民共和国核出口管制条例)[39] the "Provisions on Administrative Penalties against Price-related Unlawful Practices," (价格违法行为行政处罚规定) the "Regulations on the Administration of Cotton Quality

[37] State Council, "Regulation on Compulsory Traffic Accident Liability Insurance for Motor Vehicles," promulgated March 21st, 2006, http://www.lawinfochina.com/law/display.asp?id=5084&keyword=.

[38] State Council, "Provisions on the Reporting Activities in China Conducted by Foreign Journalists during the Beijing Olympic Games and the Preparatory Period," November 1st, 2006, http://www.lawinfochina.com/law/display.asp?id=5708&keyword=.

[39] State Council, "Decision of the State Council on Amending the Regulation of the People's Republic of China on the Control of Nuclear Export," promulgated November 9th, 2006 http://www.lawinfochina.com/Law/displayModeTwo.asp?id=5740&keyword=.

Supervision," (棉花质量监督管理条例)[40] and the "Interim Regulations of the People's Republic of China on City and Town Land Use Tax" (中华人民共和国城镇土地使用税暂行条例).[41]

## IV. *Legislation Evaluations and Predictions*

Legislation work in 2006 was based on the practical demands of Chinese society and the process of strengthening legislation work. In addition, legislation was extensive whether it concerned the formulation of laws or the formulation of administrative rules and regulations. Overall, compared with former years, the legislation in 2006 made great progress in the areas of legislation, technology and direction.

### A. *The Promotion of Legislation Technology and the Theoretical Improvement of Legislative Structure*

In 2006, further developments were made in the area of legislation technology. The systematization of laws and regulations was carefully considered (in independent legislation), while the connections and the division between laws and regulations were no longer overlooked. For example, much of the content of the "Law of the People's Republic of China on the Supervision of Standing Committees of People's Congresses at Various Levels" (各级人大常委会监督法)[42] correspond with the Legislation Law and the "Organic Law of the Local People's Congresses and Local People's Governments at Various Levels" (地方各级人民代表大会和地方各级人民政府组织法) and so on, thereby maintaining the criteria of internal unity. The "Law of the People's Republic of China on Agricultural Product Quality Safety" also coordinates with other laws concerning quality supervision and so on. A good

---

[40] State Council, "Decision of the State Council on Amending the Regulation on the Administration of Cotton Quality Supervision," promulgated July 4th, 2006, http://www.lawinfochina.com/law/displayModeTwo.asp?id=5348.

[41] State Council, "Decision of the State Council on Amending the Interim Regulations of the People's Republic of China on City and Town Land Use Tax," promulgated December 31st, 2006 http://www.lawinfochina.com/Law/display.asp?id=5767&keyword=.

[42] Standing Committee of the National People's Congress, "Law of the People's Republic of China on the Supervision of Standing Committees of People's Congresses at Various Levels," promulgated August 27th, 2006, http://www.lawinfochina.com/law/display.asp?id=5421&keyword=.

part of the legislation promulgated in 2006 exhibited an adjustment to the standards regarding the current social circumstances. For example, even if the "Regulations on the Protection of Information Transmission through the Network" is a legislative product of the internet era, it still reflects the requirements of actual societal changes in society which merit the augmentation of the inadequacies of previous laws. This is also the case of laws such as the "Law on the Protection of Minors" and the "Law on Eradicating Money Laundering" etc. This structure of these newly formulated or amended laws and administrative rules and regulations also tends towards a more rationalist ideology, and no longer solely emphasizes the right of government power. The standards also emphasize the definition and protection of citizens' rights while also promoting the authority of public rights.

### B. *Legislation that Emphasizes the Detail and Strengthens Legal Liability*

Previously, much of the legislation promulgated tended towards a macroscopic and abstract view, which resulted in a lack of operability and practicality in certain laws. The legislation of 2006 was based on basic demands at the macroscopic level; and the laws and the administrative rules and regulations all strengthened the standards of legal liability, while emphasizing the operability of the laws on a microscopic level. For example, they emphasized the concrete implementation of legislation responsibilities. This is not only advantageous to the implementation of legislation ideas and content, but also it has also played a vital role in the protection of citizen's rights. For example, in determining supervision authority, the "Banking Supervision Law" focuses more on the implementation of specific responsibilities undertaken in the supervision of illegal acts; and the "Compulsory Education Law" emphasizes the importance of strengthening the legal liabilities of the responsible government and education departments. Additionally recent legislation has determined procedures and connections through the specific and clear standards, and no longer makes only abstract and general provisions. For example, the "Law on Eradicating Money Laundering" has stipulated that, in the investigation of questionable transactions, there shall be no fewer than 2 investigators, who will show their legal certificates as well as the investigation notice produced by the correlative administrative department of the State Council or by its proxy organization at the provincial level. A transcript will be made for all inquiries and will be checked by the person being interrogated.

All of these examples indicate the fact that current legislation emphasizes concrete standards at the microscopic level which has resulted in specific and practical legislation.

### C. *Emphasizing Awareness of Legal Rights and Decreasing the Role of Management*

In 2006, legal rights were the focus of the general legislation activity. Even in the standardizing of government authority, the ultimate goal was the protection of citizen's rights. For example, the "Compulsory Education Law" stipulates that "A teacher shall, during the course of education and teaching, treat his students equally, pay attention to the individual differences, teach students on the basis of their aptitude and shall promote the full development of students." One of key contents of the "Business Partnership Law" is both the establishment of a limited partnership system and the establishment of protection for limited partnership rights. Simultaneous to the growing emphasis on legal rights in legislation, the role of management in laws and the administrative rules and regulations has lessened. This legislation direction reflects the necessities of a legal system in the era of human rights. While legislation work for2006 has ended, legislation work for 2007 has just begun.

According to the legislation plan for 2007 to the beginning of 2008, the number of effective current laws in China will reach 230, which will form the initial stage of a more complete socialist legal system of standards and will lay a solid legal foundation for building a harmonious society.

In looking at the content of legislation, the legislation plan in 2007 has strengthened social legislation while refining economic legislation, such as the "Law on Emergency Responses," (突发事件应对法) the "Urban and Rural Planning Law" (城乡规划法) and the "Employment Promotion Law" (就业促进法) and so on. Simultaneously, in 2007, legislation will further improve the democratic and scientific nature of the legislation process, in order to guarantee improvement in the quality and level of legislation. For example, while soliciting written opinions regarding the draft laws, the opinions of the deputies and all levels of society will be directly listened to through special investigation and study and through the holding of forums, deliberation meetings and evidentiary hearing etc. Additionally the lessening of formality for all kinds of legislation participation forms is guaranteed, which in turn should guarantee scientific and democratic legislation, and enhance the quality of the reviewing and revising of drafts. Serious problems and various opinions involved in the draft laws will be thoroughly investigated and studied, and full deliberation will be conducted, related opinions will be earnestly heard and legislation will be submitted to a vote after it conforms sufficiently to China's national condition.

# COMBINING PUNISHMENT WITH LENIENCY, IMPLEMENTING TEMPORARY MEASURES AND RADICAL MEASURES: AN EXPLORATION OF THE CRIMINAL "RULE OF LAW"

Liu Renwen[1] and Zhou Zhenjie[2]

In 2006, the national public order was stable. The quantity of registered criminal offense cases of the public security organizations was equal to those of 2005, a total of 4.653 million cases. The quantity of registered criminal offense cases in 15 provinces, municipalities and autonomous regions had fallen. The percentage drop of criminal cases in 5 provinces and municipalities was over 5% in Qinghai, Chongqing, Sichuan, Guangdong, Shandong and so; the drop was 5.1%, 5.7%, 5.7%, 5.8% and 6.8% respectively. Serious violent offenses also decreased in varying degrees throughout the year. The national public security organization altogether registered 532,000 cases concerning serious violent offenses, such as arson, illegal use of explosives, murder and so on. This was a reduction of 22,000 cases compared to 2005, a drop of 4%. In addition, in 2006, the crimes of "pornography, gambling, drug abuse and trafficking" had also reached their lowest point in recent years. The national public security organizations altogether registered 113,000 cases of "pornography, gambling, drug abuse and trafficking," a reduction of 22,000 cases compared to 2005, and a drop of 16.2%. Finally, in 2006, underage crime also decreased markedly. Of the criminal offenders captured, 679,000 were 25 years old or below, a reduction of 40,000 people compared to 2005, and a drop of 5.5%, the largest decrease in recent years. The proportion of underage offenders within the total percentage of criminal offenders dropped from 46.8% in 2005 to 43.5%.[3]

---

[1] Liu Renwen is a researcher at the Law Research Institute of Chinese Academy of Social Sciences.

[2] Zhou Zhenjie is a doctoral student at the Law Research Institute of the Chinese Academy of Social Sciences.

[3] The Ministry of Public Security, "Criminal Offenses had 5 Characteristics in 2006 and Crimes Concerning Pornography, Gambling and Drug Abuse and Trafficking Reached their Lowest Level," http://news3.xinhuanet.com/video/2007–02/06/content_5702631.htm, (February 24, 2007).

The criminal 'rule of law' achieved new progress in 2006. First, the NPC Standing Committee reviewed and approved the "Amendment to the Criminal Law of the People's Republic of China (VI)" ( 刑法修正案(六)) on June 29 to amend the crimes of public security, destruction of the socialist market economic order, infringement on individual citizen's democratic and individual rights, disruption of social administration and bribery and embezzlement. Additionally focus on revision of charges and adjustments to statutory sentences were carried out. Next, the supreme judicial organizations jointly or alone approved certain important judicial interpretations. For example, the Supreme People's Court and the Supreme People's Procuratorate jointly promulgated the "Provisions on Certain Issues concerning the Court Trial Procedures of the Second Instance of those Cases Involving the Death Penalty (for Trial Implementation)" (关于死刑第二审案件开庭审理程序若干问题的规定(试行))[4] in September, 2006.

Additionally, both entities jointly approved "Interpretations of Certain Issues of Specific Application in the Handling of Criminal Cases Concerning the Stealing of Oil or Gas and the Destruction of Oil-gas Equipment" (关于办理盗窃油气、破坏油气设备等刑事案件具体应用法律若干问题的解释) in November. The Supreme People's Procuratorate also promulgated the "Provisions on Standards for Cases of Crimes of Infringement through Malfeasance" (关于渎职侵权犯罪案件立案标准的规定) in July, 2006. And, the Supreme People's Court promulgated "Interpretations of Certain Issues Concerning the Specific Application of Law in the Trial of Criminal Cases Involving Environmental Pollution" (关于审理环境污染刑事案件具体应用法律若干问题的解释)[5] in July, 2006. Additionally the "Interpretations on the Concrete Application of Law in the Trial of Criminal Cases of Smuggling (II)" (关于审理走私刑事案件具体应用法律若干问题的解释(二))[6] and the "Interpretations on Some Issues Concerning the

[4] Supreme People's Court and the Supreme People's Procuratorate, "Provisions on Some Issues concerning the Court Trial Procedures for the Second Instance of the Cases Involving Death Penalty (for Trial Implementation)," promulgated on September 21st, 2006, http://www.lawinfochina.com/law/display.asp?id=5573&keyword=.

[5] Supreme People's Court, "The Interpretation of the Supreme People's Court on Some Issues Concerning the Specific Application of Law in the Trial of Criminal Cases Involving Environmental Pollution," promulgated July 21st, 2006 http://www.lawinfochina.com/law/display.asp?id=5397&keyword=.

[6] Supreme People's Court, "Interpretations of the Supreme People's Court on the Concrete Application of Law in the Trial of Criminal Cases of Smuggling (II)," promulgated November 14th, 2006 http://www.lawinfochina.com/law/display.asp?id=5676&keyword=.

Specific Application of Law in the Trial of Criminal Cases Involving Minors" (关于审理未成年人刑事案件具体应用法律若干问题的解释)[7] were promulgated in November. These provisions made the registration and prosecution of related criminal cases, the applicability of punishment and the application of punishment more detailed. Finally, the judicial departments implemented the criminal policy of combining punishment with leniency in a positive manner, developed special administration work regarding commercial bribery and so on, and investigated and prosecuted a series of major criminal cases. For example, the counterfeit drug case of the Second Pharmaceutical Limited Company (齐二药), Heilongjiang Province; the case of judge corruption in Fuyang, Anhui Province as well as the case of social security funds in Shanghai and so on.

This report discusses several important events in the area of criminal legislation in 2006, in order to approximately describe the basic condition of criminal "rule of law" in that year.

## I. *The Era of Combining Punishment with Leniency: Using Leniency to Support Punishment*

After the Fourth Plenary Session of 16th Central Committee of the CCP put forward the concept of "establishing a socialist harmonious society" in 2004, and the sixth Plenary Session of 16th Central Committee of the CCP held in October, 2006 made a special comprehensive effort to establish a socialist harmonious society, and determined that the criminal policy of combining punishment with leniency was an important part of this initiative. The "Resolution of the Central Committee of the CCP on Major Issues Regarding the Building of a Harmonious Socialist Society" (中共中央关于构建社会主义和谐社会若干重大问题的决定)[8] approved in the Sixth Plenary Session of the CCP required "the implementation of a criminal judicial policy combining punishment with leniency, the reformation of the legal system in regards to minors,

[7] Supreme People's Court, "Interpretation of the Supreme People's Court on Some Issues Concerning the Specific Application of Law in the Trial of Criminal Cases Involving Minors," promulgated January 11th, 2006 http://www.lawinfochina.com/law/display.asp?id=4916&keyword=.

[8] Network of Social System Engineering, "Resolution on Major Issues Regarding the Building of a Harmonious Socialist Society," October 11th, 2006, http://60.10.6.113/sseweb/ShowArticle.asp?ArticleID=1512.

and the establishment of positive community correction." Hereafter, the National Working Conference for Politics and Law held on 27~28 November proposed once more that, in building harmonious society, all levels of political and law institutions should be capable at all times of preventing and reducing crime using the criminal judicial policy of combining punishment with leniency.

In the fourth session of tenth National People's Congress held before this, the reports of the Supreme People's Procuratorate and the Supreme People's Court had also separately indicated that the criminal policy of combining punishment with leniency was a basic policy of current judicial work. The report of the Supreme People's Procuratorate pointed out that, earnestly implementing a criminal policy of combining punishment with leniency should maintain divergent approaches: to firmly punish serious criminal offenses, and to prudently arrest and prosecute minors, first offenders, casual offenders and negligent offenders with subjectively minor malicious intent and those who have committed slight criminal offenses. In those cases where arrest is not necessary, offenders should not be arrested. And in those cases where prosecution is not necessary, offenders should not be prosecuted. The report of the Supreme People's Court explicitly expressed that, the criminal policy of combining punishment with leniency must be maintained in 2006 in regards to those offenders condemned to death for circumstances of lenient or lesser punishment or dispensable immediate execution, should be given a stay of execution or life imprisonment. Those offenders with criminal infringements of lesser punishment, mitigation or penalty below the minimum statutory prescription and remitting punishment should be given lenient punishment according to law.

The criminal policy of combining punishment with leniency is the proper ideology of a socialist harmonious society, and is also an inevitable requirement of establishing such a society. This policy symbolizes the significant transformation of penalty protocol from a focus on punishment and retribution to a focus on punishment, education and correction.

### A. *The Manifestation of a Criminal Policy of Combining Punishment with Leniency*

In 2006, the criminal policy of combining punishment with leniency was promoted to the strategic level. At the criminal legislation stage, taking the "Amendment to the Criminal Law of the People's Republic of China (VI)" as an example, "punishment" was manifested as a rapid response to the social reality, and amendment and legislation was made to corresponding legal provisions or revisions of defined crimes.

Expanding the scope of criminal punishment and increasing statutory sentencing, increasing the strength of punishment or increasing new crimes, will bring those lacking legal statutes into the overall effort of revision of the criminal code. For example, safety accidents have occurred frequently in practice and have resulted in heavy casualties. In order to severely punish acts of violation of safety standards in production, Article 134 of the "Amendment to the Criminal Law of the People's Republic of China (VI)" implemented an amendment to the original Criminal Law that specifically emphasizes "Where anyone forces any other person to conduct risky operations by violating the relevant provisions so that any serious casualty or any other serious consequence is caused, he shall be sentenced to a fixed-term imprisonment of not more than five years or detention. If the circumstances are extremely severe, he shall be sentenced to a fixed-term imprisonment of five years or more." It deletes the contents of the original Article 135 "after the departments concerned or the unit staff has proposed amendments regarding the hidden risk of accident and they are still not fixed."

Additionally, the amendment stipulates that "When the facilities or conditions for safe work fail to meet the relevant provisions of the state so that any serious casualty or any other serious consequence is caused, the persons-in-charge who are held to be directly responsible and other directly liable persons shall be sentenced to a fixed term imprisonment of no more than three years or detention. If the circumstances are particularly severe, he shall be sentenced to a fixed term imprisonment of not less than three years but not more than seven years." This amendment has simplified the important constructive conditions of crime, and has expanded the scope of punishment. Moreover, the legislation aimed at the prevention of the organization of minors to beg, and the intentional harming of minors in forcing them to beg, the "Amendment to the Criminal Law of the People's Republic of China (VI)," increases the crimes related to this act, and stipulates that "Where anyone organizes any disabled person or any minor below the age of 14 by force or coercion to beg, he shall be sentenced to a fixed term imprisonment of not more than three years or detention, and shall be fined. If the circumstances are serious, he shall be sentenced to a fixed term imprisonment of not less than three years not more than seven years, and shall be fined."

In the "Amendment to the Criminal Law of the People's Republic of China (VI)," "leniency" was manifested in the consideration by legal organizations of the situation, the decriminalization of certain acts based on their level of social harmfulness in accordance with humanitarianism and the criminal policy, and the deliberation of these acts using a non-criminal method such as administrative penalties and economic penalties and so on. For example, the act of illicitly identifying the sex of a fetus had been included in the draft of the "Amendment to the Criminal Law of the People's Republic of China (VI)." However, when carrying out the third consideration of the draft, the NPC Standing Committee decided to remove this provision for further study and argumentation, which was correct. Because of the fact that "Presently, the act of artificially terminating a pregnancy because of fetal sex identification mainly occurs in rural areas, which reflects both the feudal idea of a man being superior to woman held in these areas and the actual problems that parents are dependent on a son for support in their later years, it is difficult for legal settlement of this issue to be dependent on criminal law. Moreover, some laws, such as the "Population and Family Planning Law" (计划生育法)[9] and others have stipulated that medical personnel who illicitly perform identification of the sex of fetus will have their licenses revoked by the authorities that issued it. If these provisions can be effectively carried out, this would be sufficient to deter a medical worker to not engage in this act." Moreover "the crimes included in criminal law consider causality between the acts and their consequences, but there is no inevitable causality between the embryo sex identification and induced abortions. For example, many urban spouses undergo procedures to identify the sex of the fetus out of a desire to know their baby's sex not out of a desire to abort. Even if, in rural areas, some spouses verify the sex of the fetus for the purpose of giving birth to a boy, the direct antecedents should be the act of seeking medical help and the medical personnel performing the abortion, and the cause should not be the identification of the sex of the fetus,"[10] therefore, decriminalizing fetal sex identification, and not

---

[9] Congressional-Executive Commission on China, "The Population and Family Planning Law of the People's Republic of China," http://www.cecc.gov/pages/newLaws/familyPlanningLaw.php.

[10] Liu Renwen, "Temporary Suspension of Punishment for Illicit Embryo Sex Identification Manifests the Principle of Cautious Punishment" http://www.iolaw.org.cn/showarticle.asp? Id=1860 (January 22, 2007).

implementing the penalties is exactly the practical manifestation of "being lenient when necessary." (当宽则宽)

At the criminal justice stage, the criminal judicial policy for minors also manifests the ideology of combining punishment with leniency. The aspect of "punishment" was manifested through legislation interpretations, and it designated some of the most serious crimes as crimes that can be prosecuted in the case of underage offenders. Article 17 (2) of 1997 Criminal Law stipulated that, "A person who has reached the age of fourteen but not the age of eighteen who commits the crimes of intentionally killing another or intentionally injuring another, to cause serious injury or death, and the crimes of rape, robbery, drug trafficking, arson, destruction with explosives, and poisoning shall all bear criminal responsibility." In practice, the above 8 acts were understood as concrete crime before, but in 2002, in view of the tendency for underage crime as well as the consequences of other serious underage crimes being more serious than these eight crimes, and in order to strengthen the deterrent of legal penalties and meet the demand of practice, "A Reply to the Scope Question on Legal Responsibilities which a Person who has Reached the Age of Fourteen but not the Age of Eighteen Should Bear" (关于已满十四周岁不满十六周岁的人承担刑事责任范围问题的答复意见) was approved by the NPC Standing Committee in 2002. This reply stipulated that, the 8 crimes mentioned in Article 17(2) of the criminal law provision referred to concrete criminal acts but not the concrete charges of these crimes. "Intentionally killing another person or intentionally injuring another person" as stipulated in Article 17 of the Criminal Law referred to the situation in which a person intentionally committed homicide and/or injury and inflicted serious injury and/or death to another person. In this case, the offender should bear the legal responsibilities of their acts. This only delineates that a person who has intentionally committed the crime of homicide or the crime of willful and malicious injury should bear legal responsibilities, but does not indicate that legal responsibility should be born for the kidnapping and killing of hostages. In the judicial practice a person who has reached the age of fourteen but not the age of eighteen who kills a hostage after kidnapping, swindles and sells woman and children and intentionally inflicts serious injury or death must be investigated and bear legal responsibilities for their acts according to the criminal law.

In the process of maintaining a stance of "punishment" and expanding the scope of legal responsibility for minors, the Supreme People's

Court's judicial interpretations as well as some practices, have also maintained a stance of "leniency" towards underage offenders. This was manifested in the "Interpretation on Some Issues Concerning the Specific Application of Law in the Trial of Criminal Cases Involving Minors" (关于审理未成年人刑事案件具体应用法律若干问题的解释) promulgated by the Supreme People's Court in November, 2006. This interpretation not only made detailed provisions regarding the scope of legal responsibilities to be borne by minors but also made provisions in favor of minors in some penalty systems, such as the reprieve of application and the release of probation and so on. For example, according to Article 6 of the interpretation, if a person who has reached the age of 14 but not the age of 16 occasionally has sex with a girl under the age of 14 and does not cause serious consequences, the act will not be considered a crime. Article 9 stipulates that, if a person who has reached the age of 16 but not the age of 18 commits the crime of theft less than three times and the amount of theft is less than the standard for a "comparatively large amount" (数额较大), and if he faithfully confesses all thefts and returns the stolen money and property, and if he played a subordinate or assistant role or was coerced in the joint theft or has any other negligible circumstances, this will not be considered a crime. If a person who has reached the age of 16 but not the age of 18 does not accomplish or suspends the crime of theft, his act may not be considered a crime. Moreover, according to Article 12 of this interpretation, if the offender has committed different criminal acts before and after reaching the age of 18, criminal acts committed before will be given a lesser punishment or mitigation of punishment below the minimum statutory prescript according to law. If the offender has committed the same criminal acts before and after reaching the age of 18, it should be considered suitable to award a lesser punishment or mitigation of punishment below the minimum statutory prescript for those crimes committed before reaching the age of 18.

### B. *The Implementation of a Criminal Policy Combining Punishment with Leniency*

In 2006, the criminal policy of combining punishment with leniency touched on various aspects of criminal "rule of law." In this article we will analyze its effect on criminal legislation and the criminal judicial system.

In the area of criminal legislation, certain crimes with a higher rate of occurrence and which cause greater harm may be considered for revisions of criminal charges, expansion of punishment, a suitable increase of certain types of punishments and an increase of punishment intensity. For example, Article 338 of the Criminal Law stipulates only that those crimes of serious environmental pollution accidents resulting in "major environment pollution, heavy losses to public and private property, or grave consequences of personal deaths and injuries" constitute crimes. However, in recent years major environmental pollution accidents have occurred frequently and the ecological environment has steadily declined. Obviously, such provisions were insufficient to deter offenders. Therefore, the condemnatory baseline should be raised, namely, changing it from a consequential offense into a potential damage offense, or even a behavioral offense. The constitution of a crime needn't cause corresponding serious consequences, but only needs to cause the danger of possibly serious consequences. In the case of the latter, for certain units (单位) committing economic offenses, the Criminal Law does not stipulate the punishment against competence, but only stipulates a pecuniary penalty. However, even in Article 9 of the "Amendment to the Criminal Law of the People's Republic of China (VI)," the provision regarding the manipulation of a listed company to commit a crime only stipulates the set term of imprisonment and the pecuniary penalty. As for the individuals or units of companies operating on the market that possess tens or hundreds of millions in capitol, these few fines are negligible and are completely lacking as deterrents. Therefore, how to increase the punishments against competence should be considered as well as how to deprive the qualifications of those individuals or units who commit similar criminal acts and who are engaged in business.

At the same time that "punishment" is implemented, "leniency" may also be carried out in the following ways. First, in regards to certain crimes, amending facts about a crime and reducing the scope of punishment may be considered. For example, according to the provision of Article 310 of the Criminal Law, which states when parents, children and spouses mutually protect each other from investigation, they also commit the crime of harboring criminals. Additionally, this offense is carries a lesser charge or criminal consequence and restriction. Even so, as the most basic cell of society, the family plays an integral role in maintaining social order and promoting social development. The harboring behaviors of parents, children and spouses reflect a mutual trust, which is advantageous to guarantee the stability of the family. Therefore, in the criminal policy for ordinary crimes, as long as it does not cause serious consequences or have serious implications, the mutual harboring of parents, children and spouses should be considered decriminalized. Second, the statutory sentences of certain crimes were adjusted and lessened. For example, the Criminal Law set the death penalty as punishment for many economic crimes and capital punishment associated with economic crime is certainly inappropriate. Therefore, abolishing the death penalty for economic crimes should be put to the agenda of study and legislation. Third, it has stipulated the abolition of a system of crime records and the institution of a system for the rehabilitation of rights. After punishment is executed for a certain number of years, the offender's crime record should be abolished to create favorable conditions for the offender's education and employment, especially in the case of minors. Fourth, in view of specific crimes or offenders, it stipulates non-imprisonment punishment such as community correction and charitable labor and so on.

Implementing the criminal judicial policy of combining punishment with leniency should pay great attention to aiding "punishment" through "leniency." First, at the pre-trial stage, the custody rate must be greatly reduced, and the prosecution rate should also be suitably reduced. Based on the "presumption of innocence," the "International Covenant on Civil and Political Rights"[11] explicitly stipulates that, "It shall not be the general rule that persons awaiting trial shall be detained in custody, but release may be subject to guarantees for trial appearance, or at any other stage of the judicial proceedings, and, should occasion arise, for the execution of the judgment." Hereby, many countries have established the pattern before trial of adopting "bail as the principle, custody as an exception" (保释为原则, 羁押为例外). For example, in Britain, the bail rate for criminal suspects has reached above 90%. However, in China custody measures, including detention and arrest of the criminal suspect, serve as the principle, and non-custody measures, including undertaking recognizance upon bail and living at home under surveillance, serve as the exception. The institutions and case handling personnel typically do not regard bail as the right of a

[11] Circumcision Reference Library, "International Covenant on Civil and Political Rights," updated September 24th, 2006 http://www.cirp.org/library/ethics/UN-covenant/.

criminal suspect, but regard it as a power at their discretion. Additionally the work ideology of these institutions is to arrest all who may be arrested to the best of their ability, but is not to provide the option of bail to all those applicable to the best of their ability.

In practice, once an individual is arrested they must be prosecuted to the utmost, and it is infrequent for one who is prosecuted to be declared not guilty. Obviously, it is extremely important for the arrest system to aid in the promotion of "punishment" through "leniency" in China. In order to achieve this, some institutional adjustments and reforms should be carried out. For example, the guarantor and the bail funds should be used jointly to strengthen the guarantor's sense of responsibility. The public prosecutor who authorizes the arrest should be relatively independent, in order to weaken his role as accuser and strengthen his neutrality. The public prosecutor who authorizes the arrest must witness the criminal offense, but cannot just give written examination and approval. The arrestee should be allowed to appeal to the court, and the court has right to overturn improper arrests.

Apart from the arrest system, the prosecution system also has huge potential for aiding "punishment" through "leniency." Thus, in the current Article 142(2) of the "Criminal Procedure Law," the provision of "relative *nolle prosequi*" (相对不起诉) has provided the authority to expand the scope of *nolle prosequi* to include procuratorial organizations accordingly. It is worth noticing that simultaneous to the expansion of deliberating not to prosecute, exploration on strengthening supervision of the exertion of power and preventing corruption in the judicature in this regard was also conducted. Moreover, in practice, some procuratorial organizations attempted to use "suspended prosecution" to good effect. This is also a manifestation of aiding "punishment" through "leniency," and it may be considered for legal status in the revision of Criminal Procedure Law.

At the trial stage, the judge's right of discretion must be used well. When the rate of punishment is at a high level, punishment should be meted out with relative leniency. It should be accepted that, at present, the criminal law of China in general has a tendency for severe punishment though promoting the ideology of "punishment" through "leniency" must be applied to the legal dimension. Consequently, this condition of "dancing in fetters" (戴着脚镣跳舞) has brought about a higher requirement for judges, as it requires them to thoroughly grasp the implications of law and to construct a network of authority with the conscience, courage and skill to realize the policy goals. Examples include the utilization of Article 13 of the Criminal Law, which states that "in those acts where the circumstances are clearly minor and the harm is not great, they are not to be deemed crimes" which is an example of "decriminalization." Additionally, the utilization of Article 37 states "when the circumstances of a person's crime are minor and do not require sentencing for punishment, an exemption from criminal sanctions may be granted," is an example of "exemption from punishment." The utilization of Article 72 of the Criminal Law to expand the suitability of the suspension of sentences, in accordance with conditions of sentence suspension, especially in the case of casual offenders, first offenders, negligent offenders and juvenile offenders in order to prevent unnecessary imprisonment. All of these measures take into account the role of the judge as the center of law and policy execution.

Certainly, utilizing these methods to realize lenient penalties will bring up certain problems, including corruption in the name of "leniency," how to carry out civil prosecution, administrative punishment or administrative sanctions on a person with an "exemption from penalties," (免刑) as well as how to consider the feelings of the victim, etc. About the latter, at present the system of reconciliation with creditors is being experimented with in many areas and has developed a new vision for the promotion of "punishment" through "leniency." Namely that, so long as there are reconciliation factors in the case and the victim and the defendant can realize reconciliation, and that the victim applies for leniency after the defendant admits guilt, provides compensation and apologizes etc., the people's court is allowed to mete out a lesser punishment. Criminal reconciliation has similar aspects with the West's "restorative justice," though it may go fundamentally farther. For example, it may not only result in lenient punishment but may also reduce and even avoid punishment all together. However this requires the revision of the "Criminal Procedure Law" in order to achieve legal status.

In the post-trial stage, the application of parole must be expanded to promote community correction. Sentence abatement and parole both must conform to the requirements of leniency, though parole is a superior transition measure. Accordingly some overseas scholars have pointed out that "parole is the most successful story in the correction system." However, presently in China's practice there exists the abnormal phenomenon that sentence abatement has a higher rate of application than parole. For example, in 2004, Beijing's rate of sentence abatement of a sentence was 30%~35%, but the rate of parole was only 2%. This situation should be reversed. China should profit from the experiences of other countries and implement a system of execution in which the parole mechanism is primary and sentence abatement is auxiliary. In addition, since the "Notice on Carrying out Experimental Work of Community Correction" (关于开展社区矫正试点工作的通知) was sent down in 2003, the experiences of some areas indicated that the use of social strength to correct criminal behavior in community correction achieved positive results and overcame imprisonment abuse, and the separation of criminals from society. These measures have manifested a leniency of penalties, and this system should be considered for comprehensive implementation based on legislative reform.

## II. *Working against Commercial Bribery: Special Administration* (专项治理) *Enters a Stage of Expansion*

"Completing the structure of a system for punishing and preventing corruption before 2010" has been established as the overall goal of opposing corruption and advocating honesty during the "11th Five-year Plan," and is a necessary act to realize the goal of carrying out key points in eradicating corruption in areas of frequent occurrence. At present, commercial bribery generally occurs in all types of commercial activities, because it is often in the name of "legitimate" (正当) commercial returns. Commercial bribery has also greatly increased concealment and fraud, which is enormously destructive and harmful to the principles of a market economy and the procedure of fair competition. It is extremely necessary to carry out special administration aimed at this type of bribery. For this reason, at the beginning of 2006, Hu Jintao, General Secretary of the Central Committee of the CCP explicitly pointed out in the sixth plenary session of the Central Discipline Inspection Committee of the CPC that it "must earnestly carry out the special work of rectifying the issue of commercial bribery, firmly correct unlawful trade acts, and investigate cases of commercial bribery according to law."[12] Thereafter, the State Council Premier Wen Jiabao stressed again in the fourth conference for honest and straightforward

[12] Qin Xuan, "The Central Committee gives a series of signals, and 'the storm against commercial bribery' is readied," http://cn.news.yahoo.com/060125/72/2gsqy_1.html (Feb. 25, 2007).

government work on the part of the State Council, various areas and various departments. He also emphasized that the government must carry out the special work of rectifying commercial bribery as a key effort in opposing corruption and advocating honesty that year. And furthermore, the problems of public welfare, which are closely associated with the people's vital interests and that disrupt the market economic order, must be settled. Additionally the issue of commercial bribery in engineering construction, land leasing, the transactions of property rights, the purchase and sale of medicine, government procurement and the development and distribution of resources etc. must be rectified.[13] These two conferences indicate the determination of the party and the state to eradicate commercial bribery, and to determine the key areas for fighting against commercial bribery, which shows that the special administration against commercial bribery has entered a stage of widespread implementation.

In fact, China's special rectification work against commercial bribery was been begun before these occurrences. In September, 2005, the leading group for rectification of commercial bribery, in which the Central Discipline Inspection Committee of the CPC took lead and 18 ministries and commissions jointly participated in, was established. On December 18 of the same year, the research office of the Central Discipline Inspection Committee of the CPC, and the State Administration for Industry and Commerce and the Nankai University etc. held the "Seminar Against Commercial Bribery and the Sustainable Development of China's Social Economy" (反商业贿赂与中国社会经济可持续发展研讨会) at Nankai University in order to conduct preparations for developing an ideology for the campaign against commercial bribery. In 2006, in order to further impel national administration work against commercial bribery, the central authority also sent down the "Opinions on Advancing the Campaign against Commercial Bribery" (关于开展治理商业贿赂专项工作的意见) and the "Opinions on the Implementation of Legally Investigation and Prosecution of Cases of Commercial Bribery According to Law" (关于依法查处商业贿赂案件的实施意见). In the "Amendment to the Criminal Law of the People's Republic of China (VI)" approved by the NPC Standing Committee in June, 2006, the provisions of criminal law involved in commercial

[13] "At the Fourth Conference, Wen Jiabao Requests an Honest and Clean Government and Proposes the State Council Adopt Rectification of Commercial Bribery as the Key Effort in the Fight against Corruption this Year," *Procuratorial Daily*, (February 25, 2006).

bribery made corresponding amendments to provide the support of the law for the campaign against commercial bribery. The supreme judicial organizations also approved corresponding judicial interpretations to inform the appropriate punishment for commercial bribery.

### A. *The Connotations and the Current Status of Commercial Bribery*

Commercial bribery is produced and gradually developed along with the development of a commodity economy. At present, it has nearly become a universal "underlying rule" in the economic life of our country. Even though China began to crack down on commercial bribery through legislation beginning of 1990's through the "Law of the People's Republic of China Against Unfair Competition," (反不正当竞争法)[14] which appeared in 1993, the "Interim Provisions on Prohibition of Commercial Bribery" (关于禁止商业贿赂行为的暂行规定) in 1996 and supplemental correlative provisions in the Criminal Law, which appeared in 1997, commercial bribery was not checked. On the contrary, it was increasingly problematic in areas such as telecommunication, finance, building and education. For example, in the national pharmaceutical industry, commercial bribery in the form of medicine kickbacks misappropriated approximately 772 million Yuan of the national assets every year, which accounted for about 16% of total annual revenues for the national medicine industry. In the transportation domain, 20 of 34 projects for high-grade highway construction were suspected of being involved with commercial bribery of which total investments reached 166.2 billion Yuan as audited by the state audit departments in 2006.[15] These statistics also indicate that, from 2000 to the first half of 2005, all levels of the industrial and commercial administrative organizations investigated and prosecuted in total 13,606 cases of commercial bribery, and the value of these cases reached 5.28 billion Yuan, with the fines or confiscated monies totaling approximately 810 million Yuan.[16]

[14] The1.com, "Law of the People's Republic of China Against Unfair Competition," posted September 2nd, 2007, http://www.the1.com.cn/infosort_the1/info/99599-1.htm.

[15] "20 of 34 projects for high-grade highway are a suspect of commercial bribery," *Beijing Youth Daily*, (June 28, 2006).

[16] Xiao Fang, "The Ministry of Commerce Promotes the Attack of Commercial Corruption," http://www.phoenixtv.com/phoenixtv/72988910451425280/20060804/858645.shtml, (February 24, 2007).

However it was two cases involving foreign corporations reported on by the Chinese media which exposed the extent to which commercial bribery had grown in 2005. The first was the Diagnostic Products Corporation Case. According to the report provided by the American Ministry of Justice on May 20, 2005, during 1991–2002, this corporation was the biggest global diagnostic instrument manufacturing business. And DPC's subsidiary in Tianjin, Tianjin Diagnostic Products Corporation, bribed the doctors of Chinese state-owned hospitals sums of 1.623 million US dollars in exchange for their purchase of DPC Corporation products. The second case was the Lucent Company case. In the case, the American Lucent Company's report disclosed on its own initiative that, when conducting a self-audit according to the "Foreign Corrupt Practices Act" (反海外腐败法), the company discovered suspect occurrences which violated this act in their operation in China. Lucent voluntarily accepted their punishment. It is important to note that these two cases have something in common, namely the criminal act occurred in Chinese territory, but the correlative offenders accepted their punishments in US territory. These two cases exposed the loopholes in Chinese market supervision and the lack of legislation and law-enforcement work against commercial bribery. It also simultaneously urged policy-making organizations to take powerful measures for administration work against commercial bribery.

At present, administration work against commercial bribery has had gradual results. Statistics indicate that, in January-December 2006, the national procuratorial organizations altogether registered and investigated 9,582 cases of commercial bribery, and the total amount involved in the cases reached more than 1.5 billion Yuan. Among them, 7,182 cases determined by the central authorities as having important influence were investigated. These cases occurred in 6 key domains and 9 different aspects and accounted for 75% of the total.[17] Examples include, the China Construction Bank Corporation original Chairman Zhang Enzhao bribery case, the China Council for the Promotion of International Trade original Vice-chairman Liu Wenjie bribery case as well as the Finance Department of the Ministry of Finance original Director-general Xu Fangming bribery case. The rectification

[17] Xiao Wei, "Wang Zhenchuan: The Procuratorial Organizations Investigated and Prosecuted 9,582 Cases of Commercial Bribery Last Year," *Procuratorial Daily* (February 16, 2007).

work against commercial bribery has facilitated a new approach in certain key domains. For example, commercial bribery has overrun the medicine field to the extent that the phenomenon is described as "the government medicine delegates are collectively hibernating" (医药代表集体夏眠).[18]

## B. *The Work of the Legal System against Commercial Bribery*

Presently, the Chinese legal system for fighting commercial bribery is mainly composed of international conventions, administrative laws, commercial laws and criminal laws.

(1) International Conventions. At present, of the international conventions against commercial bribery, the most important is the "United Nations Convention against Corruption (UNCAC)"[19] ratified by the NPC Standing Committee in October 2005. Of the 11 types of crimes of Chapter 3 of the Convention ("Criminalization and law enforcement") involved in corruption crime, 4 belong to the category of, or involve in some way, commercial corruption: Article 15 "The Bribery of National Public Officials," Article 16 "The Bribery of Foreign Public Officials and the Officials of Public International Organizations," Article 18 "Trading in Influence" and Article 21 "Bribery in the Private Sector."

(2) Administrative law system. The "Law against Unfair Competition" (反不正当竞争法) promulgated in 1993 made explicit provisions regarding commercial bribery for the first time. However, this law does not determine what "commercial bribery" actually is. Hereafter, the "Interim Provisions on the Prohibition of Commercial Bribery" (关于禁止商业贿赂行为的暂行规定) promulgated by the State Administration for Industry and Commerce in November 1996 made specific provisions regarding the connotations and the extension of commercial bribery for the first time. At the same time, the "Economic Contract Law" (经济合同法), the "Law on Commercial Banks" (商业银行法),[20] the "Land Administration Law" (土地管理法),[21] the "Pharmaceutical Administration

[18] Zhou Ming, "The Rectification of Commercial Bribery Acts: Medical Representatives Collectively Banned," *City News*, (June 21, 2006).

[19] United Nations, "UNODC and Corruption," http://www.unodc.org/unodc/en/corruption/index.html.

[20] Chinese Law in English Online (法律英语网), "Law of the People's Republic of China on Commercial Banks," 2008 http://www.21lawyer.cn/english/02a/10.html.

[21] CN-Teacher, "Regulations for the Implementation of the Land Administration

Law" (药品管理法),[22] the "Law on Administration of Urban Real Estate" (城市房地产管理法),[23] the "Foreign Trade Law" (对外贸易法)[24] and the "Telecommunications Regulations" (电信条例)[25] etc. which were promulgated consecutively, have formulated prohibitive and penal criteria regarding commercial bribery. For example, according to Article 9 of the "Interim Provisions on the Prohibition of Commercial Bribery," commercial bribery that does not yet constitute the crime may be amerced "more than 10,000 Yuan and less than 200,000 Yuan. If illegal earnings exist, these earnings should be confiscated according to law." According to the provisions of the "Pharmaceutical Administration Law," the pharmaceutical businesses and the medical institutions which commit commercial bribery may be subject to a "revoking of their business licenses, permits for pharmaceutical production and permits for pharmaceutical operation and a revoking of the certificate to practice in the case of doctors" and so on. In addition, some years ago the State Council promulgated "Interim Provisions on the Punishments for Embezzlement and Bribery of Civil Servants of State Administrative Organizations" (国家行政机关工作人员贪污贿赂行政处分暂行规定) and "Provisions on State Administrative Organization and its Personnel Regarding the Prohibition of Giving and Receiving Gifts in Domestic Official Functions" (国家行政机关及其工作人员在国内公务活动中不得赠送和接受礼品的规定) etc. which by nature can be classified as prohibitive and penal administrative rules and regulations aimed at eradicating bribery. Additionally, these provisions can be classified as belonging to a legal system of attacking commercial bribery.

(3) The commercial law system. It is generally believed that, the commercial law of our country is mainly consists of Company Law, Securities Law, Receipt Law (票据法), the Insurance Law, the Bank-

---

Law of People's Republic of China, posted May 3rd, 2007 http://www.cn-teacher.com/yyjy/flyy/flyy1/200705/209803.html.

[22] CN-Teacher, "Measures for the Implementation of the Pharmaceutical Administration Law of the People's Republic of China," promulgated February 21st, 1989 http://www.cn-teacher.com/yyjy/flyy/flyy1/200705/209855.html.

[23] CN-Teacher, "Law of the People's Republic of China on Administration of Urban Real Estate," promulgated July 5th, 1994 http://www.cn-teacher.com/yyjy/flyy/flyy1/200705/209622.html.

[24] CN-Teacher, "Foreign Trade Law of the People's Republic of China," posted May 3rd, 2007 http://www.cn-teacher.com/yyjy/flyy/flyy1/200705/209665.html.

[25] China Law and Practice, "PRC Telecommunications Regulations," promulgated September 25th, 2000 http://www.chinalawandpractice.com/Article/1694304/PRC-Telecommunications-Regulations.html.

ruptcy Law and the Maritime Law. Among them, the Company Law and Securities Law contain prohibitive measures against commercial bribery. For example, Article 59 of the Company Law stipulates that "directors, supervisors or managers of a company are not allowed to exploit their position to accept bribes or other illegal income." Article 198 stipulates that "members of a liquidation group may not abuse their powers to accept bribes or other illegal income." Article 22 of Securities Law stipulates that "securities companies may not solicit securities that underwrite business by means of unfair competition" etc.[26]

(4) The criminal law system. Criminal law is the most important protective and supplementary type of law, and is the most important component of the legal system in the efforts to eradicate commercial bribery. The crimes of commercial bribery include the following crimes stipulated as stipulated in the Criminal Law: Article 163 stipulates the crime of bribery of company and business personnel, Article 164 the crime of bribery to company and business personnel, Article 184 the crime of bribery of staff in financial institutions, Article 385 the crime of bribery, Article 387 the crime of units accepting bribes, Article 389 the crime of giving bribes, Article 391 the crime of giving bribes to work units, Article 392 the crime of giving introduction bribes, and in Article 393 the crime of unit bribery. Although Criminal Law in 1997 did not use the expression "commercial bribery," many provisions were formulated without a doubt in regards to commercial bribery, especially in Articles 163 and 164 the provisions regarding the bribery of company and enterprise personnel.

In 2006, in response to the lack of standards in criminal law, the "Amendment to the Criminal Law of the People's Republic of China (VI)" carried on pertinent revisions. First, it has expanded the scope of classification for acceptance of bribes on the part of company and business in order to settle the problem of defining the crime of employees which has been difficult to convict in practice. Article 163 has been amended as: "when any of the employees of any company or business or any other entity takes advantage of his position or accepts any money or property of any other person so as to seek any benefits for such person, and if the amount is considerably large, he shall be sentenced to a fixed-term imprisonment of no more than five years or

[26] Qu Xuewu, "Legal Theory on Refining China's 'Rule-of-Law' System against Commercial Bribery," *Hebei Law Science* Issue 6, (2006).

detention. If the amount in questions is significantly larger, he shall be sentenced to a fixed-term imprisonment of less than five years, and his properties may be confiscated." Simultaneously it has also been stipulated that, "when any of the employees of any company or business or any other entity violate relevant provisions of the state by taking advantage of position to accept kickbacks or commissions in any form and keeps them for individual use, they shall be penalized according to the preceding paragraph." Next, coordinating amendment of Article 163, Article 164(1) is amended as, "anyone who gives a considerably large amount of money or property to any of the employees of any company or business or any other entity for the purpose of seeking illegal benefits shall be sentenced to a fixed-term imprisonment of no more than three years or detention. If the amount is large, he shall be sentenced to a fixed-term imprisonment of not less than three years but no more than ten years, and shall be fined."

Finally, other correlative crimes have also been amended to increase the punishment strength. For example, Article 312 of criminal law is amended as: "when anyone who obviously knows that the income or the proceeds generated are obtained from the commission of any crime or if he harbors, transfers, purchases or sells them as an agent or disguises or conceals them by any other means, he shall be sentenced to a fixed-term imprisonment of no more than three years, detention, or surveillance, and/or shall be fined. If the circumstances are serious, he shall be sentenced to a fixed-term imprisonment of no less than three years but not more than seven years, and shall be fined." This measure has expanded the scope of the object regarding harboring, transferring, purchasing or selling stolen goods, so as to help deprive the income of commercial bribery offenders and to increase the strength of the penalties.

### C. *Faults in Legislation and Law Enforcement*

Presently, the special rectification against commercial bribery has achieved certain results. However it has also experienced certain setbacks in the areas of legislation and law enforcement.

First, the relaxed and uncritical "rule of law" system against bribery has created a massive bribery problem. The key areas for relaxing the severity of legal punishments in China are in property punishment and qualification punishment for commercial bribery. Some countries often allot extremely severe property punishments, or qualification punishments that revoke the qualifications of the listed company and the securities exchange as punishments for commercial bribery. In China however, even though different types of commercial and economic laws and regulations are used, the punishment strength of the protective law within the penal code is severely lacking. For example, whether in regards to the provisions of original Articles 163 and 164 of the Criminal Law or the correlative provisions of "Amendment to the Criminal Law of the People's Republic of China (VI)," all are lacking provisions regarding qualification punishment and revoking operation qualifications. In addition, because the main perpetrator of a crime can only be a person as stipulated in Articles 163 and 164 of the criminal law, in related crime cases, according to corresponding provisions, even if all properties are seized and the individual is sentenced to pay the maximum amount of fines, for organizations or business entities with abundant assets, the affects are extremely negligible.

Speaking critically regarding legislation, the defense line of our country in the area of bribery is too lax. On the topic of bribery, legislation requires the individuals who receive bribes and solicit bribes to "seek gains for other people" (为他人谋取利益). In addition, "the material subject-matter" (标的) that is given and received through bribery is only considered to be "property" (财物). And moreover, "promising" (承诺) an object for delivery absolutely cannot be regarded as bribery, only the object that is actually delivered can be constituted as bribery in criminal law. Obviously, the effectiveness of law of our country to eradicate bribery is misdirected and overly general. In the area of law enforcement at present, commercial bribery has gradually become an "underlying rule" for participation in trade, and has spread unchecked domestically. Additionally because of various reasons, the rate of case investigation, discovery and processing is low. For example, of the total number of cases registered by the public security organizations from 2000 to June 2006, only 2,529 cases of accepting bribes on the part of business personnel were registered, and 564 cases of bribery on the part of business personnel. Overall commercial bribery cases accounted for an extremely small portion of the total economic crimes, less than 1%. However this statistical data possibly does not reflect the actual objective situation of China concerning commercial bribery in recent years. At present, the cases investigated and dealt with are only the tip of the iceberg.[27]

[27] Wang Doudou, "Investigated Commercial Bribery Cases are Only the Tip of the Iceberg: Interview with Head of the Ministry of Public Security, the Leading Group Office Working against Bribery Crimes," *The Legal Daily* (June 16, 2006).

Second, the act of bribery is composed two opposing acts, giving bribes and receiving bribes Therefore when carrying out anti-bribery initiatives and penalization, various countries also vigorously punish the bribers. For example, US "Foreign Corrupt Practices Act" is a special act that specially regulates the "bribes" of US overseas subsidiaries or branches with headquarters located in US territory. In 2002, in the Schenker (Taiwan) & CO. case, although the Schenker International Corporation, which is located in the US territory, voluntarily disclosed the Taiwan branch's bribery, the US Ministry of Justice still filed the criminal prosecution, and sentenced the company to pay 2 million US dollars in fines. For a long time in China, efforts have been lacking in the regulation of bribery and its punishment, whether in the area of legislation or law enforcement. Its target of attack throughout has been corrupt officials who are accepting bribes. Generally speaking, in recent years, the number and the proportion of bribery crimes registered and investigated has risen, 1,298 criminal suspects of bribery were investigated and prosecuted in 2000, which accounted for 12.5% of total bribery cases registered and investigated. This continued to increase to 1,952 suspects in 2004, which accounted for 17.3%, of the total.[28] However discrepancies between those cases registered and prosecuted and the estimated number of instances of bribery happening is vast.

### D. *Suggestions for Legislation and Law Enforcement*

In targeting the above problems of legislation and law enforcement in their present work against commercial bribery, the following aspects can be refined.

First, increase corresponding types of punishment, and build a punishment system combining punishment with leniency. This punishment system would not increase the level of punishment, but would use civil and administrative punishments and other types of punishments to exert possible pressure on the defendant. On this point we can refer to the provisions of the US 'Foreign Corrupt Practices Act. According to this Act, if the individual or the company violates the provisions of commercial bribery, they are sentenced to the following three possible punishments. (1) Criminal punishment: company or commercial orga-

[28] Zhang Zhongfang, "Punishing the Crimes of Bribery According to Law," http://theory.people.com.cn/GB/49150/49153/3524687.html, (February 25, 2007).

nizations in violation are sentenced to pay up to 2 million US dollars in fines. High-level clerks, directors, stockholders and employee's agents can be ordered to pay individual fines of as high as 100,000 US dollars and be sentenced to 5 years imprisonment. (2) The US Securities and Exchange Commission institutes legal proceedings of civil compensation against the companies and correlative individuals in violation. When sentencing, the court may also determine another fixed amount of fines according to the benefits attained by the defendant through bribery or its degree of illegality. For the individual, the fine can run from 5,000 US dollars to 100,000 US dollars, and the fines for companies or commercial organizations are heavier, running from 50,000 US dollars to 500,000 US dollars. (3) The administrative sanctions of the American government: according to the implementation guide issued by the US Department of Management and Budget, any individual or company which violates this Act will have its qualifications of government procurement participation revoked. If its illegalities are confirmed by the court, it will lose the qualifications necessary for exportation qualification. The U.S. Securities and Exchange Commission could also forbid the organization from participation in the securities businesses. The US Commodity Futures Trading Commission and the US Committee on Foreign Investment are also able to forbid participation in areas under the agencies. Moreover, the illegal paying of funds may not be included in the costs of operation to be deducted from the dutiable funds and so on.

"Leniency" may be integrated into policy in the following two ways. First, procedures which conform to business practice should be accepted in the legislation. For example, if an act promotes or accelerates the practice of "normal government acts" (正常政府行为) or the implementation of laws forbidding related acts then it may be defined as not constituting commercial bribery. Such acts could include obtaining government documents, providing policy protection, providing communication services (such as electric power or water supply), and loading and unloading goods etc. In addition, when determining the scope of "prohibited" actions for businesses and individuals, the "allowable" scope should also be determined to eliminate unclear legislation and to avoid a "gray area" in law enforcement. Second, in the handling the cases of commercial bribery crimes, if the offending entity discloses their illegal activities in a timely manner, and cooperates with the law-enforcement departments, the judicial departments may rule *nolle prosequi* or forgo punishment.

Next, procedural legislation must be strengthened. At present, the cases of commercial bribery investigated indicate that commercial bribery is closely associated with government authority, and transparent, public and comprehensive procedures would be an effective way to supervise government acts and prevent commercial bribery. For this reason various countries pay extremely close attention to procedural legislation in the legislation against corruption, and emphasize legal consequences for the violation of procedure. This facilitates societal supervision of government acts, and provides relief for the public when their rights are infringed upon by acts of the government. This is of vital significance for China, because China's many legislation entities lack correlative procedure safeguards, and there is a shortage of provisions regarding the legal consequences public organizations should bear when violating the procedure, as well as regarding how the citizens can obtain effective relief.

Therefore, we should consider formulating a general "Administrative Procedure Law" to furnish provisions for the concrete issues of administrative actions. This would be especially applicable towards the unsuccessful legal consequences borne by the government when violating administrative procedure and for methods of securing relief on the part of the citizens. In addition, special legislation for especially important procedures of preventing corruption could be considered. For example, a separate "Law of Information Publications" aimed at the public information procedure could be drafted, and the government should establish an open information definition scope and expand the methods and the procedure by which citizens obtain government information, as well as the consequences for government violation of the procedure of information publication.

Finally, the law-enforcement system must be unified, and the law enforcement strength increased. So called unity is in opposition to "a system" which attacks commercial bribery. Therefore the law-enforcement agency is not the only restricted agency, and various agencies must be unified into a comprehensive "rule of law" system. Specifically, all levels of economic administrative organizations should become law-enforcement agencies for all types of commercial bribery. However in light of the fact that this type of agency also has other administrative affairs to handle every day, if all handling of commercial bribery cases are their sole responsibility there would be a shortage of manpower. Therefore, it is necessary to set up a special institution that coordinates and handles bribery cases, such as the Anti-Corruption Agency of South Korea and Singapore's Corrupt Practices Investigation Bureau,

CPIB.[29] At present, China has many organizations working against commercial bribery, and the State Council had also set up the supervision bureau and the Anti-Corruption and Anti-Bribery Bureau within the procuratorial system. However these types of organizations are either entities targeting specific behaviors or specific criminal cases, and as a result some commercial bribery acts evade punishment. The establishment of a special law enforcement agency or coordination institution that would target commercial bribery and improve resource sharing and the information exchange would be helpful in eradicating commercial bribery and in enhancing the efficiency and the quality of rectification work.

### III. *Working against Money Laundering: Obstructing the Flow of Illegal Funds*

In the legislative area in June, 2006, the NPC Standing Committee amended Article 191(1) of the Criminal Law regarding the crime of money laundering in the "Amendment to the Criminal Law of the People's Republic of China (VI)" to expand the scope of crimes related to or causing money laundering, and approved the "Law against Money Laundering" (反洗钱法) in October, 2006. In the law enforcement area, according to the press conference held jointly by the Ministry of Public Security and the People's Bank of China in December, 2006, altogether 7 major cases of illegal money changing houses (地下钱庄) were uncovered in 2006. 44 criminal suspects were arrested, and the capital that was seized and frozen was worth more than 58 million Yuan. The funds involved in this illegal operation reached more than 14 billion Yuan. A series of money laundering cases involving large sums were investigated and prosecuted. These cases included the Guangdong case in which Zhuhai Li and others illegally absconded with public savings, the Hangzhou, Zhejiang case in which a company stole investments and fled, the Ningbo, Zhejiang case of laundering money involved in the gambling and taxes and the Guangxi case of Huang Guangrui's money laundering and so on.[30]

[29] Qu Xuewu, "Legal Theory on Perfecting the "Rule of Law" System of China Working against Commercial Bribery," *Hebei Law Science* vol. 6, (2006).

[30] "Altogether 7 Cases of Major Illegal Money Changing Shops are Uncovered, and the Money Involved in the Case Reaches to More than 14 billion Yuan," http://news.xinhuanet.com/legal/2006-12/19/content_5507828.htm, ( March 2, 2007).

### A. *The Methods and the Harmful Effects of Money Laundering*

As evidenced by the cases being investigated and prosecuted presently, domestic money laundering is mainly perpetrated in the following ways: (1) the purchasing of tangible assets or securities and stocks with unlawful earnings. For example, houses and real estate or cars, precious metals, diamonds and jewelry, antiques, calligraphies and paintings etc. (2) The use of double invoices. For example, a company intentionally raises its prices to order cargo from the overseas subsidiary companies. For instance, the actual value of certain cargo is only 800,000 US dollars, and is actually sold at 1 million US dollars. The company pays, according to its invoice, 1 million US dollars as recorded by the subsidiary company, however the subsidiary company records the actual value invoice at 800,000 US dollars. The difference in price between the two constitutes illegal money income, and is deposited in a special overseas account by a subsidiary company, which covers the illegal money income with legitimate sources through legitimate trade. (3) Abscond with a sizable sum of money and flee the country. Namely secretly transport the cash overseas, and then deposit it in an overseas financial institution. (4) Transfer criminal incomes through illegal money changing institutions. For example, in a case investigated by the Shanghai public security organization in 2006, the accused was conducting illegal remittances and currency exchange between Singapore and China from a leased residence in Shanghai since 2004. The scope of the business conducted covered 25 large and medium-sized cities in China, and the volume of illegal business reached 5 billion Yuan.[31] (5) Transferring funds using bank bills or the letters of credit. Specifically, money launderers take the cash to the bank, and through a series of transactions, exchange small bills for large bills for carrying convenience, and also exchange cash for treasury bills, bank bills, letters of credit, traveler's checks or other financial instruments. (6) False investment. For example, investment in a registered dummy corporation or a company that only exists on paper that does not participate in actual commercial activity, as it is only a channel for capital or negotiable securities circulation. (7) False donations. (8) Laundering money by using a gaming house. For example, in the case of "Zhejiang 8.27

[31] Chen Weisong, "Typical Cases in which the Ministry of Public Security and the Central Bank Jointly Attack the Crimes of Money Laundering," http://news.xinhuanet.com/legal/2006-12/19/content_5506355.htm, (March 1, 2007).

money laundering with gambling funds" investigated and prosecuted by the law-enforcement agency in 2003, a Macao gambling house loaned money to Mainland gamblers, and then on the Mainland exchanged the Renminbi collected through the foreign black-market into Hong Kong dollars, and then transferred those funds to Macao via Zhuhai Port etc. (9) Mixing illegal incomes with lawful incomes; for example, in "the case of Guangzhou Wang Zhao on money laundering crime" judged by Guangzhou Haizhu District People's Court in 2004, the offender bought 60% of stock rights of Guangzhou Rainforest Wood Co., Ltd. with drug-related money, a total of 5.2 million Hong Kong dollars. The offender then moved the drug-related money as transferred funds. Using a method of deficit accounts, the company changed drug crime related funds into legitimate earnings.[32]

## B. *Building a System to Eradicate Money Laundering*

Although the Criminal Law amended as early as 1997 determined money laundering was a crime,[33] a comprehensive mechanism for fighting money laundering and law-enforcement network were not actually established. Moreover the fact that corrupt officials often fled to other countries indicates that criminal legislation limiting crimes related to or causing the crime of money laundering such as "drug-related crimes, the organized crimes, terrorist crimes and smuggling crimes" were affecting the results of special administration initiatives. The absence of international legislative cooperation against money laundering was an impediment to prosecuting acts of transnational money laundering. Thus, money laundering grew increasingly rampant. The officials of concerned Chinese departments indicated that the illegal money laundered out from the Chinese inland through illegal money changing houses every year had reached at least 2,000 billion Yuan, which accounted for 2% of Chinese GDP.[34] According to the "Report against

[32] Sun Liyun "The First Report against Money Laundering Discloses Five Typical Cases of Money Laundering," *Oriental Morning Post*, (July 14, 2005).

[33] Article 191 of the Criminal Law in 1997 stipulates: "Whoever commits any of the acts listed below to cover up or withhold the source or nature of what is known to be obtained from narcotics crimes, organized crimes, or crimes of smuggling, or gains obtained through such crimes..."

[34] Jiang Yong and Li Hongwei, "Ilegal Money Changing Shops Launder 200 billion Yuan Yearly, Chinese Officials Travel to the USA to Research," *Global Times* (December 9, 2003).

Money Laundering" issued by the People's Bank of China in 2005, various Chinese financial institutions of bank class reported 4.6391 million questionable large-sum Renminbi transactions in 2004, with the volume of trade adding up to 16582.075 billion Yuan. 4.3162 million questionable large-sum foreign exchange fund transactions were reported, and the volume of trade added up to 1198.166 billion US dollars. The Central Bank and the State Administration of Foreign Exchange assisted public security organizations in successfully uncovering 50 cases of money laundering and correlative crimes, and the money involved in these cases reached as high as 570 million Yuan and 447 million US dollars. The Ministry of Commerce's statistics also showed that up until 2004, approximately 4000 Chinese corrupt officials had fled to other countries, and the funds they carried reached 50 billion US dollars.[35] For this reason China has been devoted in recent years to refining the system to eradicate money laundering, and has built a network to undertake this work.

First, China signed and ratified international conventions to carry on international cooperation against money laundering. In 2000 and 2001, China signed the "United Nations Convention against Transactional Organized Crime"[36] and in 2005, China signed the "International Convention for the Suppression of the Financing of Terrorism." China also ratified the "United Nations Convention against Corruption." These Conventions played a vital role in the suppression of transnational money laundering. In addition, China made visible progress in international cooperation against money laundering, and achieved certain results in acceding to the international organizations against money laundering and in the development of bilateral and multilateral international cooperation. In October, 2004, China and Russia, Kazakhstan, Tajikistan, Kyrgyzstan and Belorussia jointly established the "Eurasian Group on Combating Money Laundering and Financing of Terrorism" (EAG) as a joint founding member state. Since 2002, under the support of other departments, the Ministry of Public Security and the People's Bank of China did massive work for China to accede to the "Financial

[35] Deng Fei, "4000 Corrupt Officials Flee the Country with 50 Billion US dollars and Offshore Companies Provide Convenient Locations for Money Laundering," *The Legal Daily*, (August 16, 2004).

[36] China Law Info.com, "United Nations Convention Against Transactional Organized Crime and its protocol resolution," 2009 http://journal.chinalawinfo.com/Article_Info.asp?Id=30469.

Action Task Force on Money Laundering (FATF)." In January, 2005, China officially became an observer of this organization. And a few days ago, under the organization of the People's Bank of China, and related departments, including the Ministry of Public Security, China smoothly completed FATF's field evaluation work.

Next, domestic legislation must be amended, and the legal system against money laundering must be refined. In the area of criminal legislation, Article 191 of the criminal law promulgated in 1997 officially defined the crime of money laundering, and stipulated that drug-related crimes, organized crime and smuggling crimes are all crimes related to or causing money laundering. In the "Amendment to the Criminal Law (III)" approved by the NPC Standing Committee in December 2001, the crime of terrorism was expanded and listed as a crime related to money laundering. In the "Amendment to the Criminal Law of the People's Republic of China (VI)" approved in June 2006, embezzlement and bribery, the crime of destroying financial control order and the offenses of financial fraud were further increased and listed as crimes related to money laundering.

In administrative legislation, in October, 2006, China officially promulgated the "Law on Anti-money Laundering" which made explicit provisions regarding the protocol for fighting money laundering, and the obligations of financial institutions working towards this goal and so on. China has gradually established a large-sum and questionable transaction reporting system through legislation. In January, 2003, the People's Bank of China issued the "Provisions on Eradicating Money Laundering in Financial Institutions,"[37] "Measures on the Administration of Reporting Large and Questionable Payment Transactions in Renminbi"[38] and "Measures for the Administration of Financial Institutions' Reports of Large-Sum and Questionable Foreign Exchange Transactions,"[39] which established an administrative management system to eradicate money laundering for the first time, and established a comprehensive

[37] People's Bank of China, "Provisions on Anti-money Laundering through Financial Institutions," promulgated November 14th, 2006 http://www.lawinfochina.com/law/displayModeTwo.asp?id=5638.

[38] People's Bank of China, "Measures on the Administration of Reporting Large and Doubtful Payment Transactions in Renminbi," promulgated January 3rd, 2003 http://new2007.lawinfochina.com/law/displayModeTwo.asp?id=2831&keyword=.

[39] People's Bank of China, "Measures for the Administration of Financial Institutions' Report of Large-Sum and Suspicious Foreign Exchange Transactions ," promulgated January 3rd, 2003 http://www.lawinfochina.com/law/display.asp?id=3774.

managerial system of financial institutions working against money laundering in the area of banking. In November, 2006, the People's Bank of China also issued the "Provisions on Anti-money Laundering through Financial Institutions" and "Measures on the Administration of Reporting Large and Questionable Payment Transactions in Renminbi" to replace the original administrative rules and regulations. In these provisions the scope of reporting large and questionable transactions was expanded to include the securities and insurance domains.

Finally, construction of the prosecution structure must be strengthened and a network established to eradicate money laundering. In April, 2002, the Ministry of Public Security established a special investigation department for money laundering crimes. In July, 2002, the People's Bank of China established a leadership group for investigating money laundering, and set up a monitoring department for payment transactions as well as a department specializing in eradicating money laundering. In 2003, the State Foreign Exchange Administration of China established specialized special agency for such work as well. Aside from these specialized agencies, in 2002, the State Council also authorized the establishment of an inter-ministerial joint conference on money laundering lead by the Ministry of Public Security, and including 16 ministries, such as the Supreme People's Court and the Supreme People's Procuratorate and so on. In May of 2003, the People's Bank of China became the leading ministry of this conference. In June, 2004, under authorization of the State Council, the number of member organizations was expanded to 23.

## IV. *Immediate Aid for Criminal Victims*

Article 77 of the Criminal Procedure Law stipulates "If a victim has suffered material losses as a result of the defendant's criminal act, he shall have the right to file an incidental civil action during the course of the criminal proceeding." Article 36 of the Criminal Law also stipulates that, "when the victim has suffered economic losses as a result of a criminal act, the criminal element, in addition to receiving criminal sanctions according to law, shall in accordance with the circumstances be sentenced to compensate for the economic loss." However in practice, if the offender does not have the ability to make this compensation, or if the case has entered lengthy judicial procedures, the victim is unable to collect compensation in a timely manner. Thus, many victims' fall into economic hardship even after winning their court cases. For example, in the extremely serious case of Shi Yuejun adjudicated by the Jilin Province Tonghua City People's Court in November 2006, although the accused, Shi Yuejun, was condemned to death, the court at the same time decided to award 830,000 Yuan in compensations for death, funeral expenses, the cost of living and the medical expenses for 6 victims and their families. The accused was incapable of payment, and the majority of victims' families felt uncertain that they would be able to collect. This kind of situation is widespread in multitudinous other criminal cases, such as the Qiu Xinghua case, the Yang Xinhai case as well as the Ma Jiajue case and so on.

According to statistics, since 2001, China registered more than 4 million criminal offenses every year, and the rate of solved criminal cases was 40%–50%. Except for those victims with relatively better economic conditions, at least a million victims every year experience economic hardship because they cannot obtain compensation from the offender.[40] Therefore, the question of how to guarantee that victims can obtain material justice after winning formal justice has become a major issue which must be solved in order to establish a harmonious society. In light of this, at the beginning of 2007, the Supreme People's Procuratorate and the Jiangxi Provincial People's Procuratorate, and scholars from the China Society of Criminology jointly drafted "Suggestions on the Legislation of Criminal Victims' State Compensations" (被害人国家补偿立法建议稿), and prepared it for submission to the legislative organization. When deploying work for 2007, the Supreme People's Court raised "studying and establishing a system of state aid for criminal victims" as an important goal; and it is reported that, at present Sichuan, Shanghai and Fujian etc. have also planned or started to explore this system.

The state rescue system for criminal victims is a manifestation and a requirement of a judicial civilization and is also a requirement for judicial harmony. In the past 20 years, China has made great progress in the protection of criminal suspects and in the rights and interests of the accused in the criminal domain, but more and more people have begun to realize that, protection for criminal victim's rights has not undergone a balanced development. An outstanding example of which

---

[40] Zhao Xiaoqiu. "State Aid is Unable to Solve all Problems," *Law and Life* second volume, (February, 2007).

would the lacking system of aid for criminal victims who have fallen into economic hardship. Such a system would be advantageous, not only in gaining the trust of the victims for the legal process by obtaining restitution for their suffering, but also by alleviating the contradictions and the enmity between victim and accused, thereby easing integration of the victim and the accused back into the community. Therefore, the establishment of a state system of aid for criminal victims should be established as soon as possible.

In the process of establishing a state system for victim aid, it is important to note that, (1) all levels of the courts must obtain the support and cooperation of the relevant committees and government departments to relieve financial hardship. Funds will be necessary to handle these affairs, and the burden of providing aid to victims cannot only fall on the courts, it must also fall on the local governments and the central government's financial resources as a guarantee. The Supreme People's Court may apply to the Ministry of Finance for special appropriate funds, and request various local governments to implement necessary appropriate funds. (2) The object and conditions of aid must be determined. The object must be the victim of a crime. If the victim had died, his/her parents, children and spouse also may be eligible for aid. The conditions to receive aid must be that the individual is experiencing economic hardship as a result of being harmed by a crime. For example, the victim is unable to pay their medical expenses or maintain the lowest living standards and so on. (3) Criteria for the amount of aid must be stipulated. Aid must not take the same form as written court judgments rather a case in which high compensation is awarded should conform to the state's level of economic development. Moreover, aid for different areas and for urban and rural victims should be handled differently according to local costs, otherwise unilateral "equality" could instead cause inequality. (4) The application, examination and approval procedure of the aid must be done according to plan. On the one hand, the application procedure should not be too complex; on the other hand, aid should pass the procedure of public transparency in order to guarantee its reasonable use.

In addition, in order to guarantee the implementation of a system of aid for criminal victims, and to obtain actual effects, some measures should be taken to settle certain related problems. First, the court may only provide aid for the victims in closed cases. However in practice, certain cases are not solved, because either the case offenders are not caught, or the case is possibly "a questionable case," or the organizations handling the case under the principle of "a doubtful crime is not a crime" (疑罪从无) deal with the accused by not arresting them, *nolle prosequi* or by declaring them not guilty. At this point, who should rescue these victims who are experiencing economic hardship as a result of being harmed in a crime? It is suggested that the Ministry of Public Security and the Supreme People's Procuratorate use this train of thought arrived at by the Supreme People's Court for reference in order to establish similar systems of aid. Doing so would assure that aid is provided for all types of criminal victims. Also, it should be clarified that once all avenues for aid for criminal victims are established it will not be necessary to wait until cases are closed before awarding aid. As long as the victim can prove that their economic hardship is a result of a crime, then regardless of whether the offender has been brought to justice or not or whether the case has progressed to a certain stage aid that is essential will be awarded beforehand. Next, for the victim's rescue to depend solely on the strength of the country is still not enough it also requires assistance from society. The reasoning here includes two ideas: one is that the national public fund is limited, and that social donations etc. collected by populist organizations are needed to make up the difference. For example in the overseas aid systems, the charitable donation is an important source of funding. Additionally victims do not merely need material rescue, but they also need psychological aid etc. Therefore, we should encourage and support those non-official organizations established specially for the victim rescue to carry out work in this respect.

Finally, in addition to material compensation for victims, there is also the system overseas for providing emotional support. However China does not presently recognize compensations for emotional damage in criminal cases, and disregards the emotional damage suffered by criminal victims. This not only out of touch with the fact that the civil judiciary practice of China is already widely applicable to compensations for emotional damage, but it also does not conform to the original intentions of aiding and supporting the victim. Therefore, legislation should recognize that the victim has the right to claim compensations for emotional damages. And when the offender evades capture or is incapable of making reparations for emotional damage, the related national and social organizations should bear the responsibility of awarding material compensations and emotional support for the victims.

### V. *The Controversy of Awarding Mitigated Punishment Based on the Payment of an Indemnity*

On November 1, 2005, the accused Wang, Lai and Zhou robbed and killed the victim Cai. While the public prosecution organization instituted criminal prosecution, the victim's family also filed an incidental supplementary civil action according to law. Because these circumstances had occurred, the victim's family fell into economic hardship, and Cai's daughter was forced to discontinue her studies. In light of this situation, the judge on the trial bench on several occasions organized careful mediation for both parties. The accused Wang family agreed to compensate the plaintiff 50,000 Yuan in advance, and the plaintiff in the end agreed to these terms. The accused also indicated he had every intention of rectifying his misdeeds. Finally, the court gave the accused Wang a lesser punishment to a certain degree in accordance with the sincere desires of both parties and the law, a stay of execution in first instance. After this, according to the introductions of the Dongguan municipal court in charge of adjudicating the case, cases resembling that of the accused Wang obtained mitigation of punishment through compensations of economic losses to the victim. This method has already been used in more than 30 instances in the two levels of Dongguan courts.[41] In addition, it was reported that this method of handling cases also exists in various degrees in other areas.

As soon as they were reported, the above mentioned facts were immediately met with opposition. Some camps believed that, despite the hopes of the court that the victim's maximum benefits could be maintained through exploration of this compensation mechanism and with the support of state compensations, individuals who have committed a crime must not only bear criminal responsibility but also must bear the responsibility for civil compensation. "The accused compensates the victim's economic loss" is an idea of justice supported by the law. However, presently the fact is that the victim often cannot gain any compensation at all even after it is awarded in a written judgment and accused is sentenced. The written judgment has actually just become a mere piece of paper. And instead, it is the victim who often negoti-

[41] "The Guangdong Dongguan Attempt to Commute a Sentence for Indemnity Payment: Thief Received a Light Sentence and a Stay of Execution after Making a Compensation of 50,000 Yuan," *Beijing Morning Post*, (January 31, 2007).

ates with the accused beforehand to reach a settlement, the accused can then obtain mitigation of punishment, and the victim can attain the compensation. These types of problems are associated with the fact that some accused lack the ability to furnish compensation, but they are also connected to the fact that when the accused intentionally transfers or conceals property, he can coerce the victim regarding the mitigation of punishment. If the victim agrees to mitigation of punishment, he will receive some form of compensation, otherwise the viewpoint of the accused is usually along the lines of "ask for money and you will get nothing, ask for life and there is one" (要钱没有, 要命有一条). Therefore, under existing judicial conditions, excessively advocating the measure of "giving a lesser punishment to the accused based on the furnishing of economic compensation" (对做出经济赔偿的被告人给予从轻处罚) can possibly become a tool bought from the judicial functionary or the victim, which obstructs the fairness of justice.[42] Some camps also point out that, implementing a protocol of "giving a mitigation of punishment based on compensation" is injurious to legal justice. And if this precedent is taken, "redeeming one's punishment with money" is taking advantage of weaknesses (in the system), and is not worth the effort of instituting. Moreover they believe, "giving a mitigation of punishment based on the compensation" lacks legal basis.[43] Also detractors are concerned with how impartiality can be guaranteed with such a practice.

Overall, the ideology of "awarding mitigation of punishment based on compensation" is worth promoting and developing. First, it has been developed in response to domestic and foreign criminal policies, and is a beneficial attempt to advance the goal of a harmonious judiciary. Since the 1970's, based on the revision of the modern criminal investigation protocol, Western society realized emphasis on the public prosecution system neglected to consider the original conflict of the crime, namely the conflict between victim and offender. In particular, the victim's emotions and benefits cannot be considered to the depth required. This initiative would result in a shift from "retributive justice" (报应性司法) to "restorative justice" (恢复性司法), namely the restoration of the

---

[42] Yang Tao, "How to Guarantee the Fairness of Commuting a Sentence based on Compensation," *Beijing Youth Daily*, (February 1, 2007).

[43] Li Kejie, "Preventing the Degeneration of Commuting a Sentence based on Compensation into Redeeming Punishment through Money," *Yan Zhao Metropolis Daily*, (February 1, 2007).

relationships between the victim and the offender, and also with the community through mediation, apology, heartfelt repentance and active compensation etc. On a related note, under the auspices of building a socialist harmonious society, China has also tried to implement a criminal settlement system as well as the system of positive compensation for victims discussed in this article. These practices are manifested in a human-oriented criminal judiciary, which is advantageous to advancing the goal of establishing a harmonious judiciary. Therefore, the Supreme People's Court Chair Xiao Yang emphasized at the beginning of 2007 that "great attention must be paid to exerting the function of mediation in the incidental civil actions of criminal procedures regarding criminal cases caused by the disputes among the people, including marriages and families etc. Positive compensation reflects the psychological viewpoint that the accused can make reparations for his crime with sincere repentance, and if he is forgiven by the victim. In this case then, lenient punishment can be helpful in reducing confrontation within society and in promoting a harmonious society."[44]

Locating a legal basis for the policy of "awarding a mitigation of punishment based on compensation" is not difficult. The premise of giving a mitigation of punishment based on compensation is that of sincere repentance, and sincere repentance means the offender is then less dangerous. According to the provisions of Article 61 of the Criminal Law, "When deciding the punishment of a criminal element, the sentence shall be imposed on the basis of the facts of the crime, the nature and circumstances of the crime, and the degree of harm to society, in accordance with the relevant stipulations of this law," this provision implies that the level of dangerousness of the individual is the basis for sentencing deliberation. Comparatively, in Article 72 of the Criminal Law, provisions on the application of criminal reprieve are more direct. According to this Article, "A suspension of sentence may be declared for an offender who has been sentenced to criminal detention or to a fixed-term imprisonment for no more than three years, according to the circumstances of his crime and his demonstration of repentance, and when applying a suspended sentence will not in fact result in further harm to society." This article specifically lists the offender's level of dangerousness as one of the conditions to

[44] Qian Huanxing, "Connecting Compensation with the Mitigation of Punishment is not Commuting by Money," *Beijing News*, (February 1, 2007).

consider in a suspension of sentence application. In addition, "Provisions on the Scope of Incidental Civil Action Criminal Procedure" (关于刑事附带民事诉讼范围问题的规定) promulgated by the Supreme People's Court in 2000 also stipulates that, "When the accused has compensated the victims material losses, the people's court may take the connection between suitable punishment and the compensation made into consideration."

Third, although "giving a mitigation of punishment based on the compensation" has certain realistic legal basis, it must be considered that, not all cases can be allowed mitigated punishment, or even abatement of criminal punishment, based on material compensations. And, not all cases are without fail allowed mitigated or abated criminal punishment so long as material compensations are made. The viewpoint of "no longer giving punishment after compensations and no longer giving compensation after punishment" (赔了就不再罚(刑罚), 罚了就不再赔) is wrong. Taking the above mentioned case as an example, if the accused possesses the property necessary for the execution of retribution, even if he is condemned the immediate execution of death penalty, he should provide the victim's family with funds for funeral expenses, expenses of parental support, payment for the support of parents and grandparents, medical service charges and compensation for deaths. Certainly, the family of the accused should assist in providing compensation; though according to the principle of "responsibility for an offence is borne by the offender alone" (罪责自负), that action is not obligated. However, if the positive compensations result in forgiveness by the victim's side and receives the Court's and even the Procuratorate's approval, out of friendship the family and friends of the accused should voluntarily give assistance when the accused lacks the financial ability to compensate. Simultaneously this does not violate the principle of "responsibility for an offence is borne by the offender alone," because the original intention of this principle in the legislation is to prevent "a crime from embroiling others" (罪及他人). This act of voluntarily assisting the accused with compensation funds is essentially very different from the act of involuntarily and innocently being implicated.

Finally, we should carefully consider how to safeguard the fairness of "giving a mitigation of punishment based on compensation" and how to guarantee that legal justice is not damaged in the process of realizing the goal of material gain. Therefore, a supporting mechanism should be established to standardize the application of "awarding a mitigation of punishment based on compensation." The following aspects could be considered for this process: First, define the scope of applicable cases. For instance, some important and serious cases and cases involving organized crime could be excluded from the scope of application. Second, the judge should solicit the opinions of the victim or his/her relatives. If the victim's side agrees, it may be arranged for the offender to meet the victim or his/her relatives, to sincerely repent and obtain forgiveness. Third, the victim or his/her relatives are guaranteed the right to voluntarily agree and accept compensation. Fourth, the offender must fulfill the obligation of compensation. The reason for this is the goal of "awarding a mitigation of punishment based on compensation" is not only to compensate the losses of the victim, but also to promote reconciliation between the victim and the offender, and to restore damaged social relations. Only a face-to-face talk can guarantee the voluntary participation of the victim, and can realize this goal.

## VI. *Reclaiming the Authority for Judicial Review of the Death Penalty: Follow-Up Work Urgently Needs to Catch Up*

On October 31, 2006, the NPC Standing Committee revised the "Organic Law of the People's Courts" (人民法院组织法). The original Article 13 of this law was revised as Article 12: "Cases involving death sentencing, except for cases with sentences imposed by the Supreme People's Court, shall be submitted to the Supreme People's Court for approval." The decision to revise the "Organic Law of the People's Courts" will be executed on January 1, 2007. In December, 2006, the Supreme People's Court made the "Decision of the Supreme People's Court on the Exclusive Authority to Review Death Penalty Cases" (关于统一行使死刑案件核准权有关问题的决定),[45] and decided that, from January 1, 2007, "Notices on Authorizing the Higher People's Courts and Military Courts of the PLA to Review Some Death Penalty Cases issued by the Supreme People's Court according to the related resolutions of the NPC Standing Committee" and the provisions of original Article 13 of the "Organic Law of the People's Courts" will be abolished. And except for those judged by the Supreme People's Court

---

[45] See text at: http://www.lawinfochina.com/law/displayModeTwo.asp?id=5741.

in pursuance of law, any death penalty case to be ruled or judged by a higher people's court or military court of the PLA will be subject to the review of the Supreme People's Court. Thus, the dispute regarding the reclaiming of authorization for the judicial review of death sentence cases was resolved.

However, reclaiming this authority for judicial review of death sentence is just the beginning of more difficult and longer journey. The reason being, the goal of this initiative is to implement the China's policy regarding the death penalty "cautious death penalty sentencing, fewer death penalty sentences" (慎杀、少杀), and to carry out the constitutional provisions regarding the "respect and protection of human rights." Therefore, after reclaiming authority for the judicial review of death sentence, how to guarantee and monitor the quality of the death sentence cases and their review is a problem that must be solved and must be solved well. Therefore, the Supreme People's Procuratorate and the Supreme People's Court jointly and independently promulgated certain judicial interpretations to determine the practical and concrete issues surrounding this initiative and to realize the ultimate goal of reclaiming authority for the judicial review of death sentence cases. For example, the Supreme People's Procuratorate and the Supreme People's Court jointly promulgated the "Provisions on Certain Issues concerning the Court Trial Procedures for the Second Instance of Cases Involving Death Penalty" (关于死刑第二审案件开庭审理程序若干问题的规定 (试行))[46] in September, 2006, and the Supreme People's Court announced the "Provisions of the Supreme People's Court on Several Issues Concerning the Review of Death Penalty Cases"[47] in February, 2007.

At present, in order to practically guarantee the realization of the goal of "cautious death penalty sentencing, fewer death penalty sentences," and to guarantee the reclamation of authority for the judicial review of death sentence will obtain actual outcomes, measures need to be undertaken to standardize the second-instance procedure of death penalty and the reviewing of death penalty cases. In order to

[46] Supreme People's Court, "Provisions on Some Issues concerning the Court Trial Procedures for the Second Instance of the Cases Involving Death Penalty (for Trial Implementation)," promulgated September 21st, 2006 http://www.lawinfochina.com/law/display.asp?id=5573&keyword=.

[47] Supreme People's Court, "Provisions of the Supreme People's Court on Several Issues Concerning the Review of Death Penalty Cases," promulgated February 27th, 2007 http://www.lawinfochina.com/Law/displayModeTwo.asp?id=5902&keyword=.

accomplish this work in the following areas should be strengthened: First, the transparency of the review procedure for the death penalty should be increased. The Supreme People's Court has indicated that, "the review procedure of death penalty is not the trial procedure but a relief procedure. Therefore, a death sentence case review is a written investigation of the facts and beliefs of the first trial and accordance of applied laws with trail protocol. Also according to law the collegiate panel is composed of 3 judges."[48] However prior experience indicates that, the written trial is easy corrupted, therefore, it is necessary to take measures to increase the transparency of the death penalty review procedure. For example, the media would be allowed to interview and report on these events, the defense attorney could apply to the court for the examination and review of important evidences, and the public would be allowed to obtain complete documents concerning the review results etc.

Second, the reasons for a ruling should be explained. Article 12 of above "Provisions of the Supreme People's Court on Several Issues Concerning the Review of Death Penalty Cases" has stipulated that, where the Supreme People's Court has approved or not approved the death penalty according to this provision, the judgment document should quote the provisions of correlative laws and judicial interpretations, as well as explanation of the reasons for the ruling. Communication of the legal and factual basis of the review to the public is advantageous in guaranteeing the quality of the death penalty review, and is advantageous for to the court's retrial work in second-instance or first-instance cases. However these measures alone are insufficient, as the chief of the Supreme People's Court stated, "the first instance is the foundation, and the second instance is the key to guaranteeing the accurate application of the death penalty sentence."[49] In order to guarantee the quality of death sentence cases from inception, the first-instance and second-instance judgments of the death sentence should all be required to explain the legal basis, the evidence situation and the causal inference of the judgment results etc. In addition the public should be allowed access to the completed judgment documents.

---

[48] Yang Zhongxu, "Looking Back over the Past 27 Year when Competence for Judicial Review for Death Sentences was Transferred to a Lower Level: from 'Rule by the People' to 'Rule by Law'," *China News Weekly*, (December 29, 2006).

[49] Chen Yonghui, "Xiao Yang: Guarantee of the Accurate Application of the Death Penalty, the First Instance is the Foundation and the Second Instance is the Key," http://politics.people.com.cn/GB/1026/4454123.html (February 20, 2007).

Third, the boundaries of "approval" (准) and "disapproval" (不准) should be approximately delineated and specified. Criminal practice has an infinite number of variables, and the method of "imposing uniformity" is certainly not feasible. However according to the introduction of the Supreme People's Court judge, at present more than 90% cases of death sentence cases involve voluntary manslaughter, intentional injury, robbery and trafficking in drugs,[50] therefore, approximately formulating a review instructive opinion or judicial interpretation for these cases, specifically defining the boundary between "approval" and "disapproval," and publicizing the results to the public could be extremely advantageous to guaranteeing the fairness of the application of the death penalty and enhancing the acceptability of judgment.

Fourth, related technical problems should be standardized. The criminal trial practice indicates that, certain simple technical problems could be causing death sentence cases to remain unsolved for extended periods of time, as well as causing protracted miscarriages of justice. For example, She Xianglin of Hubei province, who originally was declared not guilty in 2005, underwent five additional trials in which he was condemned to death twice. He was then innocently detained for more than 10 years, because the "Criminal Procedure Law" did not stipulate a number of second instance trials, retrials or other restrictions.[51] In reviewing death penalty cases, these problems are inevitable. For example, according to the provisions of Articles 3, 4 & 5 of the above mentioned "Provisions of the Supreme People's Court on Several Issues Concerning the Review of Death Penalty Cases," it is written: "when after reviewing, the Supreme People's Court believes that the facts verified in the original judgment of a death penalty case are unclear and the evidences are not sufficient, or that the facts verified in the original judgment of a death penalty case are true but, according to law, the death penalty should not have been sentenced, and that the People's Court of the first instance death penalty trial violated legal procedures, which could have affected the fair trial of the case, it shall make a ruling of disapproval, cancel the original judgment and remand the case for retrial." However this provision does not restrict the number of times which the case may be remanded for retrial. If

[50] Li Dongyang, "Death Penalty Review Suggests Court Hearings," *West China Metropolis Daily* (January 28, 2007).

[51] Zhang Lin, "She Xianglin is Unwilling to Become a Defendant Six Times," *Orient Today*, (April 13, 2005).

lower level court condemns the accused to death time after time, but all sentences contain the same issues, can the Supreme People's Court also indefinitely remand the case for retrial? From the standpoint of trial fairness and judicial benefits, these technical problems should be resolved as soon as possible. For instance, in the case of the above mentioned problems, it could be stipulated that, after the Supreme People's Court remands the case for retrial twice, and when the sentence of death penalty submitted for review by the lower level court still contains corresponding faults, the Supreme People's Court may directly change the original judgment.

# ANALYSIS OF THE RESPONSE TO ADMINISTRATIVE REVIEW (行政复议) AND ADMINISTRATIVE LAWSUITS

Fang Jun

According to a comprehensive analysis of the statistical data concerning administrative review from 31 provinces, autonomous regions and municipalities nationwide, as well as 60 State Council departments holding the responsibilities of administrative review and administrative litigation in 2005, the countrywide administrative review work this year maintained a steady upward trend based on the growth in 2004. Additionally, the total number of administrative review cases reached a new high. In this article, administrative review cases, administrative responses to prosecutions and the construction of a support system for administrative review will be summarized.

## I. *Regarding Administrative Review Cases*

### A. *The Acceptance of Cases*

In 2006, across the country 31 provinces, autonomous regions and municipalities and the State Council departments with the responsibility of administrative reconsideration received on average of 91,667 applications for administrative review, of which they accepted 81,197, refused 7,429, and made other handling arrangements for 3,041. Of the overall distribution of local and departmental cases, 31 provinces, autonomous regions and municipalities received in total 89,664 applications for administrative review, of which they accepted 79,847, refused 7,174, and made other handling arrangements for 2,643. In the 60 departments of the State Council, 39 departments received in total 2,003 applications for administrative review (the 21 other departments did not receive applications of administrative reconsideration at all), of which they accepted 1,350, refused 255, and made other handling arrangements for 398 (see Table 5.1).

Table 5.1: Distribution of the Applications of Administrative Review in 2006

Table 5.1–1: Applications for Administrative Review Received by Provinces, Autonomous Regions and Municipalities

| Province | Quantity | Province | Quantity | Province | Quantity | Province | Quantity |
|---|---|---|---|---|---|---|---|
| Guangdong | 9263 | Hunan | 3517 | Anhui | 2639 | Inner Mongolia | 966 |
| Henna | 8255 | Shanghai | 3354 | Beijing | 2529 | Hainan | 775 |
| Shangdong | 6288 | Guangxi | 3265 | Yunnan | 1885 | Shanxi | 640 |
| Jiangsu | 5021 | Hubei | 3265 | Heilongjiang | 1803 | Gansu | 584 |
| Liaoning | 4832 | Hebei | 3240 | Shaanxi | 1749 | Ningxia | 336 |
| Zhejiang | 4190 | Sichuan | 3151 | Xinjiang | 1564 | Qinghai | 258 |
| Jiangxi | 3912 | Fujian | 2888 | Tianjin | 1543 | Tibet | 91 |
| Chongqing | 3598 | Guizhou | 2785 | Jilin | 1478 | Total | 89664 |

Table 5.1–2: Applications for Administrative Review Received by the Departments of the State Council

| Department | Quantity | Department | Quantity | Department | Quantity | Department | Quantity |
|---|---|---|---|---|---|---|---|
| State Tax System | 496 | State Food and Drug Administration 监督局 | 33 | State Administration of Work Safety | 9 | State Administration of Radio, Film and Television | 2 |
| General Administration of Customs | 335 | Ministry of Justice | 26 | Ministry of Education | 9 | National Tourism Administration | 2 |

Table 5.1–2 (*cont.*)

| Department | Quantity | Department | Quantity | Department | Quantity | Department | Quantity |
|---|---|---|---|---|---|---|---|
| State Intellectual Property Office | 166 | Ministry of Finance | 22 | Ministry of Information Industry | 9 | China Banking Regulatory Commission | 2 |
| State Administration for Industry and Commerce | 162 | Ministry of Public Security | 21 | State Foreign Exchange Administration | 8 | Government Offices Administration of the State Council | 1 |
| Ministry of Land and Resources | 153 | General Administration of Quality Supervision, Inspection and Quarantine | 21 | General Administration of Press and Publication | 7 | Ministry of Supervision | 1 |
| Ministry of Labor and Social Security | 111 | Ministry of Civil Affairs | 19 | Ministry of Communications | 6 | State Tobacco Monopoly Administration | 1 |
| Ministry of Construction | 92 | Ministry of Personnel | 18 | Ministry of Agriculture | 6 | | |

Table 5.1–2 (*cont.*)

| Department | Quantity | Department | Quantity | Department | Quantity | Department | Quantity |
|---|---|---|---|---|---|---|---|
| People's Bank of China | 68 | China Insurance Regulatory Commission | 17 | General Administration of Civil Aviation | 4 | | |
| Ministry of Health | 55 | Ministry of Railways | 14 | Ministry of Science and Technology | 3 | | |
| National Development and Reform Commission | 38 | Ministry of Commerce | 13 | Ministry of Water Resources | 3 | | |
| China Securities Regulatory Commission | 37 | State Environmental Protection Administration | 11 | Commission of Science, Technology and Industry for National Defense | 2 | Total | 2003 |

In 2006, the quantity of applications for administrative review received by the provinces, autonomous regions and municipalities and the State Council departments increased by 1.15% over the total of 90,624 in 2005. The applications of administrative review included in this figure, received by the provinces, autonomous regions and municipalities increased by 1.17% over the total of 88,630 in 2005. The applications of administrative review received by the 13 provinces, autonomous regions and municipalities of Tibet, Beijing, Guangdong, Jiangxi, Jiangsu, Qinghai, Yunnan, Shandong, Inner Mongolia, Xinjiang, Gansu, Hainan and Hebei etc. experienced an increase over those of 2005. Among them, Tibet, Beijing, Guangdong and Jiangxi respectively increased by 89.58%, 55.92%, 42.97% and 23.45%. At the same time, the applications of administrative litigation received by the other 18 provinces, autonomous regions and municipalities experienced a decrease, and the majority of provinces, autonomous regions and municipalities also experienced a lesser drop. Overall, the quantity of countrywide applications of administrative review maintained stability, and even increased slightly (see Table 5.2).

In 2006, countrywide administrative review cases increased slightly over 2005, recording 90,000 cases above the 2005 numbers. However, this trend was unbalanced. Looking at the growing trend for the administration review cases presented, the primary reasons for the rise were: first, various local authorities and departments worked in tandem with the State Council to advance administration according to law and enhance public understanding of the importance of administration review work. The initiative for administrative review was continuously refined, and the overall quality regularly improved. The procedure of handling cases of administrative review was also refined frequently, in particular certain local organizations and departments made attempts to effect protocol innovations focused on impartial review, and to strengthen the neutrality, specialty and publicity of administrative review. These efforts advanced the quality of administrative review significantly, and greatly enhanced the credibility of the administrative review for the public. Second, along with the gradual improvement of the socialist market economy system, the idea of an administrative ideology centered around benefiting the people and the idea of protecting the people's rights according to law also increased, as well as the level to which the social public was able to learn, understand and use the law. When administrative disputes occurred, certain administrative counterparts were more and more inclined to report the appeal through legal remedy channels, including the administrative review and administrative proceedings etc. Concurrently, public faith in the unofficial channels, such as traditional petitions or complaint letters, was waning. Because its level of specialty was higher, and it had a lower cost and was a flexible way for both parties to maintain "face," administrative review had increasingly become the first choice for the public.

Third, because administrative system reform still had not reached its designated goals and the consciousness and abilities of certain basic governments and departments to administer by law were still lacking, the phenomenon of administrative violations and the administrative infringements of rights also repeatedly occurred in certain areas and departments and these phenomena caused the rate of administrative disputes in certain areas to plateau. Certainly, the widespread occurrence of administrative disputes was not the inevitable result of the growing number of administrative review cases. The quantity of applications for administrative review received by certain local organizations and departments has possibly dropped, but the administrative law enforcement conditions had by no means been perfected. And in fact, this phenomenon reflects insufficient understanding of the status and function of administrative review on the part of the leaders of these local organizations and departments, and an insufficient focus on the comprehensive implementation of the administrative review system and its functions. Additionally, the administrative review structure of certain municipal and county-levels of governments, especially county-level governments, was still incomplete, the personnel of administrative review did not achieve designated goals, the organization was unstable, and the efficiency and the quality of administrative review was also insufficient. In turn, these factors then caused the public to question the authority of administrative review, which affected the desire of plaintiffs to apply for administrative review.

Table 5.2: A Comparison of the Fluctuation of Administrative Review Applications Received by Provinces, Autonomous Regions and Municipalities in 2005 and 2006

| Province | 2005 | 2006 | Rate of fluctuation (%) | Province | 2005 | 2006 | Rate of fluctuation (%) |
|---|---|---|---|---|---|---|---|
| Tibet | 48 | 91 | 89.58 | Hubei | 3336 | 3265 | –2.13 |
| Beijing | 1622 | 2529 | 55.92 | Guangxi | 3355 | 3265 | –2.68 |
| Guangdong | 6479 | 9263 | 42.97 | Henna | 8700 | 8255 | –5.11 |
| Jiangxi | 3088 | 3812 | 23.45 | Guizhou | 3007 | 2785 | –7.38 |
| Jiangsu | 4396 | 5021 | 14.22 | Liaoning | 5256 | 4832 | –8.07 |
| Qinghai | 229 | 258 | 12.66 | Ningxia | 369 | 336 | –8.94 |
| Yunnan | 1739 | 1885 | 8.4 | Chongqing | 3958 | 3598 | –9.1 |
| Shangdong | 5846 | 6288 | 7.56 | Zhejiang | 4637 | 4190 | –9.64 |
| Inner Mongolia | 911 | 966 | 6.04 | Shaanxi | 1953 | 1749 | –10.45 |
| Xinjiang | 1499 | 1564 | 4.34 | Heilongjiang | 2014 | 1803 | –10.48 |
| Gansu | 574 | 584 | 1.74 | Shanghai | 3785 | 3354 | –11.39 |
| Hunan | 3466 | 3517 | 1.47 | Anhui | 3030 | 2639 | –12.9 |
| Hebei | 3224 | 3240 | 0.5 | Jilin | 1690 | 1478 | –12.54 |
| Tianjin | 1549 | 1543 | –0.39 | Shanxi | 782 | 640 | –18.16 |
| Fujian | 2911 | 2888 | –0.79 | Sichuan | 4390 | 3151 | –28.22 |
| Hainan | 787 | 775 | –1.52 | Total | 88630 | 89664 | 1.17 |

## B. *Regarding Applicant Distribution*

In 2006, of the 91,667 applications for administrative review received by all levels of administrative reconsideration entities, 68,957 of the applications were filed by citizens, which accounted for 75.23% of the total number. And, 22,710 applications were filed by legal persons or other organizations, which accounted for 24.77% of the total. As in previous years, applications by citizens still comprised the majority of applications for administrative review (see Table 5.3).

Table 5.3: Status of the Applicants for Administrative Review in 2006

| Applicants | Quantity | Percentage of the Total Administrative Review Applications Received |
|---|---|---|
| Citizens | 68957 | 75.23% |
| Legal persons or other organizations | 22710 | 24.77% |
| Total | 91667 | 100% |

## C. *Regarding the Party against Whom an Application is Filed*

Of the 91,667 applications for administrative review in 2006, 6,436 applications were from village and town governments, which accounted for 7.02% of the total. 9,694 applications were filed against county-level governments which accounted for 10.57% of the total. 41,386 applications were filed against county-level government departments, which accounted for 45.15% of the total. 1,619 applications were filed against municipal (regional) level governments, which accounted for 1.77% of the total. 19,484 applications were filed against municipal (regional) level government departments, which accounted for 21.25% of the total. 1,165 applications were filed against provincial ministry-level institutions, which accounted for 1.27% of the total. 3,553 applications were filed against provincial-level government departments, which accounted for 3.88% of the total, and 8,330 applications were filed other institutions or organizations, which accounted for 9.09% of the total. Of the parties against whom an application was filed, county and township-level governments and the county-level government departments accounted for 62.74%, municipal and county-level government departments accounted for 66.4%, and county-level government departments accounted for 45.15%. See Table 5.4.

## D. *Classification of the Applications for Administrative Review*

Of the 91,667 applications of administrative litigation received by all levels of the administrative organizations in 2006, 38,981 applications refused to accept the decision of administrative punishment, which accounted for 42.52% of the total. 6,133 applications refused to accept the decision regarding administrative licensing, which accounted for 6.69% of the total. 9,287 applications refused to accept the decision of administrative coercive measures, which accounted for 10.13% of the total. 1,897 applications refused to accept the decision of administrative charges, which accounted for 2.07% of the total. 3,096 applications believed there was misconduct on the part of the administration, which accounted for 3.38% of the total. Additionally 32,273 applications were filed for miscellaneous circumstances, which accounted for 35.21% of the total (see Table 5.5). From the cause of action, nearly half of the administrative review cases were caused by the administrative penalties. Other causes of action included in turn the administrative coercive measures, the administrative license measures as well as nonfeasance and administrative charges.

Table 5.4: Distribution of the Parties against whom an Application was Filed for Administrative Review in 2006

| Administrative organ | Village & town governments | County-level governments | County-level government departments | Municipal-level governments | Municipal-level government departments | Provincial ministry-level institutions | Provincial-level government departments | Others | Total |
|---|---|---|---|---|---|---|---|---|---|
| Quantity of cases | 6436 | 9694 | 41386 | 1619 | 19484 | 1165 | 3553 | 8330 | 91667 |
| Proportion | 7.02% | 10.57% | 45.15% | 1.77% | 21.25% | 1.27% | 3.88% | 9.09% | 100% |

Table 5.5: Classification of Applications for Administrative Review in 2006

| Items | Administrative penalties | Administrative licenses | Administrative coercive measures | Administrative charges | Nonfeasance | Others | Total |
|---|---|---|---|---|---|---|---|
| Quantity | 38981 | 6133 | 9287 | 1897 | 3096 | 32273 | 91667 |
| Proportion | 42.52% | 6.69% | 10.13% | 2.07% | 3.38% | 35.21% | 100% |

### E. *Trial results of Administrative Review Cases*

In 2006, all levels of administrative review entities adjudicated altogether 72,029 cases of administrative review, which accounted for 88.71% of the total 81,197 cases accepted. Additionally, the closure rate increased by 3.31 percentage points over 2005 and 9,168 cases were not adjudicated, which accounted for 11.29% of the total cases accepted. Of the cases closed, 43,645 upheld the original specific administrative action, which accounted for 60.59% of the total; 8,014 case quashed the original specific administrative action, which accounted for 11.13% of the total; 1,336 changed the original specific administrative action, which accounted for 1.85% of the total cases closed; 560 confirmed the original specific administrative action was illegal, which accounted for 0.78% of the total; and 656 ordered the party against whom an application was filed to fulfill their lawful duties, which accounted for 0.91% of the total cases closed. In 13,627 cases, applicants withdrew their applications which accounted for 18.92% of the total cases closed and 4,191 employed other methods of handling, which accounted for 5.82% of the total cases closed (see Table 5.6). In comparison with the trial results of nationwide administrative review cases in 2005, the rate of administrative reconsideration cases upholding original verdicts rose 1.05 percentage points in 2006, and the cancellation rate dropped 1.86 percentage points. The rate of administrative review cases upholding prior verdicts rose for three years, and the cancellation rate dropped.

## II. *Regarding Cases of Administrative Litigation* (行政应诉案件)

### A. *Regarding the Acceptance of Cases*

In 2006, there were in total 52,792 cases of administrative litigation of which 31 provinces, autonomous regions and municipalities had 52,502 cases of administrative litigation. Of the 52 departments of the State Council that reported statistics regarding cases of administrative litigations, 26 departments had 290 cases of administrative litigation (see Table 5.7), and the other 26 departments did not have cases of administrative litigation.

Table 5.6: Adjudication Status of Administrative Review cases in 2006

| Result | Application Withdrawal | Maintenance | Cancellation | Change | Affirmation of Misfeasance | Mandated Implementation | Others | Total |
|---|---|---|---|---|---|---|---|---|
| Quantity | 13627 | 43645 | 8014 | 1336 | 560 | 656 | 4191 | 70863 |
| Proportion | 18.92% | 60.59% | 11.13% | 1.85% | 0.78% | 0.91% | 5.82% | 100% |

Table 5.7: Administrative Litigation Cases in 2005 Table 5.7–1:
Administrative Litigation Cases from Provinces, Autonomous Regions and Municipalities

| Province | Quantity | Province | Quantity | Province | Quantity | Province | Quantity |
|---|---|---|---|---|---|---|---|
| Shandong | 9647 | Heilongjiang | 2084 | Hunan | 1095 | Gansu | 340 |
| Henan | 6620 | Anhui | 2064 | Guizhou | 975 | Inner Mongolia | 291 |
| Guangdong | 4071 | Shanghai | 1719 | Hebei | 908 | Hainan | 208 |
| Zhejiang | 3089 | Chongqing | 1633 | Fujian | 810 | Shanxi | 172 |
| Liaoning | 2463 | Guangxi | 1570 | Shaanxi | 742 | Ningxia | 115 |
| Jiangsu | 2288 | Hubei | 1324 | Jiangxi | 525 | Qinghai | 104 |
| Beijing | 2112 | Jilin | 1324 | Yunnan | 506 | Tibet | 21 |
| Sichuan | 2109 | Tianjin | 1119 | Xinjiang | 454 | Total | 52502 |

Table 5.7–2: Administrative Litigation Cases from the Departments of the State Council

| Department | Quantity | Department | Quantity | Department | Quantity | Department | Quantity |
|---|---|---|---|---|---|---|---|
| State Tax System | 146 | Ministry of Health | 5 | Ministry of Public Security | 2 | State Environmental Protection Administration | 1 |
| General Administration of Customs | 36 | Ministry of Finance | 5 | China Securities Regulatory Commission | 2 | Ministry of Land and Resources | 1 |
| State Intellectual Property Office | 30 | Ministry of Railways | 5 | Press and Publication Administration | 2 | Ministry of Agriculture | 1 |
| Ministry of Justice | 9 | China Banking Regulatory Commission | 5 | Ministry of Civil Affairs | 2 | State Administration for Industry and Commerce | 1 |
| People's Bank of China | 8 | State Food and Drug Administration | 4 | National Development and Reform Commission | 2 | Ministry of Commerce | 1 |
| Ministry of Water Resources | 7 | China Insurance Regulatory Commission | 3 | Commission of Science, Technology and Industry for National Defense | 2 | | |
| General Administration of Quality Supervision, Inspection and Quarantine | 6 | Ministry of Labor and Social Security | 3 | State Administration of Work Safety | 1 | Total | 290 |

B. *Regarding the Defendants*

Of the 52,792 cases of administrative litigation in 2006, in 2,986 cases the defendant was a village or town government, which accounted for 5.65% of the total cases. In 8,869 cases the defendant was a county-level government, which accounted for 16.8% of the total. In 21,517 cases the defendant was a county-level government department, which accounted for 40.76% of the total. In 2,558 cases the defendant was a municipal (region) level government, which accounted for 4.85% of the total. In 11,437 cases the defendant was a municipal (region) level government department, which accounted for 21.66% of the total; and in 634 cases the defendant was a provincial ministry-level institution, which accounted for 1.2% of the total. Additionally in 1,694 cases the defendant was a provincial level government department, which accounted for 3.21% of the total; and in 3,097 cases the defendant was a miscellaneous institution or organization, which accounted for 5.87% of the total cases. Of the defendants, county & township governments and county-level government departments accounted for 63.21% of the total, municipal and county-level government departments accounted for 62.42%, and county-level government departments accounted for 40.76% (see Table 5.8).

13,842 cases of litigation underwent administrative review, which accounted for 26.22% of the 52,792 total cases of administrative litigation in 2006. This figure was 4.13% less than the rate of 30.35% in 2005. Additionally it accounted for 19.53% of the 70,863 total cases closed in 2006, and was 2.78% more than the rate of 22.31% in 2005. Of this figure, in 2,444 cases the defendant was an administrative review organization, which accounted for 4.63% of the total cases in 2006 and 3.45% of the total 70,863 cases of administrative review closed this year (see Table 5.8).

C. *Regarding the Trial Results of Cases of Administrative Litigation*

In regards to trial results, nationwide of the 52,792 cases of administrative litigation, 43,706 cases were closed, which accounted for 82.79% of the total; and 9089 cases were not closed, which accounted for 17.21% of the total. Of the cases closed, 18,288 cases were sentenced to uphold the original judgment, which accounted for 41.84% of the total cases closed; 4,276 cases quashed the original judgment, which accounted for 9.78% of the total cases closed; 526 cases changed the original judgment, which accounted for 1.21% of the total cases closed; and 570 case were given a set time to fulfill their obligations, which accounted for 1.31% of the total cases closed. The plaintiff in 13,374 cases withdrew their accusations, which accounted for 30.6% of the total cases closed. 6,669 cases were handled by alternate means, which accounted for 15.26% of total cases closed (see Table 5.9).

### D. *Regarding the Adjudication of Cases of Administrative Litigation after Administrative Review*

Of the 13,842 cases of administrative litigation which had undergone the administrative review process, 11,576 cases were adjudicated, which accounted for 83.63% of the total; and 2266 cases were not adjudicated, which accounted for 16.37% of the total. Of the cases adjudicated, 6,854 cases upheld the original judgment, which account for 59.21% of total cases adjudicated, and the rate of upholding original judgments in cases of administrative litigation after undergoing the administrative review process was 23.61% higher than those which did not undergo the process. 1,260 cases were quashed, which accounted for 10.88% of total cases adjudicated; 148 cases were changed, which accounted for 1.28% of the total cases adjudicated; and 87 cases were given a set time to fulfill their obligations, which accounted for 0.75% of the total cases closed The plaintiff in 2,147 cases withdrew their accusations, which accounted for 18.55% of the total cases adjudicated. And, 1,080 cases were handled using alternative methods which accounted for 9.33% of the total (see Table 5.10).

## III. *Regarding the Development of Administrative Review*

In 2006, the establishment of the State Council's administrative review organization made important progress. When the "Administrative Reconsideration Law" (行政复议法)[1] endowed the State Council with the responsibility of undertaking administrative review cases for more

[1] National People's Congress, "Administrative Reconsideration Law of the People's Republic of China," promulgated April 29th, 1999 http://www.lawinfochina.com/law/display.asp?id=5279.

Table 5.8: Classification of the Defendants in the Cases of Administrative Litigation in 2006

| Administrative Organizations | Village & Town Governments | County-level Governments | County Government Departments | Municipal-level Governments | Municipal Government Departments | Provincial Ministry-level Institutions | Provincial Government Departments | Others | Total | Administrative Reconsideration Organizations |
|---|---|---|---|---|---|---|---|---|---|---|
| Quantity of cases | 2986 | 8869 | 21517 | 2558 | 11437 | 634 | 1694 | 3097 | 52792 | 2444 |
| Percentage of Total | 5.65% | 16.8% | 40.76% | 4.85% | 21.66% | 1.2% | 3.21% | 5.87% | 100% | 4.63% |

Table 5.9: Outcome of the Adjudication in Cases of Administrative Litigation in 2006

| Outcome of Adjudication | *Nolle prosequi* | Maintenance | Cancellation | Change | Execution of Duty within a Definite Time | Others | Total |
|---|---|---|---|---|---|---|---|
| Case | 13374 | 18288 | 4276 | 526 | 570 | 6669 | 43706 |
| Percentage of total adjudications | 30.6% | 41.84% | 9.78% | 1.21% | 1.31% | 15.26% | 100% |

Table 5.10: Adjudication Status of Cases of Administrative Litigation after Review in 2006

| Situation of Adjudication | *Nolle prosequi* | Maintenance | Cancellation | Change | Execution of Duty within a Definite Timeframe | Others | Total |
|---|---|---|---|---|---|---|---|
| Case | 2147 | 6854 | 1260 | 148 | 87 | 1080 | 11576 |
| Proportion of Total Adjudications | 18.55% | 59.21% | 10.88% | 1.28% | 0.75% | 9.33% | 100% |

than six years, the Legal System Office of the State Council, under the authorization of the Central Organization Commission, set up an administrative review department to specifically undertake administrative review for the State Council. According to the official website of the State Council Legal System Office, the administrative review department mainly undertakes the following tasks: receive the applications for administrative review submitted to the State Council by applicants, for initial examination and recording; draft those decisions refused; investigate and collect evidence from related organizations and personnel and investigate documents and data. In addition, the department must examine whether the specific administrative action applied for administrative review is legitimate and suitable, draft administrative review decisions; handle or pass on application for examination of the related provisions in Article 7 of the "Administrative Review Law," provide handling opinions regarding the acts of administrative organizations which violate the provisions of the "Administrative Review Law" according to jurisdiction and the procedure stipulated. Alongside these responsibilities, the department must instruct and supervise national work of administrative review and administrative litigation; compile statistics and analysis of cases of administrative review and of administrative litigation; provide suggestions to refine the system for administrative review and administrative litigation, implement interpretations of specific applications of the "Administrative Review Law"; undertake work regarding letters or visits concerning administrative review; and handle other work assigned by the leaders of the legal system office of the State Council.

In September, 2006, in order to meet the demands of establishing a harmonious society, the state entities concerned set a series of requirements to further expand the settlement of administrative disputes and to refine the administrative dispute settlement mechanism. In December, 2006, the State Council held a national forum for administrative review work in Chongqing, and undertook important measures to refine administrative review work under these new conditions and promote the establishment of a harmonious society. The State Council member and concurrent secretary general of the State Council, Hua Jianmin gave an important speech on behalf of the State Council. The parties concerned and this forum put forward administrative review work as an important issue in the construction of governing ability for the first time. Simultaneously the parties concerned and the forum also requested to include the expansion of administrative review work as an important agenda for all levels of the government. Some of the ideas put forward had vital significance in the development of a system of administration review, and they include the following:

First, strengthen the leading role of administrative review work. The parties concerned proposed that, great attention must be paid to promoting the prominent superiorities of administrative review which is convenient for the public, in that it is highly effective, flexible and strongly specialized. Also every effort must be made to resolve administrative disputes in the basic units, in their initial phases and within the administrative organizations, this means establishing administrative review as the main channel for settling administrative disputes in China.

Second, expand the institution of an administrative review entity. All levels of administrative review entities, especially at the municipal and county-level government level must fulfill their administrative review responsibilities according to law, and take effective measures to do so including establishing a system of administrative review personnel qualifications to strengthen the construction of organizations and teams. Additionally measures should be taken within local administration limitations, to focus on the regulation and implementation of personnel necessities within the administrative review system in order to earnestly resolve those problems reported by the public, such as the non-acceptance of cases, not rectifying existing mistakes and exceeding the term of handing cases caused by organization and personnel deficiencies, etc. These measures signify that the establishment of professional review personnel has made new advancements.

Third, according to the requirements of lawfulness, fairness, publicity, timeliness, convenience and convenience for the public, the construction of administrative review ability for all levels of governmental agencies must be vigorously advanced, and the administrative review personnel's political quality and the service quality must be continuously developed in order to guarantee the quality, efficiency and effect of administrative review work. A government system must be formulated and established which will carry out the responsibility of administrative review work assessment and investigate the fulfillment of duties. This system, regardless of desire or capability, must implement the function of settling administrative disputes by administrative review as an important indicator in assessing the work achievements of all levels of governmental agencies and its leading cadres. These measures would signify that administrative review will become a central initiative of the government, no longer relegated to the sidelines.

Fourth, the refinement of the administrative review working system must be ongoing as well as the further standardization of the procedure of administrative reconsideration, and research of new protocols and new methods that conform to the characteristics of administrative review work. In regards to major complex cases of influence that are widely followed by the public and involved in the community, a system of public hearings and "face to face" debates can be gradually introduced so as to enhance the transparency and public credibility of administrative review case handling. Protective and incentive protocols of administrative review work must be established and refined, a system for the notification of administrative review rights must be implemented, legal channels for government agencies to fulfill administrative supervision and self-correction should be opened, the handling of benefit appeals among all parties of administrative disputes should be handled legally and safely, and the basic interests of the most primary levels of society should be upheld. These measures would signify the administrative review system will progress towards a moderate "judicial" position, and that administrative review will be established as a quasi-legal system.

Fifth, supervision and guidance for national administrative review work should be increased, and research into countermeasures for dispute and controversy in areas of focus, difficulty and importance should be expanded such as land requisition, relocation, business reform and labor social security and so on. Additionally, the vital function of administrative review in settling administrative disputes should be comprehensively promoted, thereby dissolving the contradictions among the people and maintaining the social stability. These measures involving administrative review would facilitate the resolution of the most complex, incisive and outstanding problems, making administrative review truly the first recourse in settling administrative disputes.

# THE DEVELOPMENT OF ADMINISTRATIVE LITIGATION (行政诉讼) AND STATE COMPENSATION (国家赔偿)

Cheng Hu[1]

In 2006, all of the courts fulfilled their judgment duties as endowed by the constitution and laws. Administrative litigation cases were accepted and non-lawsuit administrative execution cases were reviewed in a stable and reliable manner. Sound development in administrative litigation and state compensation issues was also maintained. The number of submitted cases increased, while the difficulties of cases hearing grew, and certain cases were linked with the implementation of State policies.

## I. *Administrative Litigation Cases and State Compensation in China, 2006*

In 2006, the total number of cases accepted and settled had a slight increase over 2005. In 2006, there were 8,092,152 new cases and execution cases and 8,105,007 cases were concluded in all of the Chinese courts, an increase of 1.34% and 2.07% over 2005 respectively. In 2006, the total number of administrative litigation cases and state compensation cases declined slightly and first trial administrative litigation cases, second trial administrative litigation cases and administrative compensation cases also declined to a greater or lesser degree. In 2006, there were 125,976 administrative litigation cases of first instance, second instance and retrial, a year to year decrease of 0.54%. The administrative litigation and State compensation cases of 2006 are described below:

### A. *General Description*

#### 1. *First Instance Trial Cases*

In 2006, there were 95,617 first instance trial administrative litigation cases accepted and 95,052 cases were settled. The year to year rate of

[1] Cheng Hu is a Judge of the Beijing Higher People's Court and a Doctor of Jurisprudence.

increase decreased by 0.58% and 0.68% in comparison with the rate of 96,178 accepted cases and 95,707 settled cases in 2005. Additionally, there were 6,538 pending cases, a rise of 9.20%. Of the first trial cases in 2006, administrative litigation cases accounted for 1.84%, a decrease of 0.02 percentage points in comparison with 1.86% in 2005.

Of all first trial instance administrative litigation cases in 2006, cases concerning resources leapt into the first rank of accepted and settled cases, experiencing considerable growth. There were 20,752 first trial administrative litigation cases and 20,643 cases settled concerning resources in 2006, a year to year increase of 9.37% and 9.60% over 2005, which had a rate of 18,974 accepted cases and 18,835 settled cases respectively. In cases concerning resources, the majority of accepted and settled cases were administrative litigation cases regarding land, in particular cases resulting from land requisition. Urban construction cases fell to second place in 2006 with 20,693 cases accepted and 20,334 cases settled. The year to year had increased by 7.79% and 7.79% over 19,197 cases and 18,864 cases in 2005 respectively. The constant rise of urban construction cases shows that urban construction was still on the rise in some places and that it triggered a rising number of administrative litigation cases regarding the demolition of urban buildings, city planning and civic building registration, etc.

In 2006, the number of public security cases accepted and settled ranked third with 9,313 cases and 9,215 cases respectively, a year to year decrease of 2.11% and 4.03% over 9,514 accepted cases and 9,602 settled cases in 2005. The decline of public security cases shows that public security organizations are becoming increasingly standardized in security administration, that there is a decrease in the quantity of administrative disputes and that there is a corresponding decline in the number of administrative litigation cases filed to courts as the "Law of the People's Republic of China on Administrative Penalties for Public Security" (治安管理处罚法) was enforced.

In 2006, the quantity of administrative litigation cases on labor and social security tried by courts still ranked fourth. There were 7,411 administrative litigation cases on labor and 7,410 administrative litigation cases on social security accepted and settled; this makes a year to year increase of 3.35% and 3.61% over 7,171 accepted cases and 7,152 settled cases in 2005. Administrative litigation cases on labor and social security are a hot topic, and social security issues have attracted more and more attention from the State and the public. Of the administrative litigation cases of first instance in China, other major case types were traffic, industry and commerce, township government, family planning, health and others.

Regarding the settlement means of administrative litigation cases of first instance, the courts maintained 16,779 cases, accounting for 17.65% of total amount of first trial cases; 9,595 administrative litigation cases were withdrawn, accounting for 10.09%; 1,457 cases were sentenced to perform certain legal obligations, accounting for 1.53%; and cases confirmed to be illegal or invalid accounted for 2.40%. In 492 cases, the judgment was compensation, accounting for 0.52%; 11,562 cases were rejected, accounting for 12.16%; and 31,801 cases were approved for withdrawal, accounting for 33.46%. In 2006, case losses of the administrative organizations accounted for about 14.54%. If the cases in which the administrative organizations changed the specific administrative acts, or the plaintiffs applied to the courts for withdrawal of their suits and withdrew them, were included in that figure, the losing percentage of the administrative organizations would be higher. The withdrawal of suits by involved parties accounts for one third of settled cases. A considerable number of them were the result of the coordination of the courts and reconciliation in the proceedings.

2. *Second Instance Trial Cases*

2006 saw a rise in the accepted, settled and unsettled second instance trial cases with an enforcement rate of 89.72%. Courts at or above the intermediate level accepted 532,427 second instance trial cases, accounting for 9.24% of all court cases; 529,527 settled cases, a year to year increase of 2.07% and 2.20% respectively; and 44,919 pending cases, a rise of 6.60%. Of this total, administrative litigation cases accounted for 5.44% of the total amount of second instance trial cases, a fall of 0.21 percentage point over 5.65% in 2005. 2006 saw an appeal rate of 10.28%, a year to year increase of 0.13 percentage point. And of this figure, the appeal rate of administrative litigation cases was 30.46%, higher than the appeal rate of criminal cases, civil cases; a decline of 0.31 percentage points over the rate of 30.77% in 2005.

In 2006, the amount of second instance trial administrative litigation cases declined slightly. In 2006, courts accepted 28,956 second trial cases, and settled 29,054 cases, at a rate of 1.67% and 0.42% over the 29,448 accepted cases and 29,176 settled cases in 2005. The rate of amendment of the original judgments and remand for retrial declined. In 2006, there were 4,054 second trial administrative litigation cases changed or remanded for retrial, accounting for 13. 95% of the total settled second trial cases, 7.26 percentage points lower than 21.21%, the rate of national second trial cases changed or remanded for retrial over the same term. Compared with 2005, this was a year to year decline of 2.19 percentage points over 16.14%, or the total of 4,710 second trial administrative litigation cases changed or remanded for retrial in 2005. This shows that the correct rate of judgments of first instance trials increases yearly. In 2006, the correct rate of first instance trial administrative judgments was 95.73%, 2.1 percentage points lower than the first instance correct rate of various cases at 97.83% over the same term, and a rise of 0.65 percentage point over 95.08% in 2005. The number of first instance trial cases changed or remanded for retrial in second instance trials accounted for 4.27% of the first instance cases, a year to year decrease of 0.65 percentage point over 4.92% in 2005. The above statistical figures show that the courts have strengthened the administrative trial capability and that the administrative judges are more qualified. Of course, in comparison with the correct rate of the first instance trial cases over the same term, the correct rate of first trial administrative judgment still leaves something to be desired.

3. *Retrial Cases*

In general, 2006 saw an overall rise in the number of accepted cases, settled cases and pending cases. In 2006, 48,214 retrial cases were accepted, accounting for 0.84% of all court cases; 47,226 cases were settled, a year to year increase of 0.65% and 1.63% respectively with a rise of 2.96% for administrative litigation cases; and there were 13,039 pending cases, or a rise of 8.19%. In the trial supervision procedure, 32.92% of retrial cases were changed and 7.32% were remanded for retrial, a year to year decrease of 1.23 percentage points and 0.14 percentage points respectively. The correct rate of judgments in effect was 99.63%.

In the area of administrative retrial in 2006, there were 1,950 cases accepted and1,870 settled, a year to year increase of 2.96% and 5.06% over 1,894 accepted cases and 1,780 settled cases in 2005. Within the trial supervision procedure, there were 459 administrative retrial cases changed, accounting for 24.55%, a fall of 3.65 percentage points over the rate of 28.20% in 2005. Additionally 149 cases were remanded for retrial, accounting for 7.97%, a rise of 1.34 percentage points over 6.63% in 2005.

4. *Administrative Enforcement Cases*
2006 saw the examination of 138,919 non-lawsuit administrative litigation cases, a year to year increase of 11.47%. Of this figure 94.93% were granted permission to be executed and 5.07% were not granted permission, a rise of 0.4 percentage points and 0.04 percentage points over 2005 respectively. This also shows that administrative organizations are more standardized in special administrative acts. In 2006, 13,717 administrative execution cases were accepted and 14,163 were executed; 230,648 non-lawsuit administrative enforcement cases were accepted and 229,826 were executed.

5. *Administrative Compensation Cases*
In 2006, China saw a considerable decline in the number of accepted and settled administrative compensation cases by the courts. In total 3,620 administrative compensation cases were accepted, a year to year decrease of 23.35%. Separate administrative compensation cases accounted for 61.38% and collateral administrative compensation cases 38.62%. Additionally, 3,236 cases were settled, a decline of 21.46%.

B. *Case Characteristics*

1. *There Are a Wide Range of Cases in the Areas of Resources, Urban Construction, Public Security, Labor and Social Security*
The administrative litigation cases tried by the courts in 2006 can be classified into over 50 categories, including industry and commerce, taxes, finance, education, public security, house property and land, trademark and patents, national assets, drug pricing, immigration management, supervision of securities, urban planning, customs, examinations and education, government procurement, international trade, etc. In 2006, the administrative litigation cases tried by courts concentrated on such administrative management fields as resources, urban construction, public security, labor and social security.

2. *New Types of Cases and New Conditions Continuously Emerged, and Policy Cases and Politics-related Cases Increased Causing Increasing Handling Difficulties*
First, there were an increasing number of lawsuits concerning public interests. In this type of case, the plaintiff after suffering harm to his minor interests proposes a question regarding the application of certain

policy documents concerning an abstract administrative act. Second, the transition of government functions and institutional changes was accelerated, though the position and power of institutions after administrative law reform is not clear, resulting in difficulties of defining the defendant's qualifications after a lawsuit is lodged. Third, there were a good many extensive and difficult cases with strong emotional and social influence. Certain of these cases are involved in complicated economic, social and legal relations. Fourth, certain cases concerned with the adjustment of State policies incurred strong political reactions and handling difficulties. Fifth, there were a growing number of civil disputes that have been developed into administrative disputes. And, more and more litigants of civil rights and interests have begun to use administrative dispute points from various angles to lodge administrative actions, even when they have disputes in civil rights and interests.

### 3. *As Group Lawsuits Increase, Trial Pressures Grow*

Group lawsuits mainly addressed land requisition, awards of compensation for removal (拆迁补偿裁决), demolition approval acts (拆迁许可行为), planning administrative permit acts (规划行政许可行为), forced demolition and removal acts (强制拆除以及腾退行为), labor and social security, approval for access to some industries. Removal of city buildings, land requisition and forced demolishment in urban areas are all conducted in several regions on a large scale and are all involved in municipal or local key construction projects, and they can have direct influence on the plaintiffs' property and other interests. These types of cases usually concern the vital interests of many citizens, so their handling is closely connected with the social stability, and they are difficult to settle.

### 4. *There was a Growth in the Rate of Administrative Litigation Cases Regarding Intellectual Property, an Issue which Concerns Various Countries and Regions*

To meet the requirements of China's entry into the WTO, China revised its Trademark Law and Patent Law in 2000 and 2001 respectively. As a result, the final administrative award of trademarks and patents is replaced by a judicial review. Since 2001, Beijing courts have accepted an ever increasing number of administrative litigation cases in the area of intellectual property. The parties concerned in these cases come from over twenty countries and regions and are affiliated with several world renowned companies. Administrative cases in intellectual property necessitate strong expertise, which requires judges to not only have a rich knowledge in administrative jurisprudence but also a certain understanding of the technical field involved, which poses difficulties for the trial.

## II. *The Major Developments of Administrative Litigation and State Compensation in the Courts in 2006*

Just as a judicial system resolves administrative disputes and coordinates relations between the government and the people, administrative litigation plays a particularly important role in safeguarding citizens' lawful rights and interests, supervising and promoting administration according to law, promoting democracy and the "rule of law" and carrying out the principal plan of ruling according to law. Establishing a harmonious society is an ongoing process of resolving social problems (矛盾). Of these problems, relations between public power and private right, between the government and the general public cover a widest range, attract the most concerns and can most easily cause disputes. This is especially so now that China is in the process of establishing and improving the socialist market economy system and achieving a shift of government functions, phenomena cause by the change and complicity of interest concerns as well as illegal or ill-formed administrative acts attributed to unavoidable administrative disputes and lawsuits. It is of vital significance to appropriately handle the relationship between the government and the general public, and the administrative organizations and their administrative counterparts.

The special function of administrative litigation is accept and try administrative litigation cases according to law; to guide each interested party to express their opinions and requirements in a lawful and reasonable way; to maintain legitimate administrative acts according to law that can correct illegal acts and demonstrate justice, coordinate a relationship between public power and civil rights, and promote social equity and justice. In this way the factors influencing social disharmony are reduced from the bottom up, and the function of reducing pressure and dissolving disputes, settling contradictions among the people, enhancing the relationship between the government and the people, and establishing a sound image of ruling according to law for the Party and the State is facilitated. This is an important judicatory guarantee for building a harmonious society. Therefore, administrative procedure is an actual mechanism for settling administrative disputes and coordinating a relationship between the government and the people, and it plays an irreplaceable role in promoting and guaranteeing social harmony. 2006 witnessed the following achievements in administrative litigation and State compensation.

A. *Adequate Protection was Given for the Parties' Right of Action* (诉讼权利)

Administrative litigation is an efficient path and mechanism for the people to use when pursuing judicial remedies or resolving administrative disputes. In 2006, the courts paid great attention to the acceptance of administrative litigation cases in order to give adequate protection to the parties' right of action under the guideline of "fair administration of justice for the interests of the people" (公正司法、一心为民) and the principle of a human-oriented (以人为本) government. Those disputes conforming to the requirements of a lawsuit were put on record in a timely manner and in the case of those long-standing issues beyond the jurisdiction of the court; plaintiffs were informed of other possible options. For disputes concerning significant reform policies difficult to resolve purely by administrative litigation, they were settled by a comprehensive coordination of the parties concerned. In 2006, new progress was made in protecting the parties' right of action in courts across the country and some difficult, complicated and new types of cases were accepted and tried by the courts according to law.

For instance, the People's Court of Chaoyang District, Beijing accepted and tried a special case in which the CEO of Moon Embassy (月球大使馆) lodged a suit against the industrial and commercial administration of Chaoyang District for failing to obtain a business license for sales of "World Cup Air" (世界杯空气).[2] According to the award of the court, the terms for a company's business scope shall conform to the "Classification Criteria of the National Economic Activities Industry" (公司登记管理条例) as specified in Article 15 of "Regulations of the People's Republic of China on Administration of Registration of Companies" (国民经济行业分类标准). Therefore the "Classification Criteria for the National Economic Activities Industry" is the reference basis for industrial and commercial administration to check and ratify the scope of business with the terms used in describing it. Also, these criteria are used as reference basis by relevant organizations supervising the order of the market such as tax authorities, quality supervision

[2] Shi Yan, "Moon Embassy CEO Lost in Suit against Industrial and Commercial Administration for sales of World Cup Air," www.chinacourt.org, December 13, 2006.

authorities, etc. in acknowledging relevant matters. In this case, the plaintiff applied for increasing operating management entities for "sales of the characteristic air in a special region." The object to sell in the application is uncertain and the industry that such operation belongs to is not acknowledged in the "Industrial Classification and Codes for National Economic Activities (GB/T 4754–84)" (国民经济行业分类与代码). So, the ruling rejecting the registration application conforms to the provisions of the above regulation and helps safeguard the economic order under the current market economy level.

According to the provisions of Article 54 of the "Regulations of the People's Republic of China on Administration of Registration of Companies'" (公司登记管理条例), the defendant, Chaoyang Industrial and Commercial Department, must have a review and hearing of the application of the plaintiff to alter the scope of management within a reasonable period of time was in accordance with the relevant laws and regulations. The plaintiff's claim that the registration organization should approve the registration application in any conditions once accepting the application is a misunderstanding of the law. So, the reason Beijing Moon Village Company claims for a withdrawal of the "Notice on Rejecting Registration Application" (登记驳回通知书) issued by Chaoyang District Industrial and Commercial Administration doesn't hold water. In the conclusive judgment of the court, the plaintiff's claim was rejected.

In another example which took place in 2006, the People's Court of Xigong District, Luoyang City, and Henan Province accepted and tried the first case that a driver filed a suit against the traffic police authorities for traffic signs that were in violation of his rights. The plaintiff filed a suit to the People's Court of Xigong District against the defendant Luoyang Traffic Police Branch as it provided plenty of commercials on the back of traffic signs on main roads of Zhongzhou Road, Jiudu Road, etc. in Luoyang City and these commercials diverted the drivers' attention and had a strong impact on driving safety, thus violating the plaintiff's right to safe driving conditions. The plaintiff requested that the court affirm that the defendant's actions violated the plaintiff's rights and order the defendant to dismantle the above mentioned commercials.[3] When receiving the indictment served by the people's court of Xigong District, Luoyang Traffic Police Branch sent persons to dismantle

[3] Chen Yougen, Wei Zhiqing, "First Driver's Claim for Safe Driving Rights Concluded with Correction and Withdrawal of Action." *The Legal Daily*, July 18, 2006.

all commercials on traffic signs in the city. The plaintiff thought the object of his lawsuit had been achieved, so he applied to the court for withdrawal of his suit. After examination, the people's court of Xigong District ruled the plaintiff could withdraw his action.

### B. *Proper Handling of Group Administrative Disputes*

In recent years, a considerable number of group administrative disputes have emerged caused by hot topics like the requisition of rural collective land, removal of urban buildings, urban planning permits, labor and social security, approval of admission to relevant industries, drug and food safety, disposition of natural resources, and environmental protection, etc. These disputes concern the public's vital interests, usually cover a wide range, contain acute contradictions and involve a considerable number of people. If they are improperly handled, these issues can easily cause significant group administrative disputes and can have a strong impact on social stability, thus the resolution of such cases is stressed. In the handling of such cases, it is required to give a comprehensive consideration to balancing the interests of all parties concerned, coordinating the relationship between policies and laws, national interests and individual interests, partial interests and overall interests and to effectively guide and interpret the handling of the case. In dealing with group administrative disputes, the courts, via trying and judgment according to law, should give careful guidance, interpretation and coordination with emphasis on safeguarding the people's lawful rights and interests and addressing these disputes within the legal channel so that the parties can express their claims through the proper channel and the right method. The courts should also aim to resolve a dispute when the suit is concluded. The courts should strive to resolve contradictions and disputes by means of coordination and mediation, to reduce the negative influence of cases to the utmost, and to prevent and avoid that improper working method which worsens the contradiction and leads to group administrative disputes.

For instance, there was a case not accepted for administrative review that in which Mr. Kong, a representative of 82 farmers, filed a class action against the State Environmental Protection Administration. On June 15, 2005, Kong, on behalf of 82 farmers filed a complaint to Bureau of Environmental Protection of Zhejiang Province, reflecting that Binhai Park hadn't carried out the Environmental Assessment Report or the environmental measures proposed by the Bureau and asked that the illegal behavior of Binhai Park be investigated, namely that the Park began operations before supporting environmental protection measures were completed.[4] The Bureau of Environmental Protection of Zhejiang Province did not make an administrative decision even after receiving the complaint. On August 29 of the same year, these farmers submitted an application for reconsideration to the State Environmental Protection Administration, requiring the State Environmental Protection Administration to order the Bureau of Environmental Protection of Zhejiang Province to make an administrative decision within a definite amount of time. On September 16, the State Environmental Protection Administration decided to not accept the application for administrative reconsideration. On September 27, 2005, these farmers filed a class action suit against the State Environmental Protection Administration to Beijing No. 1 Intermediate People's Court, requiring the State Environmental Protection Administration to accept their application for reconsideration within a definite amount of time. On June 14, 2006, Beijing No. 1 Intermediate People's Court judged that the State Environmental Protection Administration should withdraw its decision to not accept the application for reconsideration from the farmers and come to a new decision within sixty days after the implementation of the judgment. On June 16, the State Environmental Protection Administration accepted the farmers' application for reconsideration.

### C. *Proper Handling of Law Application and Policy Guidance*

According to the relevant provisions of the "Administrative Litigation Law" and the Legislation Law, it is the people's court that tries administrative litigation cases according to laws, administrative regulations, local regulations, regulations on the exercise of autonomy and separate regulations, in accordance with relevant rules and regulations. At this point China's legal system is still forming, however, the existing laws and regulations are not yet sufficient to provide for actual needs. For those areas not defined by law but needing regulation, the state authorities

[4] Qie Jianrong, "Suit Against the State Environmental Protection Administration, Zhejiang Farmers Succeed in Administrative Review," www.legaldaily.com.cn, (November 26, 2006).

concerned will inevitably give specific interpretations on application and formulate other regulatory documents to guide law operations or implement administrative measures. Administrative organizations usually use these specific application interpretations and other regulatory documents as the direct basis for specific administrative acts. These specific application interpretations and other regulatory documents are not official sources of law like laws, regulations and rules and have no binding force for the people's courts in the sense of law. However, they are a lawmaking supplement to existing laws, regulations and rules in consideration of the current social situation, the unsound lawmaking environment and the status quo of exercising administrative rights. Their flexibility and groundbreaking nature play an important role in promoting administration according to law. Therefore, when administrative trial judges carry out judicial reviews, so long as the specific application interpretation and other regulatory documents based on special administration actions are verified to be lawful, valid, reasonable and proper, they shall consider fully the contents and ideas and acknowledge their efficacy in reviewing the legality of special administrative actions.

For instance, Changzhou Tianning District People's Court accepted the domestic first administrative litigation caused by road maintenance tolls in September 2006. Zhang, a lawyer of Changzhou City, was discontented with the Changzhou Highway Administration for charging a road maintenance toll.[5] The plaintiff claimed in his suit that the plaintiff bought a private car in December 2005 and Changzhou Highway Administration collected the road maintenance toll of 1,560 Yuan for a period of 12 months from 2005 to 2006. Then the plaintiff found that the Highway Law, revised on October 31, 1999, had cancelled the provision of collecting road maintenance tolls from vehicle owners and revised its provisions to be "the State shall raise funds for highway maintenance by means of taxation in accordance with law" and other contents, and that the revised Highway Law came into effect upon adoption. According to the above contents, the plaintiff thought that the administrative act of the Changzhou Highway Administration collecting road maintenance tolls was illegal. So the plaintiff filed a

---

[5] Shang Dong and Tian Xing, "Case of Changzhou Lawyer's Suit against Road Maintenance Toll Tried, and the Plaintiff Lost," www.chinacourt.org, (Oct. 18, 2006).

suit to the court, requesting a withdrawal of the defendant's collection of road maintenance tolls from the plaintiff. Upon trial, Changzhou Tianning District People's Court thought that the act of Changzhou Highway Administration, collecting a road maintenance toll of 1,560 yuan from the plaintiff, was clear in fact, irrefutable in evidence and lawful in procedure and correct in application of laws, regulations and regulatory documents, so it supported the administrative act. It is the plaintiff's due obligation to pay road maintenance roll according to law for the plaintiff's purchase and use of vehicle on the precondition that the fuel oil tax has not been launched in China. The judgment affirmed the administrative act that Jiangsu Changzhou Highway Administration collected a road maintenance toll of 1,560 Yuan from the plaintiff for his vehicle. Zhang was discontented and lodged an appeal to a higher court. Changzhou Intermediate People's Court tried the case according to law and upheld the judgment of the first instance trial.

It could be said that in the trials of first instance and second instance, the courts coordinate the relationship between laws and policies. In this case, the basis is the provision of Article 36 of the "Highway Law of the People's Republic of China" (中华人民共和国公路法), "The State shall raise funds for highway maintenance by means of taxation in accordance with law, and the specific measures and steps for implementation shall be formulated and taken by the State Council." According to the provisions of the "Highway Law of the People's Republic of China," the departments concerned from the State Council jointly formulated the "Executive Plan for Traffic and Vehicle Tax Reform" (交通和车辆税费改革实施方案), which was promulgated in October of 2000 after being approved by the State Council. The "Executive Plan for Traffic and Vehicle Tax Reform" specifies that: "before the official launch of tax on vehicle purchase, or fuel oil tax, it should be expanded by collecting a vehicle purchase surcharge, road maintenance toll and other state regulated government funds and administrative institutional fees in all regions and the department concerned to ensure the collection of various incomes in full." In a circular approved by the State Council, it was announced that: "to expedite the reform in traffic and vehicle tax, the State Council decided to begin to levy taxes on vehicles purchased in replacement of the vehicle purchase surcharge as of January 1, 2001 and the date of implementation for fuel oil tax shall be decided and announced additionally by the State Council according to the fluctuation of crude oil prices on the international markets." Thus it can be seen that the "Highway Law of the People's Republic of China" authorizes the State Council to formulate a concrete tax levying method and steps, and the State Council also plans to replace the road maintenance toll with the fuel oil tax.

The reform of traffic taxes was decided by the implementation steps taken by the State Council upon the authorization of the Highway Law. Before the fuel oil tax is launched, road maintenance toll and other traffic charges should be levied according to the existing provisions which conform to the provisions of the law. When the law concerning fuel oil tax was still not yet launched in China, the State Council established the No. 2 and No. 34 regulatory documents requiring the continued levy of road maintenance tolls and other traffic charges, which is the right of the State Council as it exercises authority over Highway Law. Therefore these actions conform to the original legislative intention of the Highway Law and also conform to the practical situation of China's current levying of road maintenance tolls. These reforms of the State Council are made according to the authorization of the Highway Law of the People's Republic of China. So based on this, the administrative act of levying road maintenance toll from Zhang by Changzhou Highway Administration conforms to the provisions of the law.

### E. *Emphasizing Coordination and Mediation as a Means to Settle Administrative Disputes*

In the area of trying administrative litigation cases, there were 31,801 cases throughout the country in 2006, in which the court's decision allowed the parties concerned to withdraw their lawsuit, accounting for 33.46% of the total. In general, there were three conditions under which the plaintiff could withdraw his lawsuit: first, the plaintiff recognized the administrative organization's decision of punishment or treatment was correct after he lodged a lawsuit, so he applied for a withdrawal of the lawsuit. Second, the defendant changed the original administrative action in the lawsuit process and the plaintiff agreed to the change and applied for a withdrawal of the lawsuit. Third, the court's coordination and mediation of the trial process resulted in the plaintiff's application for withdrawal of the lawsuit. Of the above three conditions, the second is usually treated as a loss on the part of the administrative organization and the third is what is known as coordination and reconciliation of the administrative procedure. The prevailing "Administrative Litigation Law of the People's Republic of China" (行政诉讼法) specifies that the mediation is not applicable to administrative litigation cases, yet in view of the legislative spirit, it is not forbidden for the parties concerned to seek reconciliation. As the situation evolves, the "Administrative Litigation Law of the People's Republic of China" also needs revising and improving.

In practice, mediation is forbidden for use by the "Administrative Litigation Law." Since the implementation of the "Administrative Litigation Law," substantial coordination work has been done in the trial of administrative litigation cases by the people's courts. This kind of coordination has many points in common with the conciliation of civil procedure. Moreover, there are a considerable number of mediation cases beyond courts. Since the implementation of the "Administrative Litigation Law," the withdrawal rate of lawsuits in administrative litigation has maintained a high rate. Of these withdrawal cases, a considerable number of cases were the result of coordination or reconciliation beyond the court except that some cases were withdrawn by the plaintiff voluntarily. In response scholars have increasingly called for the establishment of a mediation system for administrative litigation. Comparatively pronounced opinions have been raised on the topic of whether it is necessary to exclude mediation in administrative litigation in aspects of theory and practice. The chief arguments are concluded below: Theoretically, mediation is an important system to settle procedure disputes. Especially in China, the application of a mediation system is an excellent traditional method for dealing with civil disputes. This is also applicable to the administrative litigation. Administrative litigation is directed at administrative discretionary powers in many cases, which provides a foundation for mediation. In addition, administrative disputes are contradictions among the people by nature and have much in common with civil disputes. So, as far as theory is concerned, it is not impossible to use the mediation system of civil procedure as a reference for administrative litigation. In practice, the court adopts coordination in addressing administrative litigation cases. Such a method is very similar I nature to the mediation adopted in civil procedure. It is better to standardize this kind of method than continue applying it in a less standard way, i.e. the mediation system should be introduced into administrative litigation in a standard way.

In recent years, some courts across the country have researched the development and establishment of coordination and reconciliation system for administrative litigations, to address those administrative actions which are considered illegal, but the cancellation of which would lead to material losses for national interests, public interests or the lawful rights and interests of other parties. It is difficult for those parties in opposition to the administration to obtain support for their claims from the court, however because of a variety of causes leading to the necessity of solving problems of practice, the contradictions between the parties involved are prominent and easily intensified, and the trails of such cases can affect social stability. Therefore in the administrative litigation cases in which the parties involved apply for coordination, that coordination must be overseen by the courts. The mediation system for administrative procedure is extensively applied in practice, but is required to abide by the following principles: The first principle is that mediation must be voluntary. The people's court should respect the opinions of the parties, especially the plaintiff's opinion. Only when the parties concerned are cooperating on a fully voluntary basis, can mediation be adopted within administrative litigation. After all, voluntary participation is a precondition for gaining consensus after reconciliation. The principle of voluntary participation contains two aspects, i.e. voluntary adoption of mediation and voluntary conclusion of a mediation agreement. The former is representative of voluntary participation in procedure and the latter in its makeup as an entity (实体). Therefore, the application of reconciliation in administrative procedure must reflect the parties' desire for voluntary participation.

The people's court is forbidden to adopt these methods against the desire of either party in order to promote mediation, for example, such actions such as "urging the adoption of mediation by force," or "pressing for adoption of reconciliation by delaying the handling of case." The second principle is that mediation must be legal, and is required to follow the administrative procedure of mediation. The administrative litigation of mediation aims to better settle administrative litigation disputes. However this does not mean it is unprincipled for the court to push forward the reconciliation of the parties, rather that the court is required to carry out mediation based on sufficient understanding of the case while distinguishing wrong and right. Otherwise, it is very possible to hurt the legitimate interests of society, the collective or the third party, which is not allowed by law and also breaches the original intention of the administrative litigation system. The third principle is that mediation be limited, which means the application scope of mediation in administrative litigation should be limited. In the view of the nature of the power of administrative organizations, mediation is not applicable to all administrative procedure cases because the principle of administration according to law requires administrative organizations to not dispose of administrative rights in a discretionary manner. Miscellaneous specific administrative litigation cases and different types of administrative litigation cases restrict mediation in administrative litigation.

In addition, if there is no limitation in the reconciliation scope of administrative litigation, it is probable that it will result in the misuse of mediation rights, which can easily result in damage to the interests of the nation and the collective public. This practice proves that mediation is practical and feasible, and that in order to adopt mediation, development and improvement is needed. Furthermore, adoption of these principles will ensure that the mediation system will address administrative disputes on the basis of fact finding and distinguishing wrong and right without harming the national interest, public interest and others' lawful rights and interests and will further the purpose of achieving an organic integration of legal and social effectiveness, increasing the mutual understanding and trust of the interested parties and the administrative organization, and promoting social harmony.

## III. *Prospects of Administrative Litigation and State Compensation*

A stable social environment is indispensable to a harmonious society. Of all of the factors influencing social stability, the relationship between the government, administrative organs and the people is the most important. The core function of administrative trial is to protect the lawful rights and interests of the parties in opposition to the administration, supervise and support administrative organizations to exert their power within the framework of law, thus coordinating the relationship between public power and civil rights. In this sense, the work of administrative trials plays a very important role in building a harmonious society, and is in fact irreplaceable. Against this background, China's administrative litigation and state compensation must make progress in the following aspects.

### A. *Establish a Diversified Protocol to Settle Administrative Disputes*

Under China's current mechanism, the protocol for addressing litigation disputes and the protocol for addressing alternative disputes are not effectively coordinated. The majority of the public are inclined to elect the system of using non-contentious letters and visits or the lawsuit mechanism to settle disputes while few select the methods of people's intermediation, arbitration and administrative reconsideration, etc. The public's choosing of the lawsuit method to settle disputes has resulted in a sharp rise in the number of dispute cases in courts and an increase in the courts' workload and a greater conflict between the public's judicial demands and the limited judicial resources of the people's courts. However, the lawsuit method cannot solve all the disputes as expected and this will result in the phenomenon of "cases being concluded with their disputes remaining unsettled" (案了事未了), which will lead to public complaints and influence the building of judicial authority. Therefore, both the administrative procedure and state compensation in China require the establishment of diversified administrative dispute solution methods, which cover dispute solution and alternative dispute resolution with due emphasis made on each in order to give full play to both. It is also required that the different demands for administrative dispute solutions be carefully responded to and different administrative dispute solutions with different values for each of the parties concerned be provided for their selection. There would be no difference in the level of legal force or in conflicts of jurisdiction for these parallel methods of addressing the issues. The only decisive factor in the selection of a resolution method would be whether it is acceptable to the party, and whether the party's procedure selection right would be respected.[6] In view of China's prevailing legal system, any issue covered in regards to acceptance in the "Administrative Litigation Law" can acquire legal remedy via lawsuit. Also, China has established a fairly definite system of letters and visits for administrative appeals and administrative redress. Relevant laws also further specify the method of administrative remedy for the system of administrative appeal of letters and visits. The party in opposition to the administration may select any of the different legal remedy methods at his own will.

[6] Ke Yangyou and Gao Yuzhen. "On the Causes, Coordination and Renovation of Action and Alternative Dispute Resolution Mechanisms," *Hebei Law Science* vol. 8, 2006.

### B. *Giving Full Play to Administrative Redress in Settling Administrative Disputes*

Looking at administrative redress cases, there were over 60,000 administrative mediation cases accepted and concluded in administrative mediation organizations at all levels from 2003 to 2005, far less than the number of administrative procedure cases accepted and concluded in courts throughout the country over the same period. In the aspect of conclusion of administrative reconsideration cases in 2005, 13,020 cases were withdrawn by applicants, accounting for 18.57%. Administrative redress organizations, after reconsideration, upheld the prior decisions of 41,732 specific administrative act cases, accounting for 59.54%; cancelled the prior decision of 9,107 specific administrative act cases, accounting for 12.99%; altered the prior decision of 1,606 specific administrative act cases, accounting for 2.29%; affirmed the illegal status of prior decisions in 527 specific administrative act cases, accounting for 0.75%; ordered the defendant to perform his duty in 700 cases, accounting for 1.00%; and adopted other of conclusion in 3,403 cases, accounting for 4.86%.[7] This indicates that after administrative redress, 18.57% of applicants for review withdrew their applications. Some of these were the results of effective mediation of redress organizations or reconciliation between the respondent and the applicant where the applicant believed their redress purpose achieved so they withdrew their applications. After redress, 17% of cases concerned were concluded with cancellation, alteration, confirmation of illegality or order of performance by review organizations. Thus it can be seen that the administrative redress procedure has played an increasing role in settling administrative disputes and it still has room to grow.

China's current administrative management still leaves something to desire, however, the administrative review system is convenient for the public, immediate and free of charge, therefore only when the number of administrative review cases is kept at twice or three times the number of administrative litigation cases can it achieve the original design target of this system. However, the facts of implementation of the "Administrative Redress Law" prove that the administrative redress system is far from fully developed. Even the dilemma of the former

---

[7] *Law Yearbook of China 2006*. Law Yearbook of China Press, 2006, p. 1009.

administrative redress rules, which have ultimately become long-term social disappointments, seems to be reappearing. A considerable number of administrative disputes have not been settled in administrative redress for a series of causes. One major factor is that administrative redress has not performed sufficiently as expected and there is not a just and efficient administrative dispute settlement mechanism formed like in legal proceedings.[8] Therefore, some measures should be taken. First, a review of legality should be applied to administrative redress decisions. The people's court should adopt a policy of effectively acknowledging the standards of acceptance for the administrative redress organizations in order to maintain the authority of administrative redress decisions, strengthen public awareness of the characteristics and advantages of administrative redress in settling administrative disputes, thus promoting administrative redress as a diversified dispute settlement mechanism. Judicial review and supervision should be conducted with administrative redress following the ideology of protecting the involved party's lawful rights and interests, promoting administrative organs to carry out administration according to the law, and promoting the sound development of administrative redress under the principle of comprehensive review and moderate review.

Second, the support for administrative redress should be strengthened. For administrative redress decisions that should be cancelled or renewed, communication with the administrative redress organization concerned should be extensive, thus improving the quality of administrative redress. Third, supervision to administrative redress should be enhanced. For issues that are beyond the conditions of legal cancellation and that influence the accuracy of administrative redress; judicial opinions should be given to the administrative redress organization concerned. Fourth, communication with administrative redress organizations should be enhanced by means of business communication, training of judicial interpretation to laws and regulations, etc. in order to gain a common understanding of the applicability of laws, working procedure, etc. For administrative redress conclusions that should be cancelled or renewed, communication with the administrative redress organizations concerned should be sufficiently conducted, thus improving the quality of administrative redress.

---

[8] Fang Jun, "On Rethinking the System Reorganization of Administrative Redress in China," *Foreign Law Translation Review*, spring issue (2004).

### C. *Establishing an Impartial, Effective and Authoritative Administrative Litigation System*

With the transition of a planned economy to a market economy, unit individual to a social individual, authoritative society to a society of rights, the entity of interest has tended to diversification and contains increased social contradictions. In recent years, China has seen a sharp rise in administrative disputes. The courts have played a growing important role in settling disputes among the state, the society, citizen groups and individuals. With the expanding economy and social advancement, China's courts have also expanded in their functions, i.e. from the traditional obligatory settling of disputes of parties to the current enrichment of extension functions like controlling society, constraining power and interpretation of laws, etc. with constant improvement to its contents. Yet it is important to understand that the court can't address all issues raised. We should define the function of the court in a scientific manner. Of course, government by law and justice is the best way to resolve social contradictions. The fundamental responsibility of the people's court is to resolve social contradictions, maintain social stability, guarantee economic development, promote social harmony and realize equity and justice. In China, criminal procedure, civil procedure and administrative litigation constitute the full jurisdiction of the people's court. Of these three procedures, the administrative procedure adjusts the administrative relation of unequal entities, exerts the responsibility of examining and supervising the legality of special administrative actions of administrative organizations at all levels, and enforces the supervision and restriction of the jurisdiction over administrative rights. Therefore, administrative litigation plays an important role in promoting administration according to law by means of examination and supervision of the legality of administrative actions and the standardization of administrative actions of administrative organizations. With the revision and improvement of the "Administrative Litigation Law," China will surely make considerable headway in establishing an impartial, effective and authoritative administrative procedure system.

### D. *Promoting the Connection between the Administrative Redress System, the Letters and Visits System* (信访制度) *and the Administrative Procedure System*

Though China's prevailing Administrative Redress Law is well specified in an academic way, it is not operable. Many of its systems need detailed improvement. In regards to the decision made after a redress examination, the existing decisions of upholding a prior decision, canceling it, altering it, and confirming the violation of law or ordering the performance of duties are far from sufficient in addressing the varied and complex nature of redress cases. The administrative redress procedure is unsound and does not conform to the principle of due procedure of law. So it is necessary that a revision of the "Administrative Redress Law" be expedited, which includes the expansion of the variety of administrative redress decisions and the strengthening of the establishment and improvement of the administrative redress procedure system.

Additionally, it is necessary that the relationship of administrative review and the Letters and Visits System be examined. Administrative redress organs at all levels should carefully study this connection, establish and improve a coordination mechanism for both so as to make them function better together in settling administrative disputes and resolving social contradictions.

The "Administrative Litigation Law" is not well coordinated with the "Administrative Review Law" regarding its acceptances, examination principles and examination scope, etc. In these aspects, the former covers a smaller area than the latter. Consequently, some cases not covered by the "Administrative Litigation Law" are decided for redress but the decision grants the opposing party the right of action, which hurts the authority of the decision of the redress organization and the court. Therefore, it is necessary to revise the "Administrative Litigation Law" as soon as possible to coordinate it with the "Administrative Review Law" in regards to its acceptances, examinations and examination principles, etc. Such measures can be taken to bring partial and abstract administrative action into accepted area of the administrative procedure and to expand the rationality of the examination area, etc.

### E. *Researching the Establishment of an Administrative Mediation System*

Coordination, reconciliation and mediation are effective legal methods, with Chinese characteristics, for resolving contradictions and disputes. As China is in this transition period of system reform, many contradictions have emerged and administrative litigation cases are increasingly complicated. It is necessary to set up a diversified administrative dispute settlement mechanism which would rely on the Party, government organizations and judicial organizations and develop the functions of public self-rule organizations and social organizations. It is also necessary to apply legal means to resolving contradictions and disputes and develop the traditional culture of "a preference for harmony" (和为贵) as well. Therefore it is emphasized that coordination and reconciliation means be adopted to settle administrative disputes. It should also be said that while administrative action is a valuable approach to resolving administrative disputes, it is not the only way. The court's supervision authority is also limited. In particular cases, it is better to combine the court's independent exercise of jurisdiction according to law and the coordination of the administrative organization. And, under the premise of abiding by existing laws and regulations, to select a way to best protect the lawful rights and interests of the administrative counterparts. Concluding a case with an overly simple judgment should also be avoided. According to the provisions of China's prevailing "Administrative Litigation Law," mediation is not applicable to the trials of the People's Court in administrative litigation cases. This provision has the following primary meanings: in trying an administrative case, the court ought to make a definite determination on whether the specific administrative act of the defendant is legal and come to a judgment according to law, and shall not violate the law by willfully infringing on public rights and the involved parties' lawful rights and interests.

This approach was positive in the initial stage of establishing an administrative action system. However with the development of the situation, especially after the Party's Central Committee put forward the significant strategic decision of establishing a harmonious socialist society, the provision that mediation is not applicable to administrative litigation cases has not adapted to the new circumstances and this influences the establishment of harmonious relationship between the government and the people. Administrative action is an independent legal remedy system for administrative counterparts like citizens, legal persons and other organizations. Its role is to safeguard the lawful rights and interests of these entities, by supervising and regulating administrative actions. With the proposal of the theory of a harmonious society, administrative trials ought to strengthen the relationship between the government and the people and resolve administrative disputes. They should also equally stress the application of legal means and coordination and reconciliation means to resolve contradictions and disputes.

The judgment procedure stresses the precise and strict nature of legal proceedings and the decision between either one of the other of the involved parties. But practice proves that judgment is not the only means to settle disputes. In certain cases, legal proceedings fail to achieve ideal results, for instance, the phenomena in which "legal proceedings are concluded but the dispute is not." As an effective way of resolving disputes while maintaining Chinese characteristics, coordination, reconciliation and mediation are more flexible, convenient and effective than judgment. They also help save the cost of judicial proceedings and relieve contradiction, while also eliminating or reducing antagonism. The "Administrative Litigation Law of the People's Republic of China" stipulates that mediation is not applicable to administrative litigation cases, yet in the view of legislative spirit, it is not forbidden for the parties concerned to seek reconciliation. This is the basic requirement of the principle of a "people-centered" government safeguarding the people's interests and this is also a necessary requirement for establishing a harmonious socialist society. As the situation develops, the current "Administrative Litigation Law" needs to be amended and improved so that it acknowledges the means of coordination and reconciliation as part of the basic system of administrative action.

# JUDICIAL REFORM AND DEVELOPMENT IN 2006

Peng Haiqing[1]

## I. *The Criminal Litigation System*

In 2006 China made new progress in the criminal litigation field in the following aspects: The first was in the legal construction of criminal litigation and the second was in criminal law enforcement practices for public security organizations, the people's procuratorates and the people's courts.

### A. *Development of Criminal Litigation*

In 2006, China's criminal litigation made considerable progress in the following areas:

First, the amendment of the "Criminal Procedure Law of the People's Republic of China" (刑事诉讼法) was listed in the State agenda again. This 1996 amendment was a milestone in the history of the criminal justice system; and the amendment is better both in form and in content than its predecessor. However, any law will demonstrate its inadequacies as time goes on; and such inadequacies become increasingly clear in the process of application. It has been more than a decade since the "Criminal Procedure Law of the People's Republic of China" was promulgated in 1996. Quite a few slips and defects have been exposed in its application practice. Furthermore, since the Chinese government signed the "International Covenant on Economic, Social and Cultural Rights," (经济、社会和文化权利国际公约) and the "International Covenant on Civil and Political Rights" (公民权利和政治权利国际公约) in 1997 and 1998 respectively and was approved to accede the "International Covenant on Economic, Social and Cultural Rights" in the spring of 2001, the "Criminal Procedure Law of the People's

[1] Peng Haiqing is a postdoctoral fellow at the Institute of Law at the Chinese Academy of Social Sciences. She is also an Associate Professor of Law at the Law School of Xiangtan University.

Republic of China" has been confronted with the pressing problem of coordinating the international community laws. The above factors caused the amendment of the "Criminal Procedure Law of the People's Republic of China" to be listed in the State agenda again as well as in the lawmaking plan in the Tenth National People's Congress. In 2006, the Commission of Legislative Affairs of the Standing Committee of the National People's Congress conducted an extensive survey on the amendment of the "Criminal Procedure Law of the People's Republic of China" and asked for opinions in preparation for the secondary amendment to this law.

Second, the promulgation of several new criminal provisions further improved the criminal justice administration. In 2006, there were over 20 laws, regulations, judicial interpretations, department rules and other standardized documents promulgated by the Standing Committee of the National People's Congress, the Supreme People's Court, the Supreme People's Procuratorate, the Ministry of Public Security and the Ministry of Justice, covering the entity endowed with the authority to approve death penalty cases, second hearing procedures, handling of the criminal cases of minors, implementation of a both strict and lenient criminal policy, and the provision of judicial assistance in criminal cases with France, Spain, Portugal, etc. The promulgation and implementation of the above standardized documents provides a basis for authoritative organizations to exercise their authority and guarantee the goals of criminal litigation: punishing crimes, protecting human rights and safeguarding a harmonious social order.

### B. *The Basic State of Criminal Litigation*

#### 1. *The Filing and Investigation of Cases by the Public Security Organizations*

In 2006, public security organizations launched a series of special campaigns to crack down on crime, strengthen and improve crime prevention and control public order, as well as effectively prevent and deter criminal activity and safeguard social stability and public order.

2006 still saw a high occurrence rate of criminal cases; however, the whole country also experienced a stable public order. In some regions, the rate of discovered criminal cases declined sharply. An overview of the criminal offense situation is outlined below:

First, the total amount of criminal cases in 2006 was almost the same as the amount in the previous year. In 2006, a total of 4.653 million criminal cases were placed on file in public security organizations, almost equal with the rate in 2005. While criminal offenses still frequently occurred in China, the public security organizations kept a record of around 4.65 million criminal cases for three straight years, which was not a big fluctuation. By region, a dramatic decline occurred in 15 provinces, autonomous regions and municipalities with five enjoying rate of decrease of over 5% in Qinghai, Chongqing, Sichuan, Guangdong and Shandong, 5.1%, 5.7%, 5.7%, 5.8% and 6.8% respectively.

Second, the number of violent crimes continued to decline. In 2006, there were 532,000 violent crimes including arson, using explosives, homicide, etc. filed with the public security organizations, a fall of 4% or 22,000 violent cases in comparison with 2005. This is the fourth straight year of decline in the amount of violent crimes since 2002 and there is a larger rate of decline this year as well. Of these violent crimes, there were 6,701 arson cases, an annual decline of 12.8%; 782 cases of using explosives, an annual decline of 20.3%; 18,000 homicide cases, an annual decline of 13.7%; and 32,000 rape cases, an annual decline of 4%. This straight decline of violent crimes shows that China's public order is improving.

Third, there was decrease in the number of robbery and theft cases. In 2006, there were 3.646 million robbery and theft cases filed with the public security organizations, a decrease of 61,000 cases or 1.6% over 2005. This was a new decline after the decline rate of 2.2% in 2005. Of all the robbery and theft cases filed with public security organizations, there were 3.144 million cases of theft, an annual decline of 0.6%, which included 1.073 million burglary cases, a decline of 4.9% and 637,000 motor vehicle stealing cases, a decline of 6.7%. Additionally, there were 310,000 robbery cases filed, a decline of 6.8%, including 26,000 indoor robbery cases, a decline of 16.1%; and 24,000 motor vehicle robbery cases, a decline of 10.8%. There were 192,000 cases of theft filed, a decline of 9.5%. The decline in the amount of robbery and theft cases, which usually account for eighty percent of the total amount of criminal cases, directly contributed to a decline in the total number of criminal cases.

Fourth, the number of "pornography, gambling and drug abuse and trafficking" cases hit a new record. In 2006, there were 113,000 pornography, gambling, drug abuse and trafficking cases filed with public security organizations, a fall of 22,000 cases or 16.2% over 2005 a new low in this category of cases in recent years. Of all pornography, gambling, drug abuse and trafficking cases filed, there were 79,000 drug cases, an annual decline of 16.4%; 21,000 gambling cases, an annual decline of 21.1%; 11,000 cases involving organizing, forcing, coercing, sheltering or suggesting of prostitution, an annual decline of 5.4%; and there were 2,854 cases regarding the production, sales and distribution of pornographic goods, an annual decline of 9.8%.

Fifth, there was a remarkable decline in the number of juvenile criminals. In 2006, of persons captured in criminal offenses, 679,000 were below the age of 25 years, a decline of 40,000 persons or 5.5% over 2005, the highest decline rate in recent years. The percentage of juvenile criminals in the total amount of criminal offenders declined from 46.8% in 2005 to 43.5% in 2006. The reduction in the amount of juvenile criminals reflects a strengthened ideological and moral education of juveniles and is an achievement in the prevention of juvenile crime.[2]

Furthermore, public security organizations also performed well in certain specialized campaigns such as eradicating organized crime, commercial bribery and prohibiting drugs, etc.

In 2006, public security organizations investigated 346 organized crime cases, referred 296 organized crime cases for prosecution and shut down 1,347 influential criminal groups that were committing offences in certain regions. All these actions have contributed to the markedly improved public order and strengthened security of the general public.

In 2006, public security organizations accepted over 1,300 commercial bribery cases, and put over 1,200 cases on record, with the total sum involved over 200 million Yuan. These organizations solved over 1,000 cases, captured over 900 involved persons and prevented economic losses of over 70 million Yuan.

From January to November of 2006, there were 36,400 drug cases discovered with the capture of 45,100 criminal suspects, 4.79 tons of heroin, 1.52 tons of opium, 4.9 tons of methamphetamine, 329,000 ecstasy pills, 1.5 tons of ketamine and 267.5 tons of chemicals which can easily be made into drugs. In the Xinjiang Kunjirup (Hongqi Lafu 红其拉甫) Port "10•22" case, 20.7 kg of heroin were seized. This case represents the single largest seizure of heroin in the "Golden Crescent" (金新月) region in China. Furthermore, forty special cases under the

[2] "Bulletin of the Ministry of Public Security on the Investigation of Homicide Cases in China in 2006" (veritable records), http://www.sina.com.cn, (February 6, 2007).

supervision and management of the Ministry of Public Security were solved; and a host of major cases such as Yunnan "3•9" large scale heroin trafficking case, "8•29" large scale multinational drug trafficking case, Guangdong "601B" drug production and trafficking case, Fujian "JDB007-A" methamphetamine trafficking case, and Liaoning "703" drug trafficking case, etc.

By case coverage, robbery and theft cases, organized crime cases, banking cases and economic cases with mass involvement frequently occurred in China in 2006.[3] Yet there were differences according to different regions. For instance, trafficking of drugs and the destruction of power equipment occurring in the southeast area of Guangdong Province were also listed as frequently occurring cases. While the Central Government is in the process of strengthening the construction of the middle and west regions, some corruption cases such as appropriation of special funds tend to occur frequently. It is predicted that robbery, and theft cases, organized crime cases and economic crime cases will also see a high occurrence rate against the background of a stronger social mobility, and a relatively larger gap between the rich and the poor, and considering the unsound social security system and government supervision system.

2. *Filing, Investigation, Arrest, Prosecution and Supervision by Procuratorial Organizations*

a. *The Situation of Registration and Investigations* In 2006, there were 33,668 cases recorded for the investigation of bribery or malfeasance, etc. with 40,041 persons involved, and 29,966 persons publicly prosecuted. Of them, 18,241 were major cases recorded for investigation on committing a crime through the misuse of official position and 623 of them concerning corruption or bribery of at least 1 million Yuan. There were 2,736 state functionaries at county level or above suspected of committing crimes through the misuse of position, which includes 202 persons at department/bureau level and 6 at the provincial/ministerial level. The procuratorial organizations, together with the public security organizations launched a "special campaign for pursuing evaders"

[3] "银行业案件高发有效遏制 18 个月挽回资金27.3亿," (High Incidence of Banking Industry Cases involve Prompt Return of 27.3 Billion Yuan of Funds over Eighteen Months) http://news.xinhuanet.com/fortune/2006-08/30/content_5023727.htm.

(追逃专项行动) and captured 1,670 escaped suspects involved in crimes of taking advantage of their official positions, a YEAR TO YEAR increase of 137. 6%. A total of 2,987 judicial functionaries were put on record for investigation for the misuse of authority, the practice of favoritism, perverting of the law, bribery, etc.

In 2006, the procuratorial organizations continually promoted a synchronized audio and video recording system for questioning suspects of official occupational crimes, and formulated, printed and distributed the "Work Flow of Overall Synchronized Audio and Video Recording Technology for the People's Procuratorates to Question Suspects of Official Occupational Crimes (for Trial Implementation)" (人民检察院讯问职务犯罪嫌疑人实行全程同步录音录像技术工作流程(试行)) and the "Specifications on Construction of an Overall Synchronized Audio and Video Recording System for the People's Procuratorates to Question Suspects of Official Occupational Crimes (for Trial Implementation)" (人民检察院讯问职务犯罪嫌疑人实行全程同步录音录像系统建设规范(试行)), which standardizes the establishment of procedures and systems audio and video recording for questioning suspects of official occupational crimes.

In the area of cracking down on commercial bribery, the Supreme People's Procuratorate supervised and managed 45 major and typical cases and directly commanded the investigation and prosecution of certain serious cases. For example, certain persons of the State Food and Drug Administration accepted bribes and conducted serious malfeasance in the process of registering, examining and approving, drugs. Procuratorial organizations at all levels focused on the fields of engineering construction, transfer of land, equity transaction, purchase and sales of medicine, government procurement, development and distribution of resources, etc. to search for clues, and put 9,582 commercial bribery cases on record for investigation concerning state functionaries, and involving a total of more than 1.5 billion Yuan.

In the area of strengthening international cooperation on anti-corruption, the Supreme People's Procuratorate sponsored the establishment of an International Federation of Anti-corruption Bureaus, which built a new platform for China to develop international cooperation in this area.

b. *Approval for Arrests and Prosecution* In 2006, procuratorial organizations approved the arrests of 891,620 criminal suspects and lodged public prosecution against 999,086 persons.

To address such frequent crimes as mafia-style syndicates, serious violent crimes, robbery and theft, the arrests of 47,228 criminal suspects were approved for the charges of intended homicide, arson, using explosives, rape and kidnapping. Additionally, 46,607 persons were referred for public prosecution; 419,578 persons were approved for arrest for robbery or theft and 445,849 persons were referred for public prosecution. In the campaign of cracking down on mafia-like gangs, investigation was adopted for handling major cases. This was approved for 18,446 criminal suspects and 8,343 persons were referred for public prosecution, an effective blow against the crime of mafia-like gangs.

In the area of preventing crimes that severely impair economic security, disturb the market order and hurt the people's life and health, arrest was approved for 24,211 criminal suspects for disturbing the market order and 27,728 persons were referred for public prosecution, annual increases of 14.2% and 11.1% respectively. To strengthen judicial protection for intellectual property and environmental resources, 3,729 criminal suspects were approved for arrest for producing and selling fake goods, violating trademark rights, copyrights and business secrets, and 3,634 received public prosecution, annual increases of 16.7% and 12.6% respectively. Arrest was approved for 7,974 criminal suspects who damaged environmental resources by causing severe environmental pollution accidents, illegal mining, etc. and 12,240 received public prosecution, annual increases of 15.4% and 24.8% respectively. The government continually investigated and prosecuted the crime of damaging the market economy order and conducting malfeasance. A total of 295 state functionaries were put on record for investigation of malfeasance, harboring or conniving in the area economic crime under market supervision.

In regards to death penalty cases, procuratorial organizations lack a special handling force and established staff for death penalty cases because no hearings were held for death penalty cases of second instance in most of the various regions for some time. In consideration of the substantial incremental workload, provincial procuratorates adopt a series of measures such as temporary internal adjustment of handling forces and borrowing support from lower procuratorates, which guarantees the smooth operation of death penalty cases of second instance.

c. *Situation of Litigation Supervision* In the area of registering, investigating and supervising, 16,662 cases that should have been registered but which were not were supervised and investigated by the appropriate organization for registration. There were additional arrests of 14,858 persons and additional prosecution of 10,703 persons. There were 2,846 man hours spent for the correction of illegal commutation, parole, and the temporary execution of sentences outside prison. The Supreme People's Procuratorate launched special inspections in some areas regarding the control or neglect of control for serving sentences outside prison with 6,074 criminals corrected; it also supervised and urged the department concerned to put 207 criminals in prison who were not qualified for execution of sentence outside prison. The Supreme People's Procuratorate also supervised and urged investigative organizations to withdraw 4,569 cases. It was decided 96,382 persons who did not conform to the conditions for arrest would not be arrested; it was decided 7,204 persons who could not be prosecuted for the criminal responsibility according to law or whose crime was not proven would not be prosecuted. There were 11,368 instances of proposals regarding illegal behavior in investigation activities. A total of 233 man hours of extended custody were supervised and corrected and the procuratorial link kept records of non-extended custody as well. The Supreme People's Procuratorate and the Ministry of Public Security organized a special examination of arrests with over 100,000 arrest cases tested, rectified and corrected to address problems of looser or stricter conditions for arrest, failure in timely execution after arrest, etc. This campaign promoted the correct application of the arrest measures according to law.

Trial supervision was strengthened to supervise the lighter or heavier trial of cases. There were 3,161 protest cases against criminal judgments and determinations that were confirmed wrong. There were 2,200 instances of proposals regarding illegal acts in criminal trial activities.[4]

3. *Trials of the People's Courts*

In 2006, the Supreme People's Court adjudicated 405 criminal cases. Local people's courts at all levels adjudicated 701,379 criminal cases of first instance with 889,042 criminals sentenced.

In 2006, all courts adjudicated 245,254 criminal cases with 340,715 criminals sentenced concerning the use of explosives, intended homi-

---

[4] Jia Chunwang, "Work Report of the Supreme People's Procuratorate," 5th Session of the 10th National People's Congress, (March 13, 2007).

cide, robbery, rape, kidnapping, mafia-style crime syndicates and other crimes that severely impaired the public order.

All of the courts adjudicated 23,733 corruption and malfeasance crime cases including 359 bribery cases involving companies and 8,310 bribery cases of state functionaries. There were 825 state functionaries at the county/division level or above, 92 at the prefecture/department level and 9 at the provincial/ministerial level were prosecuted for crimes against the socialist market economy order according to law. There were 16,679 cases adjudicated involving the production and sales of fake or faulty products, smuggling, damage of the financial management order, etc. with 22,944 criminals sentenced. Drug crimes were punished by adjudicating 31,582 cases involving production and trafficking of drugs and sentencing 37,256 criminals. All of the courts adjudicated 2,277 criminal cases that violated intellectual property including counterfeiting and pirating, etc. with 3,508 criminals sentenced. Of the total number of criminals, 153,724 were sentenced to at least five year fixed-term imprisonment, life imprisonment or the death penalty.

To guarantee the exclusive authority to decide death penalty cases beginning January 1, 2007, the Supreme People's Court made preparations in the areas of ideology, systemization, organization and the provision of material equipment. First, the Supreme People's Court improved the first instance, second instance and review system for death penalty cases. Second, it and the Supreme People's Procuratorate formulated the "Provisions on Several Issues Concerning the Hearing Procedure of Death Penalty Cases of Second Instance" (关于死刑第二审案件开庭审理程序若干问题的规定), which established the complete hearing of death penalty cases of second instance. Also experienced personnel were selected to join in the trial work and two sessions of training courses for national criminal trial judges were held. And finally, various ways were implemented to instruct local people's courts to unify their legal understanding and fulfill the criminal policy of strict control and application of death penalty sentencing to ensure that death penalty is only applicable to a small minority of criminals who have committed serious crimes with heavy social damage, and that only those with confirmed and sufficient evidence of crime and should be sentenced the death penalty according to law.

The people's courts at all levels guarantee the defendants may exercise various rights of action according to law; and counsel was assigned for 17,221 defendants who were qualified to receive legal aid. In accordance with the constitutional principle of "the State respecting and preserving human rights" (尊重和保障人权的宪法原则), the courts handled cases in strict accordance with law to ensure that the innocent are free from criminal prosecution, for this reason a total of 1,713 criminal defendants were acquitted. Additionally, in order to protect the lawful rights and interests of the injured parties and their families, research has been conducted into the methods of providing aid for the injured party of criminal cases. According to the statistics of ten higher people's courts that carry out trial work, a total of 7.8024 million Yuan were provided for 378 injured parties and their families for the purpose of reducing their losses.

Adopting the policy of "education, reform and rescue" (教育、感化、挽救方针) and implementing a combination of education and punishment for juvenile criminals, the people's courts helped 83,697 delinquent youth. The courts also carried out a publication and hearing system before any commutation or parole was made, and settled commutation for 429,852 criminals and parole for 20,254 criminals, thus encouraging them to turn over a new leaf. Summary procedure was applicable to 38.87% of criminal cases of first instance in the people's courts at all levels. For cases under the trial supervision of the superior court or extensively complained about by the general public, efforts were made to discover illegal trial acts and enhance the prosecution for perversions of justice, for accepting or giving bribes and for conducting malpractices for personal benefit through the manipulation of judicial and executive rights. There were 292 persons prosecuted for violation of laws and disciplines. Of them, 109 were prosecuted for criminal responsibility according to law.[5]

### C. *Review of the Major Issues*

#### 1. *Reform of Death Penalty Case Procedure*

Procedural reform of death penalty cases was the most striking improvement in the criminal litigation field in 2006. Death penalty is the severest sentence in the system, and it deprives the criminal of their right to live. It is China's lawmaking and judicial standpoint to strictly restrict death penalty, to implement a death penalty policy of cautious execution and few executions, and to prevent the excessive

[5] Xiao Yang, "Work Report of the Supreme People's Court," 5th Session of the 10th National People's Congress, (March 13, 2007).

application of the death penalty beyond a reasonable level. Based on the consideration of the strict restraint of the death penalty application, the Standing Committee of the National People's Congress, the Supreme People's Court, and the Supreme People's Procuratorate have issued legal measures reforming the death penalty procedure, which cover and review the subject of the death penalty and the second trial procedure of death penalty cases.

a. *Authorizing Death Sentence Cases* Since the founding of the People's Republic of China, the power to authorize the death penalty has been established and recalled several times. The "Organic Law of the People's Procuratorates of the People's Republic of China" promulgated in 1954, stipulates that death penalty cases are subject to approval by the Supreme People's Court and the higher people's courts. The amended "Organic Law of the People's Procuratorates of the People's Republic of China" was adopted at the Fourth Session of the First National People's Congress in 1957. It stipulates that the immediate execution of death penalty is subject to the review and approval of the Supreme People's Court, and that the death penalty with a reprieve of two years is subject to the review and approval of the higher people's courts. The Criminal Law, the Criminal Procedure Law and the "Organic Law of the People's Procuratorates" of 1979 all definitely stipulate that the power to authorize the death penalty is held by the Supreme People's Court. By that point, the authority to approve the immediate execution of the death penalty was held by the Supreme People's Court.

In the 1980s however, China experienced a deteriorating public security situation and an increase of vicious criminal cases. It was decided at the 13th Session of the Standing Committee of the National People's Congress in February 1980 that the Supreme People's Court could authorize other higher people's courts to review those serious crime cases facing the death penalty such as active homicide, rape, robbery, using explosives, and arson, for the period of 1980. The "Decision on Issues Concerning the Power to Approve Death Penalty" (关于死刑核准权问题的决定) adopted at the 19th Session of the Fifth Standing Committee of the National People's Congress in June 1981 states that, a death penalty case for the crime of homicide, robbery, rape, using explosives, arson, poisoning, destruction of dams, or damage to traffic or electric facilities, etc. sentenced by a provincial higher people's court of last instance or by an intermediate people's court where the defendant doesn't file a appeal, does not need to be presented to the

Supreme People's Court for approval if the death penalty is sentenced by a higher people's court of first instance.

On September 2, 1983, the Sixth Standing Committee of the National People's Congress passed the decision to amend the "Organic Law of the People's Procuratorates of the People's Republic of China." Article 13 of this law was amended as: the Supreme People's Court may, when it deems it necessary, authorize higher people's courts of provinces, autonomous regions, and municipalities directly under the Central Government to exercise the power to approve cases involving the implementation of death sentences for homicide, rape, robbery, using explosives and other actions gravely endangering public security and disrupting social order." Later the Supreme People's Court issued the "Notice Authorizing the High People's Courts to Review Some Death Penalty Cases" (关于授权高级人民法院核准部分死刑案件的通知) on September 7, 1983 according to the post-amendment "Organic Law of the People's Procuratorates of the People's Republic of China." This Notice states: "The Supreme People's Court authorizes the higher people's courts of the provinces, autonomous regions, and municipalities directly under the Central Government, and military courts of the PLA to exercise the power to approve those cases involving the implementation of the death sentence for homicide, rape, robbery, using explosives and other actions gravely endangering public security and disrupting social order." Moreover, the Supreme People's Court notified the higher people's courts of five provinces Yunnan, Guangdong, Guangxi, Gansu and Sichuan they were authorized to review certain death penalty cases involving drug crimes from 1991 to 1997 respectively. Over this period, the power to approve certain death penalty cases was transferred to a lower level. In fact, the power to approve death penalty cases was exercised by the Supreme People's Court and the higher people's courts to address different cases.

The "Decision Concerning Amendments of the Criminal Procedure Law of the People's Republic of China" (关于修改《中华人民共和国刑事诉讼法》 的决定) adopted at the Fourth Session of the Eighth National People's Congress on March 17, 1996 and the amended Criminal Law adopted during the Fifth Session of the Eighth National People's Congress in March 1997 both stipulate that the power to review death penalty cases was reserved for the Supreme People's Court.

However, the Supreme People's Court issued the "Notice on Authorizing Higher People's Courts and Military Courts of the PLA to Review

Certain Death Penalty Cases" (关于授权高级人民法院和解放军军事法院核准部分死刑案件的通知), which states: "since the amended Criminal Law came into force on October 1, 1997, the Supreme People's Court continues to authorize the higher people's courts of the provinces, autonomous regions and municipalities directly under the Central Government and the military courts of the PLA to approve those sentenced death penalty cases (excluding cases adjudicated by the Supreme People's Court and foreign-related cases) for the crimes prescribed in Chapter II, Chapter IV, Chapter V, Chapter VI (excluding drug crimes), Chapter VII and Chapter X. However death penalty cases concerning parties from Hong Kong, Macao or Taiwan must be reported to the Supreme People's Court for internal examination and approval before a sentence of first instance can be made." This means that the power to approve death penalty cases is continuously transferred and it remains this way today.

Thus it can be seen that after the founding of new China, the power to approve death penalty cases has experienced a cyclical process going from the centralization of approval power, to the transfer of approval power, to the recall of approval power, and back to the transfer of approval power. This cycle shows that China's law vacillated between justice and efficiency according to changes in the public order. Excessive workload is one of the more important reasons why the Supreme People's Court would transfer the authority to approve the death penalty, because this would effectively relieve the workload of the Supreme People's Court, shorten approval time and ensure that death penalty cases can be adjudicated quickly, thereby ensuring a serious and rapid crack down on those crimes that severely disrupt national security and public order and an improvement of the public order as soon as possible. Thus, China's policies regarding the approval power of death penalty prioritize efficient and targeted measures. However, there are some problems with the transfer of death penalty approval power of death penalty both according to legal principle and legal practice:

First, the principle of rule of law is violated and the authority of the law is challenged. The transfer of the approval power of death penalty started with the decision of the Standing Committee of National People's Congress and its amendment of the "Organic Law of the People's Procuratorates of the People's Republic of China," which breaches basic legal and constitutional principles. The "Organic Law of the People's Procuratorates of the People's Republic of China," the

Criminal Law and the "Criminal Procedure Law" are all basic laws enacted by the National People's Congress. Even the Standing Committee of the National People's Congress does not have the power to make breakthrough amendments to the basic laws. In disregard of the provision that the approval power of death penalty is exclusively exercised by the Supreme People's Court as stated in the "Organic Law of the People's Procuratorates of the People's Republic of China," this amendment was enacted by the National People's Congress and the Standing Committee of the National People's Congress, without authorization, authorizing the higher people's courts to approve certain death penalty cases and permitting the Supreme People's Court to authorize the higher people's courts to exercise approval power in times of need thereby amending the Organic Law. This action hurt the lawmaking authority of the National People's Congress. The amended Criminal Procedure Law and the Criminal Law adopted by the National People's Congress in 1996 and 1997 respectively, definitely state that the death penalty is subject to the approval of the Supreme People's Court. There is no addition to these provisions that states that the Supreme People's Court can authorize the higher people's courts to approve certain penalty cases for immediate execution as occasion requires.

Additionally there is no amendment to the "Organic Law of the People's Procuratorates of the People's Republic of China (1983)." Therefore as the Criminal Law, the Criminal Procedure Law and the "Organic Law of the People's Procuratorates of the People's Republic of China" are in the same category of law, the provision transferring the approval power of death penalty of the "Organic Law of the People's Procuratorates of the People's Republic of China (1983)" should be invalid according to the legal principle that a new law shall supersede an old law that regulates the same matters. In September 1997, the Supreme People's Court issued the "Notice of the Supreme People's Court on Authorizing the Higher People's Courts and Military Courts of the PLA to Approve Certain Death Penalty Cases," which invests the higher people's courts with this authority. It is evident that such an act has no legal basis. The ambiguity and the delay of legal measures make it necessary for the judiciary to offer concrete and operable interpretations on how to apply the law, however "the first duty of the judicial organ is to follow and apply statutory laws. Once we admit that a judge can amend the law, all guarantees of freedom will be lost." In this way, the judiciary's judicial interpretation will violate the principle of rule of law and hugely hurt the authority of legislation and of justice.[6]

Second, the applicable standards of death penalty cases are numerous, working against the control of capital punishment. China's judges also have varying degrees of ability in regards to making correct decisions in death penalty cases, and a wrong sentence can occur even if it is based on the discussion of the judicial committee. Moreover, there are differences in understanding in regards to the standards for death penalty application in different provinces, which leads to the different standards for death penalty application cross the country. Owing to the capability of judges and differences between the provinces in the standards for death penalty, the transfer of approval power for death penalty cases results in different application standards for the death penalty, which violates the principle of formal justice, that "equal treatment be provided for equal circumstances" (对相同的情况予以相同的对待), and results in the excessive application of the death penalty.

Third, the procedure and approval of death sentence case review cannot be effectively realized, hindering the realization of impartial justice. According to the Criminal Procedure Law, it is the intermediate people's court which acts as the court of the first instance for cases facing life imprisonment or the death penalty. If the defendant is dissatisfied with the outcome and files an appeal or the procuratorial organization lodges a protest, the court of the second instance must be a higher people's court. As the Supreme People's Court has authorized higher people's courts to review some death penalty cases, the higher people's court also acts as the court reviewing death penalty cases. In this way, the procedure of the second instance and the procedure of reviewing death penalty are both operated by the same court. In practice, the higher people's court usually adopts a method of combining the procedure of second instance and the procedure of death penalty review in dealing with the death penalty cases that it is authorized to review. Judgments upholding the decision of first instance made by the higher people's court are both judgments of the second instance and judgments of the approving the use of the death penalty. It is estimated that since the Criminal Law and the Criminal Procedure Law came

6 Enrico Ferri, trans. Guo Jianan, *Criminal Sociology* (Publishing House of the Chinese People's Public Security University), p. 126.

into force in 1979, the transfer of the approval power for the death penalty has resulted in at least two thirds of death penalty cases not undergoing the review procedure. In the past, some comrades in the judicial department believed this kind of method would help simplify the procedure and increase handling efficiency, and would ensure handling quality. Because every death penalty case undergoes judgment of the key facts by a collegiate bench and a judicial committee, etc. before being sentenced, the quality of legal attention is high, and for the Supreme Court to review the sentence of the lower court would only be a repeat of these measures. It is the opinion of the author however, that legislation which expands the review procedure guarantees the quality of death penalty cases, and furthermore that the judiciary should not violate the intentions of the legislation regarding judicial procedure in order to prioritize efficiency because such a choice would result in the procedure of reviewing death penalty cases existing in name only. The function of the power to approve death penalty is diminished in the procedure of second instance. The experience of the Supreme People's Court shows that there are always some death penalty cases whose original sentence is amended by the Supreme People's Court, which indicates that it is difficult to guarantee the quality of the cases without a review procedure, and such an omission could hurt both substantive and procedural justice.

In light of this, the "Decision of the Standing Committee of the National People's Congress on Amending the Organic Law of the People's Courts of the People's Republic of China" (全国人民代表大会常务委员会关于修改《中华人民共和国人民法院组织法》的决定), which was adopted at the 24th session of the Standing Committee of the 10th National People's Congress of the People's Republic of China, modified Article 13 of the former "Organic Law of the People's Courts of the People's Republic of China" into Article 12: "All death penalties, except for those that should be adjudicated by the Supreme People's Court according to law, shall be reported to the Supreme People's Court for examination and approval." The Decision came into force as of January 1, 2007, ending 26 years of transferring the power to approve certain death penalty cases to the lower level courts. According to Article 12 of the amended "Organic Law of the People's Procuratorates of the People's Republic of China," the "Decision of the Supreme People's Court on the Exclusive Exercise of the Power to Approve Death Penalty Cases (FS[2006] No. 12)" (最高人民法院关于统一行使死刑案件核准权有关问题的决定) was adopted at the

1409th Meeting of the Judicial Committee of the Supreme People's Court. An outline of its contents is below:

The power to approve death penalty cases shall be subject to the exclusive exercise of the Supreme People's Court as of January 1, 2007 and all legal instruments concerning the transfer of the power to approve death penalty shall also be abolished at the same time.[7]

The exclusive exercise of approval power for the death penalty by the Supreme People's Court is of far reaching importance. First, it conforms to the requirements of the principles of rule of law and is beneficial to the protection of the authority of law, beneficial to unifying standards for the application of the death penalty and for exercising strict control over death penalty cases, and finally it is beneficial to guaranteeing justice through the power to approve death penalty cases. Furthermore, just as Liu Jiachen, the former vice president of the Supreme People's Court, stated "This [reclamation] not only addresses the issue of impartial justice; it is also a milestone event for China's judicial system. It will promote significant change in the judicial system, and the criminal justice system in particular, as the formulation of criminal sentencing is very important in the criminal justice system. In the whole criminal trial, from the filing and investigation to prosecution and hearing, all stages of the process must return to the issue of "fitting the punishment

[7] The following notices issued by the Supreme People's Court on authorizing higher people's courts to approve some death penalty cases shall be abolished as of the effective date of this notice; (1) "Notice of the Supreme People's Court on Authorizing the Higher People's Courts to Approve Some Death Penalty Cases Involving Several Categories of Flagrant Dereliction" (promulgation date: March 18, 1980); (2) "Some Notices of the Supreme People's Court on Implementing the Decision of the Standing Committee of the National People's Congress on the Issue Concerning of Approval of Death Penalty Cases" (promulgation date: June 11, 1981); (3) "Notice of the Supreme People's Court on Authorizing the Higher People's Courts to Review Some Death Penalty Cases" (promulgation date: September 7, 1983); (4) "Notice of the Supreme People's Court on Authorizing the Higher People's Court of Yunnan Province to Approve Some Death Penalty Cases Involving Drug Crimes" (promulgation date: June 6, 1991); (5) "Notice of the Supreme People's Court on Authorizing the Higher People's Court of Guangdong Province to Approve Some Death Penalty Cases Involving Drug Crimes" (promulgation date: August 18, 1993); (6) "Notice of the Supreme People's Court on Authorizing the Higher People's Courts of the Guangxi Zhuang Nationality Autonomous Region, Sichuan Province and Gansu Province to Approve Some Death Penalty Cases Involving Drug Crimes" (promulgation date: March 19, 1996); (7) "Notice of the Supreme People's Court on Authorizing the Higher People's Courts to Approve Some Death Penalty Cases" (promulgation date: June 23, 1997); (8) "Notice of the Supreme People's Court on Authorizing the Higher People's Courts and Military Courts of the PLA to Approve Some Death Penalty Cases" (promulgation date: September 26, 1997).

to the crime" and it is in the end the court which has the final word in deciding whether to execute or not, condemn or not. Now that the approval power for death penalty cases has been reclaimed by the Supreme People's Court, the issue of scientific structuring will be involved within the entire criminal sentencing system, which is just what is described by the principle of "leadership in one area can change the whole (牵一发而动全身)."[8]

Although the correctness of the Supreme People's Court exercising exclusive decision making power in death penalty cases is unchallenged, the Supreme People's Court will be confronted with a considerable workload after the reclamation, which has to be considered. Therefore, the Supreme People's Court seeks to rely on the procedure of second instance to control and reduce the application of the death penalty and in order to realize this corresponding goal to the reclamation process, it is necessary that second instance hearings be held for death penalty cases.

b. *The Second Trial Procedure of the Death Penalty* The Criminal Procedure Law (刑事诉讼法) of the People's Republic of China does not outline special provisions regarding the procedure of a second instance death penalty case. According to the provisions of the Criminal Procedure Law which are in force, the procedure of second instance is same for death penalty cases as it is with other cases. It states in Article 187 of the "Criminal Procedure Law of the People's Republic of China" that: "A People's Court of second instance shall form a collegiate panel and open a court session to hear a case of appeal. However, if after consulting the case file, interrogating the defendant and listening to the opinions of the other parties, defenders and the agents acting on their behalf, the collegiate panel believes the criminal facts are clear, it may decide to not open a court session." It states in Article 253 of the interpretation of the Supreme People's Court that, "if after consulting the case file, interrogating the defendant and listening to the opinions of the other parties, defenders and their agents, the collegiate panel believes the criminal facts are clear, it may decide to not open a court session." Thus it can be seen that there are two modes for second trial

[8] "The former vice president of the Supreme People's Court: good reasons for approving no hearings for death penalty cases." See http://www.sina.com.cn, (March 10, 2007).

criminal cases, i.e. open trial court hearings (开庭审理) and "closed" written trials (书面审理).

In practice, different courts apply the two modes in different percentages. One intermediate court in Shanghai conducted the experiment of having a 100% rate of open trials of the second instance, but this was later changed. Qingdao Intermediate Court in 2001 began to coordinate its methods with Shanghai but finally stopped the attempt. The reason for the double failure of this practice lies in the discovery that it does not conform to reality. Currently, Qingdao Intermediate Court carries out open and closed trials at a rate of roughly half and half, and in those cases where the parties concerned requested open trials then that was the method adopted. Those cases not holding hearings had clear criminal facts, were accurate in applicable law, and had no objections. While in Zhuhai Intermediate Court, only 5% of criminal cases of second instance adopt open trial. It is dominated by the closed trial method.[9] Presently the issue of whether to open a court session for all cases of second instance is still disputed. According to the practical experience, it is not necessary to open court sessions for all trials of second instance, however the prevailing method of closed trials is also not appropriate.

In consideration of the status quo of second trial of criminal cases and to ensure the quality of handling the cases involving death penalty, the "Provisions on Some Issues concerning the Court Trial Procedures for the Second Instance of the Cases Involving Death Penalty (for Trial Implementation)" (关于死刑第二审案件开庭审理若干问题的规定(试行)), was adopted at the 1398th meeting of the Judicial Committee of the Supreme People's Court on August 28, 2006 and the 60th meeting of the Procuratorial Committee of the Supreme People's Procuratorate on September 11, 2006, and was implemented as of September 25, 2006. The Provisions consists of twenty articles and the important points are outlined below:

(1) Court sessions shall be opened for second instance trials of death penalty cases. When the people's court of the second instance hears a case in which the defendant files an appeal or the people's procuratorate lodges a protest after the defendant is sentenced to the immediate execution of death penalty in the first instance, it shall open a court

[9] See also: Haiqing Peng, *Research on Setup of Criminal Litigation Procedure*, (China Legal Publishing House, 2005).

session according to the laws and relevant provisions. Article 2: "When the people's court of the second instance hears a case in which the defendant files an appeal after he is sentenced with the death penalty with a reprieve of two years in the first instance, it shall open a court session in case of any of the following circumstances: (a) The defendant or his defender puts forward new evidence that will affect the conviction or determination of punishment, and a new court session is required; or (b) There is any of the circumstances for opening the court session as prescribed in Article 187 of the "Criminal Procedure Law." With respect to a case in which the people's procuratorate lodges a protest to the death penalty with a two-year reprieve sentenced by the people's court of the first instance, the people's court of the second instance shall open a court session.

(2) Establish the review principle of both comprehensive examinations and specifically focused examinations (注意重点审查). The substance of this examination is the review of cases filing an appeal or lodging a protest for the people's court of second instance. When the people's court of the second instance opens a court session to hear a case of appeal or protest involving death penalty, the collegial bench shall, before the court session, carry out an overall examination of the case files, and shall mainly examine the following contents: reasons for the appeal or protest, whether new facts or evidence are put forward; confessions and defenses of the defendant; opinions of the defender as well as the conditions on the adoption thereof by the people's court of original trial; whether the facts are clearly ascertained and the evidence is truthful and sufficient in the judgment of original trial; whether the laws are correctly applied and the sentence was properly decided in the judgment of original trial; whether there is any circumstance of violation of litigation procedures prescribed in the laws during the course of investigation, prosecution and trial; opinions of the collegiate bench and the judicial committee of the people's court of original trial; and other contents that could affect the conviction of crime or determination of punishment.

(3) Specific requirements are prescribed for second instance court hearings. The specific requirements on holding hearings principally covers trial groups, pretrial preparations, witnesses, expert witnesses, circumstances in which the injured party ought serve as a witness at court, trial steps, argument and service of judgment documents and the supervision of court trial of the people's procuratorate, etc. Some of the key points are outlined below: In regards to trial groups, a

collegiate bench shall be formed with three to five judges for hearings of the second instance of appeals or protests of death penalty cases. It shall be the president of the people's court or the chief judge of the division that acts as leading judge in handling difficult, complicated or significant death penalty cases.

As for pretrial preparation, the collegiate bench should ascertain relevant circumstances and complete the following preparations before holding a hearing to confirm whether any report was made by the defendant after the judgment of the first instance thereby exposing actions which require verification or whether there are any circumstances that may result in a postponed trial. This would also be an opportunity to question the defendant if necessary and develop the trial outline and define the issues to be presented at court. The People's Procuratorate should be informed of the time and place of the hearing three days before the session is held, and the People's Procuratorate, the defendant and the defender should provide lists of the witnesses and expert witnesses five days before the hearing session is held. Summons and notices should be served to the parties involved and to the defendant, witnesses, expert witnesses and interpreters three days before the hearing session is held. When the people's procuratorate submits new evidence to the people's court of second instance, the people's court of second instance ought to inform the defendant's lawyer or other authorized defender to consult the files in the people's court before the hearing session is held; and when the defendant and his defense submit new evidence to the people's court of second instance, the people's court of second instance ought to inform the people's procuratorate to consult the files in the people's court before the hearing session is held.

As to the circumstances in which the witnesses, expert witnesses, and injured parties ought to serve as a witness at court, it outlines these as: when the people's procuratorate, the defendant and his defender have opinions differing with the expert conclusion, when the procedure of the expert evaluation goes against the relevant regulations or when there is obvious questionable points in the expert conclusion; when the people's procuratorate, the defendant and his defender have opinions differing with the witness testimony or the injured party's presentation, and when the witness' testimony or the injured party's presentation affects the punishment of the crime; as well as in other circumstances where the collegiate bench believes it to be necessary.

Specific requirements for the court hearing are: The leading judge can read out the judgment of the first trial or just read the primary coverage of the judgment including the brief of a case, material fact, evidence and text of the judgment, etc. During the court investigation, for a case on appeal, the appealer or his defender shall read out the petition or present the grounds of appeal. For a case being protested, it is the procuratorial personnel that handle the protest. For a concurrent case of appeal and protest, the procuratorial personnel shall read the protest first and then the appealer or the defender reads out the petition or presents the grounds for appeal. The court investigation focuses on the facts, evidence and newly submitted evidence, etc. against the judgment of the first trial. Facts and evidence for which the people's procuratorate, the defendant and his defender do not have differing opinions can be omitted from investigation at the court. Additionally evidence adopted in the judgment of first trial that the people's procuratorate, the defendant and his defender have no differing opinions of, can avoid repeated confrontation and cross-examination. It is the procuratorial personnel that speak first in forensic argument for a protest case; it is the appealer and his defenders that speak first for an appellant case; for a case of appeal and protest, the procuratorial personnel speaks first and then argumentation is made in turn. The defendant of a joint offense that is not sentenced to death penalty and has not filed an appeal, and who is not needed by the people's procuratorate and the defender for inquisition and cross-examination before the hearing session is held, can be excused from court summons. The offence of any other defendant that has not been sentenced to death penalty and is clear in fact can be omitted in the court hearing. A crime that is one of the several offences of the defendant and that carries other penalties, is clear in facts and holds no differing opinion from the people's procuratorate, the defendant and his defender, can be omitted in the hearing.

The hearing of second instance for a death penalty case presents the testimony and cross-examination in court of the prosecuting and the defending parties, which carries out the principle of participation in procedure. Based on this, the judge works out the judgment and the need for procedural justice is well met. This procedure will surely advance the quality of death penalty cases and control the number of death penalty cases. For instance, the prescription of Article 13 of the "Regulations on the Circumstances under which the Witness, Expert Witness and the Injured Parties Ought to Appear in Court" will increase the appearance rate of witness and expert witness in trials of death penalty cases, thus realizing the cross-examination right of the prosecuting party and the defending party, and the defending party in particular, and facilitating the work of the judges to formulate judgments. The prescriptions of Article 14 of the "Regulations on Major Investigation into Issues in Dispute" help to focus the hearing of second instance on settling the dispute, eliminating questionable points in the case and preventing erroneous judgment. Practice has proved that there have been a decreasing number of death penalty cases since the hearing of second instance was put into operation on July 1 of last year, ahead of the schedule.

However practice has also proved that some problems exist in hearings of second instance on death penalty cases. For example, problems of sending defendants under escort, where the defendant is typically detained at a jail (看守所) at the prefecture/county level. When holding a hearing of second instance, this system increases the possibility that that the defendant may escape. As another example, a second instance open trial has demanding requirements for the quality and quantity of senior people's judges, which increases the working pressure of the higher people's courts. Again, according to the requirement of the regulations, the witness must appear in court in some cases, but there are not definite regulations on the safeguard mechanism for the appearance of witnesses such as compensation, protection and consequences of nonappearance, etc. Thus, it is questionable whether the regulation on the appearance of witness can be put realistically put into operation. Therefore, much work is needed to realize the regulations concerning the hearings of death penalty cases after they are issued.[10]

---

[10] Relevant work has been carried out in various other areas. For instance, Shanxi Higher People's Court has supplemented 46 judges and court policemen, and transferred ten excellent judges with extensive trial experience from other tribunals to the criminal tribunals to take charge of second trial death penalty cases, and impose strict education and training on all criminal justice professionals. Hunan Higher People's Court increased staff for No. 1 Criminal Tribunal and No. 2 Criminal Tribunals by eighteen people, and adjusted and supplemented the collegiate bench. The Court, the Provincial Procuratorate, the Provincial Public Security Department and the Provincial Justice Department jointly issued the "Provisions on Certain Issues Concerning the Hearings of Death Penalty Cases of Second Instance," which provides stipulations on the procedure and work of procuratorial personnel, counsels and witnesses, the appearance of expert examiners, the defense, searching for case files, custody of criminals, etc. Shandong Higher People's Court increased one criminal tribunal by 30 staff members. To prevent the death penalty trial of second instance from becoming too formalistic, Shandong Higher People's Court formulated some provisions such as the "System of Preparations for Death Penalty Trial of Second Instance" and the "Specifications on Trial Procedure and Operation of the Death Penalty Trial of Second Instance." The Sichuan Higher People's Court also selected ten excellent criminal trial judges from

The provisions also have many defects and have led to some problems which are apparent in the issues outlined below:

The first is the issue of the safeguard mechanism for the attendance of witness. According to the requirements of the provisions, the witness must appear in court in certain cases, but there is not a definite regulation on a safeguard mechanism for the appearance of witnesses such as compensation, protection and the consequence of nonappearance, etc. Thus, it is doubtful whether the regulation on the appearance of witness can actually be put into operation.

The second is the issue of assigned counsel quality. The provisions stipulate that the court shall assign a counsel for the defendant, i.e. providing legal aid for the defendant. However, in China's legal aid practice, an outstanding issue is the low quality of legal aid as a result of the fact that the compensation for a legal aid case is low, so that skilled lawyers with successful businesses are often unwilling to participate in such legal aid cases. Those lawyers who do provide legal aid usually lack experience and capability. The provisions do not regulate the business capability (in terms of years of professional service) of lawyers providing legal aid for death penalty trials of second instance, so it is difficult to guarantee the quality of the defense and to achieve the original intention of making use of the hearing of death penalty cases of second instance in order to restrict and reduce the application of the death penalty.

The third is the issue that no special stipulation exists regarding the trial period. As the provisions do not make special regulations regarding the trial period of cases of second instance, the trial period of a death penalty case of second instance still adopts the regulation of Article 196 of the "Criminal Procedure Law of the People's Republic of China," "after accepting a case of appeal or protest, a People's Court of second instance shall conclude the trial of the case within one month, or one and a half months at the latest." Under one of the situations provided in Article 126 of this law, the period may be extended by one month upon the approval or decision by the Higher People's Court of a province, autonomous region or municipality directly under the Central Government. However, with respect to cases of appeal or

basic people's courts and intermediate people's courts to specialize in the death penalty trial of second instance. Criminal justice professionals have been equipped with laptop computers, and the criminal tribunal was equipped with six new service cars to facilitate business. See: www.legalinfo.gov.cn/misc/2006-05/25/content_321608.htm.

protest accepted by the Supreme People's Court, the matter shall be decided by the Supreme People's Court itself. In the author's opinion, it would be better to stipulate a longer trial period for death penalty cases of second instance than the current trial period of general cases so as to guarantee the quality of death penalty cases.

The fourth is the issue of risk regarding the sending of defendants to court under escort. In order to hold a hearing for a death penalty case of second instance, the defendant is required to appear in court. The defendant is usually detained at a jail (看守所) at prefecture/county level, thus to send the defendant under escort increases the risk of the defendant escaping.

The fifth issue is the increasing working pressure of the higher people's courts. Court hearings of second instance have demanding quality requirements and requirements of quantity for senior people's judges, which will increase the working pressure of higher people's courts.

Therefore, much work needs to be accomplished for the regulation concerning the hearings of death penalty cases to be realized after it is issued.

2. *The Continuing Appeal for the Resolution of Homicide Cases* (命案必破)

The label homicide case refers to eight categories of cases, i.e. intentional homicide, intentional infliction of bodily injury resulting in death, the use of explosives, the use of hazardous substances, arson, robbery, rape, and kidnapping. It basically covers all criminal cases resulting in the death of victims, which are the most malicious and dangerous of all the criminal cases. To address the severe public security situation of a high rate of homicide cases and a low investigation rate, the Ministry of Public Security formulated the appeal that "homicide cases must be cracked" (命案必破) in order to respond to the low investigation rate of homicide cases in 2004.

In 2006, "homicide cases must be cracked" was still one of the special campaigns stressed by the Ministry of Public Security. Following the spirit of the "Nanjing Meeting" (南京会议) and the "Zhengzhou Meeting" (郑州会议) on resolving the problem of homicide, local public security organizations have cracked down on violent crimes with considerable progress. In 2006, the investigation rate of standing homicide cases was up to 91.4%, a YEAR TO YEAR growth of 3.6 percentage points. In 2006, the investigation rate of the eight categories of homicide cases was 91.40%. More than 25 provinces, autonomous regions and municipalities directly under the Central Government achieved an investigation rate of over 90%. Of them, Jiangsu Province ranked first in the detention rate with 95.38%. The international metropolis of Beijing also had an investigation rate of 89.40%. There were 9,110 homicide case criminals of homicide captured who were wanted online, 7 escaped homicide case criminals classified as Wanted Order A by the Ministry of Public Security, and 70 escaped homicide case criminals classified as Wanted Order B by the Ministry of Public Security. A batch of long-pending homicide cases and many influential cases supervised and managed by the Ministry of Public Security were also solved.

Incidents of homicide tended to decline yearly compared to the general occurrence of criminal cases. Based on the year to year fall of 6.2% in 2005, homicide cases classified within the eight categories in 2006 decreased by 8.2% over 2005, and homicide cases decreased by 13.7%. 2006 saw a yearly decline of 22.3% of escaped intended homicide offenders wanted online in China. In addition, a great many units achieved the goal of having no homicide cases and solving all homicide cases held. In 2006, 501 units at the county/municipal/district level had no homicide cases, accounting for 14.48% of all units qualified for registering criminal cases at the county/municipal/district level. Additionally 1,785 units at county/municipal/district level solved all homicide cases held, accounting for 51.59% of all units at the county/municipal/district level.

Practice has proven that the campaign of "homicide cases must be cracked" has achieved considerable progress, however criticism has been continuous. Criticism of this campaign is mainly limited to the following two aspects: First, that it violates the recognized litigation laws; second, the campaign could easily result in the extortion of confessions by torture. Additionally in Henan Province in 2004, four leaders of public security bureaus were dismissed for practicing fraud in connection with this campaign.

While acknowledging the positive intentions of the campaign of "homicide cases must be cracked," it is necessary to realize that the campaign's appeal is a kind of guiding requirement. As to whether a homicide case can or cannot be solved, apart from relying on the positive initiative of investigation personnel, it is also is dependent on certain objective factors that are beyond human determination. Therefore, it is a normal phenomenon that a certain number of homicide cases have not yet been solved. In some places, public security organizations set up investigation deadlines for certain homicide cases. If the detectors concerned fail to discover a case by the stated period, they are punished. This action actually violates recognized litigation law, which is inadvisable indeed.

Furthermore, it is necessary to emphasize observation of the legally formulated procedure responding to the campaign of "all homicide cases must be cracked." It should especially be strictly prohibited to adopt any illegal method to solve a case, such as extorting a confession by torture. To extort a confession by torture violates human rights and the evidence obtained in this way is usually untrue, thus resulting in the occurrence of unjust, false and wrong cases. There are provisions that strictly prohibit extorting a confession by torture in the "Criminal Procedure Law," though because of the lack of provisions on exclusionary rules of illegal evidences and the feudalistic ideas of "guilt being decided by confession" and "the presumption of guilt," it is normal to extort confession through torture in judicial practice. The most influential misjudged cases of Sun Wangang, Li Jiuming and Yu Xianglin are all related to extorting a confession by torture. On the other hand, even if the evidences acquired by illegal means such as extorting a confession by torture were true and based on this some cases were solved, this kind of method dispraises the value of procedural justice and violates fundamental human rights, and it is also counterproductive to the goal and pursuit of value in criminal litigation. Such acts are neither legal nor reasonable, and should be strictly prohibited.

### 3. *The Criminal Policy of Combining Punishment with Leniency* (宽严相济的刑事政策) *is Implemented in Procuratorial Work*

On December 28, 2006, "Certain Opinions on Implementing the Criminal Judicial Policy of Compining Punishment with Leniency in Procuratorial Work" (关于在检察工作中贯彻宽严相济刑事司法政策的若干意见) was adopted at the 68th Meeting of the Tenth Procuratorial Committee of the Supreme People's Procuratorate. It is the first special guidance document on implementing the criminal justice policy of combining punishment with leniency formulated and issued by the Supreme People's Procuratorate. The opinions cover four areas, i.e. carrying out the philosophy and principle of the criminal justice policy of combining punishment with leniency for the procuratorial organizations, implementing the requirements of the criminal justice policy for performance of the authority of legal supervision, establishing and improving the procuratorial work mechanism and handling mode, and amending concepts and strengthening instructions. Its primary points include:

(a) Defining the contents of the criminal policy of "combining punishment with leniency." It is clearly proposed in the opinions that: To carry out the criminal justice policy of combining punishment with leniency, the procuratorial organizations are required to make a difference in exercising legal supervision according to law in consideration of the public order and different criminal circumstances, and to emphasize the organic unification of punishment and leniency in an appropriate way by strictly cracking down on indictable offences and maintaining leniency in dealing with minor crimes. In addition, the policy of balancing punishment with leniency for lenient circumstances in severe crimes and the severe circumstances in minor crimes should be carried out. The policy will be demonstrated both by dealing with the criminal entities and through the applicable legal proceedings.

(b) Proposing that the prosecution organizations should institute the judicial policy of leniency and severity and maintain its principles. These principles include: complete familiarity with the details, tailor treatments to differences, administer in strict accordance with law and emphasize outcomes.

(c) Proposing requirements to completely implement the criminal justice policy of combining punishment with leniency in exercising the legal supervision function. These requirements include: Rigorously crack down on crimes that disrupt the public order and the market economy order according to law. Solemnly prosecute work-related crimes of state functionaries like corruption, bribery, malfeasance, and infringement according to law. Strictly control the arrest condition of "necessary arrests" (有逮捕必要) and be prudent in applying arrest measures. Correctly grasp the conditions for prosecution or non-prosecution and apply non-prosecution according to law. Grasp key points for recording and supervision, and emphasize supervision on indictable offences or cases with extreme social influence and serious results caused by illegal recording for investigation. Attach great importance to protests against improper sentencing and weighing of penalties. Be lenient in dealing with juvenile cases. Be lenient in dealing with minor criminal cases caused by problems among the people. Be lenient in dealing with first offenders and causal offenders of minor crimes according to law. Hold to the principle of punishing the minority, and striving to unite and educate the majority in dealing with cases of group incidents.

(d) Establish and improve the procuratorial work mechanism and handling mode when carrying out the criminal justice policy of combining punishment with leniency. Further improve the regular work mechanism in the procuratorial arm in carrying out the "strike-hard" (严打) policy. Strengthen the construction of an investigation mechanism, and improve discovering, investigating and prosecuting abilities for work-related crimes. Professionalism in handling cases is also proposed, as well as the establishment of a protocol for the timely handling of minor criminal cases, the correct application of a summary procedure and simplified trial procedure according to law, and the reformation and improvement of the method of handling juvenile cases.

(e) Strengthen departmental instruction and interdepartmental coordination and cooperation. The relevant business departments of the Supreme People's Procuratorate and the provincial people's procuratorates should strengthen work instruction, inspection and supervision of their departments in carrying out the criminal justice policy in the responsible regions. The higher-level people's procuratorates should intensify current management and regular examination, improve the supervision and restriction measures, and prevent any deviation of implementation. The procuratorial organizations at all levels should strengthen connection and coordination with public security organizations, the people's courts and the judicial administrative organizations by establishing a regular coordination protocol to study the measures of carrying out the criminal justice policy in criminal litigation activities and to solve those issues arising from the implementation of the policy, in a timely manner.

The policy of combining punishment with leniency is a basic criminal policy that has been adhered to and maintained by the Party and the country. It plays a positive role in the reasonable disposal of judicial resources, in the targeting of serious crimes, in the effort to "educate, reform and rescue" minor offenders including delinquent youth, and in safeguarding criminal and social outcomes. However there are also certain issues which have emerged as a result of the implementation of this policy. For instance, the punishment of crimes in the "strike-hard" (严打) campaign was excessively pursued, and instances of breaking the law and breaching the legal procedure were not uncommon. The law enforcement offices' illegal administration of justice hugely hurt the authority of law, which was a substantial cause of criticism of the "strike-hard" campaign. "Some Opinions on Implementing the Criminal Judicial Policy of Combining of Punishment with Leniency in the

Procuratorial Work of the Supreme People's Procuratorate in 2006" (关于在检察工作中贯彻宽严相济刑事司法政策的若干意见) specifically defines the policy of combining punishment with leniency and stresses that "striking-hard' and lenient treatment must both be conducted according to law, which shows that the law enforcement offices have improved their understanding of the concept of rule of law and their understanding of the administration of law. Additionally these opinions have had important operational significance in changing negative phenomena associated with the "strike-hard" campaign, such as the illegal administration of the law and the violation of human rights.

In order to carry out the criminal justice policy of combining punishment with leniency, to improve litigation efficiency, preserve judicial resources, resolve social contradictions in a timely manner, realize the organic combination of legal and social outcomes in handling cases and to build a harmonious socialist society, according to the relevant provisions of the "Criminal Procedure Law" and combining the reality of procuratorial work experience, the "Opinions of the Supreme People's Procuratorate Concerning Rapid Handling of Minor Criminal Cases According to Law" (最高人民检察院关于依法快速办理轻微刑事案件的意见) was adopted at the 68th meeting of the Tenth Procuratorial Committee of the Supreme People's Procuratorate. These opinions state that minor criminal cases with simple details, clear facts, sufficient and true evidence, and the confessions of criminal suspect and defender, can be simplified through work flow and that the handling period can be shortened on the premise of following legal proceedings and proscribed periods and ensuring handling quality. To rapidly handle minor criminal cases according to law, the following principles ought to be followed: the principal of strict implementation according to law, the principle of unifying justice and efficiency, the principle of sufficiently guaranteeing the right of litigation for litigant participants and the principle of settling social contradictions in a timely manner. The opinions also give restrictive provisions on the details of rapidly handling cases such as the time limit for the approval of arrests, and the examination of the prosecution.

The "Regulations of the People's Procuratorate on Handling Criminal Cases with Minor Offenders" (人民检察院办理未成年人刑事案件的规定) was adopted at the 68th meeting of the Tenth Procuratorial Committee of the Supreme People's Procuratorate on December 28, 2006. The regulations require the people's procuratorates to carry out the policy of "educate, reclaim and save" and to uphold the principle of giving priority to education with punishment as the subsidiary means. Generally, special working institutions or special working groups shall be set up to handle juvenile criminal cases; if this is not possible, a special person should be assigned to handle the case. This should usually be undertaken by such procuratorial personnel as are familiar with the physical and mental development characteristics of juveniles and who excel at providing ideological education for minors. Special regulations are also made to address the approval of arrests, the prosecution, and the support of public prosecution in court as well as the inspection of appeal. For instance, it should be noted in examination of approving the arrest of a juvenile criminal suspect whether the juvenile threatened to commit the crime, whether there was an adult abetting the juvenile, imparting criminal methods or taking advantage of the minor for delinquency. In order to examine the prosecution of a juvenile criminal suspect, to the examining entity should hear the opinions of the juvenile's parents or other legal representative, the defense representative, and the injured juvenile and his legal representative. Social investigation can be adopted in order to familiarize the examining entity with the juvenile criminal suspect's growth experience, home environment, personal characteristics, social activity, etc. by investigating the organizations and personnel concerned in the juvenile's school, community and home, etc. so as to provide reference for handling the case, etc.

In practice, the procuratorial authorities' criminal policy of "combining punishment with leniency" has been adopted for some time. For instance, the People's Procuratorate of Changning District, Shanghai took the lead in adopting the method of reprieve prosecution of minor's cases (then addressed as investigation before prosecution) in 1992. By the end of 2003, prosecution of a total of 20 juvenile crime cases was postponed. Except for four cases, which were slated for public prosecution, the rest were handled with no prosecution. Those minors who were not prosecuted all went to a college or started to work.

Absorbing the concept of restorative justice, Shandong Yantai People's Procuratorate started to adopt the procedure of "reconcilable justice" (平和司法) in 2006, which is one form of the criminal reconciliation system. The primary aim of "reconcilable justice" is to address minor criminal cases such as eligible juvenile crime, unintentional crime, or crimes of slight damages, in which the injured party and the injuring person come to common understanding on the handling of the case. This happens under a presiding community comprehensive treatment institution along with the initiation, participation and supervision of a procuratorial organization. The participation of the procuratorial organization will assure that the injuring party amends the injury and will assure that the injured party receives timely and sufficient compensation for material and emotional losses, and that the procuratorial organization does not impose punishment or imposes light punishment to the injuring party.[11] This practice has achieved positive results.

The "Opinions of the Supreme People's Procuratorate Concerning Rapid Handling of Minor Criminal Cases According to Law" and the "Regulations of the People's Procuratorate on Handling Criminal Cases with Minor Offenders" are pretty definite standards for the procuratorial organizations to use in carrying out the criminal policy of "combining punishment with leniency." They make the criminal policy operable to some degree and help guarantee that the prosecution of minor criminal cases and cases involving minors are handled leniently and to promote the transition of the purpose of criminal penalty from retributive to preventative.

However there are still two more issues which merit inquiry:

First, the content concerning the rapid handling of minor criminal cases according to law in the "Opinions of the Supreme People's Procuratorate Concerning Rapid Handling of Minor Criminal Cases According to Law" is not prescribed in the "Criminal Procedure Law" in force. While it does not outright contradict the "Criminal Procedure Law," it still cannot be said that it conforms to its requirements. This is because in effect the "Criminal Procedure Law's" summary procedure in fact is just a type of simplified judicial procedure, the simplification of procedure and the omissions of litigation phases only happens during the trial stage. Although there are shortcomings in this type of stipulation in the "Criminal Procedure Law," China's application practice of summary procedure shows that the simplification of summary procedure needs improvement. The form of summary procedure ought to be diversified with expanding application to cases and application lawsuit stages, etc. However, according to general legal principle, state organizations will be incapable of exercising power that is not prescribed by law. In this way before amending the "Criminal Procedure Law," the prosecution organizations took the lead in reforming summary pro-

[11] 烟台首推 "平和司法" 程序, "Yan Taishou Pushes the 'Reconcilable Justice' Process," July 26th, 2007, http://www.shm.com.cn/newscenter/2006-07/26/content_1768606.htm.

cedure, which could be viewed as a violation of the law enforcement. Furthermore, there are definitely some contents which merit further discussion in the opinions.

For instance, Article 6 of the opinions uses the work-intensive nature of the task and the shortage of personnel for handling cases as the reason of restricting the time period for examining appeals and forbids the extension of the handling period. Obviously, such a provision is unreasonable, as the examination of an appeal should have time to consider the case properly and the period of handling an individual case with a heavy workload should not be restricted. Such methods will inevitably influence the case quality. As another example, as to whether the scope of criminal cases applicable to rapid handling according to law as stipulated in Article 3 and Article 4 of the opinions are appropriate, etc. all these issues need to be standardized within the "Criminal Procedure Law."

Second, the "Opinions of the Supreme People's Procuratorate Concerning Rapid Handling of Minor Criminal Cases According to Law" and the "Regulations of the People's Procuratorate on Handling Criminal Cases with Minor Offenders" are both judicial interpretations issued by the Supreme People's Procuratorate and are only legally binding to procuratorial organizations. However in China, criminal litigation includes the stages of filing, investigating, protesting, and trying, as well as execution. To make criminal policy produce substantial results in criminal litigation, it is not enough to rely on only the procuratorial authorities but it also needs the aggressive action and mutual coordination of other authority organizations like the public security organization, the people's court, jails, etc. It would also need the legislature to stress this issue in amending the "Criminal Procedure Law," to sum up the experiences and lessons drawn from the two judicial interpretations of the procuratorial organ in practice, and to conduct an overall amendment and improvement of the summary procedure, thus making the authorities concerned in criminal litigation work in this respect better demonstrate the spirit of the criminal policy of "combining punishment with leniency."

### D. *The Prospects of Criminal Litigation*

In 2006, the legislature made active preparations for the amendment of the "Criminal Procedure Law of the People's Republic of China." The Commission of Legislative Affairs of the NPCSC conducted surveys and asked for opinions on the amendment of the "Criminal Procedure Law." The academic community responded positively and the departments handling practical affairs also actively researched it. According to the lawmaking plan for 2007 of the Standing Committee of the National People's Congress, the amendment of the "Criminal Procedure Law" will be deliberated at the 30th Session of the Standing Committee of the National People's Congress. This amendment of the "Criminal Procedure Law" will address pressing issues in criminal justice practice according to the tenet of advancing the guarantee of human rights (in reference to the provisions of the international human rights covenants and common legal rules of developed countries of "rule of law" that carry out the Continental Law System or the Common Law System). Progress is desired on the following fronts:

1. *Basic Principles of the "Criminal Procedure Law of the People's Republic of China"*

The basic principles of the "Criminal Procedure Law" exist throughout the overall process or major stages of the criminal litigation. They are the ground rules required of the special State authorities and litigant participants in order to engage in criminal litigation activities and they contain extensive instruction for criminal litigation. Therefore, the amendment of these basic principles will influence the renewal of ideology as well as the system construction of the entire "Criminal Procedure Law."

This amendment should give prominence to the establishment of the three basic principles: the presumption of innocence, privilege against compulsory self-incrimination and prohibition against double jeopardy. Additionally, amendments ought to be made within relevant systems, for example the cancellation of the provision that "the criminal suspect shall answer the investigators' questions truthfully." Additionally, the relevant provisions on procedure for trial supervision should be changed, etc.

2. *The Criminal Litigation System*

The amendment of certain content in the advocacy system, the enforcement measure system and the evidence system is urgently needed.

In regards to the system of advocacy, amendments are suggested in the following areas: The first is to guarantee the essential conditions of defending such as the guarantee of the right to meet, the right of investigation and the right of collecting evidence, etc. The second is to respect the function of defense, which is mainly reflected in the case handlers hearing the opinion of the defender in the litigation procedure. Also these case handlers should specify the cause and record it on the litigation document if they have a different opinion.

In regards to the enforcement measure system, procedural fairness for enforcement measures should be improved and the current situation should be changed so that it is the prosecuting organ that exclusively decides to give or take away the basic rights of the criminal suspect such as the right of personal liberty and property rights.

In regards to the evidence system, compulsory stipulations on the appearance of special witnesses, expert examiners in court, etc. should be granted and the prosecuted should be ensured the right to cross-examine. Exclusionary rules for illegal evidence should be established in order to standardize the authorities' evidence collecting behaviors and prevent the violation of the lawful rights and interests of the prosecuted.

3. *Criminal Litigation Procedure*

In regards to criminal litigation procedure, it is necessary to improve the death penalty review procedure, the summary procedure and the litigation procedure for minors' cases.

For the death penalty review procedure, one necessary amendment is to define the review scope of death penalty cases including material content and procedure content. Another is ensuring that the judge be neutral in the review method. It is necessary to stipulate that the prosecutor shall furnish evidence of guilt and take charge of eliminating the questionable points of a case. Finally, the last improvement is the stipulation that the demand of proof of a death penalty review case ought to be higher than the demand of proof of other cases just as is prescribed in Article 4 of the "Safeguards Guaranteeing Protection of the Rights of Those Facing the Death Penalty (1984)," that "Capital punishment may be imposed only when the guilt of the person charged is based upon clear and convincing evidence leaving no room for an alternative explanation of the facts."

As to the summary procedure, it ought to sum up the experience and lessons of judicial departments and bring about improvements in diversifying the summary procedure so as to change China's single summary procedure and increase the efficiency of criminal litigation. This should also facilitate the reasonable allocation of judicial resources. For instance, we can refer to the provisions of the German law to increase the penal order procedure, etc.

It is also necessary to increase the criminal litigation procedure to address the cases of minors. There is no separate litigation procedure to address the cases of minors in the "Criminal Procedure Law." Minors are still growing both physically and mentally and have low socialization and awareness abilities. To some degree, their natural character eclipses their social character and instinct eclipses their rationality. Therefore, there should be a different litigation procedure to address the crimes of minors. It should differ from the litigation procedure for adults in aspects of basic principles of litigation, pretrial procedure and judicial procedure.

## II. *The Civil Litigation System*

2006 saw progress made both in lawmaking and administration of law in the civil litigation field.

### A. *Development of Civil Litigation*

In 2006, the Commission of Legal Affairs under NPC Standing Committee worked out the first draft of the amendment to the "Civil Procedure Law of the People's Republic of China" (刑事诉讼法) after several consultations with the relevant authorities. In 2006, several legal documents concerning civil litigation were issued by the Standing Committee of the National People's Congress and the Supreme People's Court mainly covering the areas of supervision, management and jurisdictional control of execution cases, service of judicial documents of cases involving foreign interests, periods of sequestration, retention, and the freezing of assets for civil execution, etc.

### B. *Civil Trial, Execution and Supervision*

In 2006, the Supreme People's Court adjudicated 673 civil cases with a total object value of 15.1 billion Yuan. The Supreme People's Court also coordinated and supervised the handling of 213 trans-regional civil execution cases. Local people's courts at all levels adjudicated 4,382,407 civil cases of first instance with a total object value of 682.78 billion Yuan. The people's courts at all levels adjudicated 1,159,437 cases concerning marriage, family or inheritance disputes, and 986,082 cases concerning ownership or infringement disputes. Of these cases, there were 31,427 neighborhood dispute cases. Also 179,637 labor dispute cases with total object value of 3.189 billion Yuan were adjudicated. The people's courts at all levels adjudicated a total of 4,755 cases on disputes arising from mergers, bankruptcy or the transfer of property right of state-owned enterprises 717,526 cases on financial disputes were adjudicated, and 2,236,888 cases on contract disputes with a total object value of 475.7 billion Yuan. The people's courts at all levels adjudicated a total of 14,056 intellectual property civil cases of first instance with a total object value of 2.71 billion Yuan. This includes 5,751 copyright infringement cases, 378 trademark infringement cases, 3,227 patent infringement cases and 1,188 illicit competition cases. Abiding by the Chinese laws and the international treaties China has accessed to respecting international practice and equally protecting the lawful rights and interests of Chinese and foreign parties, the people's courts at all levels adjudicated 7,375 maritime and maritime trade cases with total object value of 4.445 billion Yuan. Moreover, the people's courts at all levels also strengthened the trial of cases concerning parties from foreign countries/regions, Hong Kong, Macao or Taiwan, and adjudicated a total of 23,313 cases concerned, a yearly growth of 16.39%. Summary procedure was applicable to 71.26% of civil cases of first instance in the people's courts at all levels.[12] The people's courts at all levels accepted and examined the parties' appeals in a timely manner against the effective judgments of the people's courts, and opposed 12,669 civil and administrative actions and proposed 5,949 suggestions on reopening inspection. These actions influenced the parties involved to withdraw 37,524 appeals against correct judgments.[13]

### C. *Civil Litigation Mediation*

According to the needs of establishing a harmonious socialist society, the Supreme People's Court further carried out the civil judicial principle of "mediation is preferential and judgment is necessary." The primary method is "the use of a combination of mediation and judgment to settle disputes thoroughly" (能调则调、当判则判、调判结合、案结事了) for the purpose of resolving social contradictions and disputes to

[12] Xiao Yang, "Work Report of the Supreme People's Court," 5th Session of the 10th National People's Congress, (March 13, 2007).

[13] Jia Chunwang, "Work Report of the Supreme People's Procuratorate," 5th Session of the 10th National People's Congress, (March 13, 2007).

the utmost in 2006. Of all the civil cases adjudicated by the people's courts at all levels, 30.41% were settled by means of mediation with 55.06% for mediation of civil cases of first instance and withdrawal of suits.[14]

China's history of applying judicial mediation in civil litigation can be divided into approximately five stages:

The first stage was before the founding of the new China when there was the Ma Xiwu adjudication method in the liberated area in north Shaanxi Province. At that time Ma Xiwu, the judge of Shaanxi Longdong Superior Court often went to the case sites to settle civil disputes by means of mediation. By using a simple and straightforward manner, this kind of trial means effectively resolved "contradictions amongst the people" and was developed in the initial stages of the People's Republic of China.

The second stage was the period before the promulgation and enforcement of the "Civil Procedure Law of the People's Republic of China" (民事诉讼法), from the 1950s to early 1980s. This means of civil mediation was excessively and dominantly stressed. The civil trial work at that time was concluded according to the following policy: "rely on the masses, investigate and study, handle cases on the spot, give priority to mediation" (依靠群众, 调查研究, 就地办案, 调解为主). As the mediation rate was excessively stressed, there appeared cases of pending mediation, compulsory mediation and cheating mediation, etc. The authority of certain courts was challenged and public confidence in the system was damaged.

The third stage was from the promulgation of the "Civil Procedure Law" to the early 1990s. In this period, the dominant method of mediation was replaced by legislation-based mediation. However because of the lack of a necessary guarantee of legal procedure, some problems such as illegal case work, and the judges bearing responsibility for the entirety of the trial (法官包揽诉讼) still existed.

The fourth stage began in the 1990s when there was a boom of adopting open trials as the core trial method in the national court system. In the process of reforming the trial method, certain regions stressed case handling by trial in court and neglected the application of mediation, thereby causing a rise in the number of appeals.

[14] Xiao Yang, "Work Report of the Supreme People's Court," 5th Session of the 10th National People's Congress, (March 13, 2007).

The fifth stage is the past few years. In order to establish a harmonious socialist society, the Committee of Political and Legislative Affairs, the CPC Central Committee and the Supreme People's Court have issued some documents pointing out that judicial mediation that combines morality and the law can facilitate the acceptance of mediation results by the parties involved with a high execution rate and it can play an exclusive role in resolving social contradictions and disputes and promoting the establishment of a harmonious socialist society.

The Sixth Plenary Meeting of the 16th CPC Central Committee was held during October 8–11, 2006. At this meeting President Xiao Yang of the Supreme People's Court spoke, saying that: "Judicial mediation is an important litigation system regulated in the "Civil Procedure Law of the People's Republic of China," and it is also an important method for the people's courts at all levels to administer justice according to law. Judicial mediation plays an exclusive role in resolving social contradictions and disputes and promoting the building of a harmonious society. Thus, judicial mediation has been promoted to a new level of importance. During October 8–11, 2006, the Supreme People's Court required that the people's courts at all levels must establish these three goals of judicial mediation in the new era: to settle disputes with the conclusion of mediation, that all parties concerned shall abide by this decision, and set a standard to end disputes (定纷止争). On November 8, 2006, Vice President Jiang Xingchang of the Supreme People's Court made a request to the people's courts at all levels: for criminal cases with civil litigation, mediation work shall be applied throughout the whole trial to assure the injured party reparations in kind according to law.

Local courts have created innovations in the forms of mediation; for instance, integrating the local tea culture in the lawsuit mediation, the People's Court of Jinjiang City, Fujian Province has invented and popularized the "tea table mediation method" (茶桌调解法). When a party comes to the People's Court of Dongguan City, Guangdong Province for filing a suit, the party can apply for selecting one of the five settlement modes out of court. The People's Court of Zhenhai District, Ningbo City, set up a special judicial mediation team, which deals with a civil/commercial case within one week at average, sometimes even within several hours.[15]

---

[15] "司法调解被提到了新高度," (Regulations on the Administration of Justice have

However some issues also appeared in the legislation and practice of civil mediation. They are mainly reflected in the following aspects:

The first is compulsory mediation. The mediation mode of "combining mediation with trial" (调审合一) has been adopted in China. Acting as mediator and adjudicator, a judge has more freedom in selecting the mode of mediation or judgment in handling a case. In order to complete an assigned mediation rate and avoid the investigation of misjudged cases, some judges disregard the parties' rights and have adopted compulsory mediation, which fails to resolve disputes for a protracted period of time, thus damaging the lawful rights and interests of the parties and hurting the authority of justice.

The second is malicious mediation. As social creditability has not yet been formulated in China, some parties usually take advantage of the judicial mediation in order to maliciously bring the other party to compromise but without performing the due obligations when a mediation agreement is concluded. This phenomenon hurts the lawful rights and interests of the other party and the authority and accountability of the court.

The third is lack of rules of procedure. There is almost no provision on the procedure of civil mediation in the "Civil Procedure Law" and related judicial interpretations, which results in excessive randomness in the mediation procedure. Although it is decided by the nature of the mediation system, "the reconciliation procedure features more liquidity and informality than our conventional litigation procedure." Therefore it is not feasible to give detailed rules of the mediation procedure. But as a system of law, mediation ought to have basic standardized requirements, which are necessary for regulating and restricting power, protecting rights and guaranteeing the successful realization of the lawmaking goal of mediation.

The fourth is the lack of a guarantee of full awareness and voluntary compromise on the part of all parties involved. A mediation agreement is formed at the cost of the compromise of the interests of both parties. According to the requirement of general legal principle, the waiving of a citizen's right granted by the constitution and the law shall be based on the voluntary full awareness of the citizen, otherwise it shall constitute a breach of law, as in the legal rules of civil media-

Reached a New High), Xinhuanet News Special Report, 2006, http://news.xinhuanet.com/legal/2007-01/01/content_5557653_1.htm.

tion in China, there is no content to guarantee of the full awareness and voluntary participation in compromise of the parties involved for waiving their rights.

The fifth is the unsound mechanism of mediation supervision. It is prescribed in Article 180 of the "Civil Procedure Law" that "with respect to a legally effective conciliation statement, if evidence furnished by a party proves that the conciliation violates the principle of voluntariness or that the content of the conciliation agreement violates the law, the party may apply for a retrial." However in practice, a mediation agreement is signed by the parties personally. Even if illegal mediation has occurred, the parties are required to undertake the evidential burden, and it is difficult to furnish evidence that "proves that the conciliation violates the principle of volunteerdom." Furthermore, the people's procuratorate has no right to lodge a protest against the mediation. So there is almost no supervision over mediation.

If the above problems can't be solved, civil mediation won't function fully or could even generate negative influence. This could even lead to such phenomenon that the more cases mediated, the more problems are discovered in those cases. Thus this issue merits further attention.

### D. *The Prospects of Civil Litigation*

According to the legislation plan for 2007 of the Standing Committee of the National People's Congress, the amendment to the "Civil Procedure Law" will be deliberated at the 28th Session of the Standing Committee of the National People's Congress in June 2007. This amendment to the "Civil Procedure Law of the People's Republic of China" should be made in order to "ensure the parties' right of appeal obtains effective guarantees and the furnishing of evidences obtains judgment and behavior in support of the social harmony, thus safeguarding social equity and justice."[16]

#### 1. *Improving the Evidence System*

The evidence system is one of the most important but also one of the weakest areas in the "Civil Procedure Law of the People's Republic of China." To make up for the shortness of the legislation and to

[16] Xiao Yang, "Work Report of the Supreme People's Court," 5th Session of the 10th National People's Congress, (March 13, 2007).

meet the needs of judicial practice, "Some Provisions of the Supreme People's Court Concerning Civil Litigation Evidence" (最高人民法院关于民事诉讼证据的若干规定) was adopted at the 10th meeting of the Judicial Committee of the Supreme People's Court Judicial Committee. These provisions regulate the party's adducing of evidence, the court's investigation and collection of evidences, and establish a time limit for adducing evidence, evidence exchange, cross-examination, examination and determination of evidences, etc. Practice has proved that these provisions help standardize the judges' and the parties' operation of evidences and solve a series of problems in the civil litigation practice. However from of the standpoint of legality, a great many contents in the provisions clashed with the provisions of the "Civil Procedure Law" such as the setup of time limit for evidential burden, etc, and the legality of judicial interpretation was diverted. Therefore these problems need to be solved in an amendment. The parts of the provisions proven feasible through actual practice can be included in legislation to make them actually legal and convenient for enforcement; contrarily, the implementation of those contents not proved through practice should be prohibited.

2. *Improvement of Summary Procedure*
Considering the single summary procedure form of civil action is inadaptable to actual demands, it is suggested the concrete forms of the summary procedure be expanded to increase litigation efficiency and save judicial resources. For instance, the procedure for objects of little value can be formulated additionally.

3. *Improve the Procuratorial Supervision System for Civil Litigation*
Procuratorial supervision of civil litigation plays a unique role in China's legal supervision system. Thus it is very necessary to improve the procuratorial supervision system for civil litigation. For example, the procuratorial organizations ought to be authorized with a larger scope for lodging protests and should have the right to lodge a protest for all judgments and orders of the people's courts including the judgment of execution proceedings, mediation agreements and the legal instruments produced in the proceedings of the trial of cases such as special proceedings applicable to the people's courts (excluding the cases concerning voters' qualification), proceedings for supervising and urging the clearance of debt, proceedings of service by publication and proceedings in bankruptcy.

4. *Improving Civil Execution Measures*

Execution is the last stage of civil litigation and is also a key stage for judgments to be put into effect. In order to address the difficulties of execution, the following stipulations should be made to improve the law:

(a) Establish a system of assisting enforcement of public security organizations actions. Referring to foreign legislation experience, it is necessary to definitely stipulate the functions of the public security organization in assisting civil execution.

(b) Establish a sound "upgraded execution" (提级执行) and designated execution system. It is necessary to set up the legal standards of "upgraded execution" and designated execution, to define the rights of the parties concerned in "upgraded execution" and the determination of jurisdiction, and to stipulate the relevant conditions. For example, the party concerned possesses property but the executing court fails to execute within one year without lawful cause, thus addressing the local protection.

(c) Establish an execution relief system. According to the "Civil Procedure Law" in force, there is no execution relief procedure to address the improper acts of execution such as not conducting sequestration according to law, delay in execution, illegal behavior in auction, etc., which influence the safeguarding of the lawful rights and interests of the parties. The law should grant the right to raise an objection against improper execution to the parties concerned and the interested parties in order to solve the problem.

(d) Improve prevention of obstructions to executions of judgments. At present the compulsory measures which are impeding execution of the "Civil Procedure Law" include: too short of a detainment time, imposed fines which are too low as well as the question of whether it is permitted to detain the relevant responsible person when the unit concerned doesn't perform the obligation of assisting in the execution. Therefore, this amendment to the "Civil Procedure Law" ought to prolong the term of detention, increase fines and define the punishment measures for the responsible person(s) of the unit concerned.

(e) Establish a system of execution for property investigation and compulsory reporting. One important cause of the difficult execution of sentences is that the applicant is not granted effective measures to search for property by the law. It is also not a smooth process for the courts to search after the property. After concluding some useful research of several local courts, it is suggested that a system of "investigation order" (调查令) be established, i.e. the court issues an investigation order and the lawyer holds it to conduct an investigation into the unit concerned.[17] The courts should be assigned the responsibility of investigating the property status as a supplement to the investigation; and should also define the assistance obligation of relevant units, etc.

---

[17] To address difficulties of investigation and collection of evidence due to the interested partys' limited procedural capacity and the influence of external factors, the No. 2 Civil Court of Jingkou District People's Court of Zhenjiang City, Jiangsu Province issued the first investigation order to the attorney of the plaintiff of a traffic accident case according to the "Opinions on Standardizing the Pretrial Procedure of Civil Cases (I) (trial implementation)" of the provincial high court. It has been reported that the issue of the lawyer's investigation order is a pioneering work in Jiangsu provincial court system and is also an innovation in China's judicial field. The implementation of the investigation order is helping to improve the party's investigation and evidence collection capabilities, and guarantee the realization of sustaining the plaintiff's various rights. The court can also order and assist a lawyer to investigate those units or individuals that are non-compliant. For those hindering the investigation and collection of evidence without just cause, the court can order them to perform the obligation of assistance, or may also investigate and collect evidence according to their authority.

# PROTECTION OF HUMAN RIGHTS AND THE ESTABLISHMENT OF "RULE OF LAW" IN CHINA

Liu Huawen[1]

Chinese society is entering a new era of rights and 2006 marks the third year since the line "the State respects and preserves human rights" was written into China's Constitution. The protection of human rights is the goal and the measure of China's establishment of "rule of law," it guides the development of this undertaking and at the same time also creates favorable conditions for the provision of a guarantee for the protection of human rights.

This year China set the development goal of building a harmonious socialist society, and it continually played an active role in the field of international human rights law. The country was elected as a member of the newly established Human Rights Council of the United Nations. And, within China the implementation of the International Covenant on Human Rights was actively promoted, authority over the judicial review of death penalty to the Supreme People's Court was reclaimed; an international seminar on "Respecting and Promoting Human Rights and Building a Harmonious World" was held in an active and open way and the first photo exhibition on human rights was sponsored. Domestic research and education on human rights also maintained momentum.

## I. *China Sets the Goal of Establishing a Harmonious Socialist Society*

The Sixth Plenum of the 16th CPC Central Committee held from October 8–11, was one of the most momentous events of 2006. It was the meeting in which the "Resolutions of the CPC Central Committee on Major Issues Regarding the Building of a Harmonious Socialist Society" (中共中央关于构建社会主义和谐社会若干重大问题的

[1] Liu Huawen is an associate research fellow at the Institute of Law at the Chinese Academy of Social Sciences.

决定) was adopted, which promoted the goal and task of building a harmonious socialist society by 2020, thus presenting a roadmap for a "harmonious society." This was an important strategic measure for China to increase the well-being of its entire people, to build a fair and just society and to realize the sustainable development of economy and society after the high-speed economic growth and the satisfaction of the basic needs of its 1.3 billion citizens for adequate food and clothing. Hu Jintao, the General Secretary of the CPC Central Committee and the Chinese President pointed out, "the harmonious society we aim for is a society based on democracy and the "rule of law" as well as on impartiality and justice. It is a society of integrity and amity; a society full of vitality, one of order and stability, and of harmony between man and nature."

The goal of building a harmonious socialist society has received positive feedback from abroad. At the EU Foreign Ministers Council in Brussels, Belgium on December 11, 2006, an official document was passed that confirmed the Chinese Government's achievements in developing its economy and eliminating poverty, and noted the Chinese Government's important strategy of promoting the concept of a "harmonious society" while advancing the balanced development of society. The Council considered the concept of "harmonious society" to be very important and it continues to encourage and support China's political and economic reforms, and strengthen international cooperation in the areas of social welfare, and the implementation of social responsibility in business and in sustainable development.[2]

The goal of building a harmonious socialist society has had great influence in China. Therefore it can be predicted that according to the ideas of the Sixth Plenary Session, the Chinese Government will guarantee social equity, further close the gap between the rich and the poor and expand employment. These goals will be realized mainly in the areas of systemization and protocol. The government will also take the lead in reforming medical treatment, education and social security in order to allow the poor to greater enjoy the achievements of the reform and development. This will have important and profound significance on the strengthening the protection of human rights at home

[2] EU Foreign Ministers Council Meeting, "Conclusion of EU Foreign Ministers Council Regarding Europe-China Strategic Partnership," Brussels, Belgium, December 11, 2006.

and in the promoting of the domestic implementation of international human rights standards.

## II. *China was Elected as a Member of the Human Rights Council of the United Nations*

The Sixtieth Session of the United Nations General Assembly passed a decision by 170 votes to replace the Commission on Human Rights with the Human Rights Council on March 15, 2006. The decision states that the 47 member countries of the Human Rights Council will be distributed according to the principle of equitable geographical distribution and elected by the popular vote of the UN with the support of majority of UN member countries required. In electing the Council members, the UN should consider the contribution of the candidate countries in promoting and protecting human rights.

On May 9, The United Nations General Assembly elected 47 member countries of the first session of the UN Human Rights Council. The secret ballot result of 191 member states was striking: forty-seven countries including China, Cuba, Saudi Arabia and Russia were elected as the first session members of the UN Human Rights Council. According to the result of lot drawing, the term for China and other 17 member countries is three years. The United States did not participate in the election for members of UN Human Rights Council.

China's election by high vote shows that China has made considerable achievements and that its accomplishments in the area of human rights have won the acknowledgement of the majority of the countries presiding. China has included the line "the State respects and preserves human rights" in its constitution and continues to promote the cause of human rights in its social development. These actions indicate China's solemn commitment to the international cause of human rights and the Chinese government's promotion of the principle of "taking people as the basis for governing" (以人为本的执政) further raised its human rights status to a new level.

In line with the comments of spokesman Liu Jianchao of the Chinese Ministry of Foreign Affairs, China's election as a member of the Human Rights Council will be beneficial for the Council in the promotion and protection of human rights across the world. The Chinese Government has been devoted to promoting and protecting human rights and fundamental freedoms and has taken an active part in international human rights conversation and cooperation. The Chinese Government supports the Human Rights Council in its handling of human rights issues in a fair, objective and open-minded way and in its strengthening of constructive conversation and cooperation between different civilizations, cultures and religions. The Chinese Government has a definite standpoint on human rights issues, and it is believed that China will play an active role in the work of the Human Rights Council.

## III. *China and the International Covenant on Human Rights*

### A. *Overview*

The Chinese government has paid great attention to the role international correspondence on human rights has played in promoting and protecting human rights. So far, China has been a signatory country of certain important international human rights conventions like the "International Covenant on Economic, Social and Cultural Rights" (经济、社会及文化权利国际公约), the "Convention on the Rights of the Child" (儿童权利公约), the "Convention against Torture and Other Cruel, Inhuman or Degrading Treatment or Punishment" (禁止酷刑公约), the "International Convention on the Elimination of All Forms of Racial Discrimination" (消除一切形式种族歧视国际公约), and the "Convention on the Elimination of All Forms of Discrimination against Women" (消除对妇女一切形式歧视公约). China has also signed the "International Covenant on Civil and Political Rights" (公民权利和政治权利国际公约) as well as the "Optional Protocol of the Convention on the Rights of the Child on the Involvement of Children in Battle" (〈儿童权利公约〉关于儿童卷入武装冲突的任择议定书) and is also studying the approval of the documents.

The Chinese Government has been carefully performing its obligations under the international human rights covenants and has submitted its first report on its performance of the "International Covenant on Economic, Social and Cultural Rights," nine reports on the "International Convention on the Elimination of All Forms of Racial Discrimination," six reports on the "Convention on the Elimination of All Forms of Discrimination against Women" and five reports on the "Convention against Torture and Other Cruel, Inhuman or Degrading Treatment or Punishment." Additionally two reports have been submitted on the "Convention on the Rights of the Child" and the first report on the "Optional Protocol of the Convention on the Rights of the Child Regarding the Dealing of Children, Prostitution of Children and Child Pornography Products." During the inspection process of these reports, the Chinese Government maintained positive conversation and communication with the human rights treaty organizations. These actions will be discussed below.

Since Hong Kong and Macao were returned to the motherland, the Chinese government, adhering to the principle of "One County, Two Systems" (一国两制), has been actively supporting the Hong Kong Special Autonomous Region (SAR) Government and the Macao SAR Government to protect human rights and to perform their obligations under related covenants. For human rights documents respectively applicable to the Hong Kong SAR and Macao SAR, the Chinese Government included the performance information written by the governments of these two SAR in the performance report of China.[3]

The Chinese Government is also preparing the 10–13th report of the "International Convention on the Elimination of All Forms of Racial Discrimination" for submission to the UN Committee on the Elimination of Racial Discrimination at an appropriate time in 2007.

### B. *China and the "International Covenant on Economic, Social and Cultural Rights"*

From April 25 to May 13, 2005, the UN Committee on Economic, Social and Cultural Rights reviewed China's first performance report on the "International Covenant on Economic Social and Cultural Rights" and passed its concluding arguments. While China's efforts in performing the Covenant and making certain achievements was acknowledged, certain issues concerning China's performance of the "International Covenant on Economic Social and Cultural Rights" and the preparation of the report were noted and corresponding improvement opinions and suggestions were proposed.

China has been actively studying how to abide by the commitments of the "International Covenant on Economic, Social and Cultural Rights." From October 12–13, 2006, the Ministry of Foreign Affairs

---

[3] From March 20 to 21, the 86th Session of the UN Human Rights Committee will review the secondary report of the Hong Kong SAR of the People's Republic of China on its performance of the "International Covenant on Civil and Political Rights."

held a seminar on China and Australia's performance of the concluding arguments of the UN Committee on Economic, Social and Cultural Rights in Urumqi, Xinjiang. More than 20 representatives from China's relevant government sectors, nongovernmental organizations and research institutions were present at the seminar and conducted constructive conversation and discussion with representatives from the Australian Human Rights and Equal Opportunity Commission on the topics of the improvement of data statistics, the right to education, women's rights, the right to work, the rights of minorities, and nongovernmental organizations' participation in the preparation of the national report. Chairwoman Virginia Bonoan-Dandan of the UN Committee on Economic, Social and Cultural Rights and the human rights representatives of China's Ministry of Foreign Affairs were also present at the seminar. Finally, it was the common understanding of participants to carry out the concluding suggestions and promote the implementation of the covenant in China.

On December 16, 2006, in commemoration of the fortieth anniversary of the "International Covenant on Civil and Political Rights" and the "International Covenant on Economic, Social and Cultural Rights" and in order to promote China's human rights theories and practice, the Research Institute of Human Rights and Humanitarian Laws at China's University of Politics and Law and the Research Center for Human Rights at the Law School of Shandong University jointly sponsored the academic seminar "Implementation of the International Covenant on Economic, Social and Cultural Rights in China" with more than forty experts and scholars present, in support of the attitudes of the above mentioned seminar.

### C. *China and the "Convention on the Elimination of All Forms of Discrimination against Women"*

On August 30, 2006, the UN Committee for the Elimination of Discrimination against Women passed the concluding suggestions on the fourth "Convention on the Elimination of All Forms of Discrimination against Women" submitted by China and proposed suggestions for improvement. The committee appraised China's efforts and its constant improvement of laws, policies and plans for eliminating discrimination against women and it also proposed many opinions and suggestions on China's work regarding women. The committee suggested that China further strengthen its collection, summary and analysis of data, as it was the belief of the committee that resolution of this issue must be based on sufficient data and information. However the collection and provision of statistics according to gender, region and nationality was difficult. Therefore the Committee hoped China would study these difficulties and take efforts to address them in order to enhance its capabilities in establishing and implementing policies and schemes to promote gender equality and women's enjoyment of human rights.

China is a developing country and has a vast territory and population. It is a heavy task to submit national reports in accordance with the "International Covenant on Human Rights," so data collection and statistical treatment continue to be a big challenge.

### D. *China and the "Convention on the Rights of the Child"*

From November 23–24, 2006, China's Ministry of Foreign Affairs held a conference in Beijing on implementing the concluding suggestions on the review of China's secondary national report on the "Convention on the Rights of the Child" for the UN Committee on the Rights of the Child. This Committee was comprised of attendants from government departments, nongovernmental organizations, experts and scholars. This conference was another positive action conducted within China in support of the national report on joining the "International Covenant on Human Rights." The officers of the United Nations Children's Fund Beijing Representative Office were present at the conference and praised it highly.

To strengthen national legislation and establish a complete legal guarantee system is an important measure for signatory states to take in performing international commitments and implementing the "Convention on the Rights of the Child." In 2006, the United Nations Children's Fund cooperated with the All China Women's Federation to amend the "Law of the People's Republic of China on the Protection of Minors" (未成年人保护法) for the purpose of including the tenets and principles of the "Convention on the Rights of the Child" of the UN approved by China in China's national legislation. On December 29, 2006, the Standing Committee of National People's Congress passed the newly amended "Law of the People's Republic of China on the Protection of Minors," of which the contents regarding the indiscrimination principle, the priority of children and respect for children's opinions, etc. reflect the provisions of the "Convention on the Rights of the Child."

China's nongovernmental organizations and academic institutions have also paid much attention to the research, popularization and implementation of the "Convention on the Rights of the Child." On August 1, 2006, the Institute of Law at the Chinese Academy of Social Sciences, the Institute for Population and Development Studies at Xi'an Jiaotong University, the China Soong Ching Ling Foundation, the United Nations Children's Fund, and the International Planning Union (国际计划联合) jointly held an international symposium on birth registration of Chinese children in Beijing. At the Symposium, the birth registration system was studied from the view of being a child's right for the first time, which is a groundbreaking effort in the implementation of the "Convention on the Rights of the Child" in the area of specific rights.

## IV. *The Supreme People's Court Reclaims Authority for Judicial Review of the Death Penalty*

The abolition or restriction of the death penalty in international human rights standards and the prospect of China's possible approval of the "International Covenant on Civil and Political Rights" (公民权利和政治权利国际公约) has driven China to carry out judicial reform related to the restriction of the death penalty.

On December 28, 2006, the Supreme People's Court issued the "Decision on Issues Related to the Exclusive Exercise of the Review of Death Penalty Cases" (关于统一行使死刑案件核准权有关问题的决定), which definitely abolishes all notices authorizing the higher people's courts and PLA military courts to approve certain death penalty cases. The Supreme People's Court has completed all system preparations and the death penalty review will be reclaimed by the Supreme People's Court for exclusive exercise beginning on January 1, 2007.

After reclaiming the exclusive exercise of reviewing death penalty cases, the Supreme People's Court will strictly standardize the procedure for death penalty review cases and firmly prevent the occurrence of any unjust, false or wrong cases. The review of a death penalty case will be handled by a collegiate bench that consists of three judges and a comprehensive review will be made. In principle, it is required that the defendant be arraigned in order to hear their opinions. The defendant is also permitted to propose his explanations to the collegiate bench by means of a letter.

Moreover, the review of the death penalty and the trial of second instance of the death penalty will be separated from one procedure into two procedures, which is an important procedural link that helps prevent the occurrence of unjust, false or wrong cases, and which also provides another opportunity for the defendants sentenced to death to express their opinions to the court.[4]

It is predicted that the quantity of death penalty cases will decline dramatically, at a rate of at least 20% once the Supreme People's Court reclaims death penalty review authority.[5] However several days before the effective date of the above decision, the higher people's courts in many provinces executed the last death penalty reviews, which caused some disputes.

2007 is the first year that the competence for judicial review of death penalty will be reclaimed by the People's Supreme Court and the practical outcome of this decision is still unknown. We must wait and see what the results will be. However, there are still a great many procedural problems in the death penalty review procedure. For instance, is the review conducted in writing or in open court? Should the trial deadline be regulated? And are the lawyers and procuratorial authorities permitted to take part in the review and the start-up proceedings of the revision? The jurisprudential circle hopes that the reclaiming of the death penalty review will create an overall reform of the criminal justice system. It is believed that all these questions will be addressed in accordance with the principle of respecting and protecting human rights.

### V. *The International Seminar on "Respecting and Promoting Human Rights and Building a Harmonious World" and the First Exhibition on Human Rights in China*

On November 24, 2006, the international human rights seminar on the subject of "Respecting and Promoting Human Rights and Building a Harmonious World" came to an end in Beijing after three days. More than seventy representatives from 19 countries in Asia, Europe, Africa and America considered and proposed their opinions and the

---

[4] Tian Yu, Zou Shengwen, Wang Yani. 2006. *Death Penalty Approval Power to Be Reclaimed by the Supreme People's Court Beginning January 1, 2007*, www.bj.xinhuanet.com (October 31, 2006).

[5] Ibid.

opinions of their colleagues open-heartedly and respectfully. Overall, the seminar could be considered a model of international human rights communication and conversation. A series of achievements were made at the seminar: first, representatives from different countries expressed their countries' and their own personal standpoints on human rights. Second, the goal of working towards a harmonious world was universally accepted as a worthy goal for all people and that is would have profound scientific effects and improve the standard of living for human beings Additionally, it was decided that the promotion of the development of human rights was an efficient path to eliminate discordant factors and establish a harmonious world. Third, representatives of different countries presented the human rights development in their own countries and their experiences in the protection of human rights, and pointed out new challenges and problems regarding human rights issues that they confronted. Fourth, the necessity of strengthening and establishing an international and domestic protocol for the protection of human rights was universally supported. Fifth, representatives expressed the hope that the attending governments and their peoples would make an effort to pay more attention to human rights issues and take effective measures to earnestly protect human rights.

In November 2006, the large-scale "Exhibition of Human Rights in China" debuted in Beijing, which was jointly sponsored by the Information Office of the State Council, China's Society for Human Rights Studies and China's Human Rights Development Foundation. The "Exhibition of Human Rights in China" is China's first large-scale exhibition on the subject of human rights. The exhibition gave a full display of the Chinese people's efforts in striving for and realizing human rights, as well as the development and advancement of the cause of human rights in China in the 57 years since the People's Republic of China was founded in 1949, in particular since the recent reforms and the increased international participation. In the exhibition, a good many photographs, charts, books, sound and image data and physical objects were used to give a true record of the promotion of the people's right to exist and right to develop in China as well as the protection of the citizens' rights in the areas of politics, economy, society and culture. The exhibition also displayed a record of China's legal guarantee of human rights in general, protection of human rights of minorities, women, children and the elderly, the human rights of the disabled; as well as China's active development of international communication and cooperation on human rights.

### VI. *The Principle of Equality and Nondiscrimination, Labor Rights, the Rights of Women and Children, and Public Interest Litigation Become Hot Topics in China and the Interdisciplinary Study of Human Rights Receives Attention*

"All citizens of the People's Republic of China are equal before the law" is China's constitutional principle. The implementation of the principle of equity and non-discrimination has become an increasingly hot topic along with the rapid development of society and the economy after entering the 21st century. The gap between urban and rural areas, gender equality, and employment discrimination are some of the most widely-followed issues and China has conducted substantial research in these areas. For instance, the Law Institute at the Chinese Academy of Social Sciences, the Oriental Public Interests Legal Aid Law Office, the Danish Institute for Human Rights and the Norwegian Centre for Human Rights jointly sponsored the seminar "Right of Equality and Litigation for Public Interests" from June 9–11, 2006, which was comprised of four discussion topics: the practice of International Human Rights Treaty entities in the protection of human rights; discrimination issues and legal guarantees in China; gender discrimination and legal aid; and public interest litigation on the right of equality in China.[6]

From Oct. 16–17, 2006, the "Fifteen Human Rights Justice Seminar" of the European Union was held in Beijing with the right to work as one of its topics.[7] On December 24, 2006, the "Labor Contract Law (draft)" (劳动合同法 (草案)) was submitted to the Tenth Standing Committee of the National People's Congress for deliberation for the second time. This draft was first submitted on December 24, 2005. Hereafter, the Standing Committee of National People's Congress publicized the draft of first instance to society for feedback on March 20, 2006. As of April 20, 2006, there were over 190,000 opinions received via the Internet, press, mail and so on, which was a rarity in the legislative history of the new China. The advice focused on "equally protecting the lawful rights and interests of employers and laborers" and "stressing the protection of laborers' lawful rights and interests." These difficult issues comprised the basis for the controversies covered by the

---

[6] Lisa Stearns Ed., "Research Outcomes on Instances of Employment Discrimination," *Prohibiting Employment Discrimination: International Standards and Domestic Practice*, Law Press, 2006.

[7] Another topic for discussion was the right of information.

"Labor Contract Law (draft)."[8] It can be predicted that this law that is so closely related to laborers, employers and the market economy will continue to attract much attention. It is increasingly necessary and important for China to improve labor legislation and formulate a series of single laws such as the "Law for the Settlement of Labor Disputes" (劳动争议处理法) (which has begun the legislation process), "Trade Union Law" (工会组织法), "Social Security Law" (社会保险法), "Labor Standards Law" (劳动标准法), and "Collective Contract Law" (集体合同法), etc.

In 2006, Hunan, Jiangxi and Heilongjiang provinces drafted and passed their own "Enforcement Regulations for the Amended Law of the Peoples Republic of China on the Protection of Rights and Interests of Women" (妇女权益保障法) thereby advancing research on gender mainstreaming.[9]

2006 was also an important year for the "Amendment of the Law of the People's Republic of China on the Protection of Minors" (未成年人保护法). The amendment process helped all circles to understand, learn about and discuss children's rights and their protection. The Beijing Representative Office of the United Nations Children's Fund organized Chinese Government officials, representatives of non-governmental organizations, experts and scholars to pay a special visit to the Innocenti Research Center and discuss the "Convention on the Rights of the Child" and related legislation reform. There were also activities regarding research, publicity and encouragement of this cause within China. On December 29, 2006, the 25th session of the Standing Committee of the National People's Congress deliberated and passed the amendment with a high vote, which provided a new opportunity for China to develop the cause of children.[10]

---

[8] Ye Doudou, "Secondary Review of Labor Contract Law," *Finance and Economics* Vol. 1 (2007): pp. 120–121.

[9] In March 2006, the first "green paper" and "blue paper" on women's development were publicized. They are: 1.) Women's Institute of the All China Women's Federation, "Report on Gender Equality and Women's Development in China (1995–2005)," Social Science Academic Press, 2006. 2.) Wang Jinling, Report on Women's Development in China, Social Sciences Academic Press, 2006. These documents review and evaluate the lives of Chinese women and their development over the past decade as well as research accomplishments and achievements.

[10] For related interpretations, please refer to: Administrative Law Office of the Commission of Legislative Affairs of the NPCSC, comp., *Interpretation of the Law of the People's Republic of China on the Protection of Minors*, China Legal Publishing House, 2007.

From October 25–26, 2006, the Norwegian Centre for Human Rights and the Raoul Wallenberg Institute of Human Rights and Humanitarian Law held the "Review of Human Rights Seminar on Interdisciplinary Research Methods." During this seminar more than twenty human rights experts of jurisprudence, economics, anthropology and medical science, etc. got together to communicate and discuss the methods and meaning of the interdisciplinary study of human rights; at this seminar many constructive proposals were made.

Human rights education also took on new characteristics. From May 20–25, 2006, the fourteenth China-Europe Human Rights Seminar was held in Vienna, which was organized by the Ministry of Foreign Affairs of the People's Republic of China and the European Union. One of the major topics was human rights education in primary and high schools.[11] As an attempt at instituting this practice, the *New Citizen Reading Book* (新公民读本) published by Peking University Press in November contained some human rights education ideas and contents.[12]

In order to popularize human rights education, some jurisprudence experts actively suggested that the Ministry of Education list human rights law in the required courses of law schools.[13] In order to summarize the teaching practice of Chinese universities on human rights law, the "Seminar on Human Rights Law Teaching in Chinese Universities in a Globalized Environment" was sponsored by the Center for Jurisprudence Research of Jilin University from December 20–21, 2006. At the seminar, human rights law scholars summarized and reflected on empirical research on human rights education in Chinese universities and colleges.[14] In June 2006, the national cadre training teaching material the *Human Rights Book of Knowledge for Cadres* (人权知识干部读本) was published.[15]

---

[11] Another topic was the discussion of the special report procedure of the United Nations and the report of Special Reporter Manfred Nowak on torture after his visit to China in 2005.

[12] Yang Dongping ed., *New Citizen Reading Book, Volume A–D for Elementary Schools*, (Beijing: Peking University Press, 2006).

[13] Guangzhou TV Station, "Human Rights Experts' Suggestion on Listing Human Rights Law as Required Coursework for Jurisprudence Majors," http://www.gztv.com/channel/news/node_16/2006/08/08/115505781064540.shtml, (August 7, 2006).

[14] See also: Sun Shiyan, "Actuality and Reflection on the Teaching of Human Rights Law in the Legal Education of Universities and Colleges," *Human Rights* Vol. 6 (2005): pp. 43–46.

[15] Cai Wu, ed., and National Cadre Training Teaching Materials Compiling and

Public interest litigation also developed considerably in 2006. The term public interest litigation became a key phrase in China's law circle and was actively practiced. Public interest litigation has great potential in the fields of environmental protection, protection of the interests of disadvantaged groups, social equity and justice. Though the legal basis for public interest litigation is still weak and limited, it has been following the development trend of society and "rule of law." Public interest litigation for public interests has attracted much attention in China but it is also still a controversial topic. However it is certain that China's public interest litigation will prosper in the same way as human rights and the "rule of law."[16]

## VII. *Human Rights Events in China in 2006*

Jan. 10: The national conference of legal aid directors was held. Legal aid had received much attention so the State and governmental responsibilities were further defined and put into operation. The budget for legal aid at all levels of government has increased yearly. In 2005, the national total appropriation for legal aid was 262.20 million Yuan; and the central fiscal budget first appropriated 50 million Yuan as a special fund to support legal aid work in poverty-stricken areas.

Jan. 11: The Ministry of Finance announced the establishment of a new protocol to guarantee funds for compulsory education in rural areas and in the west and appropriated in advance 3.69 billion Yuan for 12 western provinces (autonomous regions, municipalities directly under the central authority), for the Xinjiang Production and Construction Corps and for pilot provinces in middle China.

Jan. 17: The Chinese migrant farmers' right claim website (www.zgnmg.org) was officially launched. Presided over by the Beijing Legal Aid Work Station for Migrant Farmers, this website specialized in helping migrant farmers protect their lawful rights and interests.

---

Steering Committee, *Human Rights Knowledge Book for Cadres*, (People's Publishing House and Party Building Books Press, 2006).

[16] Li Lihong, "Practice, System and Value of Litigation for Public Interests and Law for Public Interests," *Chinese Journal of Law* Vol. 6 (2006), pp. 148–158. Beijing Oriental Public Interests Legal Aid Law Office, *Public Interest Litigation, Volume 1 and Volume 2*, (China Procuratorial Press, 2006). Several websites on public interest law and public interest litigation have been launched in China: Pursuing the Public Interests (http://www.dfpilaw.org), Public Interest Litigation (http://www.pil.org.cn), etc.

Feb. 4: The Ministry of Civil Affairs announced that the "Plan of Tomorrow" (明天计划) which was under implementation had helped 13,000 disabled orphans obtain healthcare, which directly improved their physical condition. According to statistics, nearly one half of the 66,000 orphans and abandoned babies adopted by Chinese welfare premises are suffering from disabilities. The Ministry of Civil Affairs started up the "Plan of Tomorrow for Disabled Orphans to Receive Rehabilitation by Operation" (残疾孤儿手术康复明天计划) in May 2004, which plans to spend three years raising a capital of 600 million Yuan for operational correction and rehabilitation of nearly 30,000 disabled orphans. This is China's first nationwide operational correction movement for disabled orphans.

Feb. 12: The State Council issued the "Regulations on AIDS Prevention and Control" (艾滋病防治条例), which was signed by Premier Wen Jiabao. The regulations regulate the responsibilities of all levels of government in the prevention and control of AIDS and define the rights and duties of infected persons and patients of AIDS. The regulations also regulate the provision of free drugs by the governments about county level against AIDS for AIDS patients in rural areas and those in urban areas with economic difficulties, and the provision of free treatment and consultations on preventing maternal-neonatal transmission of AIDS for pregnant women and new mothers who have been infected with AIDS.

March 1: China's first "Green Paper for Women" (妇女绿皮书), a "Report on Gender Equality and the Progress of Women in China (1995–2005)" was launched in Beijing.

March 9: The Information Office of the State Council published the "Human Rights Record of United States" in 2005 to respond to the US State Department's national report on human rights practices for 2005. This was the seventh successive year the "Human Rights Record of the United States" issued by the Information Office of the State Council to respond to the US' annual "National Report on Human Rights Practices."

March 14: The Eleventh Five-Year Plan for National Economic and Social Development was approved at the fourth session of the 10th National People's Congress in the morning. Thus a program of action guiding China's economic and social development over the next five years was born. China adopted new legal procedures to establish the precept of the new five-year plan as the country's program of action.

March 15: The Sixth United Nations General Assembly passed a decision on establishment of Human Rights Council with 47 seats that replaced the Commission on Human Rights headquartered in Geneva of Switzerland with 170 votes for, 4 against and 3 abstentions.

March 20: The Standing Committee of National People's Congress published the "Labor Contract Law (draft)" to society in order to solicit opinions.

March 27: "Several Opinions of the State Council Concerning the Settlement of Rural Migrant Workers' Issues" (国务院关于解决农民工问题的若干意见) was issued. The opinion, which allows for China's current situation and upholds the "people-oriented" (以人为本) principle, gives detailed regulations on a series of issues concerning the interests of rural migrant workers. These opinions also demonstrate the Chinese Government's regard and care for its 120 million rural migrant workers.

April 5: The International Conference on "Village Self-Governance in China: Past, Present and Future" was held in Beijing sponsored by the EU-China Training Program on village governance. As of this point, village self-governance has been basically achieved in 615,000 village committees in China. The Ministry of Civil Affairs will continue to implement the core contents of village self-governance, i.e. democratic election, democratic decision-making, democratic management and democratic supervision. As stated in the "Report on Civil Affairs Development in 2005" issued by the Ministry of Civil Affairs in May, 470 million farmers participated in the election of village committees with 368,000 village committees elected in 2005.

April 11: Deputy Director Wang Guoliang of the State Council Leading Group of the Office of Poverty Alleviation and Development stated in the "Seminar on Gender, Poverty Alleviation and China's New Socialist Countryside Construction" that Chinese women had experienced significant improvement in the areas of poverty, education, employment and social participation. The number of poor women in rural areas decreased from 35 million at the end of 1994 to over 12 million at the end of 2005. This seminar was aimed at discovering appropriate ways to combine the gender problem with China's poverty alleviation activities and policy intervention.

April 13: Fifteen organizations of the Ministry of Civil Affairs, the Office of the Central Committee for Comprehensive Management of Public Security, the Supreme People's Court, the National Development and Reform Commission, the Ministry of Education, the Ministry of

Public Security, the Ministry of Justice, the Ministry of Finance, the Ministry of Labor and Social Security, the Ministry of Construction, the Ministry of Agriculture, the Ministry of Public Health, the National Population and Family Planning Commission of China, the Central Committee of the Communist Youth League of China and the All China Women's Federation jointly published the "Opinions on Providing More Aid to Orphans." The opinions require the establishment of a protocol to aid and protect orphans, led by the government, sponsored by civil administration, coordinated by departments concerned and involving social participation. The opinions also define divisional responsibilities, formulate preferential policies, increase capital input and extensively mobilize social forces in order to meet the primary demands of orphans in their lives, education, rehabilitation, medical treatment and employment, and aims to create a favorable social environment for protecting the lawful rights and interests of orphans and facilitating their healthy development.

April 16: The Research Office of the State Council issued the "Report on Rural Migrant Workers in China."

April 16: An exhibition of China's achievements in the protection of intellectual property rights was held in Beijing, which was the first large exhibition in China on this subject.

May 9: After three rounds of secret ballot, the Sixth United Nations General Assembly elected 47 members for the first session of the newly founded Human Rights Council of the United Nations; among these members, China, France, Russia and Britain, were included as four permanent members of the United Nations Security Council.

May 16: Some officers of the All-China Federation of Trade Unions announced that the Federation had not only been emphasizing and actively promoting the establishment and improvement of a minimum wage guarantee system and had also effectively promoted the appropriate adjustment of the minimum wage standards. At this point, a minimum wage guarantee system had been established in all of the provinces, autonomous regions and municipalities directly under central authority and the minimum wage standards were adjusted properly according to relevant regulations. Twenty-three provinces, autonomous regions and municipalities directly under the central authority have formulated minimum hourly wage standards; and 26 provinces, autonomous regions and municipalities directly under the central authority have set minimum wage standards by referring to social security charges, and housing accumulation funds payable for laborers.

May 16: The Ministry of Public Health issued a notice requiring health administration departments and medical institutions at all levels to focus on addressing the issues of rural migrant workers' medical care, and the protection of their lawful interests and rights and guarantee of justice and equal treatment without discrimination. The notice required those health administration departments and disease prevention and control organizations serving rural migrant workers to strengthen rural migrant workers' disease prevention and control, intensify health education for them and disease monitoring of their living quarters, and carry out State policy by providing free treatment for specific infectious diseases such as AIDS, tuberculosis and schistosomiasis. The notice also required the authorities to provide preventive vaccinations for children of rural migrant workers according to the local immunization plan and take effective measures to increase the rate of vaccination under the State immunization plan.

May 29: The Ministry of Foreign Affairs held the founding ceremony for the Counselor Protection Office of the Department of Consular Affairs. Minister Li Zhaoxing of the Ministry of Foreign Affairs said the Chinese government emphasized the protection of the lawful rights and interests of overseas Chinese citizens and legal persons.

June 1: The All-China Federation of Trade Unions issued the "Blue Paper" on the "Role of Chinese Trade Unions in Safeguarding the Legitimate Rights and Interests of Workers (2005)" (2005 年中国工会维护职工合法权益蓝皮书).

June 5: The State Environmental Protection Administration issued the "White Paper" on "Environmental Protection in China (1996–2005)" (中国的环境保护 1996–2005).

June 6: The Ministry of Labor and Social Security issued certain measures to expedite rural migrant workers' participation in employment injury insurance, to implement and improve policies concerning rural migrant workers' use of insurance, to aid in the identification of work injury, to assess labor abilities, to compensate for work injuries, to facilitate the involvement of rural migrant workers in the insurance system and their enjoyment of equal treatment. According to the words of the principal of the Ministry of Labor and Social Security, China will basically achieve the participation of rural migrant workers in employment injury insurance who work in colliery and non-colliery enterprises and most of construction enterprises countrywide by the end of 2008.

June 8: The China Disabled Persons Federation issued the Eleventh Five-Year "Development Outline of China for the Disabled (2006–2010)." The outline promises that China will strive to make the general life of the disabled reach a comparatively well-off level initially in the Eleventh Five-Year period.

June 8: China's Legal Aid Foundation set up a special fund for legal aid for the elderly. Its setup helps protect the lawful rights and interests of the elderly through the legal channel. "The Legal Aid Workstation for the Elderly" also began to provide legal aid for the elderly.

June 14: The All-China Federation of Trade Unions, State Administration for Work Safety and State Administration for Coal Mine Safety decided to jointly launch the "special campaign for rural migrant workers' life safety and health" with a focus on mining, construction and processing industries. In this campaign, rural migrant workers will be provided with safety knowledge, documents outlining laws and regulations concerning their safety and health (such as the "Trade Union Law of the People's Republic of China" (农民工发放工会法), the "Labor Law of the People's Republic of China" (劳动法), the "Law of the People's Republic of China on Work Safety" (安全生产法), and the "Law of the People's Republic of China on the Prevention and Control of Occupational Diseases" (职业病防治法) in order to raise awareness and understanding of their individual rights and obligations.

June 19: The Human Rights Council of the United Nations held its first conference in Geneva. Vice Chairman Yang Jiechi of the Ministry of Foreign Affairs proposed five proposals at the conference that created a new environment for the international cause of human rights. These actions were based on the principle that the enjoyment of human rights necessitates a peaceful environment, sustainable development, a harmonious and comprehensive society, constructive conversation and cooperation, and the guarantee of effective protocol.

July 1: The Qinghai-Tibet Railway, known as the "Road to Heaven," was opened to traffic in the full line, thus beginning a new chapter in the development of Tibet.

July 10: According to information from the Ministry of Public Health, there were 1,369 counties (cities, districts) carrying out trial operations of a new rural cooperative medical service by the end of March 2006, accounting for 47.83% of the total number of counties (cities, districts) in China. The agricultural population involved was 473.5402 million, accounting for 53.44% of the total national agricultural population.

Additionally, there were 374.3585 million persons participating in cooperative medical service, accounting for 42.25% of the total agricultural population with a participation rate of 79.06%.

July 11 is World Population Day (世界人口日). China proposed the theme of "Care for Girls, Spring into Action" (关爱女孩，行动起来) for World Population Day, 2006. The National Population and Family Planning Commission announced that China paid great attention to the problem of gender imbalance in the birth population in recent years and that it took necessary measures to address this problem and actively create a favorable living and development environment for girls.

July 24: The national conference of legal aid directors was held. Since "Several Opinions of the State Council Regarding the Settlement of Rural Migrant Worker Issues" (国务院关于解决农民工问题的若干意见) was issued officially in January 2006, legal aid departments have taken active measures to carry it out by widening the censorship standard on economic difficulties, simplifying the examination and approval procedure, creating innovation in working methods and expanding service sectors to facilitate the applications of rural migrant workers' and the timely provision of illegal aid.

July 25: The election at the expiration of the official term of the people's congress at the county and township levels was launched with 900 million voters involved across the country. This was the first election simultaneously held at county and township levels after the official term of the representatives of the people's congress at the township level was changed to five years from three years in the constitutional amendment of 2004.

July 25: A videoconference on the three-year action plan for implementing a system of labor contracts was convened. Wang Zhaoguo, the vice chairman of the Standing Committee of National People's Congress and the chairman of the All-China Federation of Trade Unions stressed in his comments and instructions to the conference a system of collective contracts needs to be actively implemented in order to affect a comprehensive system of labor contracts. He also pointed out that the mechanism for the coordination of the labor relationships between three parties and the system to address labor disputes must be improved.

July 26: The Supreme People's Procuratorate held a press conference to promulgate the "Provisions of the Supreme People's Procuratorate on the Criteria for Dereliction of Duty and Rights Infringement" (最高人

民检察院关于渎职侵权犯罪案件立案标准的规定). Deputy Procurator-general Wang Zhenchuan of the Supreme People's Procuratorate said at the conference that the new standards demonstrated stronger emphasis on the safeguarding of human rights.

July 27: To celebrate the tenth ceremony of promulgation of the "Law of the People's Republic of China on Protection of the Rights and Interests of the Elderly" (老年人权益保障法), the Office of the National Working Committee for the Elderly held an exhibition of achievements in the cause of supporting the elderly in Beijing.

August 7: The minimum wage standard for workers in Shanghai was adjusted from existing 690 Yuan/month to 750 Yuan/month. This was the fourteenth raising of the standards since Shanghai introduced the pioneer minimum wage system in China in 1993. The minimum wage is realized income, and an individual's basic social security and housing accumulation funds are paid by his/her employer separately. These minimum wage standards are the highest in China, and were put into operation on September 1.

August 9: Wal-Mart East China Stores Co. Ltd. declared that Wal-Mart would assist the All-China Federation of Trade Unions to organize trade unions at the grass roots level in all the Wal-Mart stores in the territory of China. As the world's largest chain retailer, Wal-Mart had not allowed the organization of trade unions since it entered the Chinese market in 1996. Since the workers of Wal-Mart Jinjiang Store organized the first trade union in Wal-Mart according to law on July 29, the workers of Wal-Mart have organized trade unions with an irrepressible force. Nov. 8: Wal-Mart China Headquarters established a trade union in Shenzhen. Thus, all operating facilities of Wal-Mart in China will establish trade unions.

August 16: Vice Chairman Chen Xiaohong of the Ministry of Public Health announced that the State Council Working Committee for AIDS Prevention and Control set up the national AIDS prevention and control social mobilization appropriation project with an annual appropriation about 6 million Yuan to support nongovernmental organizations and social groups and institutions to carry out the prevention and control of AIDS.

August 27: The "Supervision Law of Standing Committee of the People's Congress at All Levels" (各级人民代表大会常务委员会监督法) was approved by the Tenth Standing Committee of National People's Congress. The Supervision Law took 20 years from drafting and deliberation to voting. The Supervision Law guarantees the authority of

China's state power organizations to exert the right of supervision. It also defines the function of supervising the "court and procuratorate" for the Standing Committee of the National People's Congress and provides provisions to guarantee courts and procuratorates exert jurisdiction and procuratorial authority independently according to law.

August 28: The General Office of the State Council printed and distributed the Eleventh Five-Year Plan on Safety in Production. This is the first special plan on safety in production organized and compiled at State level since the founding of the new China. It is also the first Eleventh Five-year Plan printed and distributed by the General Office of the State Council.

August 29: The China Research and Training Base on Minority Women and Gender was established in Beijing.

Sep. 1: The amended "Compulsory Education Law of the People's Republic of China" (义务教育法) was put into operation today, which will further guarantee children in rural areas and children of floating population enjoy the right to compulsory education.

Sep. 14: The Work Committee for the Disabled of the State Council and the Work Committee for Women and Children of the State Council held a symposium in Beijing, studying how to promote the rehabilitation of handicapped children. Vice Chairman Gu Xiulian of the Standing Committee of National People's Congress stated at the symposium that aid for rehabilitation of handicapped children was required in order to solve practical problems. He also said it was necessary to establish a long-term mechanism for the rehabilitation of handicapped children, to promote the formulation and amendment of relevant laws and to improve the policy and law system; as well as to further mobilize social forces to care for and help handicapped children and create a favorable environment for this cause.

Sep. 18: The spokesman of the Ministry of Foreign Affairs Qin Gang announced that China was strongly dissatisfied with and objected to the content concerning China in the US State Department's "International Religious Freedom Report of 2006."

Sep. 21: The Office for the Elderly of the State Council issued the Eleventh Five-Year Plan for China's Elderly Cause, which was approved by the State Council.

Sep. 23: The Minister Tian Chengping of the Ministry of Labor and Social Security said at the first annual meeting of China Social Security Forum that social security had expanded its coverage and the funds' supporting capacity had expanded with the advancement of the reform. In 2005, the gross domestic income from five kinds of social security funds was 696. 8 billion Yuan, the gross domestic expenditure was 540.1 billion Yuan, and the funds had accumulated to 606.6 billion Yuan.

Oct. 8–11: The Sixth Plenary Session of the Sixteenth CPC Central Committee was held and the "Resolution on Major Issues Regarding the Building of a Harmonious Socialist Society" (中共中央关于构建社会主义和谐社会若干重大问题的决定) was passed.

Oct. 12: The All-China Federation of Trade Unions delivered the news that there was an increase of 6.50 million rural migrant workers joining trade unions countrywide in the first half of 2006. It took just half a year to complete the desired annual goal. Some officials said the enforced joining of trade unions by rural migrant workers helped guarantee their democratic rights and lawful rights and interests.

Oct. 19: The special workgroup concerning stay-at-home children in rural areas was established in Beijing by twelve organizations including the Joint Conference Office for Rural Migrant Workers of the State Council and the All China Women's Federation. This workgroup is devoted to solving China's increasingly serious problem of children left at home in rural areas while their parents go out working. So far, stay-at-home children in China amount to 20 million and the number is still rising. These children are confronted with many problems of education, living, psychology and safety, etc. finding an adequate solution for this issue is very urgent.

Oct. 25: The Foreign Minister Li Zhaoxing published an article in the People's Daily in commemoration of the People's Republic of China's recovery of her lawful seat in the United Nations for its 35th anniversary. In this article, the author announced that China had submitted 22 international covenants on human rights; carefully implemented its international human rights obligations and extensively developed communication and cooperation in the international human rights field.

Nov. 13: The State Council approved and transmitted the Eleventh Five-Year Plan "Outline for Developing the Cause of Labor and Social Security (2006–2010)" by the Ministry of Labor and Social Security and the National Development and Reform Commission. The State Council required the people's governments of the provinces, autonomous regions and municipalities directly under central authority, and the ministries and commissions and institutions directly affiliated with the State Council to execute the outline carefully.

Nov. 17: The "Exhibition of Human Rights in China" debuted in Beijing, and was jointly sponsored by the Information Office of the State Council, the China Society for Human Rights Studies and the China Human Rights Development Foundation. This was the first comprehensive exhibition on a large scale with the subject of human rights in China. This exhibition contained more than 250 law documents and over 330 human rights books.

Nov. 22: The international human rights seminar on the subject of "Respect and Promote Human Rights and Building a Harmonious World" was held in Beijing, and was sponsored by China Society for Human Rights Studies. More than seventy Chinese and foreign human rights experts, scholars and officials from 19 countries attended the seminar.

Nov. 23: The Ministry of Labor and Social Security declared that social security supervision committees had been set up in 27 provinces. These committees consist of a government leader (acting as chairman), representatives of relevant department and enterprises, and experts. They coordinate the efforts of different circles and study effective ways to address social security as a whole in a way that preferably combines administrative supervision from the Ministry of Labor and Social Security, special supervision from the fiscal auditing department and other departments as well as social supervision of the public and the media.

December 1: On World AIDS Day, Premier Wen Jiabao and Vice Premier Wu Yi of the State Council, in red ribbon, welcomed a group of special guests, i.e. 15 orphans from Henan Province, Yunnan Province, Liaoning Province, Anhui Province and Shanxi Province, etc. with parents who have died of AIDS or who have suffered from AIDS.

Dec. 7: The symposia on national health planning and financial management came to an end. In 2006, a special appropriation of 5.41 billion Yuan was provided from the central fiscal budget for local budgets with the main application being to the fields of public health, rural health, and the prevention and control of major diseases. In addition, the central fiscal budget expanded free treatment of critical infectious diseases and the construction of a grassroots hygiene structure by providing a subsidy of 4.27 billion Yuan for the new rural cooperative medical service and a special fund of 3.18 billion Yuan for capital construction.

Dec. 12: The Information Office of the State Council issued a "white paper" on the "Development of the Cause for the Elderly in

China" with contents covering State protocol concerning the elderly, the retirement guarantee system, medical care for the elderly, social services for the elderly, cultural education for the elderly, participation of the elderly in social development and the guarantee of their lawful rights and interests.

Dec. 13: The 61st United Nations General Assembly discussed and adopted the "Convention on the Rights of Persons with Disabilities" at UN Headquarters in New York. This convention is the first international convention with legal bonding force, which is aimed at safeguarding the rights of the disabled, and promoting the cause of the disabled. The Chinese government actively participated in the drafting of this convention.

Dec. 15: The United Nations Children's Fund issued a report on the state of the World's children in 2007 (Chinese Version) in Beijing. The foundation's representative in China called on the Chinese government to further promote gender equality and bring about "double dividends" in the area of improving women and children's lives.

Dec. 22–23: The meeting on rural labor of the CPC Central Committee was held in Beijing. Hui Liangyu, member of the Political Bureau of the CPC Central Committee and vice premier of the State Council was present at the conference and spoke. At the conference, it was first proposed to actively pursue the establishment of a social security system covering urban and rural residents as well as a minimum standard of living guarantee system (最低生活保障制度) in rural areas across the country.

Dec. 28: The Supreme People's Court promulgated the "Decision of the Supreme People's Court on the Exclusive Exercise of the Power to Review Death Penalty Cases" (关于统一行使死刑案件核准权有关问题的决定), which clearly abolishes all notices authorizing the higher people's courts and the PLA military courts to approve certain death penalty cases issued according to law, and reclaims all authority to authorize the death penalty for the supreme people's court for exclusive exercise beginning January 1, 2007.

Dec. 29: The amended "Law of the People's Republic of China on the Protection of Minors" (未成年人保护法) was adopted at the 25th Session of the 10th Standing Committee of the National People's Congress.

## VIII. *Conclusion and Prospects*

In 2006, China made remarkable achievements in the protection of human rights, an item included in the establishment of "rule of law."

The Chinese government regarded building a harmonious socialist society as a leading development goal, which predicts a positive future for the implementation of the constitutional principle of respecting and safeguarding human rights. China became a member of the Human Rights Council of the United Nations and actively participated and cooperated in international human rights protection. Both government organizations and nongovernmental organizations attached great importance to the concluding arguments approved by the UN treaty organization after reviewing the performance report submitted by the Chinese government. China also actively engaged in domestic and international communication and cooperation activities in the area of human rights and strived to integrate international human rights standards in the domestic law in order to strengthen its effective implementation at home. The Supreme People's Court reclaimed competence for judicial review of the death penalty, a substantial step towards restricting the application of the death penalty and protection of human rights. China also witnessed vivid human rights practice in the reform of legal proceedings, the strengthening of judicial guarantees, advocating authority and the social mainstreaming of gender, discussing new governmental and social mechanisms and pushing forward the development of legal aid and litigation for public interests. Relevant research and teaching also developed steadily.

In 2007, the Chinese government will focus on strengthening the lawmaking aimed at improving the people's lives and establishing a harmonious society. Certain important laws like the Property Law, the "Labor Contract Law" and the "Employment Promotion Law" will be adopted or expedited in the lawmaking process. The decision-making leaders exhibit a strong political will to push forward social security and other programs concerning the people's lives. In the area of international human rights law, the Chinese government will submit a combined report for the tenth to thirteen reports of China on implementing the "International Convention on the Elimination of All Forms of Racial Discrimination" to the UN Committee on the Elimination of Racial Discrimination. China will also continue to work to adopt certain international human rights documents like the "International Covenant on Civil and Political Rights," part of the "International Bill of Human Rights," and the "Convention of the Rights of Persons with Disabilities" the first human rights UN covenant of the 21st century, as well as the International Labor Organization's "Convention Concerning Forced or Compulsory Labor."

For a long time, legislation and the work of establishing legal goals was a primary target in the establishment of "rule of law." Now based on democratic participation and the overall improvement of lawmaking, law enforcement has become an important area that is expected to be implemented and strengthened in all circles. Though of course, lawmaking cannot dissolve all problems, promoting a legal consciousness in society, carrying out administrative, institutional and judicial reform and guaranteeing law enforcement in a true sense, have become goals which increasingly form the foundation for establishing "rule of law." Additionally, as far as the protection of human rights and construction of "rule of law" goes, opportunities and challenges do exist. However their foundation in society is stronger, experiencing more favorable conditions and greater room to develop.

# REPORT ON THE RESOLUTION OF RURAL DISPUTES

China's Legal & Social Development Research Group

## I. *Background of Research on the Resolution of Rural Disputes*

### A. *Research Issues and Methods*

Dispute resolution is an important aspect of legal practice. In the area of legal regulation, dispute resolution can clarify the meanings and requirements of the laws, and can correct and recover social order. In the area of protecting rights, dispute resolution can help the involved parties achieve their rights and investigate illegal behaviors. In the same way, dispute resolution in rural areas is also an important legal matter for the following reasons. For one, there are also problems of standardizing social order and safeguarding rights via laws in rural areas. Additionally, there is sharp difference in social environment between rural and urban areas. Rural areas have experienced many changes in recent years. Therefore dispute settlement in rural areas requires extensive research and attention. Moreover, it is important that the strategic plan to build a new countryside, include the protection of the social order and that a new system of benefits be established as part of the coordination of the reform process. Additionally the development of these efforts can be reflected on a large scale in the in the adoption of dispute resolution methods. Therefore, on the subject of "dispute resolution in rural areas," we have carried out on-site research on rural area disputes and their settlement. Specifically, this survey focuses on two aspects of dispute settlement, i.e. the situation of disputes in rural areas and the settlement of such disputes. The latter also contains two categories, one is successful dispute resolution and the other is dispute resolution with existing problems.

The situation of disputes in rural areas refers to the major issues and areas of dispute in rural areas, and the social environment causes and system causes for the frequent occurrence of such contradictions and disputes. There are a great many types of contradiction and dispute with different division standards. In this article we will focus on those issues discovered in our research to address those serious contradictions and disputes.

China has a system of unified basic laws and regulations to address such disputes. However within the uniform system framework, there may be great differences in the dispute situations and there is considerable variability in the physical measures used to address disputes, which leads to differences in the dispute resolution practice in different rural sectors. These types of difference may be attributed to some extent to the influence of economic development, geographical position and traditional culture, etc. Taking into account these differences, we, in order not to lose the objectivity of field research, conducted research that integrated national and economic development and geographical and historical conditions and selected four regions as the targeted research areas. These four regions are: a certain county in Shanxi Province, a certain city in Hubei Province, a certain town in Nanjing, Jiangsu Province and a certain county in Zhejiang Province.

### B. *Social and Economic Development in These Four Regions*

The county in Zhejiang Province is located in the area of Zhejiang Province that borders Shanghai and Jiangsu Province. It is in the very north of Zhejiang Province, known as the first stop on the way to Shanghai. This area is the national base producer of commodity grains, and has the reputation of being the "rice sack of Zhejiang Province and the vegetable basket of Shanghai (浙江的米袋子，上海的菜篮子)." The whole county had a permanent population of 380,500 by the end of 2005 and covers an area of 506 square kilometers. The land is flat here and water accounts for about 14% of the total county area. "The whole county has 458,000 *mu* of cultivated area with 436,000 *mu* of paddy field and 1.2 *mu* per person."[1] Thanks to the advantageous geographical location, a good traffic system, fertile land and developed industry, this county enjoys a higher standard of economic and cultural development. According to the State statistics, this county is among the top 100 counties of China. Of the "Top 100," it ranked 26th in 2004 and 64th in 2005.

The town in the Jiangning District of Nanjing had a population of about 72,000 in 2006, a land area of 215 square kilometers and

[1] Translator's Note: A *mu* (亩) is a Chinese unite of measurement equivalent to one sixth of an acre or 0.0667 hectares.

cultivated area of about 124,000 *mu* including dry land, vegetable plots and irrigated paddy fields. The total area of the paddy fields was more than 100,000 *mu* with per capita area about 1.5 *mu*. This town is located on the border of the Jiangsu and Anhui Provinces; it is 30 kilometers from downtown Nanjing and faces the Lukou International Airport across the river. Compared with the other townships and towns of the Jiangning District, this town is poorer and it receives assistance from other more powerful economies in the region.

The subject city is located in the center of Hubei Province, slightly to the east. It has a land area of 1,103.4 square kilometers and its total population was 672,900 as of the end of 2005. The city's total area of cultivated land is 597,500 *mu*; of which 595,700 *mu* is cultivated land for common use and 1,900 *mu* is used as temporary cultivated land. Of the cultivated land, the area of paddy fields accounts for 72.7%; and dry land 27.3%. The per capita cultivated area is 0.89 *mu* and the per capita paddy field area is 0.65 *mu*. This city is comparatively behind in its economic and cultural development, and falls below the average. It is one of the poorer regions of the four areas researched.

The county in Shanxi Province is situated in the Weifen River bottomland along the Yellow River, in the north of the Luliang region. It borders on Kelan and Lanxian Counties in the east, Linxian County and Fangshan in the south and Baode in the north, with Shenmu County of Shaanxi Province across the Yellow River to the west. This county is abundant in mineral resources with 23 kinds of minerals evident in the initial stages of appraisal. However this county also has several unfavorable conditions: (1) the land here is sterile and water loss and soil erosion is grave. The areas affected by water loss and soil erosion account for 77% of the total land area. (2) It suffers severe drought with poor vegetation cover. The total resources of surface water and underground water sources in the whole country are 179.77 million cubic meters with a per capita stock size of 671 cubic meters, a litter more than the provincial per capital level of 525 cubic meters and the regional per capita level 546 cubic meters, and far below the national per capita level of 2,300 cubic meters. (3) As coal is the dominant fuel in the county, the countryside here is studded with poorly-equipped coking plants, aluminum plants and iron works, leading to severe environmental pollution. Currently, this county lags far behind in general socioeconomic development. In 2005, the per capita gross regional product was just 1,550 Yuan, far lower than the national and the provincial average. It is the poorest region of the four regions surveyed.

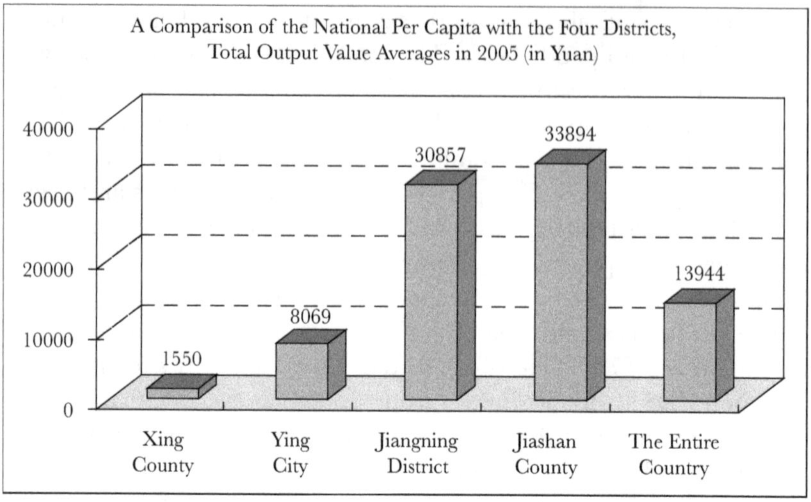


Figure 9.1: A Comparison of the National Per Capita with the Four Districts Total Output Value Averages in 2005 (in Yuan)

The per capita gross regional product reflects a region's socioeconomic development level to a great extent. The four regions we researched were specifically selected for their different socioeconomic development levels. As shown in Figure 9.1, in reference to the national per capita GDP, the subject county in Zhejiang Province and the Jiangning region in Jiangsu Province are both well developed regions with a per capita GRP far higher than the national average. While the per capita GRP of the subject county in Shanxi Province and the subject city in Hubei Province are considerably lower than the national average. This is especially the case of Xingxian County of Shanxi Province which is counted among the poorest in terms of ecological environment, agricultural production conditions and socioeconomic development. On the contrary, the subject county in Zhejiang Province is among the best in terms of agricultural production conditions and socioeconomic development, of the four regions surveyed.

## II. *Principal Situation of Disputes in Rural Areas*

In regards to the existing contradictions and disputes in rural areas, there are some unique problems as well as some universal problems in the four regions of Zhejiang Province, Jiangsu Province, Shanxi Province and Hubei Province.

### A. *Contracting Disputes over Land Management Rights in Regions Suitable for Cultivation are Universal*

In this case, "regions suitable for cultivation" refers to an area with favored natural land conditions that is suitable for farming. Of the four regions surveyed, the subject county in Zhejiang Province is located in a northern plain, the subject town in Jiangsu Province in the downstream plain of the Changjiang River, and the subject city in Hubei Province is in the Jianghan Plain. These three regions have with favorable natural land conditions, and could be called regions suitable for cultivation. However the subject county in Shanxi Province is located in the Luliang mountainous region and has uneven topography, less rainwater and sterile land. So it is not suitable for farming.

The General Office of the State Council pointed out in its "Urgent Notice on Adequate Solutions for Disputes Occurring over the Contracting of Land in Rural Areas in April 2004" (关于妥善解决当前农村土地承包纠纷的紧急通知), "This year, the CPC Central Committee and the State Council have promulgated a series of policies to support grain production and promote an increase of farmer incomes, which has greatly encouraged farmers to develop grain production and appears to have resulted in the favorable status of agricultural production. Accompanying this enthusiasm for cultivation, some disputes over the contracting of land have occurred, and in some places mass events have happened, which has brought about adverse impacts on rural economic development and social stability." We conducted a relatively complete field survey of these types of disputes and contradictions. The survey shows that disputes concerning the contracting management rights of land frequently occurred in regions suitable for farming, i.e. the subject county in Zhejiang Province, the subject town in Jiangsu Province and the subject city in Hubei province. Comparatively, such disputes seldom occurred in the Xingxian County of Shanxi Province where there are poor natural conditions for agricultural production.

#### 1. *Quantity of Disputes over the Contracting of Land*

Statistics of letters and visits (信访) in the period from January to September of 2006 in the subject county in Zhejiang Province show that disputes over the contracting of land ranked third with a total of 71 cases, accounting for 5.92% of the total amount of letters and visits. The issues ranking first and second in volume are also related to land, i.e. compensation for land requisition and curtilage

(宅基地) respectively. The county agricultural management bureau dealt with four or five disputes on land contracting per month on average. Of these disputes, in 1/3 of these disputes the land in question was contracted by a large contractor and farm households wanted to recover use of their land from the contractor; and the other 2/3 were situations such as unfair distribution or unreasonable compensation for land requisition. Most of these disputes occurred after the cancellation of the agricultural tax.

As evidenced by the relevant statistics, township (sub-district) judicial mediation centers across the county mediated 299 disputes in 2005, including 13 concerning issues of land contracting, which accounted for 4.3% of the total. The People's Mediation Committee dealt with 1,698 disputes in 2005 including 44 concerning land contracting, which accounted for 2.6% of the total.

In 2005, the courts in the county accepted 1,779 civil and commercial cases, including 7 concerning land contracting. There were not large numbers of such cases, but they were difficult to deal with.

In comparison with the subject county in Zhejiang Province and the subject surveyed region in Hubei Province, the research group only surveyed one town in Jiangsu Province, but disputes over land contracting rights were still a noteworthy social issue in the locality.

The subject city in Hubei Province presented a similar situation. Since 2004, when the agricultural tax was exempted, disputes concerning land contracts became one of the major contradictions and conflicts for the whole of Hubei Province. Because of the frequency at which this type of dispute occurred, Hubei Province started improvement of second-round contracting extensions at the end of 2004.

According to the statistical data of the Yingcheng Judicial Bureau, the People's Mediation Committees of the whole city mediated 723 disputes in 2005 including 80 concerning land contracts, accounting for 11.1% of the total. And from January to September of 2006, the People's Mediation Committees in the city dealt with 690 disputes including 74 concerning land contracts, accounting for 10.7%. In the last two years, the total quantity of disputes over land contracts has risen slightly; the proportion however has slightly decreased. And comparatively speaking, the quantity of disputes lodged in the courts was not large. According to the statistics of the city courts, there were 12 dispute cases concerning the contracting of land in 2005 and 6 during the period of January through September 2006, a slight decline. One court official stated, "Generally such disputes are resolved by the administrative organs of villages. It is a sensitive issue, so the Party committee deals with them independently in most of cases." What is handled in a court then is such dispute that cannot be settled by the government and is complained about on a large-scale by the public.

In general, disputes over land contracts have two features. One is this kind of dispute usually occurred in last few years. And the second is that the superintendents of the departments concerned basically complained that the quantity of this type of case was not large but the process of resolving such cases was very difficult, containing acute contradictions and involving a considerable number of people.

### 2. *Type of Disputes Concerning Contracts for Land Management and Related Causes*

In the regions surveyed, the most frequently occurring disputes in the area of land contracts are as follows:

First, farm households privately transferred possession of their contracting management rights at low price or free of charge; and then after cancellation of the agriculture tax sought to recover those rights. It was at this point that a dispute usually occurred. The parties concerned were typically ordinary villagers.

This type of dispute occurs under two different types of circumstances, the first happens before the second round of land contracting, with a private transfer of land happening between farmers, i.e. a farm household with more land transfers part of his land to a farm household with less land. During the second round contracting, such land is transferred under the name of the latter farmer household and the transfer was acknowledged by the village organization. However, when the land appreciated, the party originally giving the land reneged, thus leading to a dispute. In the other type of circumstance, such presentation or transfer is not reflected in the certificate of contract for land management, i.e. a villager gave or transferred his contracted land to other villager at a low price but still holds the certificate for contracting the land. Now the land value has risen, the certificate holder wants to recover the land.

In the second type of condition, some villagers gave up their contracting management rights partially or fully during the first round contracting period. Then when it came to the second round of contracting, the rising land value induced them to try and recover their abandoned land, thus causing a dispute. This kind of dispute mainly occurred between villagers and the collective, and sometimes between a large-scale farmer and other villagers. This kind of dispute is complicated in practice with different types and circumstances. First, the contracted land was given up in oral form or in writing. As specified then, the abandonment of land must be accompanied by a written certificate. Most of the abandoners signed written documents but a few didn't, which then led to the later disputes. And in fact, some farmers who gave up the contracted land in writing also asked for land from the collective later. Second, some abandoned land was kept by the collective as public land and flexible use land, and was not contracted. Some of the land has also been contracted by other farm households in the second round contracting. The former condition is relatively easy to handle, but the latter involves several interested parties, and is difficult to deal with. Third, some villagers want to recover their abandoned land, and some want to receive a compensation and relocation allowance for abandoned land that has been requisitioned.

In the third type of condition, a villager entrusted partial or full contract of his land to the village collective for uniform subcontracting. When the land value rose, the villager desired to recover such land, thus leading to a dispute. The contents under dispute are including two categories, i.e. more funds are demanded for the transfer of land or a return of the land is demanded.

As the contracting management right of the land is still held by the villagers, villagers have the right to reclaim the land from the view of policy and law and also to increase the transfer fee. Therefore, there shouldn't be any dispute. However, the village collective is sometimes incapable of or unwilling to meet the villagers' requirements for two reasons. First, the village collective after being entrusted with the contract can gain definite financial profits for the collective. If the farmer households (农戶) want to increase the transfer fee or reclaim the land, this will definitely influence the income of the village collective. This is a contradiction that frequently occurs in the transfer stage. And there is certainly would be a conflict of interest between improving the second round contracting and ensuring the interests of the farmer households, and the village collective as the abolition of the agricultural tax has reduced the economic income of the village collectives. Second, the village collective usually signs a contract of subcontracting, which specifies the transfer fee and contracting period. Such contract terms feature lower transfer fees and longer contracting period. When farmer household's proposed to increase the transfer fee or reclaim the land, some contracts were not yet expired. Under these conditions, the village collective had difficulty meeting the farmer household's requirements.

Fourth, collective land is expropriated by various means, which leads to disputes. Some village land was not contracted and used as public land, and when the land value rose, villagers occupied the land by various means for the purpose of gaining compensation and relocation allowances when the land was requisitioned in the future. There is a concept in the rural areas "if land plot is covered in my contracting certificate, then the neighboring public land is certainly mine." (我这块田地在我的权证上面, 旁边的公地肯定是我的)

Fifth, the status of a private plot is unclear, which can easily cause a dispute. The central government has not issued any policy regarding the problems of private plots. There is no mention of private plots in the first and second contracting. Some villagers have proposed that though they left the land the ownership rights are still theirs. And furthermore is the land was requisitioned, they should receive some relocation allowance. Current land requisition is subject to the interpretation of the Land Administration Bureau. The county authority has issued a policy that private plots are not eligible for relocation allowances. However villagers believe that private land should be treated equally with the contracted land and dealt with properly when requisitioned.

Sixth, some villagers returned the contracted land to the collective in order to obtain permanent residence in a city. However now that the land return is considerable, they want to recover the previously contracted land.

3. *Causes of Disputes over Land Contracts*

Though the causes mentioned above are specific, there are still some general common factors that cause or induce disputes over land contracts.

The first and most basic cause is the substantial increase of land value, which leads to a rising enthusiasm on the part of the farmers for farming and owning land, thus leading to conflict. All of these disputes are aimed at obtaining the recently accrued value. This value may be the earnings from cultivation or the transfer fee or compensation from land requisition, etc., and the increase of land value is generally the result of exemption to the agricultural tax, development of profitable agriculture, or probability of compensation from land requisition, etc. Therefore there are difficulties involved in approximating past land appreciation. Certain villagers who, when the land value was relatively low or negative, dealt with their contracted land by abandoning farming, contracting, transfer, etc., regretted their actions when the land suddenly appreciated and desired to reclaim their land contracts, leading to inevitable disputes.

Secondly, the procedure for abandoning and transferring land contracting management rights is not standardized, which increases the difficulty of settling such disputes. However such non-standard procedure is not the leading cause of the disputes. Rather, the leading causes are as follows: first, although there is no written agreement, the abandonment and transfer is not denied in many cases, instead the villagers justify their actions with the change of policies and circumstance, holding the idea that "who could know the current policies would be so favorable." Second, even if the procedure for abandoning the contracted land was standardized and definite, some villagers desire to recover their land. For instance, some villagers who gave up the land in order to apply for urban resident status or gave up the land in written statements still return to reclaim the land. Third, some villagers put forward similar claims and requirements not on the basis of "their rights being violated" but on the basis of necessity "asking for help from the government," or "for the sake of their lives."

Thirdly, it is the basic principle of justice of farm households cultivating the land that it is harmful to the land to let it lie idle, and they are therefore unwilling to return the land after cultivating it. There are some articles, such as houses or cars, which have the characteristic that if they are not used, it is adverse to their maintenance. Cultivated land is the same way, if it is desolated, its fertility and infrastructure will be damaged. Furthermore, because of this characteristic when one villager abandons his land, another claims it to cultivate it. Then the latter farmer believes he has contributed to maintaining the land when the agricultural taxes were considerable and is unwilling to return the land when the value of the land appreciates.

Fourthly, the economic problems of the village collective can also be the cause for some disputes.

4. *Disputes over Land Contract Management Rights are Few in Areas where the Land is Unsuitable for Cultivation*

There were few disputes over land contract management rights in the survey subject county in Shanxi Province. There are three major causes for this phenomenon: first, as a whole, this county in Shanxi Province has little rainwater, poor irrigation conditions, steep land slope and poor land fertility all of which lead to low land output. In such conditions, the earnings from agricultural cultivation are lower. Even after the exemption of the agricultural tax, the earnings from cultivation are not high, so farmers are not active in their cultivation. Second, urban development and land development are slower in this area, so there is little chance to receive compensation from land requisition. These circumstances also reduce the ownership value of the right to contracted management of land to some degree. Third, owing to low earnings from land cultivation and environmental damage, the policy of reusing cultivated land for forestry has been implemented in recent years. Although there have been some disputes over the distribution of compensation for reusing cultivated land for forestry, the quantity of disputes concerning land contract management rights have reduced considerably.

a. *Conflicts and Disputes Regarding Compensation for Land Requisition are Extensive* In the four regions surveyed, disputes concerning compensation for land requisition were a universal social phenomenon.

For instance, in the subject county of Zhejiang Province, compensation for land requisition and relocation is one of the major social conflicts. Since second round contracting was put in to operation, disputes concerning land contracts ranked first, with disputes concerning land requisition and relocation second, and disputes concerning labor and capital and work injury third. Of all the letters and visits accepted in 2006, issues concerning land requisition topped the list. From January to September of 2006, there were 120 calls concerning land requisition, accounting for 10.76% of the total. The second largest issue was disputes concerning curtilage, and the third was the contracting of land.

As the regional economic development and urbanization is below average, land requisition and relocation in the surveyed county of Shanxi Province was conducted on a limited scale. However, even with this small scale land requisition and relocation, there were still acute contradictions and disputes.

According to the local township, town officers and law service staff, there was a fierce armed conflict between the government and farmers caused by a dispute over the standard of compensation for land requisition in regards to the requisition of about 1000 *mu* land for the building of a train station at Weijiatan. According to the words of an interviewee, the land up for requisition was suitable for twice a year planting but was only compensated with 27,000 Yuan per *mu*. In the opinion of the farmers losing the land, the land should have been compensated by 80,000–100,000 Yuan/*mu*.

To sum up, conflicts and disputes occurring because of compensation for land requisition and relocation in the four regions are reflected in the following aspects:

First, after the relocation funds were spent, farmers came to the government for retirement support and life insurance. In the mid-90's, two patterns were adopted for compensation of farmers, i.e. lump sum monetary payment and endowment insurance (养老保险). The former paid over 10,000 Yuan at one time and the latter, operated by social security funds, provided a monthly stipend to a male after the age of 60 and a female after the age of 50. At that time, many farmers selected this option. However, after spending these funds, they were unable to make a living because of the loss of land. At this time they would come to the government to ask for help, with the reasoning of necessity, i.e. "I have to live and I need life security." Some young people have selected monetary settlement at first but then when they get older, they also want the choice of endowment insurance.

Second, villagers believed the government's compensation standard was too low and required improving. Different time periods were provided with different amounts of compensation. For instance, the endowment insurance was 160 Yuan in 1995. Now the same location receives a payment of 200 Yuan. For this reason it is believed the previous allowance is too low and should be properly increased. This kind of contradiction exists when land is requisitioned in advance. For instance, land requisitioned was advance in 1996 with a payment of 100 Yuan at that point, but then the project was not launched. In 2000, the land requisition fees rose to 200 Yuan, thereby leading to a dispute.

Third, some of the public are not accepting of the method of pricing different areas of land differently.

Fourth, there are disputes over the distribution of land compensation. According to the provisions of Article 26 of the "Regulations on the Implementation of the Land Administration Law of the People's Republic of China" (土地管理法实施条例), land compensation shall belong to the rural collective economic organization; and compensation for land attachment and "green crops (青苗)" shall be possessed by the land attachment and "green crop (青苗)" possessors. However in practice, some villagers don't accept such methods of distribution.

Fifth, there are disputes over compensation for land requisition related to land contracts. In the area of compensation for land requisition and relocation, allowances are distributed to farmers who lose their land, and farmers who lose their land refer to farmers who lose contracted land. Therefore, it is important for the distribution of allowances to acknowledge the owner of the contractual management rights of land requisitioned. However in reality, there are many disputes over the ownership of the contractual management rights of land, which is a very real obstacle for settlement work. To sum up, there are four major types of disputes: first, in the middle and later 20th century, agricultural management was under a heavy burden. Some villagers gave up partial or full contracted land in the second round of contracting and the contracting certificate for land was altered. Now that the land given up has been requisitioned or expropriated, the original contractor wants to receive allowances. Second, the land transfer happened privately and was not reflected in the contracting certificate. When such land was requisitioned or expropriated, a dispute arose over the right to allowances. Third, some village public land was cultivated by some of the villagers. When such land was appropriated, the villagers made a claim for allowances. Forth, the dispute concerns the villagers' private plots.

Sixth, the dispute over compensation for land requisition is related to curtilage (宅基地). Some of the compensation for land requisition is designated to address land attachment such as buildings, "green crops," etc. and some is designated to address the land itself, such as land ownership, contractual management rights, the right of using curtilage, etc. Of these, compensation for the removal of buildings is one special type of dispute. In this type, the ownership of curtilage is vulnerable to dispute in practice. And in fact the basis for dispute is that the transfer of the property rights of a building is concurrent with non-transferability of curtilage in the areas of system and policy, thus leading to a dispute regarding the true ownership of the curtilage and then also a dispute over compensation. Right to use curtilage (or a building), after being sold directly or indirectly, cannot be transferred with ownership. When relocation compensation is made, it may lead to disputes among several parties such as the buyer, the seller, the village collective, the relocation compensation provider, etc. Another condition of dispute is when because of some reason like inheritance, a shift from agricultural resident status to non-agricultural resident status, or becoming a cadre, etc. the building owner gains non-agricultural population status. If the building has not been removed, the owner can continue to live there. If the building has been removed, the non-agricultural population cannot enjoy the curtilage policy which is aimed at the collective curtilage of the agricultural population, thus leading to a dispute.

Seventh are the disputes which happen as a result of previous compensation for land requisition; this type of dispute can be divided into two classes. The first is that that the villagers concerned were organized to work when their land was appropriated but due to unforeseen circumstances, such as the employer going bankrupt or the villagers being fired, contradictions and disputes have broken out. The second condition is that the land charge was too high and villagers accepted land requisition at a lower price or for free. And, now that land resources have increased substantially in value, the villagers are trying to reclaim the land for compensation, thus leading to contradictions and disputes.

b. *Analysis of the Reasons for Contradictions and Disputes* According to the above description, there are quite a few types of contradictions and disputes over compensation for land requisition with different causes. The causes can be classified into the following six groups:

First, from the viewpoint of procedure, the pricing mechanism for the compensation for land requisition is not reliable for the public. The questions of how to calculate the appropriate compensation price for one *mu* land is essentially a question of intangible justice. However, if a fair procedure does not exist; such essential justice will never be achieved. And a fair procedure, under the market mechanism, could help achieve a fair price for both parties to some extent.

Of course, if one land plot involves the interests of a considerable number of villagers, it may lead to a higher transaction cost, thus influencing the effective development of land resources. However if we refer to the practice of developed market economies, this concern can be eliminated because as far as China is concerned, the compensation price for land requisition is unilaterally decided by the government as this pricing is closely related to the government's interests. According to the provisions of the "Law of Land Management" (土地管理法), for the compensated use of newly increased construction land, 30% of it shall be turned in the central treasury and 70% shall be set apart for the local people's government for special applications in the development of cultivated land. In reality, this method of income has entered local public finance to a great extent. And in fact, these are important methods to attract investment and business for the local government to increase GDP, and are usually based on the prior condition of land requisition. So in fact, it is difficult for the government to be indifferent to the establishment of a compensation price for land requisitioned in consideration of the need for local fiscal revenue and GDP growth. Therefore, any price the government sets is controversial and leads to contradictions and disputes.

Second, even considering the outcomes, the current compensation price for land requisitioned is on the low side. This phenomenon can be explained in two ways. First, that there is a big gap between the compensation price and transfer price of land requisitioned. Taking the subject city in Hubei Province as an example, the compensation allowance for one *mu* of land is about 20,000–30,000 Yuan. However, one *mu* of land in the area connecting town and country can be transferred at a price of up to 500,000 Yuan. One must consider the government's investment in infrastructure in the case of the latter; though the price differential is still considerable after such investment is deducted.

According to an officer of the Municipal National Land and Resources Bureau, the compensation for land requisition is 27,000 Yuan/*mu*, or 40.5 Yuan/square meter. After the land is requisitioned the government will invest about 200 Yuan/square meter into the land. As to the transfer price, land in a prime area can reach up to 1,000 Yuan/square meter and even land in a less desirable area can reach as high as 500–600 Yuan/square meter. If we take the surveyed town as an example, the cultivated area of the agricultural population is 1.89 *mu*/person and every 1.89 *mu* of land provides one person with an endowment insurance of 200 Yuan/month. Locally, the rental of land has already exceeded that amount. As stated by the town officer, one *mu* of land is charged with a rental about 300 Yuan and the rental for 1.89 *mu* of land is about 567 Yuan. We did not take into consideration also the fact that the rental price of the land will appreciate (which it almost certainly will). Even if compared with the existing price, the compensation price for the land requisitioned is far lower than the rental.

Third, there are many hidden dangers in arranging compensation for the labor force. One of the compensation arrangements is settling for labor. In practice, some regions ask the land requisition units to arrange the work force. However this method can lead to disputes because the operations and profits of the land requisition units are not stable and they can become bankrupt. Let us use as an example the "leasing" dispute over land for a golf course in the surveyed county of Jiangsu

Province. The land using unit promised to arrange employment when expropriating the land (as in the case of permanent leasing). However the golf course project violates the state system and policies and cannot begin normal operations, thus delaying the employment of farmers who had lost their land and resulting in consequent contradictions and disputes.

Fourth, the system by which land compensation is collected by the village collective is not reasonable. Since the household contract responsibility system (家庭联产承包责任制) was implemented in the rural areas, the rural economic collective has lost its economic functions and the villagers' committee has become a service organization. Our survey shows that village committees, especially those in the subject county of Zhejiang Province and the subject county in Jiangsu Province, undertake many important functions. However by their nature, these functions are extensions of public management. In fact, these committees work for the township/town governments. In this sense, it is not very reasonable for village committees to earn income from land compensation and apply them to the maintenance of their operations, because this means that the township/town government transfers its fiscal burden to its villagers. In addition, even if it is reasonable to collect such fees, it is not reasonable to collect from farmers who have lost their land as the villagers' committee is more than just the collective of those farmers. Moreover, on the occasion that the village budget experiences problems, the allowance of collection of land compensation fees indeed encourages village collectives to throw themselves into promoting land requisition (or expropriation in disguised form) regardless of whether such expropriation conforms to the public policy and farmers' long-term benefit. Moreover, similar motives regarding land requisition on the part of the village collective and of the government may result in a community of benefit consisting only of the above parties, forcing the land using party into the game of land requisition, which will put farmers in a more disadvantageous position in negotiating with government and the land using units. The above worry is not theoretical but in fact, frequently occurs in reality.

Fifth, some problems are not caused by relocation settlements but the extension of land contracting. The compensation for land requisition is primarily based on the ownership of contractual management right of land. However disputes frequently arise regarding such ownership, thus leading to dispute over compensation for land requisition. For instance, some villagers gave up their contracted land in various ways or transfer or exchange their contracted land. Now that there is compensation for land requisition available, a dispute may occur regarding the ownership of compensation rights between villagers or between the villager and the village collective.

Sixth, some problems are not caused by relocation settlement but by the extension of curtilage. Disputes frequently occur regarding the ownership of curtilage. For instance, there are many cases of trading curtilage (or house property). As curtilage cannot be transferred with the ownership according to the system, especially in the case of those buyers and sellers who are not in possession of a living place and registered permanent residence, there may be disputes over compensation for relocation between the government, the village collective, the seller and the buyer. Moreover, when the registered permanent residence has shifted from agricultural population status to non-agricultural population status or been altered for moving, the removal of house property may lead to some contradictions and disputes over compensation for loss of curtilage.

### C. *The Situation Concerning Disputes over the Transfer of Curtilage in Developed Areas is Grave*

The four regions we surveyed all exhibit problems regarding the transfer of curtilage to some degree. And, it is most common in Jiashan County of Zhejiang Province as this county is the most developed of those areas studied and the dispute problem caused there is also the most serious.

#### 1. *Types of Disputes over the Transfer of Curtilage*

According to the introduction of the department concerned, there are three major types of disputes regarding curtilage transfer in the surveyed county of Zhejiang Province. First, owing to an increase in land or building value, sellers denied the validity of the sales contract after the curtilage was sold. Second, when the curtilage was sold, the other family members of the seller declared the sale invalid. Third, the dispute occurred in the compensatory process of land requisition but it was still rooted in the legal effects of curtilage being transferred. As stated by the superintendent of Jiashan County Letters and Visits Bureau: private trading led to some problems. The individual, once he has acquired curtilage, erects a new building on the site. However if the curtilage is expropriated, the owner of the curtilage is still the village not the buyer. Its requisition will lead to a conflict of interests between the villager and the buyer, thus forming a triangular dispute.

2. *Causes for Disputes over the Transfer of Curtilage*

The reasons causing this type of dispute can be broken down into the following three areas:

First, the transfer of curtilage is a universal phenomenon. According to the testimony of the superintendent of the county national land and resources bureau, it is a common phenomenon for villagers to trade curtilage and house property, especially those in areas linking the town and the country. As explained by the superintendent of the department concerned, there is a wide range of transfer methods for curtilage. One kind is the trade of curtilage along with the trade of house property. The superintendent of the County National Land and Resources Bureau explained: "some villagers have transferred their registered permanent residence to towns or cities, so they sold their empty houses in the countryside." Another condition is that the transfer of curtilage cannot be transferred with ownership, so such action lacks any legal guarantee. When the curtilage or rental rate increases, the original seller may claim invalid sales. In order to combat this legal uncertainty, a method of leasing has appeared to replace of sales, i.e. "To lease one hundred years, two hundred years, the payment shall be made in one lump sum."

Secondly, as it is forbidden to transfer curtilage according to law and policy, the transfer of curtilage is not acknowledged or protected by law or policy. The practical rights and obligations formed after such circulation are not stable. According to the provisions of China's Constitution and the "Law of Land Management," land is forbidden to trade but the usage rights to land can be transferred according to the requirements of the law. To an individual villager, curtilage rights means some usage rights of the collective land, but this type of usage right can only be enjoyed by a member of the collective economy. Therefore the curtilage is non-transferable and cannot at the very least belong to an individual outside the collective economy. The Ministry of Land and Resources specifies this point in the "Opinions on Strengthening the Management of Rural Curtilage" (关于加强农村宅基地管理的意见) in November 2004: "It is strictly prohibited that town residents purchase curtilage in the rural areas and that any land use certificate be issued to the residence of an urban resident who has purchased and built a residence in a rural area. It is forbidden to approve any application for new curtilage ownership when the villager applicant has sold, leased or given away his original house property."

Third, substantial increases in house property and curtilage values provide economic incentives to the sellers for amending or cancelling the transfer of curtilage. In such developed regions as the surveyed county in Zhejiang Province, the economy is rapidly growing while the migrant worker population is rapidly rising; a situation which has sharply increased the value of house properties and curtilage. Under these circumstances, those sellers who had sold their house property or curtilage directly or indirectly at previously lower prices cancel the sales for the reason of the transfer being null. The appreciation of curtilage or house property values has several effects. One is the higher market price of house property or curtilage; another is that house property has seen higher earned income on lease, which indirectly raises the value of curtilage; third, compensation for the requisition of curtilage or house properties may be far higher than the former transfer price.

It is worth noting that the three situations mentioned above are interrelated. First, the universal existence of curtilage transfer is the precondition of the disputes. Second, the lack of protection from laws or policies make the transfer of curtilage unstable, which leads to probable disputes. However, the existence of these two factors alone is not enough to result in such a wide-scale occurrence of disputes regarding the transfer of curtilage. As the rest of the four regions also experience a heavy volume of curtilage transfer without suffering from as many as disputes under the same conditions of laws and policies offering no protection in this matter. This indicates that the third aspect, i.e. the swift growth of house property and curtilage value is also an important reason. It is this value increase that is the immediate cause for the sellers' claims of null sales contracts; and it is just the third cause that differs by region. Generally, there are more disputes regarding the transfer of curtilage in developed coastal areas experiencing swift economic growth and an increase in the migrant worker population.

### D. *The Growth of the Migrant Population in Coastal Developed Areas Challenges Social Management*

#### 1. *Coastal Development Areas Experience a Rise in the Migrant Worker Population*

Of the four regions we surveyed, the surveyed county in Zhejiang Province is a coastal development area and its economic development is far higher than the national average. On the other hand, Xingxian County of Shanxi Province and Yingcheng City of Hubei Province are situated in middle-west inland, and both have a comparatively lagging economic development rate. This is especially the case in Xingxian County, where the economic development level is far lower than the national average (see Fig. 9.1). We discovered through our research that the situation of economic development in the eastern coastal areas and the middle-west inland areas varied greatly; for example a sizable amount of the rural population of the inland left that area and a sizeable amount of migrant workers immigrated to the coastal development areas.

In the inland area of the middle-west, the numbers of individuals that are willing to work in other areas is increasing, which is consequently causing a sharp reduction in the number of actual local residents. As most of the persons who leave to work are young, those left are composed of a small number of young people and a majority of seniors, women and children. The rural population from the inland mainly flows into the local county or provincial capitals, and coastal development areas. In the subject county of Shanxi Province, there is a trend that rural residents move to the county and the county residents move to the provincial capital. There are three townships and towns with a registered permanent population over 20,000 but just about a half live there with the rest going out.

Contrarily, there are substantial migrant worker populations either in the urban areas or in the rural areas of the eastern coastal areas. The term "migrant population" primarily refers to rural migrant farmers from inland provinces. The subject county of Zhejiang Province has a population over 380,000. According to the latest statistics, the migrant population was over 270,000 by September 2006. They have been registered in public security authorities with temporary residence certificates and are called "new person X" (新 x 人) by the local management authorities. The "new person X" population is distributed in a concentrated way, in the surrounding areas of the county, the areas connecting the urban and rural areas, in emerging development areas, and some in townships and towns that have seen rapid industrial development. In one of the villages we surveyed, the population was 2,136 persons including 1,430 migrant workers, who leased 126 households' houses, or 11 tenants per owner. The neighboring village is crowded with factories. Ninety percent of the employees in these factories come from other places. According to the introduction of the county Party committee officer, "so far, we have registered nearly 280,000 "new person X's," of whom 218,000 persons work in the factories, 13,300 do business and 11,400 persons work in the service sector. There are 33,000 persons under the age of 18 and about 10,000 children between the ages of 0–7."

### 2. *The Rising Migrant Population in Coastal Developed Areas Raises Challenges for Social Management*

The inverse population changes in the two types of regions interact as both cause and effect to some degree; the increase of the migrant population in the coastal areas in the southeast is just the result of the decreased population in the rural areas of the inland provinces. From the view of social conflict and dispute, such changes of population just lead to negative results. In the rural areas of the inland provinces, the significant outflow of the young and prime population has attributed to the substantial decrease of conflicts and disputes in the countryside. On the contrary, the considerable amassing of migrant workers in the coastal areas in the southeast has resulted in many conflicts and disputes. In the subject county of Zhejiang Province that we surveyed, these kinds of contradictions and disputes are very common and the social problems caused were frequently discussed by cadres from all levels and the villagers in our interviews. According to the explanation of the head of the county Party Committee Office, the floating population had increased rapidly in the county and brought large pressure to bear on the social management system especially in the areas of environmental and public security. The issue of social welfare being another significant problem, as while most of migrant population is peaceable, according to statistics, crimes like prostitution, drug use, stealing and robbery can be attributed to this population. One important cause for the large amount of offenses committed by the migrant workers is their inability to reside locally with a fixed residence, thus they less liable to feel shame for committing crimes. As the vast majority of migrant workers are laborers, some labor disputes are also involved with migrant workers.

The county has seen a swift growth in the number of labor disputes in recent years, which is the fasted growing type of dispute. As almost every town in the Yangtze River Delta (长三角地区) is equipped with an industrial development park. In these towns, labor disputes fall just below land disputes in number. Since 2004, this kind of disputes has accounted for nearly one third of the disputes among the people in the town. As shown in the following table, in the subject city in Hubei

Table 9.1: Comparison of Disputes in Jiashan County, Zhejiang Province and Yingcheng City, Hubei Province in 2005

| Region | Total # of disputes among the people | Total # of labor disputes among the people | Percentage of labor disputes of the total |
|---|---|---|---|
| Yingcheng City, Hubei Province | 723 | 52 | 7.2% |
| Jiashan County, Zhejiang Province | 1698 | 402 | 23.7% |

Province, which is an inland region, there were 723 disputes among the people including 52 labor disputes or a total of 7.2% in 2005. While in the subject region in Zhejiang Province, the disputes among the people amounted to 1,698 in 2005, of which 402 were labor disputes, accounting for 23.7%. By comparison, the subject region in Zhejiang Province was higher than the inner region both on total quantity and relative percentage.

## III. *Successful Experiences in Settlement Protocol for Addressing Rural Disputes*

### A. *Land Disputes are Settled Flexibly*

Currently rural areas are experiencing swift social development, acute land conflicts and complicated profit networks. The existing laws and policies are insufficient to effectively dissolve the amount of conflicts and disputes. Under the circumstances, many competent authorities have adopted flexible methods to address the problems based on the basic principles of the laws and policies with some success. In addressing disputes concerning the contracting of land, the principle of maintaining a steady relationship regarding the contracting of land is adhered to decide cases as specified by the contractual management certificates for the land.

In order to help solve the environmental and public security problems caused by the influx of migrant workers as well as to maintain the rights and interests of the migrant population and strengthening management of this population, the surveyed county of Zhejiang Province set up a special management model with "new persons X" as the core subject.

This measure signifies two things, one is a more updated conception of the migrant population, acknowledging their contribution to local social and economic development and raising them to a better status. To some degree, the migrant population is also regarded as the "persons X." This update has been strongly promoted through the introduction of a new title, "new persons X." The address to migrant population is replaced by "new persons X" in all files and announcements, and speeches of the government.

In addition, the surveyed county of Zhejiang Province set up a special department to address the issues related to the migrant population. In November 2004, the county established the "New Persons X Administration Committee," which acts as the general authority in implementing management and service for this population. On April 8, 2005, the Administration Committee was officially put into operation. The management and services for the "new persons X" covers all aspects, such as children's education, improvement of housing conditions, public security, settlement of disputes and maintenance of rights, etc. A "Comprehensive Administration, Justice, Letters and Visits Service Center" was set up in this county in Zhejiang Province. Realistically, many conflicts and disputes are intertwined with several sectors and different involved parties; so the coordination of several sectors is needed. On the most basic level, comprehensive administration is needed. In order to strengthen this kind of comprehensive administration, the surveyed county in Zhejiang Province set up a comprehensive administration organization "Comprehensive Administration, Justice, Letters and Visits Service Center" while in the process of establishing "two stations and one court" (police station, judicial station and people's court). This action establishes the "Service Center" at the level of township/town with the judicial station serving as the routine office. This center is responsible for coordinating the work of the judicial station, the police station, the people's court, the letters and visits office and the comprehensive administration office. The Center adopts the work protocol of "one window towards the outside" (一个窗口对外) and "five in one" (五统一). The motto of "five-in-one" signifies uniform acceptance, uniform distribution, uniform coordination, uniform supervision and uniform registration for the purpose of better serving the masses and improving work efficiency. Over several years' practice, the work ideal of an "coordinated programs center" (联动中心) has been emphasized by the municipal Party committee and the municipal government and acknowledged by the Zhejiang provincial

Party committee, the political and law committee, and the provincial department of justice. This protocol was praised for its innovation and popularized across the province.

To shorten the channel for letters and visits and integrate government resources in a timely manner in order to resolve social contradictions, the surveyed county of Zhejiang Province began to establish a regular integrated reception system at the county level in 2004. Since 2004, leaders of many county organizations were present in the Letters and Visits Bureaus to interview visitors on the 5th day, 15th day and 25th day of each month. During this reception process, the divisional directors concerned are able to be contacted directly. As there were many complaints made concerning the laws, officials of the public security organizations, procuratorial organizations and the people's courts are invited to provide services in a special reception room of the Letters and Visits Bureaus. Now that this system has matured from formal structure to tangible contents after development over these years, the channel for letters and visits is smoother and more efficient. This type of system has made remarkable achievements and was acknowledged by leaders from the State Bureau for Letters and Visits.

In order to strengthen the comprehensive administration of public order, some cities in Hubei Province established relevant organizations at the county and township/town levels and defined their relationship, power and responsibilities. At the county level, under the political-legal committee is a comprehensive administration office at the deputy section level, responsible for coordinating related departments, and political-legal departments in particular, in order to carry out comprehensive administration of public order. At the township/town level, a comprehensive administration office is set up to coordinate the strength and resources of police station, judicial station, people's court, and office for letters and visits for effective and efficient settlement of social conflicts and disputes.

According to our survey of the people's courts in the surveyed county in Hubei Province and the surveyed county in Zhejiang Province, the quantity of civil cases has taken a downturn since 2000.

In the subject city of Hubei Province, statistical data from the court shows that there were 1,629 civil and business cases in 2005 but that during the period from January to September of 2006, there were only 1,018 a marked decline. This same situation also occurred in the surveyed county of Zhejiang Province. In 2004, there were 1,779 civil and commercial cases. But at its peak there were 5,000. As a whole, civil cases have experienced a decrease in recent years.

According to the analysis of the judiciary, the decrease in the quantity of civil and commercial cases can be attributed to the following two causes: first, various social activities and economic operations became more standardized. For instance, rural contracting and financial credit have been implemented in a more standardized way, thus reducing the occurrence of disputes. Secondly, legal actions are conducted in a more standardized way with more prudence exhibited in the employment of power, which contributes to a reduction in the number of cases to some degree. Also, the standards for filing a case are more demanding.

## IV. *Major Problems Facing Settlement Protocol Addressing Rural Disputes*

### A. *Inland Underdeveloped Areas: the Legal Remedy Channel Does Not Function Well*

Of all the methods available for resolving disputes, the lawsuit (or legal remedy) is a very important one. Not only because lawsuits in and of themselves possess dispute resolution abilities, but also for the following reasons: (1) a lawsuit is implemented in strict accordance with laws and procedures and can effectively coordinate the interests of parties concerned in a dispute, especially in the protection of public interests. (2) For the parties concerned, a lawsuit is more than a settlement of disputes or conflicts, it is also a reliable way to remedy and achieve rights. (3) The characteristics of a lawsuit, i.e. justice, enforceability and finality play an important and indirect role in guiding and promoting the settlement of disputes outside of the lawsuit, also known as "bargaining in the shadow of the law" (法律阴影下的交易). However, our survey indicates that the lawsuit method is problematic in some less developed rural areas of the inland provinces. Moreover, the lawsuit is not accepted in these places as an effective way to address disputes.

One important cause for this phenomenon is the people's lack of confidence in the capability of the lawsuit and the judicial administration. This belief is primarily rooted in two causes. One is that some cases are beyond the scope of the court. In some cases, farmers are embroiled in fierce conflict with the government, but they do not select the resolution channel of a lawsuit and rather resort appealing to the higher authorities for help because these conflicts involved complicated social dynamics. Namely, as some local Party and government sectors are involved in the dispute, the lawsuit may be rejected by the court or the case can't be settled effectively. Another cause is difficulty in executing judgments. Even if the court concludes a case, it is still unknown whether it can be executed. This weakens the people's confidence in the lawsuit to some degree. Another reason is the high economic cost of a lawsuit, which results in the people's continued avoidance of using this legal remedy.

### B. *Land Disputes: Judicial Administration is Difficult to Endure*

Although land conflicts and disputes everywhere include disputes concerning land contracts, disputes over allowances for land requisition and disputes regarding the approval and transfer of curtilage, such contradictions and disputes are difficult to address through the judicial administration. Even if they are placed under the handling of administration organizations, they cannot be effectively resolved only by means of official laws and policies.

First, land conflicts and disputes are common throughout the country; and they are handled generally through administrative means with little judicial intervention. The cases handled in court are those disputes that cannot be settled by the government and that are strongly complained of by the public. This is reflected in the quantity of disputes handled by the different government organizations. In the surveyed county of Zhejiang Province, there were only seven disputes regarding the contract of land accepted by courts in the whole county and over fifty disputes handled by the County Bureau of Rural Economy. Additionally, there were 13 disputes handled by the township/town (sub-district) judicial mediation centers and 44 disputes under the mediation of the people's mediation committees in 2005. In the surveyed county of Hubei Province, there were only 12 disputes regarding the contract of land addressed by courts in the whole year of 2005, and 80 by the people's mediation committees. According to the statistics collected from January to September of 2006, there were only 6 disputes over the contract of land addressed by courts and 74 by people's mediation committees.

Second, this type of dispute is difficult to resolve using the existing laws and policies. Much work is needed in the comprehensive consideration of the interests of all parties as some cases have been brought to court but are still difficult to handle. Conflicts are also more frequent regarding in the second contract of land. Additionally, the current policies are different than the former ones. And the collection and reallocation of land involves a great many legal problems and political issues, with the latter being particularly difficult to solve.

Third, administrative mediation usually cannot resolve contradictions, which results in a high number of letters and visits regarding land. According to the statistical data of letters and visits in the surveyed county of Zhejiang Province from January to September of 2006, the quantity of conflicts regarding land requisition ranked first, which shows that land contradictions and disputes are acute, complicated, and difficult to handle.

Fourth, as the available judicial and administrative means cannot address land conflicts and disputes effectively, it is necessary to establish a special arbitration organization to address land disputes. However there is no such special organization in the four regions we surveyed. According to the provisions of the "Law of the Peoples Republic of China on Land Contracts" (土地承包法) promulgated in 2002, a dispute arising over the contractual management of land, "where the parties are not willing to have it settled through consultation or mediation or consultation or mediation is not successful, they may apply to an arbitration entity in charge of arbitrating rural land contracts, or directly file a suit in the People's Court." As required in the "Urgent Notice Concerning Appropriate Settlement of Existing Disputes over Rural Contracts of Land" (关于妥善解决当前农村土地承包纠纷的紧急通知) issued by the General Office of the State Council in April 2004, competent authorities of agriculture at all levels shall make great efforts to experiment with the arbitration of disputes over rural land contracts and strengthen the arbitration of disputes over land contracts. However according to the "Methods for the Organization of Implementing Experimental Projects for the Arbitration of Disputes over Rural Land Contracts" (农村土地承包纠纷仲裁试点设施建设项目组织实施办法) issued by the Ministry of Agriculture in November 2005, the arbitration of these disputes is still in the experimental stage, and has not yet been completely popularized. No arbitration system addressing disputes over rural land contract had been set up in the three regions we surveyed.

The difficulties of resolving lawsuits involving land are the same difficulties which the official laws and policies need to address. This indicates to some extent that rural land problems are a part of social reform, and that every type of profit relationship is both acute and complex even though certain laws and regulations lag behind evolving circumstances and there is still no consensus regarding the establishment of new laws and policies. Therefore based on certain basic principles, those authorities concerned should pursue the fundamental justice of each individual case in order to find adequate solutions for conflicts and disputes. However it is not the particular strength of the judiciary to pursue the essential justice of individual cases and this type of approach is also not in conformity with the principle and concept of a "rule-of-law" nation.

### C. *Developed Areas: Difficulties Reconciling Law Enforcement Standards and Law Enforcement Results*

The above two conditions have made improvement in relatively developed areas where the law enforcement is implemented in a more strict, standardized and humanized way. However, these areas suffer from another problem, expressed by cadres at all levels in our interviews, which is the demanding requirements of standardization of law enforcement may weaken judicial organizations performance in cracking down on illegal and criminal behaviors.

According to the explanation of public security authorities at the basic level, this weakening is caused by the fact that the standardization of regulations requires substantial police force, thus influencing the efficiency of law enforcement. The power of the public security organizations, procuratorial organizations and people's courts at the basic level in the coastal areas is not sufficient, in particular in regards to the public security organizations. As migrant workers move into those coastal areas with quickly developing economies, many conflicts have emerged. Furthermore, the quality of the law enforcement workers leaves something to be desired which makes it difficult to ensure the efficiency of judicial administration.

(Written by: Ran Jingfu)

# THE DEVELOPMENT OF MECHANISMS FOR SETTLING DISPUTES THROUGH LEGAL CHANNELS

Li Lin and Mo Jihong

Social disputes objectively exist throughout human culture. Though the establishment of the socialist system basically eliminated the economic, political and social causes for opposition and conflicts among the people, social disputes resulting from contradictions between the people will still continue to exist for a long time. In the historical context of "rule of law," the question of how to prevent and settle social disputes through legal means in order to guarantee social harmony and stability has become an important topic for China's Party and government in this new century.

## I. *The Types, Causes and Nature of Existing Social Disputes as well as their Influence on the Harmony and Stability of Society*

### A. *Analysis of the Types, Causes and Nature of Existing Social Disputes*

#### 1. *The Main Types and Nature of Existing Social Disputes*

As a result of China's advancement in reforming the economic system, the per capita GDP has exceeded USD 1,000 and the gap between the urban and the rural areas, the rich and the poor, the east, the middle and the west have been further widened and the quantity of social contradictions and social disputes has steadily increased. In particular group disputes caused by land requisition and removal, and the reform of state-owned enterprises, etc. are outstanding among existing social disputes. As of this point, the statistics regarding all social disputes arising across the county cannot be obtained. However, some knowledge about the change in quantity of social disputes in recent years can be gleaned from researching dispute settlement by lawsuit or other methods (see Table 10.1, Figure 10.1, Figure 10.2 and Figure 10.3).

Table 10.1: Breakdown of the Cases Handled by the Supreme People's Court and the Local People's Courts at All Levels

| | | |
|---|---|---|
| The Supreme People's Court handled and closed 3,668 cases, a YEAR TO YEAR growth of 14.77%.<br>The local people's courts at all levels handled and closed 8,105,007 cases, a YEAR TO YEAR growth of 2.07%. | | |
| | There were 245,254 criminal cases adjudicated and 340,715 criminals were sentenced, for committing the crimes of using explosives, willful murder, robbery, rape, kidnapping, etc. There were 825 state functionaries at county/divisional level, 92 at prefecture/department level and 9 at provincial/ministerial level. Of the total number of criminals, 153,724 were sentenced to fixed-term imprisonment over five years, life imprisonment or given the death penalty. | |
| Criminal Trials | Equal Emphasis on Criminal Punishment and the Protection of Human Rights | A total of 1,713 criminal defendants were acquitted of crimes according to law. A relief fund of 7,802,400 Yuan was provided for 378 victims of crime and their families. |
| | Participation in the Comprehensive Administration of Public Order. | A total of 83,697 juvenile delinquents were sentenced to correctional measures. A total of 429,852 criminals had their sentences commuted and 20,254 criminals were released on parole according to law. |
| Civil Trials | A total of 1,159,437 cases were adjudicated on marriage and family and succession of estates. A total of 986,082 cases were adjudicated on disputes concerning ownership and infringement. A total of 179,637 labor lawsuits were adjudicated with a total object value of 3. 189 billion Yuan. | |
| | Regulation of Economic Matters According to Law | A total of 4,755 cases were adjudicated on disputes concerning mergers, bankruptcy and the assignment of property of state-owned businesses. A total of 717,526 cases were adjudicated on relating to disputes of finance. A total of 2,236,888 cases were adjudicatedonvariouscontractdisputeswith a total object value of 475.7 billion Yuan. |
| | Judicial Protection for Intellectual Property | A total of 14,056 civil cases on intellectual property with trial of first instance were adjudicated with a total object value of 2. 1 billion Yuan. |
| | Maritime and Maritime Trade Trials | A total of 7,375 maritime and maritime trade cases were adjudicated with a total object value of 4. 445 billion Yuan. |
| | The Trial of Cases Involving Foreign Countries and Regions, as well as Hong Kong, Macao, Taiwan | A total of 23,313 cases were adjudicated concerning parties from foreign countries or regions, and Hong Kong, Macao or Taiwan, a YEAR TO YEAR growth of 16.39%. |

Table 10.1 (*cont.*)

| | |
|---|---|
| The Supreme People's Court handled and closed 3,668 cases, a YEAR TO YEAR growth of 14.77%.<br>The local people's courts at all levels handled and closed 8,105,007 cases, a YEAR TO YEAR growth of 2.07%. | |
| Administrative Trials | There were 14,250 administrative litigation cases cancelled, changed or affirmed illegal or invalid. Those administrative litigation acts which should have been upheld were affirmed, with a total of 37,360. |
| Execution | 780,000 long term-pending cases were enforced involving a total of 216 billion Yuan. |
| Retrials | A total of 48286 cases were retried according to law with 47,270 cases adjudicated and 15,568 cases amended. |
| Reform of the Judicial System and its Working Protocol | The exclusive exercise of the review of death penalty cases has been implemented since January 1, 2007, which ended a 26 years history of transferring some right-of-review of death penalty cases to the lower level courts.<br>The system of people's assessors was put into operation with 48,211 people's assessors participating in the trial of 339,965 cases;<br>The system of direct filing of cases in the people's courts was advanced, with 6,520 people's courts becoming equipped with this qualification. A "One-stop" hall for registration has been set up in 328 intermediate courts and 2,307 basis-level courts.<br>The applicability of summary procedure has been expanded according to law with 38. 87% of criminal cases and 71.26% of civil cases adopting summary procedure for trial of first instance. Parties facing economic difficulties were provided with timely legal aid with 282,581 man-hours spent in total and 1.211 billion Yuan of legal costs put on hold, reduced or exempted over the whole year. |

The data in the three graphs below show that China has maintained an upwards trend in settling disputes by lawsuit.

China has seen a wide range of complicated social disputes. Social disputes can be divided into four categories according to the subject of the dispute: the first category is comprised of disputes arising from government agencies' exercise of authority on the general public. The second category is comprised of disputes arising between government agencies due to their performance of their duties. The third category is comprised of disputes arising inside government agencies, businesses, pubic institutions and social organizations. The fourth category is comprised of disputes among the general public. Of them, the first and the fourth categories compromise the majority of existing social disputes.

According to the "Work Report of the Supreme People's Court" in the Fifth Session of the 10th People's Congress, 2006 witnessed a

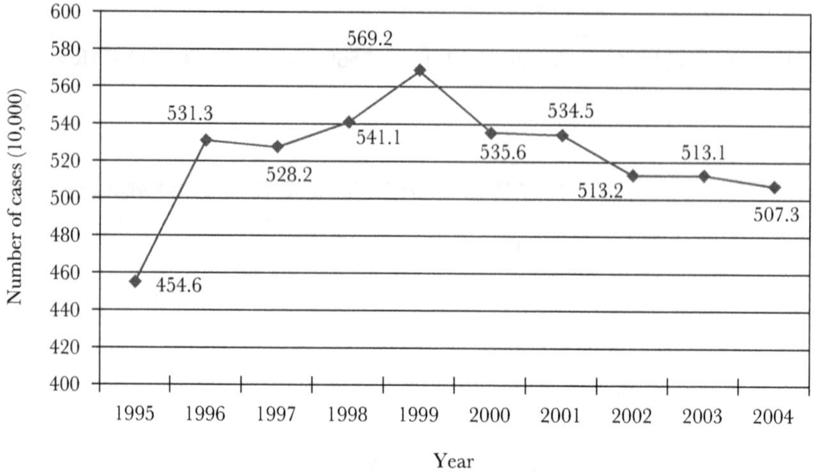


Figure 10.1: Cases Accepted by Courts for Trial of First Instance (1995–2004)[1]

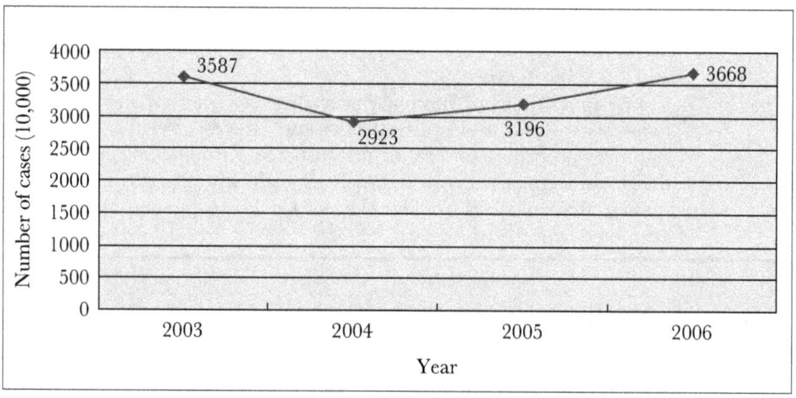


Figure 10.2: Cases Adjudicated by the Supreme People's Court (2003–2006)[2]

[1] *Statistical Yearbook of China (1996–2005).*
[2] Work Report of the Supreme People's Court (2004–2007).

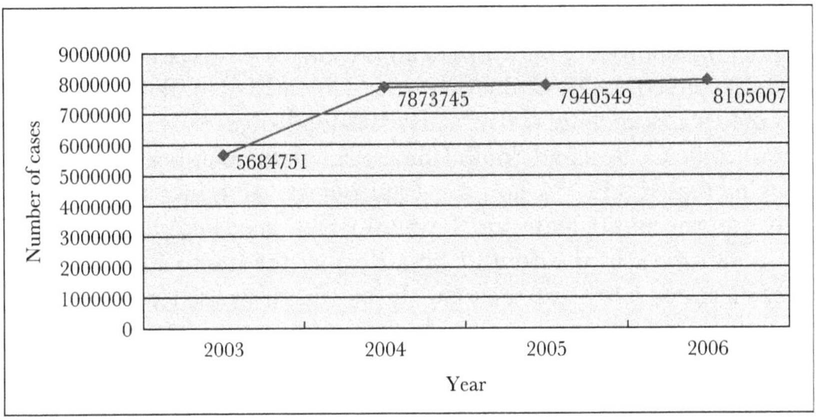


Figure 10.3: Cases Adjudicated by Local People's Courts (2003–2006)[3]

considerable increase in the number of social disputes settled by the people's courts at all levels and the courts played a more important role in resolving these social disputes.[4]

At the National Arbitration Work Symposium 2007 held in Beijing from January 23–25, 2007, Yuan Shiming of the Law Office of the State Council explained in the status report on China's arbitration work development that China's 185 arbitration commissions accepted 60,844 cases in 2006, an increase of 12,505 cases over 2005 or a growth rate of 21%. The total object value of these cases amounted to 72.5 billion Yuan, an increase of 7.1 billion Yuan over 2005 or an increase of 10%. In the whole year, the people's courts revoked 124 arbitration awards, accounting for 0.2% of the total number of accepted cases. Additionally the people's courts did not execute arbitration awards in 71 cases, accounting for 0.12% of the total number of accepted cases. In general, China's arbitration work maintained development though the regional case acceptance numbers and total object values increased only by a small margin or even declined for some arbitration organizations, a phenomenon which must be seriously considered.

In 2006, the work conditions of the eight national regions are outlined as follows: in the North China Region, the number of accepted cases increased 19.1% and the total object value increased 66.9%. In the Northeast China Region, the number of accepted cases increased

[3] Work Report of the Supreme People's Court (2004–2007).
[4] *Legal Daily*, (March 14, 2007), p. 2.

13.1% and the total object value increased 35.1%. In the East China Region, the number of accepted cases increased 6% and the total object value decreased 7.3%. In the Southeast China Region, the number of accepted cases increased 0.4% and the total object value decreased 8.6%. In the Central and South China Region, the number of accepted cases increased 117.1% and the total object value increased 33.6% with the rate of increase for the number of accepted cases ranking first nationwide. In the South China Region, the number of accepted cases increased 6.6% and the total object value increased 20.2%. In the Southwest China Region, the number of accepted cases decreased 3.8% and the total object value increased 22.6%. In the Northwest China Region, the number of accepted cases increased 30.3% and the total object value increased 73.1% with the latter ranking first nationally. In view of the arbitration work in 2006, comrades from each region held the opinion that although there was fluctuation in the total number of accepted arbitration cases, it continued to advance as a whole, and played a positive role in establishing a socialist market economy and a socialist harmonious society.[5]

As a whole, China's existing social disputes can still be categorized as normal social contradictions and conflicts, which are inevitable in the social transition and developing process. Most of these social disputes are contradictions among the people and can be settled through legal channels and systems.

2. *Characteristics of Existing Group Disputes*

Group disputes are the category of social disputes that most negatively impact social harmony and stability. Our analysis of the group disputes is as follows:

(a) Some group disputes are large in scale and number of participants involved. Some group disputes involved more than one thousand persons. Such a large scale dispute is difficult to control for the government. For example, around 14:00 on January 4, 2004, more than two thousand motorcycle drivers drove their motorcycles to block Chaoyang Municipal Government Office in Liaoning Province.

(b) A minority of group disputes lasted a long time and produced strong negative side effects in society. From the strike beginning on September 14, 2004 and ending on November 1, a group dispute

[5] *Legal Daily*, (March 18, 2007), p. 14.

lasting 48 days and involving thousands of employees occurred at the Xianyang China Resources Textiles Co., Ltd.

(c) Some large-scale group disputes developed from small-scale group appeals. Because the related government agencies failed to take effective measures to address them, the disputes worsened. For instance, hundreds of teachers of several towns and townships in Xinmin City, Liaoning Province appealed to the municipal governments for in-arrears wages on April 12, 2004. This caused a chain reaction in which teachers in the secondary and primary schools of over ten towns and townships went on strike and classes were suspended.

(d) Some group disputes received organizational support, which aggravated the difficulty of resolving the issues. For instance, some migrant workers and businessmen in a certain province of the south often got together and participated in mass demonstrations for the so-called "protection of rights," which resulted in physical brawls and disturbances. Some disputes evolved into vicious criminal cases. This type of situation has become a new hidden danger for local level security and stability. For instance, many workers have been invited to take part in certain underground activities of "villager organizations" (老乡会), by signing an agreement to receive the protection of these organizations before working in the factories in Guangdong. The reasons for these phenomena are, one, migrant workers are vulnerable to invasion of their personal rights and interests. These infringements are not resolved for a variety of reasons, so more and more people begin to look for more extreme methods to resolve them. Second, migrant workers alone have slight power, so they are easily bullied, and investigation into these "villager organizations" can easily result in disturbances. Third, the majority of people believe that the law won't punish the public because of their organization of a "villager organization."

(e) Many group disputes resulted in sharp mass conflicts with the police, even bloodshed. Some group disputes were not emphasized enough and were dealt with in an overly simplified way, which worsened the overall situation. For instance, about one hundred employees of a bankruptcy enterprise in Chongqing were not satisfied with the employment provision issues and held a sit-in demonstration for two continuous days on June 1 and June 2 of 2004. There were dangerous conflicts with the police in the process.

In a word, group disputes have occurred more frequently and have had increasing influence. They have become a hidden danger in the establishment of social harmony and stability and merit the attention of the government at all levels as well as those departments concerned.

3. *Analysis of the Causes of Social Disputes*

Existing social disputes are caused by complicated issues with different features. As a whole, different types of social disputes have some commonalities but also maintain their own separate causes.

History, tradition, economy, society, culture, systems and concepts, etc. have all become common causes for some social disputes. However from the viewpoint of the legal system, the top cause of the majority of China's social disputes and the ineffective settlement of disputes is the incomplete legal system, i.e. the low quality of legislation, the non-observance of laws, the lack of strict law enforcement, the lack of effective prosecution of illegal behaviors, illegal administration, unjust jurisdiction, complicated legal methods for settling disputes and an unsound protocol, etc.

Among the typical causes of social disputes, the most serious are group disputes caused by land requisition and removal, the reform of state-owned enterprises, job placement for the laid-off, labor and capital contradictions, environmental pollution, right of management for taxis, protection of lawful rights and interests of special groups and widespread corruption, etc.

On a macroscopic level, some frequently occurring social disputes can be classified as "normal" social phenomena. These disputes can be resolved by legal regulation and control, by use of institutionalized and standardized means as well as by the application of morality, discipline and education. However some social disputes are caused by specific causes during a specific period, appearing suddenly and not frequently. Therefore, these disputes require special measures in handling their resolution.

In general, strengthening the construction of a legal system to settle disputes and enhancing the function of legal dispute settling in order to contain them within allowable scope of the system is required. On the other hand, protocol should be established and improved to prevent and respond to new disputes with a focus on those group disputes that are the most influential, intense and complicated.

## B. *The Influence of Present Societal Disputes on Social Harmony and Stability*

The frequent and varied occurrence of group disputes in recent years has attracted widespread attention and tremendous dissatisfaction from the general public, which has had a considerable influence on social harmony and stability.

An example related to land requisition in rural areas is outlined as follows: On the morning of June 18, 2004, more than 100 farmers of Wushan Village in a certain eastern city clashed with the builders of the relevant unit because of dissatisfaction with land requisition, an encounter which left at least 10 people injured. Just one year ago there was a large-scale group dispute which occurred here, which also injured over 10 people. The facts of this group dispute case are: on November 16, 2001, the municipal government approved the real estate development project of Lian Huashan Haide International Community with a total planned area of 1,388 *mu* encompassing the land of Wushan Village and other villages. However investigation results show the municipal government opened the bidding without going through any of the typical procedures for change of use, or requisition and evaluation of land prices before signing a contract with the estate developer; an action which violated the lawful rights and interests of the local farmers. The leading reason why farmers objected to the land requisition was their concerns for living security and in addition they were dissatisfied with the compensation for land requisition, as in a certain neighboring county compensation was larger. It is reported that the system of "land for social security" (土地换社保) has spread through in some cities of Zhejiang Province but it was not carried out in this particular city because of fiscal difficulties.

On March 17, 2005, in a dispute caused by forced demolition and relocation in a city, hundreds of villagers in the economic and technological development zone of city X were dissatisfied with the large-scale land requisition being conducted by the local government in order to introduce an iron and steel project. When this group went to appeal these actions at the office building of the management committee of the development zone, there was an encounter with the police, and several villagers were injured. In addition, more than one hundred fishermen appealed to the Liaoning Provincial Government at a rate of requesting one "petition" (请愿书) per person, and announced "we shall go to Beijing to appeal if the provincial government fails to settle the issue." Three issues leading to the dissatisfaction of these farmers were: 1) forced removal by the government; 2) compensation standards and failure to deliver said compensation in a timely manner; 3) living standards were not guaranteed after the land requisition. However some officials have explained that the project was rushed and the government was lacking in funds; also standards of compensation for land requisition were established according to the State policies and laws, and changes were not permitted.

In a dispute caused by the systemic reform of a state-owned business, and dissatisfaction with a business merger and the job placement plan, hundreds of staff of at a certain Qiulin Group Corp. refused to assume their posts on January 6, 2004. Then they appealed to the provincial Party committee for three straight days.

In a dispute regarding the violation of lawful rights and interests of taxi drivers, taxi owners in a certain city of Sichuan Province were dissatisfied with the municipal government's reform measure of withdrawing management's right to public bidding. They first went on strike for ten days from November 24, 2003 to December 3, 2003 and then started a second strike from December 17, 2003 to early January 2004 with occurrences of damaging operating taxis and beating drivers happening in this time. Some taxi owners went on strike by parking 100 taxicabs near the railway station of the city and more than 50 taxicab owners went to appeal in Beijing and Chengdu.

As example of a dispute concerning labor and capital conflicts, on November 3, 2004, the labor and capital conflict in the industrial zone of a certain city led to a large-scale group dispute in which thousands of civilian workers blocked certain sections of the No. 104 National Highway. The police's attempts to disperse the civilian workers worsened the situation, and civilian workers burned and damaged several cars including police cars, official cars and buses. These actions were caused by in-arrears wages at a small-sized leather shoe factory. Civilian workers had made claims to their superior, but he fled. The workers then went to the town government for settlement but were denied. Finally, workers from neighboring factories joined with them and blocked the national highway in order to impose pressure on the town government and thereupon clashed with the police.

In an example of a dispute concerning massive corruption, 540 villagers signed an appeal to expose the corrupt actions of the former villagers' committee director and village Party secretary La Zhanshan, who despite diverting and appropriating collective or villagers owned property valued at 3.52 million Yuan, was acquitted. The general understanding of the villagers regarding La Zhanshan's acquittal was that his son played a role in his release as he worked at the execution division of the county court.[6]

---

[6] Wen Yiwei, Ga Ma, and Liu Yuehua, "A Corrupt Qinghai Village Head Steals 130,000 and is Judged Not Guilty, Causing 540 Village Heads to Jointly Sign and

According to the latest statistics, the letters and visits system touches on the following five issues which are the subject of the most public complaints: land requisition, demolition and relocation due to urban construction, environmental protection, the business reorganization and bankruptcy systems, and complaints regarding laws and litigation. These issues have become key points of the new stage of the letters and visits system.[7]

All social disputes and group disputes in particular, disturb normal production, life and legal order to different degrees and impose a negative influence on social harmony and stability.

A socialist harmonious society is not a society without contradictions or disputes but rather a society whose contradictions and disputes can be prevented, controlled and dissolved through legal channels and means in order to reduce the negative influence of social disputes in maintaining social harmony and stability to the utmost degree.

First, social disputes should be regarded as a normal social phenomena and should be resolved by means of laws and systems. Social disputes are the necessary result of conflicts and contradictions in the people's social discourse and are differences between the expression of will and the demands for interests. This type of contradiction will be particularly reflected in a social transition period with diversification of interests. Therefore, social disputes, just like other social affairs, should be brought under routine management in a normal social system and the prevention and settlement of social disputes should be seen as important contents of the system construction in its design.

Second, the study of the characteristics of different social disputes is necessary in order to master and control development trends, from the aspects of policy and physical measure, etc. For instance, more than one thousand taxi drivers demonstrated on the main road of a certain city on July 29, 2004. The cause was the taxi drivers' heavy dissatisfaction with the clause, "the operating period will be regulated for operators who have obtained the operation right of taxicabs for urban passenger transport" in the "Management Methods on Payable Use of the Operation Right of Taxicabs for Urban Passenger Transport" (城市客运出

---

Appeal," http://news.tom.com/1002/3291/20041212-1639470.html, (December 12, 2004).

[7] Li Yajie and Wei Wu, "Public Reports Intensify the Five Aspects of Outstanding Problems: Making them Priorities of The Letters and Visits System" http://politics.people.com.cn/GB/1026/5534212.html, (March 28, 2007).

租汽车经营权有偿使用管理办法) that was to be put into operation on August 1 of that year. In the opinion of the taxi drivers, most of the car owners did not own the right of management for ten full years according to the regulations of the "Management Method" and they faced difficulties in recovering their investment in the remaining time because of the overly high cost of purchasing a taxicab. It is stipulated in the city that a taxicab will be discarded after eight years operation. Yet if the taxicab is discarded during the payable serviceable life of the right of management, it is difficult to buy a new car and secure a profit, which leads to the problem of owning the right of management but not owning a car. When the payable term of service for the right of management expires, it is difficult for the car owner to raise money to obtain the right of management at such a high cost.[8]

On the afternoon of August 2, 2004, the autonomous regional government held a special meeting and took effective measures to address the issue from seven different angles: first, the municipal government declared to all taxi drivers via the media that the municipal government will not enforce Document 107 and Document 108 of 2004, i.e. the "Management Method for Paid Use of the Operation Right of Urban Taxicabs in City X" and the "Management Method on the Replacement of Urban Taxicabs in City X"; and the former method will remain in effect until a new method is issued. Second, the municipal government will publish a bulletin asking taxi drivers to be objective and return to operation within a specified time period; those refusing to return to operate may be punished by the revocation of their operating licenses. Third, the municipal government planned to hold a hearing according to law in the second half-year and issue new rules based on consideration of the opinions of all circles and promised to put these into effect as of January 1, 2005. Fourth, a leadership team of City X will be established to manage the standardized operation of the taxicab industry and implement overall supervision over the issuing of the new methods. Fifth, publicity of those laws pertaining to the taxicab industry will be intensified to increase instruction and education. Sixth, those persons committing illegal behaviors such as provoking, organizing and threatening drivers to protest, fight and loot, etc. shall be prosecuted with criminal punishment according to the law. When the dispute is settled,

[8] Wen Yiwei, "La Zhan Mountain Case is Called into Question," http://www.qh.xinhuanet.com/2004-12/28/content_3468947.htm, (December 28, 2004).

a special force will immediately be organized to rectify and reform the taxicab operation companies. Those taxicab operation companies and individuals that resold the taxicab operation licenses for profiteering shall be prosecuted according to the law.

Additionally, sudden disputes, and sudden group disputes in particular should be treated with care and dealt with prudently by the Party committee and the government at all levels. For instance, in order to address new conditions in the letters and visits system and the practical situation of increasing group disputes, the Guizhou Provincial Party Committee and Provincial Government decided to take the following measures:

(1) Strengthen leadership and put the leadership measures into operation. A joint conference was sponsored by the deputy secretary of the provincial Party committee; three members of the standing committee of the provincial Party committee and one secretary-general of the provincial government were its convenors and its members included first and second heads of provincial and municipal departments, bureaus and judicial organizations with a total of 28 participants. Thus, cooperation in dealing with sudden issues in letters and visits system and group disputes was facilitated.

(2) The unequivocal duties of a joint conference were defined for all departments concerned and their leading members, to take charge of understanding and mastering outstanding letters and visits complaints and the conditions and trends of group disputes. Additionally this joint conference analyzed and studied the situation of social stability and put forward plans, counter-plans and suggestions in a timely manner to handle outstanding issues and group disputes. Also, the joint conference organized and coordinated the parties concerned in the handling of multi-industry and trans-regional issues and group disputes, etc.

(3) The joint conference implemented a strict responsibility system, and carried out its duties in accordance with the principles of territorial administration, assigned responsibilities according to levels, and professional administration, etc. The goal of the joint conference was to settle issues from the root cause and in its initial stages. These efforts brought the settlement of outstanding ombudsman issues and group disputes into the legal channels, and solved theoretical problems while also solving practical problems.

(4) To address those newly emerging subjects reflected in letters and visits, the Guizhou Provincial Joint Conference for Safeguarding Social Stability set up five special working teams: a group specializing on rural

land requisition issues, a group specializing in urban demolition and relocation issues, a group specializing in state-owned business restructuring issues, a group specializing in issues concerning complaints about law and litigation and a group specializing in issues concerning cadres in businesses transferred the from army. These five working groups are led by the Provincial Land and Resources Department, the Provincial Construction Department, the Provincial State Assets Administrative Committee, the Provincial Politics and Law Committee and the Provincial Office of Personnel Services with their group leaders taking on primary responsibilities.[9]

Finally, it is not necessary to magnify the contradictions and negative impacts of social disputes to the extent that composure is lost; but it is necessary to maintain a high level of vigilance and prevent future issues with occasional and resolute measures. For instance, the Shaanxi provincial Party committee reviewed the settlement of the group dispute of Xianyang China Resources Textiles Co., Ltd. and realized that it was caused by deep and accumulated contradictions in the enterprise: first, the enterprise had stifled democratic practices for a long period of time, and the patriarchal management had seriously infringed on the interests of the staff.

Additionally, the privileges of the cadres let to high levels of staff resentment. Second, the restructuring of the business was not conducted stably or connected with effective measures. For instance, the placement of workers was not discussed and decided by holding a meeting of workers' representatives but rather was decided by a meeting of leading workers supposedly acting as the workers' representatives. Third, the businesses staff and workers were kept unaware for a long time and the business heads were unwilling to introduce the China Resources Group and publicize the company among the staff, which led to the staff's boycott of the group. Fourth, the Party organization and work unions within the business were weak and the factory leaders and the intermediate leadership were not respected by the staff. The experiences learned from this dispute settlement are: delineating handling responsibilities for sudden group disputes is necessary, as well as a strong sense of politics and the adoption of resolute measures to resolve the dispute

[9] Wang Zhengfu, "Speech Given at the Province-wide Symposium on Implementing 'Regulations on Letters and Visits'," *Gazette of Guizhou Provincial People's Government* vol. 9, http://www.gycity.com:81/zb_2/huichui_detail.asp?id=1815, (2005).

in its infancy. As soon as the dispute occurred, the provincial Party committee and the provincial government dispatched a working group to address the dispute. However owing to insufficient force, disagreement among the businesses' leadership, significant difficulties in mediation and the protracted time taken to respond to the reasonable appeals of the staff, the situation worsened. In addition the company organization after the merging and restructuring was lacking, and it failed to work on a fundamental level for some time, thus prohibiting the optimal occasion to resolve this dispute.[10] In conclusion, social disputes should be treated as normal social occurrences and should be handled through routine work by establishing and improving a preventive mechanism against disputes and by resolving them by means of laws and systems.

## II. *Dispute Resolution through Legal Channels*

### A. *Summary*

There are a wide range of social disputes in China, which are caused by various causes and settled by different means. From the view of standardization and effectiveness in addressing these disputes, resolution methods can be divided into two categories, i.e. legal channels and other channels. The legal channels used to address disputes are based on fairly definite legal rules and are supported by institutions and legal procedures with certain legal outcomes for the settlement of disputes. Compared with other channels, the legal channels exhibit stability, clear outcomes and standard procedure. The legal channels follow a principle of justice, impartiality and openness to effectively handle the contradictions and conflicts of dispute parties, and accomplish the purpose of establishing a harmonious and stable social order.

So far, there are two categories of legal mechanisms used to address disputes through legal channels. The first category is based on litigation, including civil litigation, criminal litigation and administrative litigation; the second category contains non-litigation means including administrative redress, internal dispute settlement protocol, the arbitration of civil and commercial cases, legal mediation, letters and visits, review of

[10] "Foundry Proofs of Domestic Developments," *Xinhua News Agency* Issue 3378, (November 8, 2004).

constitutionality, etc. Litigation is the most effective legal channel and is the ultimate legal means for settling social disputes. Non-litigation is an important auxiliary channel that uses legal means other than litigation to settle social disputes.

## B. *Litigation Methods*

Litigation is the most effective and final channel and means to settle disputes legally. In China, the litigation channel covers the majority of social disputes. Litigation is best applied in the settlement of a dispute as it grants the parties involved sufficient rights of litigation and can effectively dissolve their dispute under a fair and open legal procedure, and it can lead to a settlement conclusion that is legally bonding for the parties involved in the dispute.

### 1. *Civil Litigation*

The laws and regulations that concern civil litigations are listed in Table 2:

Table 10.2: Laws and Regulations that Concern Civil Litigation

| Type | Name of Document | Promulgation Time |
|---|---|---|
| Law | "Civil Procedure Law of the People's Republic of China" | 04.09.1991 |
| | "Decision of the Standing Committee of the National People's Congress Regarding Perfecting the System of People's Assessors" | 08.28.2004 |
| Judicial Interpretation | "Opinions of the Supreme People's Court on Several Issues Concerning the Application of the Civil Procedure Law of the People's Republic of China" | 07.14.1992 |
| | "Several Regulations of the Supreme People's Court on Civil Litigation Evidence" | 12.21.2001 |
| | "Regulations of the Supreme People's Court on Several Issues Concerning Civil Mediation by the People's Court" | 08.18.2004 |
| | "Regulations of the Supreme People's Court and the Ministry of Justice on Legal Aid in Civil Litigation" | 09.22.2005 |

In recent years, China's judicial organizations have dealt with a considerable number of civil cases through the mechanism of civil litigation. China's courts adjudicated over 4.734 million civil cases of first instance in 2000, over 4.73 million in 2001, over 5.075 million in 2002, over 4.834 million in 2003, over 4.303 million in 2004 and over 4.36 million in 2005 (see Fig. 10.4).

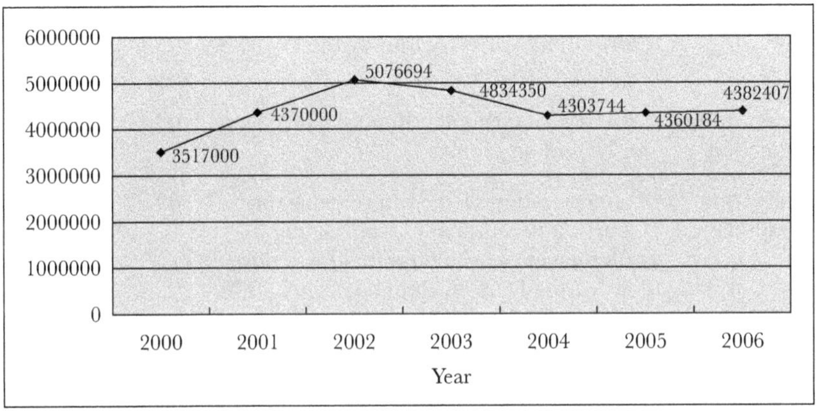


Figure 10.4: Civil Cases Adjudicated in People's Courts at All Levels in China (2000–2006)[11]

Generally, the quantity of civil litigations tended to increase. The people's courts have handled civil cases according to law in order to dissolve contradictions among the people and this has contributed a lot towards maintain a harmonious and stable society. The courts have adopted mediation as a means to settle disputes and keep harmony between the parties involved in the dispute by focusing on finding fact and distinguishing responsibilities in dealing with cases concerning debts, real estate, and the dismantlement of houses, labor disputes, land and forests, in cases that are prone to escalation. In the administration of justice, protection of the lawful rights and interests of women, children, the elderly and the disabled according to law is emphasized. The people's courts deal carefully with various civil lawsuits according to the law and resolve social conflicts in a timely manner, thus preventing the occurrence of crimes and maintaining social stability.

[11] Work Report of the Supreme People's Court (2001–2007).

2. *Criminal Litigation*

The laws and regulations concerning criminal litigations are stated in Table 3:

Table 10.3: Major Legal Basis for Criminal Litigation in China

| Type | Name of Document | Promulgation Time |
|---|---|---|
| Law | "Criminal Procedure Law of the People's Republic of China" | 03.17.1996 |
| Administrative Regulation | "Rules of the People's Republic of China on Detention Homes" | 03.17.1990 |
| Judicial Interpretation | "Interpretation of the Supreme People's Court on Several Issues Concerning the Enforcement of the Criminal Procedure Law of the People's Republic of China" | 09.02.1998 |
| | "Supreme People's Procuratorate: Rules on the Criminal Procedure for the People's Procuratorates" | 01.18.1999 |
| | "Several Opinions on the Application of Summary Procedure in the Trial of Guilty Plea Cases by the Supreme People's Court, the Supreme People's Procuratorate and the Ministry of Justice (trial implementation)" | 03.14.2003 |
| | "Several Opinions on the Application of Ordinary Procedure in the Trial of Guilty Plea Cases by the Supreme People's Court, the Supreme People's Procuratorate and the Ministry of Justice (trial implementation)" | 03.14.2003 |
| | "Regulations on Legal Aid for Criminal Proceedings by the Supreme People's Court, the Supreme People's Procuratorate, the Ministry of Public Security and the Ministry of Justice" | 09.28.2005 |

Table 10.3 (*cont.*)

| Type | Name of Document | Promulgation Time |
|---|---|---|
| Other Documents | "Regulations on Several Issues Concerning the Implementation of the Criminal Procedure Law by the Supreme People's Court, the Supreme People's Procuratorate, the Ministry of Public Security, the Ministry of State Security, the Ministry of Justice and the Commission of Legal Affairs under NPC Standing Committee" | 01.19.1998 |

For a long time, the people's courts, people's procuratorates and public security organizations at all levels have played an important role in resolving disputes by means of criminal litigation. In 2000, China's courts adjudicated 539,000 criminal cases of first instance, a year to year increase of 12.27%; and sentenced over 600,000 criminals, a year to year increase of 14.02%. In the same year, a total of 5,878 defendants whose behaviors did not constitute crimes were acquitted. Thus, the guilty were punished and the innocent were not legally accountable. In 2001, the local people's courts at all levels as well as specific people's courts adjudicated 729,958 criminal cases in total, and a total of 6,597 defendants were acquitted. In 2003, the local people's courts at all levels adjudicated 735,535 criminal cases and sentenced 933,967 defendants in total, a year to year increase of 1.21% and 1.51% respectively. A total of 4,835 defendants whose behaviors did not constitute crimes were acquitted according to law, including 2,467 criminal defendants who were privately prosecuted and 2,368 defendants who were publicly prosecuted. In 2004, the local people's courts at all levels adjudicated 644,248 criminal cases and sentenced 767,951 defendants in total, a year to year increase of 1.5% and 2.8% respectively. A total of 2,996 defendants of private prosecution and public prosecution cases were acquitted according to law because their behaviors did not constitute criminal acts. The defendants' right of litigation was guaranteed according to law; and a total of 91,296 defendants who were qualified to receive legal aid were assigned counsel.

In 2005, the local people's courts at all levels adjudicated 683,997 criminal cases and sentenced 844,717 defendants in total, a year to year increase of 6.17% and 10% respectively. In the same year, the people's courts at all levels acquitted 2,162 criminal defendants. Defendants' right to counsel was guaranteed according to law; and a total of 117,407 defendants who were qualified to receive legal aid were assigned counsel. In 2006, the local people's courts at all levels adjudicated 701,379 criminal cases of first instance and sentenced 889,042 criminals, a year to year increase of 2.54% and 5.25% respectively. By the year's end, 1,713 criminal defendants were acquitted and 17,221 defendants who were qualified to receive legal aid were assigned counsel according to law (see Table 10.4).

Table 10.4: Criminal Cases of First Instance Adjudicated in People's Courts at All Levels in China (1998–2006)

| Year | 1998 | 1999 | 2000 | 2001 | 2002 |
|---|---|---|---|---|---|
| Number of Decided Cases | 480000 | 539000 | 558000 | 729958 | 523042 |
| Year | 2003 | 2004 | 2005 | 2006 | |
| Number of Decided Cases | 735535 | 644248 | 683997 | 701379 | |

3. *Administrative Litigation*

Since the "Administrative Litigation Law of the People's Republic of China" (行政诉讼法) was promulgated 17 years ago, the people's courts at all levels have supervised and supported administrative organizations in administering according to law, in protecting the lawful rights and interests of citizens, legal persons and other organizations, and in maintaining administrative order according to the provisions of laws and regulations. Because they have dealt with a significant number of administrative disputes, they contribute to the maintenance of social stability, and the effective elimination of conflicted and strained relations between administrative organizations and administrative counterparts, thus playing a very important role in building a harmonious society. The laws and regulations concerning administrative litigations are listed in Table 10.5:

Table 10.5: Laws and Regulations Concerning Administrative Litigations

| Type | Name of Document | Promulgation Time |
|---|---|---|
| Law | "Administrative Litigation Law of the People's Republic of China" | 04.09.199. |
| | "Law of the People's Republic of China on State Compensation" | 05.12.1994 |
| Judicial Interpretation | "Interpretation of the Supreme People's Court on Certain Issues Concerning the Execution of the Administrative Litigation Law of the People's Republic of China" | 11.24.1999 |
| | "Regulations of the Supreme People's Court on Certain Issues Concerning Evidence in Administrative Litigation" | 06.04.2002 |

With the strengthening of the government's social management and public service functions in recent years, the harmony and balance between public power and the citizens, legal persons and other organizations is becoming an increasingly important matter attracting extensive public concern. Since 2005, the Supreme People's Court adjudicated 62 major administrative litigations and State compensation cases in the aspects of urban planning, dismantlement of houses, labor and social security, environmental protection, industrial and commercial administration, etc. Local people's courts at all levels adjudicated 95,707 administrative litigation of first instance in 2005, an increase of 3.81% over 2004. Those administrative litigation decisions infringing upon the interests of the general public were corrected resolutely. A total of 16,895 administrative actions were revoked, modified or affirmed illegal or invalid. Administrative organizations were supported determinedly by the administration of law to ensure the performance of their social management functions. A total of 37,192 administrative cases of administrative organizations were affirmed; and the parties' right of litigation was sufficiently respected. A total of 41,620 cases were approved for withdrawal by the prosecutors as the administrative organizations changed special administrative litigation. In addition, a total of 124,629 administrative cases were handled outside the lawsuit system; and 2,991 State compensation cases were adjudicated and handled with a total compensation of 37.51 million Yuan (see Figure 10.5, Figure 10.6).

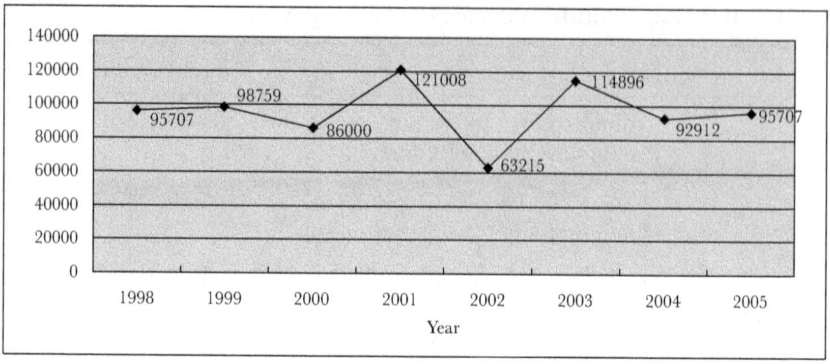


Figure 10.5: Administrative Cases of First Instance Adjudicated in People's Courts at All Levels in China (1998–2006)[12]

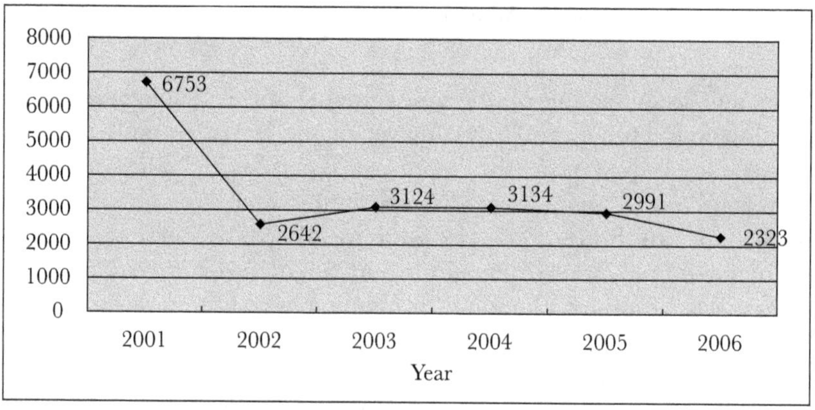


Figure 10.6: State Compensation Cases Adjudicated by Local People's Courts at All Levels in China (2001–2006)[13]

4. *Problems of Litigation in the Settlement of Disputes*

Presently, the role of litigation as a principal method for resolving social disputes has not been sufficiently promoted as many disputes cannot even enter the litigation channel because they cannot pass the judicial proceedings of the court to reach a final settlement. Furthermore, as the courts adopt the system of the court of second instance as the final instance, it is difficult to effectively implement a trial supervision procedure. Also, many disputes cannot be settled by litigation obtain

[12] Work Report of the Supreme People's Court (1999–2006).

[13] Work Report of the Supreme People's Court (2002–2007).

sufficient and effective settlements. As a result, a considerable number of disputes that cannot enter the litigation channel for settlement or that fail to be effectively resolved litigation through, resort to alternative dispute solutions. In particular the method of letters and visits, thus increasing the workload of the letters and visits system and the difficulty of handling these complaints as well, resulting in repeated litigation and complaints which severely influence social stability and disturb the normal work order of government organizations.[14]

Because abstract administrative actions have not been brought within the examination scope of administrative litigation, it fails to effectively resolve the disputes between administrative organizations of the State and their administrative counterparts, i.e. citizens, legal persons and other organizations. This also results in long-term conflicts, thus influencing the routine work of the administrative organizations, increasing the government's fiscal expenditure, deteriorating the relationship between cadres and the masses, influencing the government's image of impartiality and authority and hurting the maintenance of social harmony and stability. Furthermore, this also leads some disputants to apply for other methods for resolution, the government's letters and visits system in particular. As these disputes are intertwined with strong policy content, it is difficult for the existing mechanism to address complaints and it is easy for these complaints to negatively affect social stability and harmony.

### C. *Non-Litigation Methods*

Non-litigation methods are an import means to settle disputes in a legal way and they are a type of auxiliary legal mechanism to resolve disputes. Currently, non-litigation methods can cover all sorts of social disputes, a considerable number of which cannot be resolved by litigation

[14] According to 2004 statistical data, the procuratorate's dispute cases accounted for 36% of the cases which had the original sentence changed, and rehearing cases decided by the court or started up by other channels accounted for 64% of the cases which had the original sentence changed. The data of 2005 also shows that the appeals of the parties concerned were the main material sources for case re-hearings. That year, the local courts at all levels examined 196,342 appeals and applications for rehearing, of which 47,902 were in conformity with lawful conditions and were accepted for the rehearing procedure, 46,468 were adjudicated and 15,867 had the original sentence changed, which resulted in 0.31% of the total cases becoming effective in the same year.

under the existing system. Therefore, non-litigation methods play a unique and irreplaceable role in resolving disputes.

1. *Letters and Visits*

China's current letters and visit system consists of two parts: one is the special letters and visit institutions set up by Party committees and government organizations at all levels. These institutions mainly deal with letters and visits containing suggestions or appeals. Many letters and visits concern disputes that cannot be resolved by litigation or other non-litigation channels. The other category is the letters and visit institutions set up within government agencies and government functional departments at all levels. These institutions mainly deal with disputes concerning the legitimate authority of the agency/department on their own. The letters and visits institutions of judicial organizations mainly handle complaints regarding laws and lawsuits. These institutions do not deal with disputes directly. Their value lies in the transfer of information and procedural guarantee, and they forward various disputes to different channels to resolve according to law. Owing to the functions of information convergence and transfer of the protocol of letters and visits in addressing disputes, this protocol also plays a role in the analysis and mastery of the status, characteristics and development trends of social disputes.

China's current letters and visits system is mainly based on the legislation listed in Table 10.6.

Since the policy of reformation and international cooperation was implemented, especially since middle 1990s, new and different types of conflict of interest and social contradictions have increased sharply. A high volume of disputes are channeled into the letters and visits system, thus leading to a so-called "flood of letters and visits" (信访洪峰). Therefore, China's existing letters and visits system is faced with rigorous challenges.

Since 1993, the amount of letters and visits across the country has risen again, with a steady growth of letters and a greater number of visits. In 2000, the amount of letters and visits accepted by the Party and government authorities at three levels at or at and above the county level in 31 provinces, autonomous regions and municipalities directly under the Central Government achieved the milestone of working 10 million man-hours on this cause for the first time. 2001 saw a year to year increase of 8.7%, 2002 of 2.9% and 2003 was almost the same as the previous year in the total number of letters and calls as a result of

Table 10.6: Major Regulations, Rules and Standardized Documents Concerning Letters and Visits

| Type | Name of Document | Time of Promulgation |
|---|---|---|
| Administrative Regulation | "Government Administration Council: Decision on the Work of Handling People's Letters and Interviewing People" | 06.07.1951 |
| | "The State Council: Regulations on Letters and Visits" | 01.10.2005 |
| | "Working Rules on the Reception of Visits for the Division of Letters and Visits of the Supreme People's Court" | 06.20.1980 |
| Judicial Interpretation | "Decision of the Supreme People's Procuratorate on Strengthening Letters and Visits Work" | 01.16.1985 |
| | "The Supreme People's Procuratorate: Rules on Prosecuting and Appealing Work of the People's Procuratorate" | 12.10.1986 |
| | "The Supreme People's Court: Certain Opinions Concerning the Reception of Supervision from the People's Congress and Its Standing Committee for the People's Courts" | 12.24.1998 |
| | "The Supreme People's Procuratorate: Measures for Implementing the First Inquiry Responsibility System of Prosecuting and Appealing for the People's Procuratorates (trial implementation)" | 06.17.2003 |

Table 10.6 (*cont.*)

| Type | Name of Document | Time of Promulgation |
|---|---|---|
| | "Regulations of Guizhou Province on Letters and Visits" | 11.27.1990 |
| | "Regulations of Wuhan City on Letters and Visits" | 07.25.1993 |
| | "Regulations of the Inner Mongolia Autonomous Region on Letters and Visits" | 05.31.1994 |
| | "Regulations of Beijing on Letters and Visits" | 09.08.1994 |
| | "Regulations of the Standing Committee of the People's Congress at All Levels in Hainan Province on Letters and Visits" | 09.30.1995 |
| Local Regulations | "Regulations of Shanxi Province on Letters and Visits" | 08.01.1996 |
| | "Regulations of Guangxi Zhuang Autonomous Region on Letters and Visits" | 09.25.1996 |
| | "Regulations of Qinghai Province on Letters and Visits" | 09.26.1996 |
| | "Regulations of Henan Province on Letters and Visits" | 01.16.1997 |
| | "Regulations of Jiangsu Province on Letters and Visits" | 10.17.1997 |
| | "Regulations of Hunan Province on Letters and Visits" | 08.04.1998 |
| | "Regulations of the Standing Committee of the People's Congress at All Levels in Fujian Province on Letters and Visits" | 11.18.2000 |
| | "Regulations of Shandong Province on Letters and Visits" | 12.27.2000 |

Table 10.6 (*cont.*)

| Type | Name of Document | Time of Promulgation |
|---|---|---|
| | "Regulations of Chongqing on Letters and Visits" | 10.08.2001 |
| | "Regulations of Jilin Province on Letters and Visits" | 12.01.2001 |
| | "Regulations of Gansu Province on Letters and Visits" | 07.26.2002 |
| | "Regulations of the Standing Committee of the People's Congress at All Levels in Guangdong Province on Letters and Visits" | 10.13.2002 |
| | "Regulations of Liaoning Province on Letters and Visits" | 08.01.2003 |
| | "Regulations of Shanghai on Letters and Visits" | 08.08.2003 |
| | "Regulations of Heilongjiang on Letters and Visits" | 10.17.2003 |
| | "Regulations of Zhejiang Province on Letters and Visits" | 01.16.2004 |
| | "Regulations of Jiangxi Province on Letters and Visits" | 03.31.2004 |
| | "Regulations of Zhengzhou on Letters and Visits" | 08.11.2004 |
| | "Regulations of Tianjin on Letters and Visits" | 10.21.2005 |
| | "Regulations of Hubei Province on Letters and Visits" | 11.26.2005 |
| | "Regulations of Anhui Province on Letters and Visits" | 12.16.2005 |

Table 10.6 (*cont.*)

| Type | Name of Document | Time of Promulgation |
|---|---|---|
| | "Provisions on Letters and Visits for Judicial Administrative Organs (for Trial Implementation)" | 01.24.1991 |
| | "Provisions on Letters and Visits for Health Authorities" | 06.29.1993 |
| | "Tentative Specifications on Letters and Visits for Labor and Social Security Authorities" | 08.12.1999 |
| | "Regulations of China Securities Regulatory Commission on Letters and Visits" | 12.12.1999 |
| | "Measures of the Ministry of Civil Affairs on Letters and Visits" | 12.23.1999 |
| Rules and Regulations of Ministries and Commissions | "Regulations of the Ministry of Land and Resources on Letters and Visits" | 05.09.2002 |
| | "Regulations of the People's Bank of China on Letters and Visits" | 10.28.2002 |
| | "Regulations on Letters and Visits for Education Authorities" | 10.26.2004 |
| | "Provisions of China Insurance Regulatory Commission on Letters and Visits" | 05.26.2005 |
| | "Scope of Letters and Visits to be Accepted by the National Population and Family Planning Commission (for Trial Implementation)" | 06.17.2005 |
| | "Scope of Letters and Visits Not to be Accepted by the National Population and Family Planning Commission (for Trial Implementation)" | 06.17.2005 |
| | "State Food and Drug Administration: Opinions on Strengthening Letters and Visits" | 07.20.2005 |

Table 10.6 (*cont.*)

| Type | Name of Document | Time of Promulgation |
|---|---|---|
| | "Provisions on the Work of Public Security Organs regarding Letters and Visits" | 08.18.2005 |
| | "Provisions of the Ministry of Finance on Letters and Visits" | 08.22.2005 |
| | "Detailed Rules of China Banking Regulatory Commission for the Work of Letters and Visits" | 10.20.2005 |
| | "Measures of the Ministry of Construction on Letters and Visits" | 11.10.2005 |
| | "Regulations of the Ministry of Land and Resources on Letters and Visits" | 01.04.2006 |
| | "Provisions of the State Physical Cultural Administration on Letters and Visits" | 03.03.2006 |
| | "Measures on Letters and Visits Concerning the Environment" | 06.24.2006 |
| | "The General Office of the CPC Central Committee, the General Office of the State Council: Provisional Regulations on Handling Letters and Visits for Party and Government Organs (Draft)" | 04.08.1982 |
| Other Policies and Regulations | "The General Office of the CPC Central Committee, the General Office of the State Council: Circular on Strengthening Letters and Visits" | 11.19.1989 |

Table 10.6 (*cont.*)

| Type | Name of Document | Time of Promulgation |
|---|---|---|
| | "Circular of the General Office of the CPC Central Committee, the General Office of the Standing Committee of National People's Congress and the General Office of the State Council Concerning Revision, Printing and Distribution of the Measures of Accepting Visits for Departments under the CPC Central Committee by Functional Division" | 05.13.1991 |
| | "Measures of the Monitoring Chamber of the Discipline Inspection Group of the People's Insurance Company of China Concerning Verification of Letters and Visits by Grading" | 07.04.1996 |
| | "Interim Provisions on Handling of Letters and Visits from Veteran Cadres" | 11.06.1996 |
| | "Interim Provisions of the People's Insurance Company of China on Management of the Work of Discipline Inspection, Supervision and Letters and Visits" | 05.04.1999 |
| | "Notice of the General Office of the CPC Central Committee and the General Office of the State Council on Printing and Distribution of the Regulations of the State Bureau for Letters and Visits Concerning Disposition of Function, Internal Organization and Staffing" | 01.11.2000 |
| | "Notice of the Office of the Bank of Communications on Printing and Distribution of the Working System of the Bank of Communications on the Work of Letters and Visits for Headquarters Organizations (Temporary)" | 12.04.2002 |

"SARS" but the total number of mass visits had a year to year increase of 5.1%. In 2004, the State Bureau for Letters and visits accepted 457,000 letters, a year to year increase of 11.7%; accepted 67,000 visits and devoted 148,000 man-hours to this work, a year to year increase of 58.4% and 52.9% respectively[15] (see Figure 10.7).

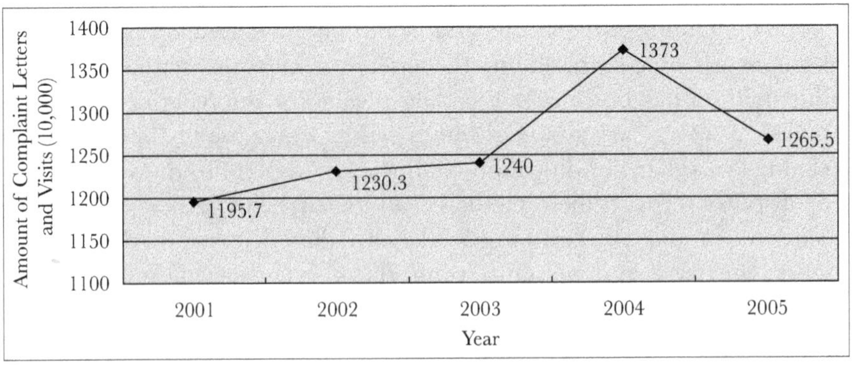


Figure 10.7: Numbers of Letters and Visits (2000–2005)[16]

In 2005, the promulgation and implementation of the "Regulations on Letters and Visits" improved the existing situation to some extent and in 2005, the constant rise of the total amount of letters and visits was brought under control with a new trend of "three declines and one improvement" (三个下降, 一个好转): a decline in the total number of letters and visits, a decline in the number of mass visits, a decline in the number of first-time letters and visits, and an improvement of order in the area of letters and visits. These changes were reflected in the following aspects: in 2005, all of the letters and visits departments of the Party and the government organizations at or above county level accepted 12.656 million letters and calls, a decline of 7.9% in comparison with 13.73 million letters and calls in the previous year. Of them, the State Bureau for Letters and Visits accepted 603,000 letters

[15] Zhou Yongkang, "Address on the Opening Ceremony of the Seminar on the Regulations Regarding Letters and Visits," (February 16, 2005).

[16] Zhou Yongkang, "Address on the Opening Ceremony of the Seminar on the Regulations Regarding Letters and Visits," http://gov.people.com.cn/GB/46737/4342648.html, (February 16, 2005).

and calls, almost equal to the previous year. The number of letters and visits accepted by departments at the provincial, municipal and county levels declined by 8.9%, 9.2% and 9.3% respectively. The trend of steady increase in the total amount of letters and visits in the previous 12 years was curbed, which marked a turning point (拐点).[17]

The principal problem in the letters and visits mechanism is the inappropriate emphasis on the role of letters and visits in addressing social disputes. Some disputes that should be dissolved through other legal means are channeled into the letters and visits institutions. In fact, this method has become the leading means for resolving certain disputes. As a large amount of disputes cannot make use of the litigation channel or other non-litigation channels for resolution, the settlement of disputes through these methods can increase the parties' economic burden. In many places, some leaders are directly concerned with the letters and visits system and have produced huge societal influence in the settlement of some disputes, which has resulted in unreasonable expectations regarding the function and effect of the letters and visits mechanism in the settlement of disputes. As a result, letters and visits institutions have been flooded with various types of social disputes. However, these institutions are just procedural organizations that have no right to handle those disputes expressed in the letters and visits, thus forming new social disputes between the petitioners and the letters and visits institutions and resulting in large scale problems. In 2003, the number of visits and expended man-hours of the State Bureau for Letters and Visits increased 33.3% and 39% over the previous year, respectively. Additionally the number of people involved in group-visits rose to over 800. Increasingly violent litigation also occurs frequently. For instance, some visitors became excited and behaved extremely; they held banners, shouted slogans and blocked the traffic, held up officers' cars, attacked government offices, damaged public goods, and beat the letters and visits officers, etc. There were also accounts of extreme behavior such as self-immolation, drowning, jumping off a buildings, etc. All of these occurrences not only disturbed the work order of the

[17] "The Chief of the State Bureau for Letters and Visits introduced the Implementation of the "Regulations on Letters and Visits'," http://gov.people.com.cn/GB/46737/4342648.html (April 29, 2006).

Party and government organizations but also directly influenced social harmony and stability.

2. *Settlement Mechanisms for Internal Disputes*

The existing internal dispute settlement mechanisms mainly address labor and personnel disputes involving state functionaries, employees in government agencies, businesses, public institutions and social organizations. There are three major systems in place: The first is a complaint mechanism, which primarily resolves disputes regarding personnel management between the State administrative organizations and civil servants. The second is a personnel dispute arbitration mechanism which primarily resolves personnel disputes between public institutions and employees, between State administrative organizations and employed public servants, and between troops and their civil personnel. The third is a labor dispute arbitration mechanism which primarily resolves disputes regarding the fulfillment of labor contracts between employers and employees.

Before 2006, the primary legal basis for addressing internal personnel disputes were the "Interim Rules for Handling of Personnel Dispute Cases" and the "Interim Provisions on Appeal and Accusation of Civil Servants" promulgated by the Ministry of Personnel in 1997, as well as the "Rules for the Handling of Personnel Dispute Cases" and the "Measures for the Administration of Personnel Dispute Arbitration Commission" were later promulgated by the Ministry of Personnel. The major legal basis for defining the rights and obligations of civil servants are the "Interim Provisions of the State Council Concerning the Rewards and Punishments of Working Personnel of National Administrative Organizations" and the "Provisional Regulations on Civil Servants." However there has been a new development after the "Civil Servant Law of the People's Republic of China" (中华人民共和国公务员法) was promulgated on January 1, 2006. There is a special chapter in this law which prescribes the rights and obligations of a civil servant. In order to protect the rights and interests of a civil servant, the "Civil Servant Law" also prescribes a related appeal and accusation procedure.[18] Namely, a civil servant may lodge an appeal with respect to eight categories of personnel disputes arising between

[18] The "Interim Provisions on Appeal and Accusation of Civil Servants," which was formulated based on the "Provisional Regulations on Civil Servants," is still effective.

the civil servant and the organization.[19] When a civil servant believes that any leader thereof has damaged his legitimate rights and interests, he may file an accusation to the organization at a higher level or the relevant special organization.[20] And it is prescribed in Article 100 of the "Civil Servant Law" that the arbitration system for personnel disputes is established by the state. When a civil servant in the appointment system has a dispute with the organization he works for due to the performance of the employment contract thereof, he may apply to the arbitration committee of personnel disputes for arbitration within 60 days as of the day when the dispute arises. This is the first time that the personnel dispute arbitration system has been incorporated into the law in China.

Moreover, some local regulations on the arbitration of personnel disputes were also issued. For instance, except Chongqing and Fujian Provinces who instituted local regulations in order to address personnel disputes, 26 provinces, autonomous regions and municipalities directly under the Central Government have established government rules and regulations to address personnel disputes. However in general, these regulations on personnel disputes mainly concern the arbitration system of personnel disputes, and focus on procedural rules. Regarding the rights and obligations of contending parties, there is no substantial legal norm, like the Labor Law, to stipulate the rights and obligations of both parties of a labor dispute; what is principally applicable in the personnel dispute arbitration procedure is the internal files of the Ministry of Personnel.

Legal norms related to the labor dispute arbitration mechanism are principally led by the "Labor Law," and the "Rules on Settlement of

---

[19] It is prescribed in Article 90 of the "Civil Servant Law" that when a civil servant is discontent with any of the following punishments concerning himself, he may apply to the original organization that has imposed the punishment for administrative redress within 30 days as of the date when he is notified of the foresaid punishment. When he is discontent with the results of the administrative review, he may appeal to the administrative department of civil servants at the same level or appeal to a level higher than the organization that has imposed the punishment according to the provisions of the state; or, he may directly file an appeal without any administration redress within 30 days of the date when he was notified of the foresaid punishment. This kind of punishments include: punishments, dismissal or cancellation of employment, demotion, being assessed as "incompetent" in the periodical assessment, being dismissed from a post, rejection of an application for resignation or retirement in advance, failing to define or deduct wages, welfare or insurance treatment according to relevant provisions, or any other circumstance as prescribed by laws or regulations on appealing.

[20] See: Article 93 of the "Civil Servant Law."

Corporate Labor Disputes" and a legal system addressing labor disputes has basically come into being. Labor dispute arbitration commissions are set up inside the labor administration departments of all levels of government and consist of a representative of the labor administrative department, a representative of the trade union at the same level of government and a representative of the employer. These commissions take charge of labor disputes arising within their administrative divisions.

Labor dispute arbitration is compulsory arbitration and is the procedure that precedes a court hearing of a labor dispute. Labor dispute arbitration award is also legally enforceable, and the parties involved must undisputedly execute the arbitration award. The current labor dispute settlement mechanism can be summed up by a line "one mediation, one arbitration and two trials" (一调一裁两审), i.e. when a labor dispute occurs, the party may apply for mediation to the labor dispute mediation commission within the business. If such mediation fails, the party may submit their complaint to the labor arbitration commission for arbitration, or the party may directly submit it for arbitration without the involvement of internal mediation. If not satisfied with the arbitration award, the party may apply to the court and the arbitration becomes a procedure that precedes a lawsuit. As the organization rate of labor dispute mediation commissions within businesses is very low, labor dispute arbitration agencies have become the foremost channel for satisfactorily resolving labor disputes. So far, labor dispute arbitration agencies have been established in 31 provinces, autonomous regions and municipalities directly under the Central Government with over 7,000 full-time arbitrators and over 10,000 part-time arbitrators drawn principally from trade unions (see Figure 10.8).

Government agencies, businesses, public institutions and social organizations have continued to develop their internal dispute settlement mechanisms in order to help resolve relevant disputes; however this mechanism is far from perfect and cannot resolve some disputes effectively. Currently, it is not only the labor and personnel disputes within businesses and public institutions that cannot be completely resolved through the existing labor and personnel dispute arbitration mechanisms, personnel management disputes between government agencies and State functionaries within government agencies also cannot be resolved thoroughly. The appeal and lawsuit mechanism under the general management system can resolve some of the disputes that fall into this category. However, because the nature of some disputes

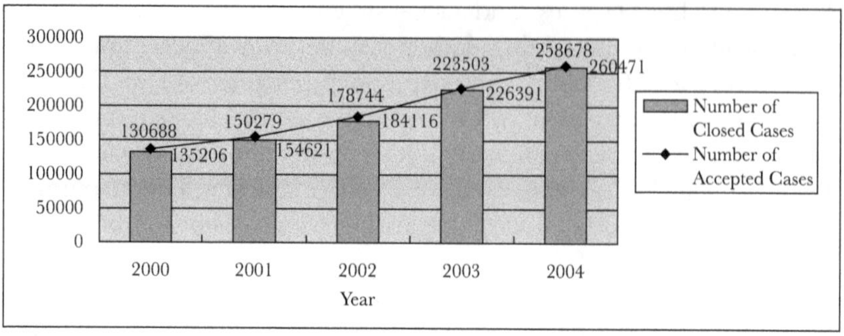


Figure 10.8: Number of Cases Accepted and Settled by Labor Dispute Arbitration Commissions (2000–2004)[21]

is unclear and the institutions addressing disputes are not reasonably set up, these disputes have been channeled into the letters and visits system, thus increasing the burden and pressure on these ombudsman institutions that seem to have "omnipotence" in addressing these disputes.

3. *Arbitration of Civil and Commercial Cases*

The purpose of arbitration of civil and commercial cases is to address property disputes occurring between equal civil subjects. This mechanism is based on the voluntary participation of the parties involved in the dispute and is arbitrated by a civil arbitration agency. This arbitration mechanism greatly supports the lawsuit mechanism and effectively relieves the work load and pressure on the latter in settling civil and commercial disputes.

Arbitration is lauded for the following characteristics: respect for the will of the parties involved, the final and binding nature of the arbitration award, its simplicity, its low cost, its diversified solutions and its confidentiality for those parties concerned. Arbitration has become an important method for resolving civil and commercial disputes. Since the "Arbitration Law of the People's Republic of China" was put into operation on September 1, 1995, the Supreme People's Court has provided over thirty judicial interpretations of the arbitration system to make up for those holes in the arbitration legislation system and in order to support the implementation of the law.

[21] *Statistical Yearbook of China (2001–2005).*

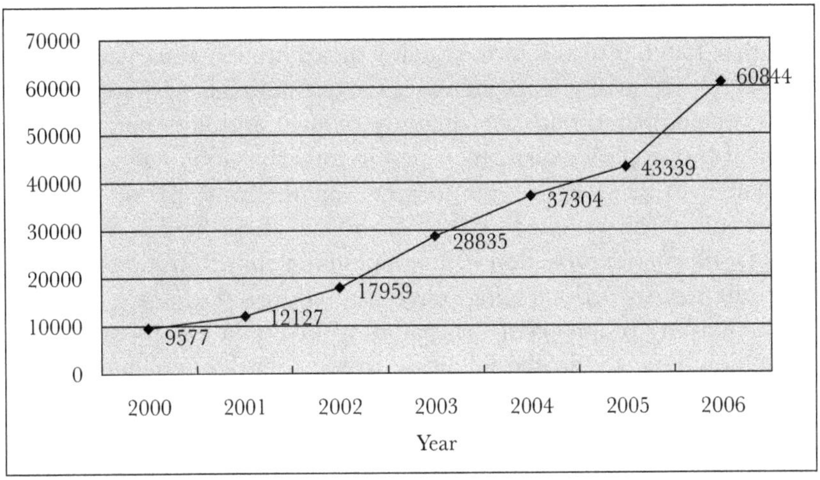


Figure 10.9: Quantity of Cases Accepted by Arbitration Commissions in China (2000–2006)[22]

There were 157 arbitration commissions established throughout the country with over 2,100 commissioners, over 1,300 working personnel and over 18,000 arbitrators from 1995 to 2000. In five years, more than 22,000 arbitration cases were assumed with an object value over 42 billion Yuan. Eighty percent of these arbitration cases were performed automatically, which shows the function of arbitration in settling disputes. By 2005, there were 183 arbitration commissions reorganized in over 270 cities that were authorized to reorganize arbitration agencies according to law. Including the existing China International Economic and Trade Arbitration Commission and the China Maritime Arbitration Commission, there were 185 arbitral agencies across the country (see Figure 10.9).

By the end of 2005, arbitration agencies had handled 140,000 civil and commercial cases in a just and timely manner with an object value amounting to over 230 billion Yuan in strict accordance with the provisions of the "Arbitration Law." Many cases involved important areas of concern affecting the national economy and the livelihood of the people and influencing the overall situation of stability, harmony and development. According to incomplete statistics, the average rate of awards made by arbitration agencies that were revoked or not executed by the judicial authorities is lower than 1%. This indicates that the

[22] *Statistical Yearbook of China (2001–2005).*

people's courts support the arbitration work on the one hand and on the other hand, proves that the quality of arbitration work is at a high level and high quality work increases the accountability of arbitration. However compared with the quantity of civil and commercial cases handled by people's courts, the quantity of arbitration cases was just equivalent to the 4.1% of the former over the same period and the object value just was 4.5% of the former.[23] These figures show that there is still considerable development potential for arbitration and that arbitration is still a developing solution to address disputes.

The existing problems of arbitration of civil and commercial cases are mainly reflected in the following issues: arbitration agencies have strong administration characteristics, the principle of party autonomy is weakened in the procedure of arbitration, and some arbitration systems are not reasonably designed, which hinders the role of arbitration in resolving civil and commercial disputes. These problems then contribute to the lack of trust in arbitration by dispute parties and their subsequent decisions not to select the arbitration method to settle civil and commercial disputes. As a result, these disputes are then channeled into the litigation system and increase the workload of the courts. In practice, some arbitration agencies are organized, and staffed and designated with sufficient authority according to the administrative model. They enjoy appropriation and office accommodations from the government, most of their members are officers of relevant government departments, and the directors are usually also competent government leaders or principal department leaders in the legal system. In some places, it is the government or the government department concerned that issues documents to popularize the arbitration system. Finally, for some difficult arbitration cases or cases receiving much social attention, the arbitration commissions or arbitration tribunals report them to the relevant government department leader and hear their opinions, etc. before making their awards.

### 4. *Non-Judicial Mediation*

Non-judicial mediation generally addresses personal or property disputes between equal civil subjects. The non-judicial mediation mechanism

---

[23] 二次创业：中国仲裁发展的必由之路 (Starting a New Undertaking: The Only Way for China's Arbitration Development), China Law Edu., March 24th, 2006, http://www.chinalawedu.com/news/18500/189/2006/3/li317121650142360021188-0.htm

includes administrative mediation and civil mediation. Administrative mediation is implemented by administrative organizations. Civil mediation is conducted by basic level autonomous mediation organizations or mediation organizations within businesses. The mediation mechanism is not a necessary procedure for dealing with civil disputes but it does help settle certain disputes that may be channeled into the litigation system or other non-litigation systems, and relieves their work load and pressure (see Figure 10.10).

As early as 1954, the Government Administration Council (predecessor of the State Council) promulgated the "Interim Rules for Organization of the People's Mediation Committee," which stipulates the establishment of a people's mediation committee to mediate conflicts among the people and that this committee be an autonomous group organization. Based on this, the State Council stipulates in the "Rules on Organization of the People's Mediation Committee" adopted on May 5, 1989 that for disputes among the people under mediation by the people's mediation committee, if the parties fail to reach an agreement or have second thoughts after reaching an agreement, they may apply to the people's government at the grassroots level to deal with it or file a suit with the people's court (Article 9). In order to further standardize the people's mediation work, the Ministry of Justice promulgated the "Regulations on the People's Mediation Work" in September 2002, which stipulates the organization and mediation forms, etc. of the people's mediation committee.

In addition, general civil disputes can be mediated by administrative departments. For instance, the Ministry of Justice promulgated the "Stipulations on Settlement of Disputes among the People (Order No. 8 of the Ministry of Justice of the People's Republic of China)" on April 19, 1990, which stipulates that judicial assistants, acting as the judicial personnel of the people's government at the grassroots level, take charge of disputes among the people.

In addition, according to the prevailing laws, regulations and administrative rules, the administrative organizations can carry out administrative mediation of civil disputes within the competent administrative management scope. Taking the field of management of public security as an example, the "People's Police Law of the People's Republic of China" (中华人民共和国人民警察法) promulgated on February 28, 1995 stipulates that the people's police should help with the citizens' demand for settlement of disputes. The "Law of the People's Republic of China on Public Security Administration Punishments" (治安管理处罚法)

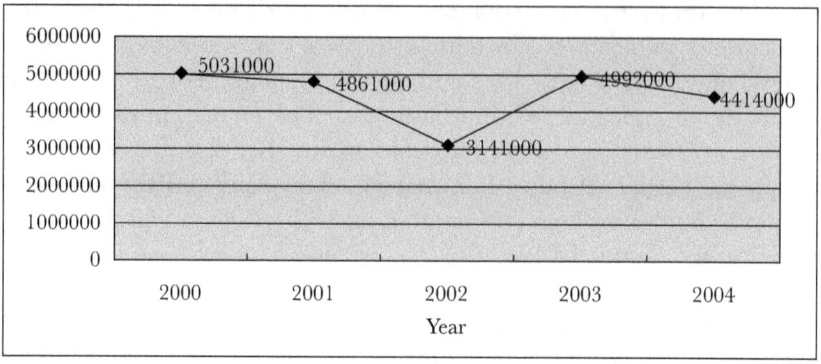


Figure 10.10: Quantity of Public Disputes Mediated by the People's Mediation Committees (2000–2004)[24]

stipulates that the public security organizations can mediate those behaviors which violate the management of public security according to circumstances; and that those mediated are free of punishment. This means that the public security organization gives priority to administrative mediation in the management of public security.

In addition, some other departments are also involved in administrative mediation of civil disputes. For example, industrial and commercial administrative departments provide administrative mediation for contract disputes and consumption disputes in implementing market supervision and control. Environmental protection departments provide administrative mediation for environmental disputes. Local people's government and relevant departments provide administrative mediation for land and other resource ownership disputes, telecommunication administrative departments provide administrative mediation over disputes between telecommunications businesses and for disputes regarding telecommunications service quality and intellectual property rights administrative departments provide administrative mediation for disputes concerning copyrights, trademark rights and patents. The health administration departments provide administrative mediation for medical disputes and the State Council electric power administrative organization and its offices provide administrative mediation for disputes of electric power, etc. (see Table 10.7)

[24] *Statistical Yearbook of China (2001–2005).*

Table 10.7: Practical Situation of Administrative Mediation in China[25]

| Dispute | Handling Organization | Handling Means | Legal Basis (or standardized document) |
|---|---|---|---|
| General civil dispute | Judicial assistant | Administrative mediation | "Stipulations on the Settlement of Disputes among the People" |
| General civil dispute | People's police | Administrative mediation | "People's Police Law" |
| Disputes among the people over the behaviors of fighting, violence or damage of another's property, etc. that breach the management of public security | Public security organization | Administrative mediation | "Law of the People's Republic of China on Public Security Administration Punishments and Procedural Provisions for the Handling of Administrative Cases by Public Security Organizations" |
| Disputes over land ownership | Land and resources administrative authorities at and above the county level | Administrative mediation | "Measures for Investigation and Handling of Disputes over the Allocation of Landownership and Land Use Rights" |
| Disputes over the right to use sea territory | Maritime administrative authorities of the people's government at and above the county level | Administrative mediation | "Mediation and Handling of Disputes Over the Right to Use Ocean Territory Measures" |
| Disputes over allocation of ownership and usage rights for grasslands | People's government at or above the county level | Administrative mediation | "Grassland Law" |
| Disputes over ownership and usage rights for water areas and mudflats for aquatic breeding | People's government at or above the county level | Administrative mediation | "Fisheries Law" |

[25] State laws, administrative regulations and administrative rules are listed here by principles, particular conditions, local regulations, local rules and standardized documents.

Table 10.7 (*cont.*)

| Dispute | Handling Organization | Handling Means | Legal Basis (or standardized document) |
|---|---|---|---|
| Disputes over fishery water pollution | Fishery supervisory authorities | Administrative mediation | "Regulations on Investigation and Handling Procedures of Pollution Accidents in Fishing Zones" |
| Disputes over allocation of ownership and usage rights for forests and woodlands | People's government at all levels | Administrative mediation | "Measures for Handling Disputes over the Allocation of Ownership and Usage Rights for Forests and Woodlands" |
| Disputes over connections between telecommunication networks | Ministry of Information Industries, Ministry of Information Industries: Telecommunications Management Office, Provincial Correspondence Management Office | Coordination | Article 20 of "Telecommunication Regulations Measures for the Settlement of Disputes over Connections between Telecommunication Networks" |
| Disputes over connections between public telecommunication networks | Telecommunication authorities | Coordination | "Provisions on the Management of Connections between Public Telecommunication Networks" |
| Telecommunication service disputes | Telecommunication administrative organization | Administrative mediation | "Interim Measures for Settling the Complaints of Telecom Users" |
| Power disputes | Power regulatory institution of the State Council and its detached offices | Administrative mediation | "Temporary Measures for the Mediation of Power Disputes" |
| Disputes over economic contracts concerning hydroelectric construction | National Mediation Commission on Disputes over Economic Contracts Concerning Hydroelectric Construction | Administrative mediation | "Provisional Rules on Mediation of Disputes over Economic Contracts Concerning Hydroelectric Construction" |

Table 10.7 (*cont.*)

| Dispute | Handling Organization | Handling Means | Legal Basis (or standardized document) |
|---|---|---|---|
| | Evaluation and Mediation Group of Disputes over Economic Contracts Concerning Construction Projects | | |
| Contract dispute | Industrial and commercial administration | Administrative mediation | "Measures for Administrative Mediation of Contract Disputes" |
| Dispute over product quality | Technical supervision administrative department at county and municipal levels | Administrative mediation | "Measures for Handling Product Quality Complaints" |
| Dispute over automobile repair quality | Road transportation administration organization under traffic administration authorities of the local people's government at or above the county level | Administrative mediation | "Measures for Mediation of Disputes over the Quality of Automobile Repairs" |
| Dispute over consumers' rights and interests | Industrial and commercial administration offices | Administrative mediation | "Interim Procedures for Industrial and Commercial Administration Institutions to Accept Consumers' Complaints and Implement Rules on Industrial and Commercial Administration Institutions to Deal with Consumers' Complaints" |
| Commercial and economic disputes | Legal organizations of commercial administration authorities | Administrative mediation | "Proposed Regulations on Mediation of Commercial and Economic Disputes" |

Table 10.7 (*cont.*)

| Dispute | Handling Organization | Handling Means | Legal Basis (or standardized document) |
|---|---|---|---|
| Disputes over road transportation service quality | Traffic administrative authorities of the people's government at and above the county level | Administrative mediation | "Provisions on the Management of Complaints about Road Transportation Service Quality" |
| Labor disputes | Labor dispute arbitration commissions | Administrative mediation | "Regulations of the People's Republic of China on Settlement of Labor Disputes in Enterprises" |
| Disputes over agricultural (rural) contracting contracts | Rural cooperative economy administration authorities | Mediation | "Opinions on Stabilizing and Improving the System of Contracting of Land" by the Policy Research Office on Rural Issues of the Secretariat of the CPC Central Committee, the "Opinions on Enhancing the Management of Agricultural Contracting Contracts" by the Ministry of Agriculture and the "Provisions on Arbitration of Agricultural Contracting Contracts in Hebei Province"[26] |
| Copyright dispute | Copyright administrative department | Administrative mediation | "Copyright Law" |
| Trademark dispute | Industrial and commercial administrative department | Administrative mediation | Article 53, etc. of the "Trademark Law" |

[26] Besides the two standardized documents listed above, there is no definite law or regulation which constitutes a basis for the arbitration of disputes concerning agricultural (rural) contracting contracts. In practice, arbitration is mainly based on the local regulations, local rules and standardized documents established by local governments.

Table 10.7 (*cont.*)

| Dispute | Handling Organization | Handling Means | Legal Basis (or standardized document) |
|---|---|---|---|
| Patent dispute | Patent administrative department | Administrative mediation | Article 57 of "Patent Law" |
| Dispute over new plant varieties | Agriculture and forestry administration departments of the State Council | Administrative mediation (applicable to the compensation issue of the above disputes) | Article 39 of "Regulations of the People's Republic of China on the Protection of New Varieties of Plants" |
| Medical negligence | Health administrative department | Administrative mediation | "Regulations on the Handling of Medical Accidents" |
| Dispute over compensation for injury from traffic accident | Traffic management sector of the public security organization | Administrative mediation | "Law on Road Traffic Safety," "Provisions on the Procedures for Handling Traffic Accidents" |
| Civil disputes caused by fishery and maritime traffic accidents | Supervision of fishing ports | Administrative mediation | "Regulations on Investigation and Handling of Fishery Maritime Traffic Accidents" |
| Disputes over state-owned business property rights | Financial authorities at and above the county level | Administrative mediation | "Work Rules on Mediation of Disputes over State-Owned Business Property Rights" |
| Disputes over liability for compensation or the amount of compensation | Competent department of environmental protection administration or another department invested by law with power to conduct environmental supervision and management | Administrative handling (administrative mediation)[27] | "Environmental Protection Law of the Standing Committee of the National People's Congress: Reply on the Correct Understanding and Execution (2) of Article 41 of the Environmental Protection Law" |

[27] The word "settle" is used in handling this kind of dispute in the second stipulation of Article 41 of the "Environmental Protection Law." The Standing Committee of

Table 10.7 (*cont.*)

| Dispute | Handling Organization | Handling Means | Legal Basis (or standardized document) |
|---|---|---|---|
| Disputes over water | People's government at or above county level or its authorized department | Administrative mediation | Water Law |
| Water pollution dispute | Environmental protection department Administrative organs of the traffic sector | Administrative handling (administrative mediation) | "Law of the People's Republic of China on Prevention and Control of Water Pollution" |
| Disputes over atmospheric pollution damage | Environmental protection department | Administrative mediation | "Law of the People's Republic of China on the Prevention and Control of Atmospheric Pollution" |
| Disputes over solid waste pollution damage | Administrative organizations of environmental protection or other supervisory management departments on prevention and control of other solid waste pollution | Administrative mediation | "Law of the People's Republic of China on Prevention and Control of Environmental Pollution by Solid Waste" |
| Disputes over environmental noise pollution damage | Administrative organizations of environmental protection or other supervisory | Administrative mediation | "Law of the People's Republic of China on Prevention and Control of Environmental Noise Pollution" |

---

the National People's Congress has defined this as "the administrative organization mediates disputes over civil rights and interests of parties concerned" in the second stipulation of the "Reply on Correct Understanding and Execution" of Article 41 of the Environmental Protection Law. Such problem also exists in the "Law of the People's Republic of China on Prevention and Control of Water Pollution." It has been amended as "through mediation" in newly enacted or amended environmental protection laws.

Table 10.7 (*cont.*)

| Dispute | Handling Organization | Handling Means | Legal Basis (or standardized document) |
|---|---|---|---|
| | management departments/institutions for the prevention and control of environment noise pollution | | |
| Economic disputes inside the railway sector | Department of Policies and Regulations of the Ministry of Railways Enterprises' legal counsel institutions | Administrative mediation | "Regulations on Mediation of Economic Disputes inside the Railway Sector" |

The administrative departments of justice and public security organizations are all authorized to mediate disputes and a considerable number of general disputes among the people have been resolved in this way. The administrative organizations of justice mediate civil disputes regarding marriage and family, building and curtilage, debts, production operations, neighborhood relations, compensation for damages, etc. Relevant statistical data shows that every year there is a large number of civil disputes in these areas submitted to relevant administrative organizations of justice for mediation. For instance, the administrative departments of justice mediated 4,491,257 general civil disputes in 2003 and 4,414,233 general civil disputes in 2004.[28] Another example concerns the mediation of public security organizations on disputes among the people. According to the existing provisions, public security organizations can carry out mediation of general disputes among the people or mediation for disputes among the people that violate the regulations of public security management. Chaoyang District, in Beijing is an example as in 2005, the Chaoyang District Public Security sub-bureau succeeded mediating 50,283 disputes among the people,

[28] 2006 年全国数据 (2006 National Information Database), posted on Gansu Province Economic Information Online (甘肃经济信息网), http://www.gsei.com.cn/ziliao/shuju/default.asp, (February 21, 2006, 21:06).

accounting for 91% of the total received. Of them, 28,489 cases were accepted for public security mediation, accounting for 51.5%; 26,783 cases were accepted for civil mediation, accounting for 48.5%.[29]

The function of China's non-judicial mediation mechanism is restrained by many factors such as lack of necessary authority for mediation agencies, no legal binding force for mediation agreements and insufficient emphasis on the function of mediation. This makes the mediation mechanism fail to work effectively in resolving disputes. In fact, most of disputes after mediation still applied for other legal procedures seeking new decisions. This situation increased the costs, the connections and the complexity in the settlement of disputes, and reduced the prestige of the mediation mechanism in resolving disputes. The mediation mechanism led by civil organizations has shrunk comparatively in China and the mediation mechanisms that still play a role in practice are certain autonomous organizations like village committees, neighborhood committees, etc. Besides this, mediation is mainly implemented by administrative organizations. According to incomplete statistics, there are more than forty administrative mediation mechanisms specified in laws, administrative regulations and department regulations. Of these, very few can mediate general civil disputes and the majority of them are aimed at mediating civil disputes in special fields such as disputes over ownership of resources, telecommunication disputes, consumption disputes, intellectual property disputes and traffic accident disputes, etc. This status indicates that China still has something to desire in the area of the general public's self-rule and self-discipline mechanism and that the intensity of administrative control is still too large. It also shows that the general public is greatly dependent on the power of the State that they are inclined to seek help by submitting their disputes to the competent authorities, which results in certain higher mediation costs and works against the building of an all-inclusive and multi-level dispute resolving mechanism. A fairly complete dispute resolution mechanism should include the prevention and the settlement of disputes.

In the area of dispute resolution, this system should guarantee that the judiciary is the last prerequisite in dispute resolution, and should form a multiple-layer dispute handling mechanism that includes media-

[29] "Police Stations Mediated 90% of Disputes," *Beijing Morning Post*, December 28, 2005, p. 6.

tion and decisions apart from lawsuits. Apart from the intervention of administrative organizations in the handling of disputes, emphasis should be placed on the role of civil mediation in dealing with civil disputes. Only when such a sort of comprehensive dispute resolving mechanism is formed, can resources be well distributed enough to provide effective prevention and settlement of disputes.

5. *Administrative Review*

Administrative review addresses personal and property disputes between State administrative organizations and citizens, and legal persons and other organizations. Administrative review is the same as administrative litigation in the nature of its dispute settlement. However as the administrative mechanism to remedy administrative disputes, administrative review resolves a high number of disputes and has independent legal status.

China's administrative review mechanism was established in the early 1990s. The "Regulations on Administrative Review" were adopted at the 71st executive meeting of the State Council on November 9, 1990 and put into enforcement on January 1, 1991. According to the regulations, citizens, legal persons or other organizations may apply to the administrative organizations for administrative redress if they think the administrative organizations violated their lawful rights and interests in their specific administrative litigations (Article 2). Review organizations administer according to law and are protected from any illegal intervention of other organization, social organizations and individuals (Article 3). Thus it can be seen that the administrative redress mechanism set up according to the "Regulations on Administrative Review" handles administrative disputes between State administrative organizations and citizens, and legal persons and other organizations via administrative redress institutions established within administrative organizations. Administrative review actually redirects some administrative disputes from entering the administrative litigation mechanism. However owing to the wider acceptance scope, the administrative review mechanism addresses a wider range of administrative disputes. The "Regulations on Administrative Review" were revised according to the "Decision of the State Council Concerning Revision of the Regulations on Administrative Review" issued on October 9, 1994, thus further improving the system of administrative redress.

The "Law of the People's Republic of China on Administrative Review" adopted at the Ninth Meeting of the Standing Committee of the Ninth National People's Congress on April 29, 1999 advanced the administrative review system to a new stage. The "Law of the People's Republic of China on Administrative Review" not only stipulates that citizens, legal persons and other organizations can apply for administrative redress with specific administrative litigation for the State administrative organizations and their working personnel, but also permits citizens, legal persons and other organizations to apply for redress based on the standardized documents of the administrative organizations when making special administrative litigation. Thus partial review of administrative organizations had been included in the administrative litigation of administrative organizations (see Figure 10.11).

Administrative review plays an important role in supervising administrative organizations' administration by law and in guaranteeing the lawful rights and interests of administrative counterparts. However this mechanism also suffers from a lack of independence and impartiality on the part of the review organizations as well as an imperfect redress procedure. The core problem is that administrative review cannot examine abstract administrative litigation completely, i.e. the abstract administrative acts that can pass the examination of administrative review are fairly limited. Even for those who are able to take advantage of the redress procedure, the examination results in the review stage are far from ideal.

### 6. *Review of Constitutionality*

The mechanism for reviewing constitutionality is based on the provisions of China's current Constitution and the Legislation Law. It is made to address disputes regarding standardized documents such as laws, regulations and rules. The government agency that is legally empowered to review constitutionality is the Standing Committee of National People's Congress; and the review of constitutionality is mainly aimed at administrative regulations, local regulations, autonomous regulations and separate regulations that are stipulated in Article 90 of the Legislation Law. The mechanism of reviewing constitutionality serves to resolve the contradictions and conflicts between laws, regulations and rules from the source and to uphold the authority of the Constitution and the uniformity of the laws.

On June 28, 2001, the "Official Reply of the Supreme People's Court on Whether the Civil Liabilities Shall Be Borne for the Infringement upon a Citizen's Basic Right of Receiving Education" was adopted at

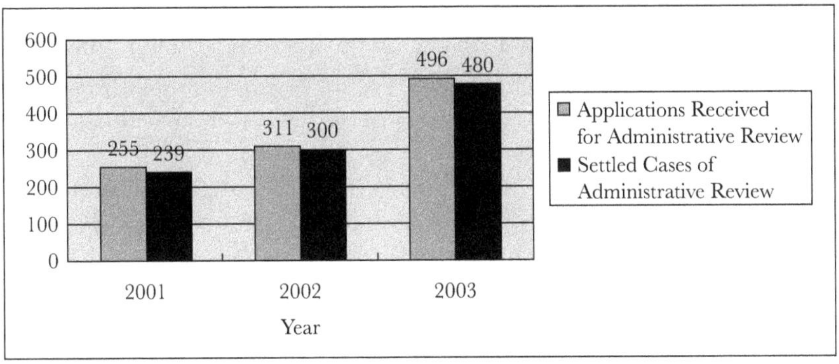


Figure 10.11: Administrative Review Cases Received and Settled by the State Council (2001–2003)[30]

the 1183rd meeting of the Judicial Committee of the Supreme People's Court, which states to the Shandong Provincial Higher People's Court: "We have received your request for instructions on the "Case Concerning the Dispute of the Right of Personal Name with Qi Yuling and Chen Xiaoqi, Chen Kezheng, Shandong Jining Business School, Shandong Tengzhou No. 8 Middle School, and the Shandong Tengzhou Education Committee.' Through research, we consider Chen Xiaoqi and others, by means of infringement of the right of personal name, infringed on Qi Yuling's basic right to receive education enjoyed pursuant to the provision of the Constitution which has led to material damage and shall undertake the corresponding civil liability."

In the above judicial reply, the Supreme People's Court defines that a citizen can obtain a civil remedy when the citizen's right to receive education as stipulated in the Constitution is infringed upon. This judicial attitude clearly shows that the Supreme People's Court, as the supreme judicial organ of the country, put forward its own judicial view on how to realize the basic rights of citizens contained in the Constitution. In fact it means that the Supreme People's Court has assumed the responsibility of guaranteeing the implementation of the Constitution, which is realized by directly applying the Constitution as the legal basis for judicial trial. The issue of the "8.13" reply of the Supreme People's Court has attracted attention from all sides. Some news media have even deemed this reply as the "No. 1 case of review

[30] *Law Yearbook of China* (2002–2004).

of constitutionality in China." This shows that the operation of the mechanism of constitutional review of has a considerable foundation with the public and society at large.

In regards to constitutional review, another event with important social influence is the "Sun Zhigang Event" (孙志刚事件) which happened in 2003. Soon after this event, three citizens submitted a suggestion letter to the Standing Committee of the National People's Congress for examination of the "Measures for Detention and Repatriation of Vagrants and Beggars in Cities," claiming violation of the Constitution and laws.

The general contents of the suggestion letter are as below:

> To the Standing Committee of the National People's Congress:
> The second stipulation of Article 88 in the "Law on Legislation of the People's Republic of China" states that the Standing Committee of the National People's Congress has the power to annul any administrative regulations which conflict with the Constitution and the laws. The second stipulation of Article 90 states that when considering administrative regulations that contradict the Constitution and the laws, citizens may submit to the Standing Committee of the National People's Congress written suggestions for examination.
>
> As citizens of the People's Republic of China, we consider the 'Measures for Detention and Repatriation of Vagrants and Beggars in Cities, which was promulgated on May 12, 1982 by the State Council and is still applicable, contradictory to the Constitution and the related laws, and therefore we submit the suggestion to the Standing Committee of the National People's Congress to examine the "Measures for Detention and Repatriation of Vagrants and Beggars in Cities."

The Standing Committee of the National People's Congress did not officially reply to the suggestion of the three citizens but due to great concerns of the general public, Premier Wen Jiabao of the State Council signed the No. 381 Decree of the State Council on promulgating "Measures for the Administration of Relief for Vagrants and Beggars without Assured Living Sources in Cities." These measures were put into effect as of August 1, 2003; and they stipulate that the "Measures for Detention and Repatriation of Vagrants and Beggars in Cities" issued by the State Council in May 1982 would be annulled. It should be noted that although the Standing Committee of the National People's Congress has not yet made any official examination on constitutional violation, it has become common understanding for the decision-making levels and the general public to use examination of constitutional violations in order to resolve conflicts and contradictions between laws, regulations and rules. However, it is not the right time to implement the examination mechanism on constitutional violations.

Presently, conflicts between laws, regulations and rules still cannot adopt examination of constitutional violations as a resolution method. Plenty of social disputes are caused by fuzzy policies or ambiguity of legal rules. The settlement of these disputes within the system completely rests with the effective settlement of contradictions between policies, conflicts between policies and laws, and between laws. According to the provisions of the Constitution and the Legislation Law, the Standing Committee of the National People's Congress has the power to interpret the Constitution and laws and also has the power to conduct examination on constitutional violation of administrative regulations, local regulations, autonomous regulations and separate regulations that contradict the Constitution and the laws. However in practice, the Standing Committee of the National People's Congress has never adopted an official legal procedure to conduct any interpretation of the Constitution or to conduct any official examination on constitutional violation. The result of this is that disputes between policies, between policies and laws, and between laws cannot be resolved effectively, thus influencing the settlement of disputes regarding policies and laws.

In practice, some local courts have decided that the local regulations enacted by the provincial people's congress were contradictory to national laws when trying administrative cases; however the judges concerned were dismissed as punishment. Thus it can be seen that the biggest resistance to the implementation of a protocol examining laws, regulations and rules regarding constitutional violations comes from the judicial departments, in particular those individuals implementing the objectives to examine constitutional violations. This shows that the establishment of an examination mechanism for constitutional violation that fully uses its authority to resolve disputes will truly be a long and arduous process. In conclusion, China has a wide range of legal mechanisms to address disputes and has established fairly complete dispute resolution systems, however effective and inclusive legal relation between these legal mechanisms is still lacking, the legal dispute resolution channel has not been effectively promoted within the system, and the potential for resolving disputes via the legal channel is not fully popularized.

The existence of these issues influences dispute settlement. With an unsound system of law, emphasis on this issue and theoretical research are needed in order to comprehensively advance the role of the legal channel in safeguarding social stability and establishing a harmonious society.

## III. *Suggestions for Measures to Resolve Disputes by Legal Channel*

### A. *Change the ideology of "extensive letters and visits,"* (大信访) *and promote the role of the lawsuit and other legal methods. Strengthen the legal construction of the letters and visits system, and guarantee the function of letters and visits in information collection and conveyance when resolving social disputes on the basis of enacting the law regarding letters and visits. Realize a centralized management system for, and specialization in, letters and visits, reduce the comments and instruction of government leaders, and improve and standardize the protocol for the letters and visits system*

The letters and visits system is just a reception procedure and a transfer procedure of incoming letters and visits conducted in government agencies. Letters and visits institutions are not authorized to deal with those disputes detailed in the letters and visits. Therefore, it is necessary to promote the role of these institutions in providing procedural guarantees for the settlement of disputes, as these institutions do not directly resolve disputes. If this is not done, these institutions will become collecting places for disputes and conflicts, which would work against the channeling function of letters and visits institutions and facilitate violation or misuse of authority, thus influencing the functions of other legal dispute resolution channels and weakening the government and the general public's understanding of resolving disputes according to law. If this problem is addressed, it will assure that letters and visits system does not exceed its authority or receive a larger workload and will facilitate the complaint letter-visit system in providing procedural guarantees by working in coordination with other mechanisms.

Reform of the letters and visits system is based on the following aspects: (1) enact the law regarding letters and visits in order to standardize the work mechanism of letters and visits, establish a work management mechanism under the unified leadership of the Party committee and the People's Congress at all levels to reduce the overlapping of letters and visits institutions, thus realizing the specialization of the work of handling letters and visits. (2) Establish "a one window"

(一个窗戶) reception system for letters and visits, avoid multiple reception and repeated reception, establish a reception center for letters and visits in the same city and improve the work efficiency of the reception of letters and visits. (3) Put a stop to government leaders' comments and instructions that promote unreasonable expectations on the part of letter-writers/visitors regarding the outcomes of disputes, which puts enormous pressure on the letters and visits institutions; and severely disturb and influence their day to day work order. (4) Further improve the resolution system letters and visits, facilitate individuals' experiences with this method, and establish a standardized and orderly working routine for letters and visits, etc.

B. *Actively and steadily promote the structural reform of justice. Improve the lawsuit mechanism in order to substantially increase the outcomes of lawsuits; and promote the lawsuit as the principal means for resolving disputes. Also establish easier methods for accessing the lawsuit system, and push forward institutional reform of trial instances as well as intensify legal execution*

To resolve social disputes by the litigation channel is to seek solutions with legal binding force through legally stipulated legal proceedings, thereby ensuring parties' sufficient access to the right of litigation and upholding the principles of a just, fair and open process. The role of the litigation channel is to resolve disputes through the resulting judgments, arbitration awards or mediation agreements all of which possess legal bonding force. This method ensures that the litigation channel enjoys the authority, justice and determinative force necessary to resolve disputes and ensures the execution of dispute solutions that use the coercive force of the State as well as prevents disputes from flowing into other resolution channels. Considering the importance of the litigation channel in resolving disputes, the overall effects of this method should be developed in accordance with its core function and the system of using the litigation channel as the final legal means to address disputes should be reasonably applied.

Therefore, it is necessary to establish as easier lawsuit access protocol and improve the acceptance system, thus ensuring the litigation channel is capable of resolving disputes that cannot be resolved in other non-litigation channels. The role of being the final means for settlement of disputes which has been played by the institution of letters and visits should be transferred to the litigation channel and the principal role of the litigation channel in dispute resolution should be defined. The legal consciousness should be raised in order to resolve social disputes according to law and prevent mafia-type organizations or other illegal organizations from interfering in dispute settlement and causing less than ideal results. The core function of the litigation channel in resolving disputes should be strengthened and the generation and development of mafia-type organizations or other illegal organizations should be effectively prevented, thus safeguarding social harmony and stability and guaranteeing the security of the lives and property of the general public.

In addition, the system of trial instances should be reformed and adjudication of third instance should be gradually implemented as the final level. Also the role of the higher people's courts in ensuring the quality of lawsuits and safeguarding justice should be further promoted. Reform of the system of trial instances can make up for the insufficient remedy methods of the trial supervision system in resolving disputes and can increase the execution strength of the people's courts. For those parties refusing to execute the decisions of the people's courts, effective enforcement measures shall be taken to ensure they perform their legal obligations thereby increasing the authority and effectiveness of the people's courts in resolving disputes through the litigation channel, and guaranteeing that litigation channel acts as the final method of resolving disputes.

### C. *Revise the "Administrative Litigation Law" and the "Administrative Review Law," establish and improve the examination mechanism for abstract administrative acts through administrative litigation and administrative review*

After the "Administrative Litigation Law" and the "Administrative Review Law" were promulgated, citizens, legal persons and other organizations could resort to administrative review and administrative litigation to resolve disputes with administrative organizations regarding the latter's implementation of specific administrative acts. However as the abstract administrative acts of administrative organizations are not completely included in the administrative review procedure or the administrative litigation procedure, disputes arising regarding administrative organizations' implementation of abstract administrative acts with citizens, legal persons and other organizations cannot be resolved by the relevant legal channels. As a result, certain administrative organizations make use of the system defect (that abstract administrative acts are not subject to administrative review and administrative litigation) to violate the lawful rights and interests of persons who are subject to their administration leading to increased administrative disputes, and even group disputes of great social influence. Therefore, to reduce the occurrence of contradictions and conflicts between state administrative organizations and citizens, legal persons and other organizations in the process of exercising administrative authority, the examination scope of administrative review regarding abstract administrative acts should be expanded and abstract administrative litigation should be included in the accepted scope of administrative litigation.

D. *Improve internal dispute settlement mechanism and bring all internal personnel disputes related with social organizations under the arbitration scope of personnel disputes. Establish a system to connect personnel dispute arbitration with lawsuits, which will provides an institutional guarantee for resolving various personnel disputes through the litigation channel. Establish a unified petition and complaint system for the working personnel of government agencies that is gradually geared towards litigation. Further improve the labor collective dispute negotiation system to protect the lawful rights and interests of employees according to law*

An internal dispute is a dispute arising between the employer and the employee regarding personnel management and fulfillment of labor contracts. This kind of dispute occurs inside government agencies, businesses, public institutions and social organizations, and if improperly resolved, can influence the involved parties' lawful rights and interests and severely disturb the day to day work of government agencies, businesses, public institutions and social organizations, and can even hurt the internal harmony and stability of the employer. As some internal disputes fail to be resolved in a timely manner, they are drawn out and can appeal to the higher authorities for help. Some disputes worsen and became criminal cases, threatening the employers' day to day work order, and the personal safety and property safety of persons concerned. Therefore the structural reorganization of institutions should be expanded to include the establishment of an internal dispute settlement mechanism integrated with the litigation channel, thus transferring internal personnel disputes to the personnel dispute arbitration mechanism.

All internal disputes regarding social organizations not exercising public administration should be handled under the personnel dispute arbitration mechanism. Also, a unified petition and complaint mechanism for working personnel of government agencies should be established in order to bring the personnel management disputes in government agencies into the legal channels. In addition, an institution for handling the petitions and complaints of government agency personnel will be established in the judicial organizations, which will bring personnel management disputes within government agencies into the litigation channel, thus guaranteeing the settlement of internal disputes of government agencies.

Currently, the labor dispute mediation system within businesses is unsound and employees' rights and interests are vulnerable to violation, thus leading to group disputes and influencing the social harmony and stability. Measures should be taken within the system to prevent large-scale group disputes triggered by the violation of employees' rights and interests. It is suggested the trade unions within businesses be established and improved, and that their duties to act as employee representative for collective negotiation and collective bargaining with the employer be defined. This would help resolve disputes in the area of business and avoids the possibility of them affecting society at large. Also the labor dispute arbitration system and the independence and impartiality of labor dispute arbitration agencies should be improved, thus ensuring labor disputes can be effectively settled in the arbitration process. Finally judicial control of labor dispute arbitration decisions should be strengthened and the examination scope of lawsuits for labor dispute cases should be expanded.

### E. *Protect the independent position of civil and commercial arbitration agencies from administrative organizations. Reform and improve the arbitration procedure of civil and commercial cases and ensure sufficient realization of the principle of party governance*

The arbitration of civil and commercial cases is an important legal channel for the resolution of civil disputes and it works within the litigation channel. Its legal character is to respect the parties' will in the process of dispute resolution. It is the parties involved who freely choose between the options of arbitration and legal proceedings. For those parties involved, acceptance of the dispute arbitration decisions is voluntary and reasonably fair. In order to allow the arbitration of civil and commercial cases to play a role in the resolution of civil and commercial disputes, it is necessary to prevent the interference of administrative organizations and ensure the relative independence of arbitration agencies. Arbitration agencies of civil and commercial cases should be disconnected from administrative organizations and arbitration agencies should be purely civil institutions aimed at resolving civil and commercial disputes according to law. The procedure of arbitration should be improved in order to give adequate assurance that it is the parties' will which governs the arbitration procedure. Additionally arbitration evidence rules, the system of adducing evidence, and the examination mechanism, etc. should be improved based on a thorough respect of the parties will, thus forming arbitration decisions or agreements with determinative force for the parties involved in the dispute parties thereby increasing the work efficiency of arbitration in resolving civil and commercial cases.

### F. *Improve the mediation system, increase the legal force of non-judicial mediation and promote mediation as assisting in the settlement of social disputes. Affirm the legal force of mediation agreements reached by civil and administrative mediation in the courts to promote the resolution of general disputes by mediation*

Those mediation agreements arrived at through civil and administrative mediation should be affirmed in the courts as legally binding in order to promote the resolution of general disputes through mediation.

Non-judicial mediation for dispute resolution is a straightforward dispute handling procedure that respects the will of the parties involved as well as their freedom to sufficiently express their opinions and claims, etc. Therefore as an auxiliary method to litigation and other non-litigation channels in the area of dispute resolution, non-judicial mediation has won the attention of the government and the general public. However, as mediation lacks legally binding force, many disputes subject to mediation went un-enforced and failed the function of channeling social disputes. In the reform of civil mediation, the combination of non-judicial mediation results is suggested, especially administrative mediation reached with the courts' affirmation mechanism. Any mediation agreement voluntarily reached by the dispute parties can be submitted to the court for affirmation of its effectiveness and can directly apply for legal execution, thus improving the function of mediation in resolving disputes and allowing the majority of simple disputes to achieve final settlement in mediation.

G. *Establish a mechanism to examine the constitutionality of laws, regulations and rules and overcome local protectionism* (地方保护主义) *and departmental protectionism* (部门保护主义) *to provide a basic system guarantee for resolving social disputes through the legal channel*

The review of constitutionality has been written into the Constitution and the Law on Legislation, and the principle that laws, regulations and rules shall not be inconsistent with the Constitution is also an important part of the Constitution. However, the Standing Committee of the National People's Congress does not effectively exercise the authority to review constitutionality in order to resolve conflicts between laws, regulations and rules. As a result, contradictions of policies and laws have attributed to many social disputes. Yet on the other hand, the people's courts at all levels including the Supreme People's Court have exercised a review of constitutionality for laws, regulations and rules and made many judicial decisions that are controversial both in theory and in practice. The review of constitutionality is also a method of dispute resolution. A mechanism of constitutional review should be established to provide a system guarantee for the resolution of disputes through legal channels. A mechanism for constitutional review is part of the litigation channel in character; however in view of the operation of constitutional review abroad, this mechanism actually plays the role of being the final step in the dispute resolution system. For instance, in Germany if a citizen uses up all general legal remedy procedures but still thinks that his/her constitutional rights have been violated then the citizen can submit such dispute to the German Constitutional Court for review. In this way the mechanism for constitutional review plays a role that other channels cannot play in effectively maintaining the uniformity of the legal system, protecting citizens' rights and providing a final level solution for various social disputes from the view of the system.

In view of China's legal channels for the settlement of disputes, China's letters and visits channel has become the final solution for parties of social disputes to address disputes. Even though the letters and visits system operates positively and effectively and is firmly established as the final stage in the resolution channel, its capability to settle disputes is still limited and so it fails to effectively resolve all social disputes. One of the major causes for this is that the letters and visits mechanism is not the final law channel for dispute resolution, a function that only the constitutional review mechanism possesses. What is worthy of mentioning is that the letters and visits mechanism cannot resolve contradictions and conflicts between legal standards of law caused by local protectionism and department protectionism. The letters and visits mechanism is dependent on constitutional review which exercises control over the constitutionality of laws, regulations and rules; and it is only through such a mechanism that those legal regulations and rules working against the Constitution be discovered and corrected and the uniformity of the legal system be safeguarded. Therefore, it is very critical that constitutional review be established at the earliest opportunity in order to maintain social stability and build a harmonious society.

In summary, the resolution of disputes through legal channels is comprised of seeking effective dispute solutions to realize the goal of concluding lawsuits according to the definite legal regulations, following legal procedure, adhering to the principle of justice, fairness and openness and providing adequate assurance of lawful rights of the parties involved.

There are two legal mechanisms used to address disputes, i.e. the litigation channel and the non-litigation channel, with the former acting as the final method to resolve disputes and the latter redirecting some disputes into different handling methods in order to increase the efficiency of the litigation channel in resolving disputes. However, from the view of resolving disputes, the non-litigation channel is only an auxiliary mechanism and it cannot replace litigation. Therefore, a principle of "rule of law" regarding the settlement of disputes is that any dispute that cannot be resolved in the non-litigation channel should be provided with the ability to apply for litigation for resolution. This ability is reflected in the various rights of litigation enjoyed by the dispute parties. However China's litigation and non-litigation channels are not well equipped. As a matter of fact, many disputes after being handled in the non-litigation channel lose the ability to be addressed through litigation, which creates an obstacle to resolving disputes by just, fair and open legal procedure.

Though many disputes are prevented from being resolved through litigation by their involvement in the non-litigation channel they cannot be effectively resolved in the non-litigation channel, thus becoming destabilizing factors for social harmony and stability.

Also, many disputes dealt with through litigation to dissatisfactory results then resort to the non-litigation channel, thus leading to a lack of definite system division between the litigation and non-litigation channels in the function of resolving disputes. Furthermore, either of these two mechanisms can continually address a dispute previously dealt with by the other, which results in a lack of ultimate purpose and authority on the part of both of these two mechanisms in resolving disputes. Therefore, the establishment of a harmonious and stable society necessitates a scientific and rational system that connects the different legal channels to resolve social disputes and form an integrated and harmonious dispute resolving system, thus comprehensively promoting the overall effect of all legal channels in this area.

Finally, the existing legal channels used to address disputes are not capable of resolving all the types of social disputes in system. As China is in a transition period, many disputes and conflicts have emerged that are apt to develop into group disputes. The general mechanism for dispute resolution faces the difficulties of social contradictions and conflicts in these intensified conditions. Therefore, it is necessary to establish a mechanism under the people's government at all levels to integrate all emergency response mechanisms and set up a unified emergency response institution that will formulate stipulations for all levels to prevent the occurrence of group disputes and respond to emergencies with emergency measures in a timely and effective manner, while also eliminating social disputes and maintaining social harmony and stability.

# INDEX

www.ingramcontent.com/pod-product-compliance
Lightning Source LLC
LaVergne TN
LVHW080846300926
849162LV00003B/347
* 9 7 8 9 0 0 4 1 7 3 0 3 3 *